Jasper County Public Library System

Overdue notices are a courtesy of the library system.
Failure to receive an overdue notice does not absolve the borrower of the obligation to return materials on time.

CLUBBING

Published by DC Comics,

1700 Broadway,

New York, NY 10019.

Printed in Canada.

DC Comics, a Warner Bros.

Entertainment Company.

ISBN: 1-4012-0370-1

ISBN: 978-1-4012-0370-2

COVER BY JOSH HOWARD

clubbing

Written by Andi Watson

Illustrated by Josh Howard

Lettering by Travis Lanham

"The coppers have nicked my corned beef
hash and Yorkshire puds and bogged off
down the motorway."

Don't have a clue what I'm talking about?
Consult my Lexicon on pages 147-151
to translate English slang into
fluent American.

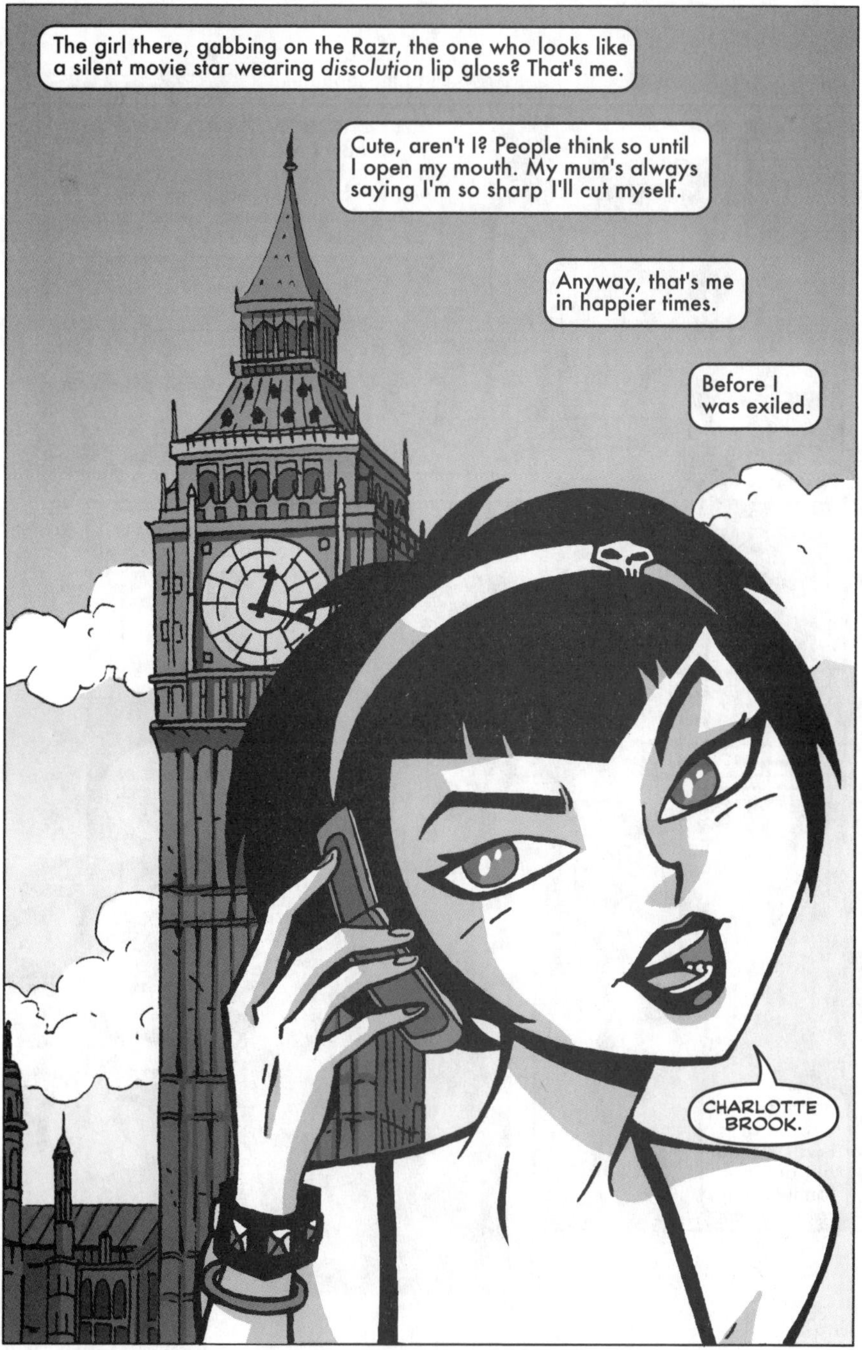
The girl there, gabbing on the Razr, the one who looks like a silent movie star wearing *dissolution* lip gloss? That's me.
Cute, aren't I? People think so until I open my mouth. My mum's always saying I'm so sharp I'll cut myself.
Anyway, that's me in happier times.
Before I was exiled.
CHARLOTTE BROOK.

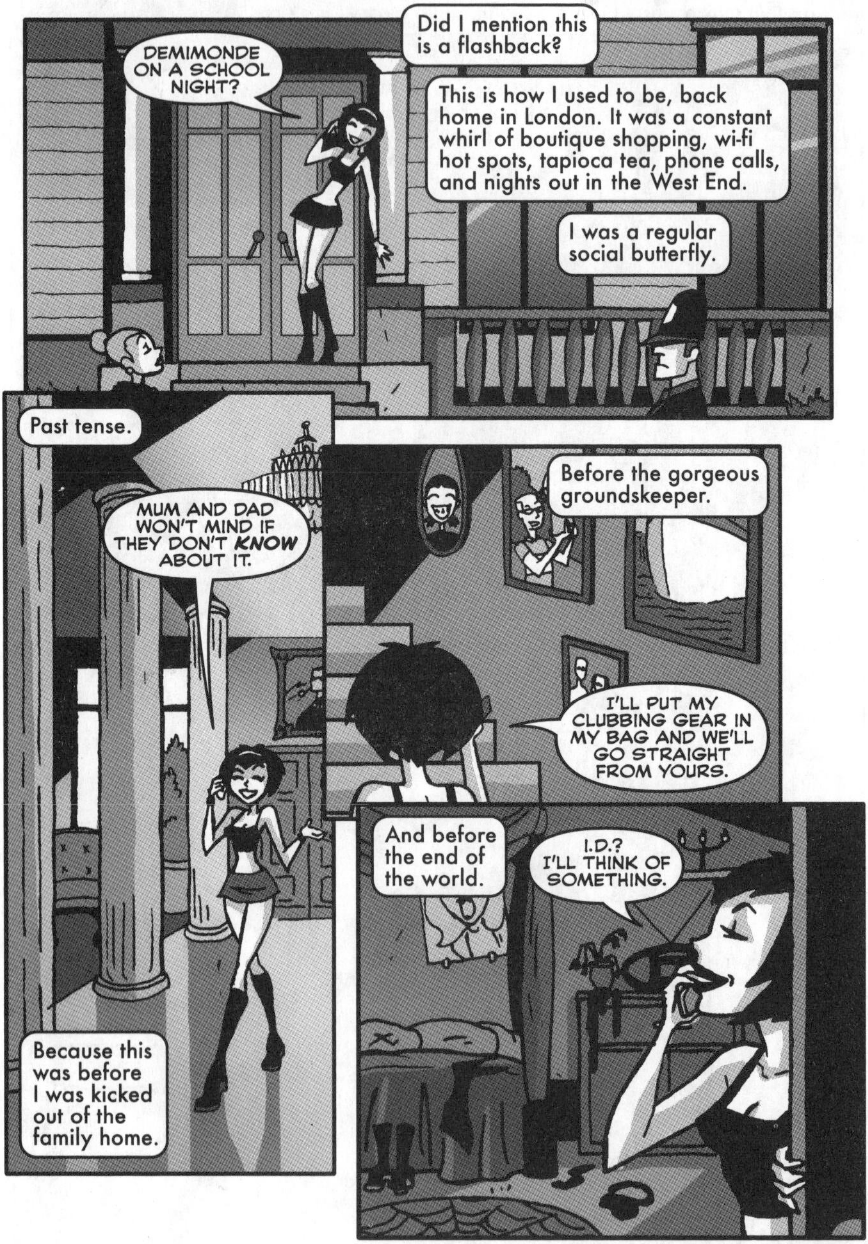
DEMIMONDE ON A SCHOOL NIGHT?
Did I mention this is a flashback?
This is how I used to be, back home in London. It was a constant whirl of boutique shopping, wi-fi hot spots, tapioca tea, phone calls, and nights out in the West End.
I was a regular social butterfly.
Past tense.
MUM AND DAD WON'T MIND IF THEY DON'T *KNOW* ABOUT IT.
Because this was before I was kicked out of the family home.
Before the gorgeous groundskeeper.
I'LL PUT MY CLUBBING GEAR IN MY BAG AND WE'LL GO STRAIGHT FROM YOURS.
And before the end of the world.
I.D.? I'LL THINK OF SOMETHING.

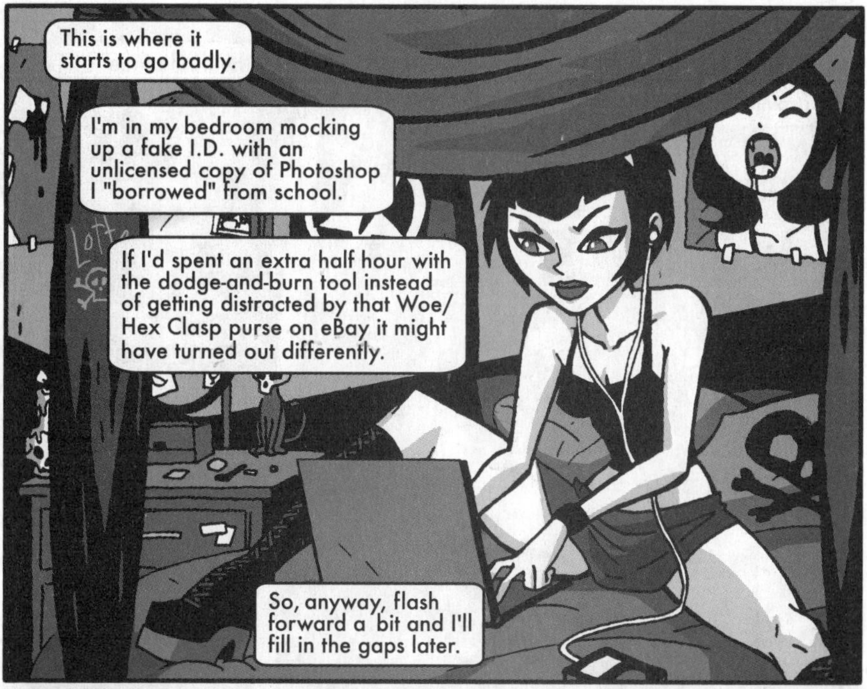
This is where it starts to go badly.
I'm in my bedroom mocking up a fake I.D. with an unlicensed copy of Photoshop I "borrowed" from school.
If I'd spent an extra half hour with the dodge-and-burn tool instead of getting distracted by that Woe/ Hex Clasp purse on eBay it might have turned out differently.
So, anyway, flash forward a bit and I'll fill in the gaps later.
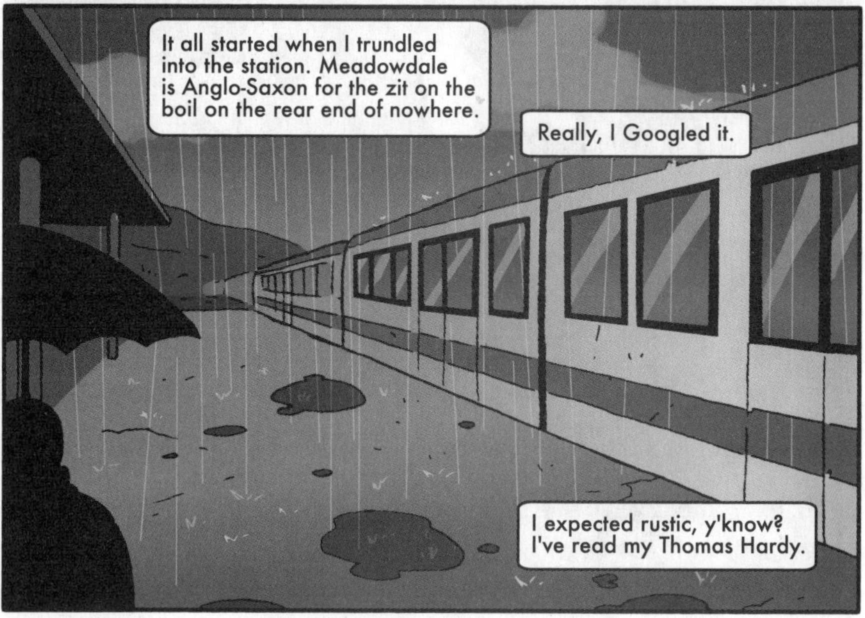
It all started when I trundled into the station. Meadowdale is Anglo-Saxon for the zit on the boil on the rear end of nowhere.
Really, I Googled it.
I expected rustic, y'know? I've read my Thomas Hardy.

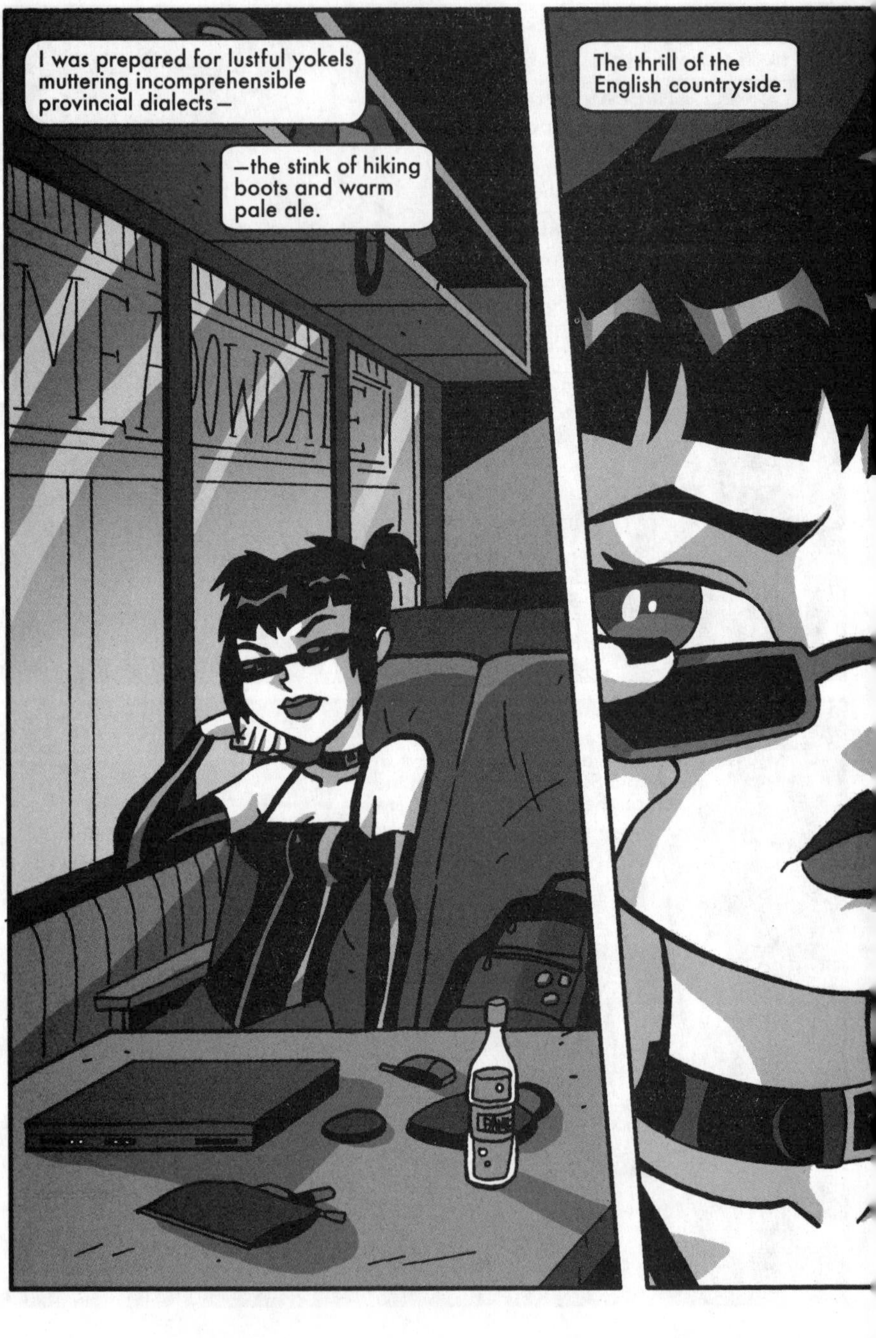
I was prepared for lustful yokels muttering incomprehensible provincial dialects–
–the stink of hiking boots and warm pale ale.
MEADOWDALE
The thrill of the English countryside.

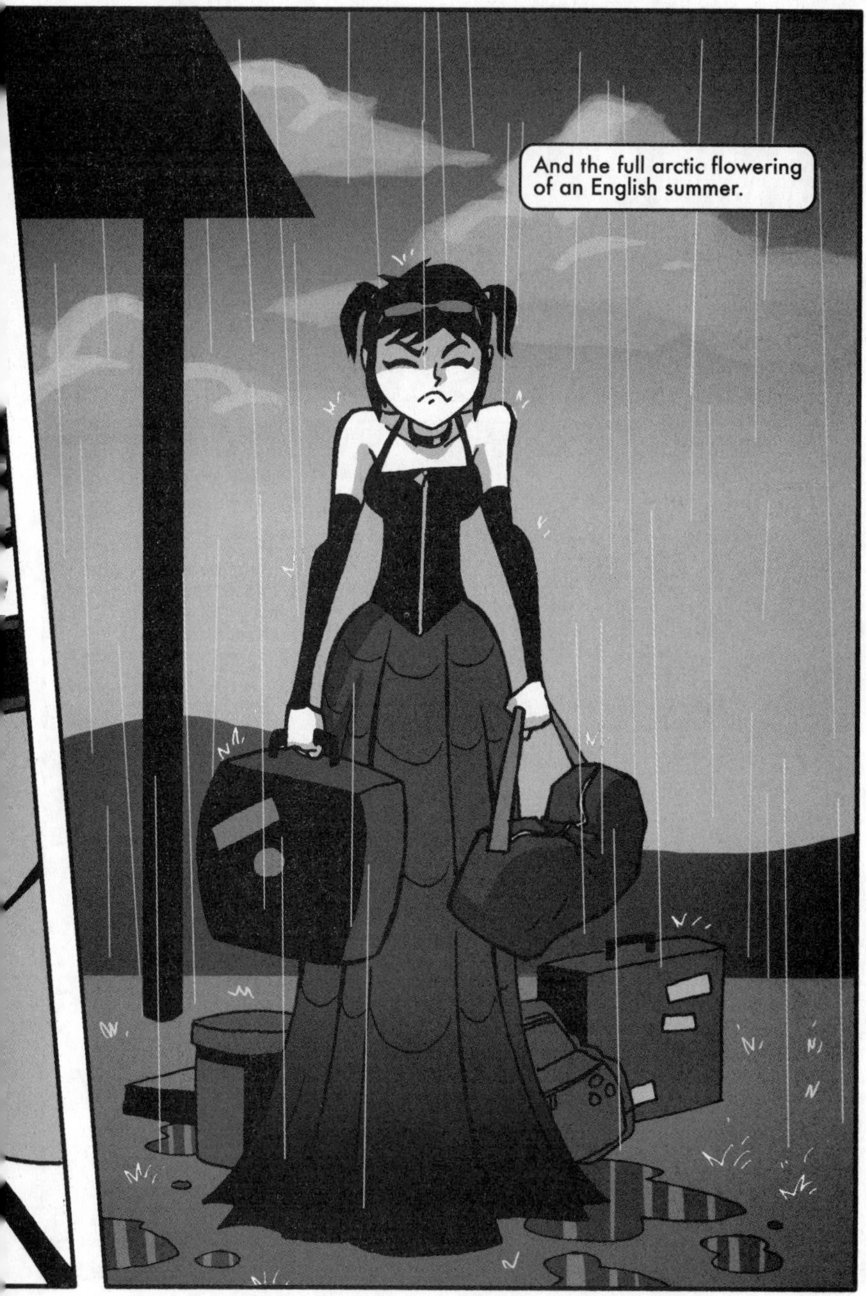
And the full arctic flowering of an English summer.

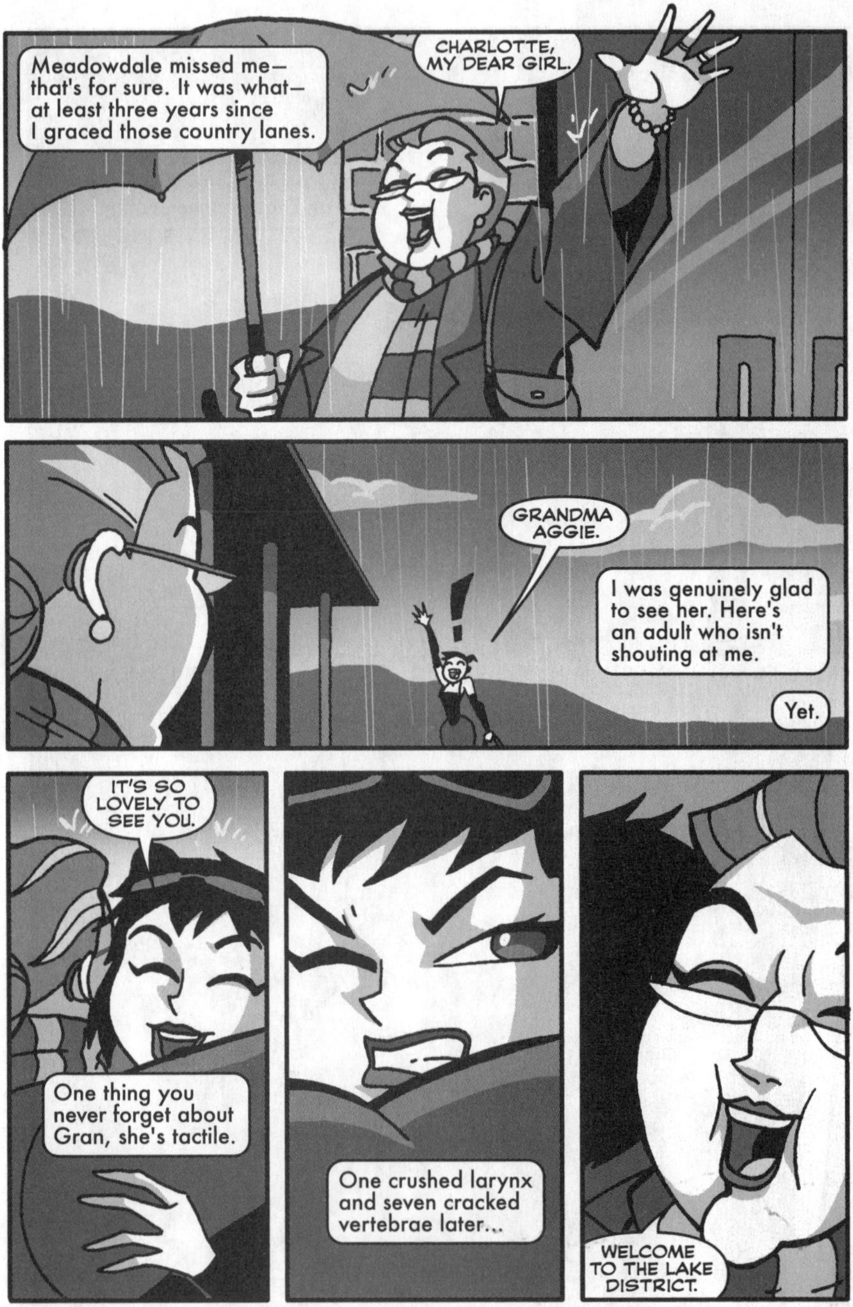
Meadowdale missed me—that's for sure. It was what—at least three years since I graced those country lanes.
CHARLOTTE, MY DEAR GIRL.
GRANDMA AGGIE.
I was genuinely glad to see her. Here's an adult who isn't shouting at me.
Yet.
IT'S SO LOVELY TO SEE YOU.
One thing you never forget about Gran, she's tactile.
One crushed larynx and seven cracked vertebrae later...
WELCOME TO THE LAKE DISTRICT.

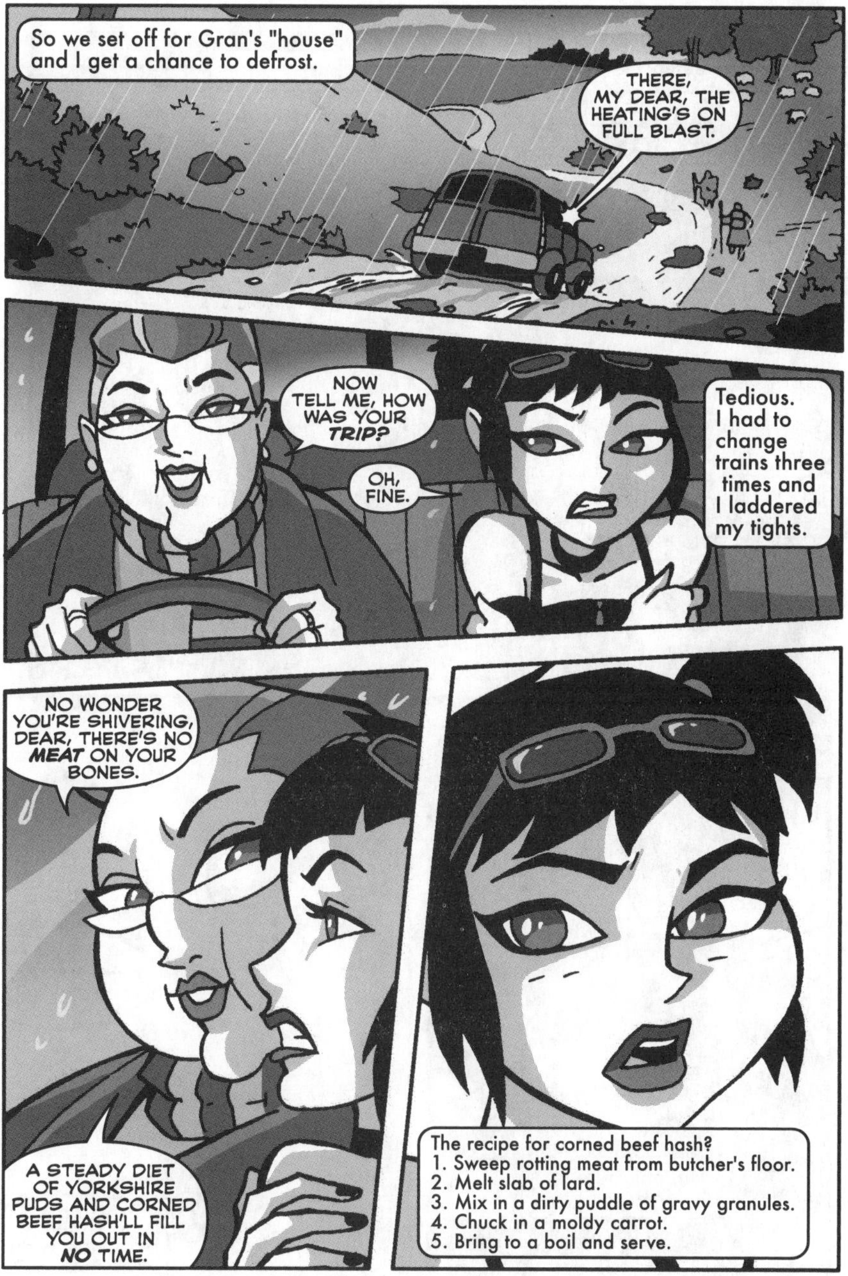
So we set off for Gran's "house" and I get a chance to defrost.
THERE, MY DEAR, THE HEATING'S ON FULL BLAST.
NOW TELL ME, HOW WAS YOUR *TRIP?*
OH, FINE.
Tedious. I had to change trains three times and I laddered my tights.
NO WONDER YOU'RE SHIVERING, DEAR, THERE'S NO *MEAT* ON YOUR BONES.
A STEADY DIET OF YORKSHIRE PUDS AND CORNED BEEF HASH'LL FILL YOU OUT IN *NO* TIME.
The recipe for corned beef hash?
1. Sweep rotting meat from butcher's floor.
2. Melt slab of lard.
3. Mix in a dirty puddle of gravy granules.
4. Chuck in a moldy carrot.
5. Bring to a boil and serve.

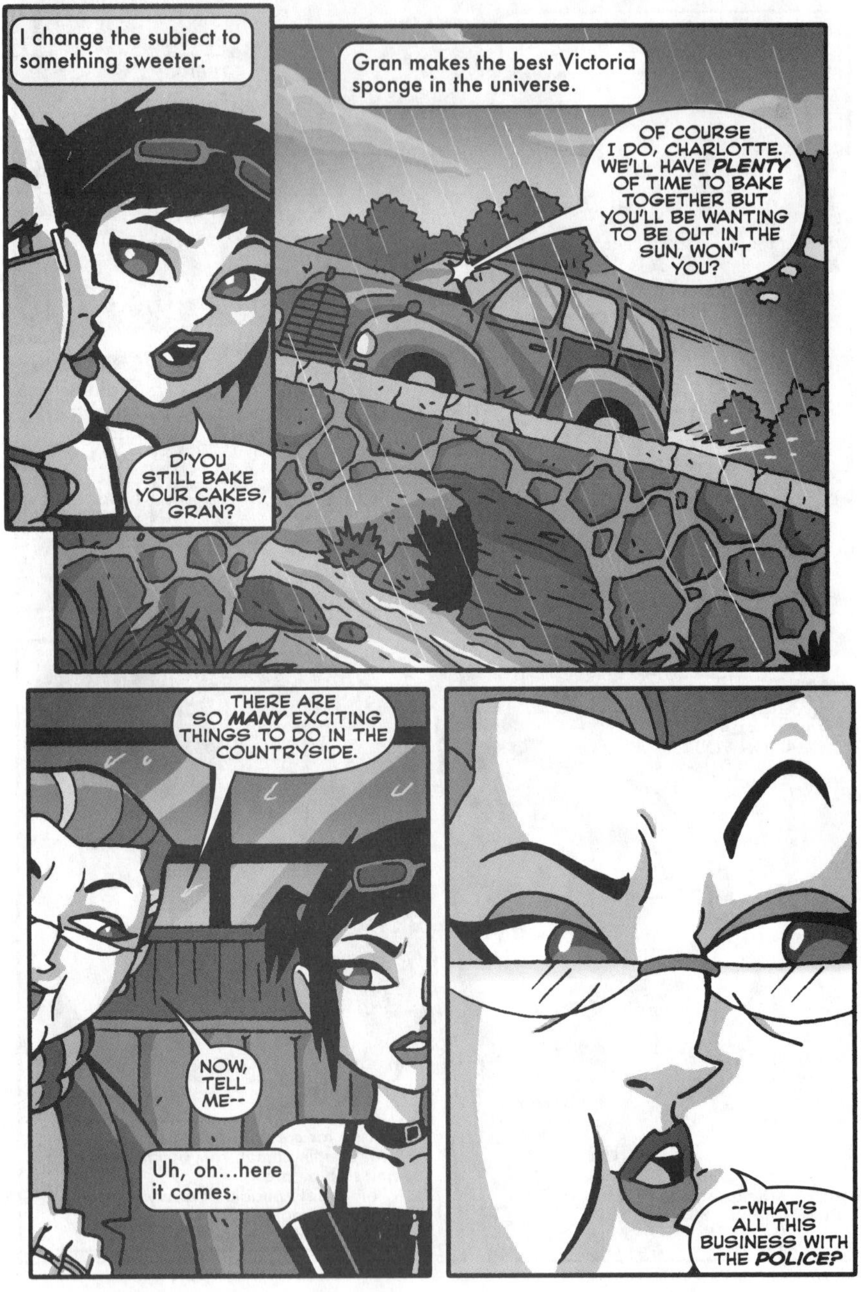
I change the subject to something sweeter.
D'YOU STILL BAKE YOUR CAKES, GRAN?
Gran makes the best Victoria sponge in the universe.
OF COURSE I DO, CHARLOTTE. WE'LL HAVE **PLENTY** OF TIME TO BAKE TOGETHER BUT YOU'LL BE WANTING TO BE OUT IN THE SUN, WON'T YOU?
THERE ARE SO **MANY** EXCITING THINGS TO DO IN THE COUNTRYSIDE.
NOW, TELL ME--
Uh, oh...here it comes.
--WHAT'S ALL THIS BUSINESS WITH THE **POLICE?**

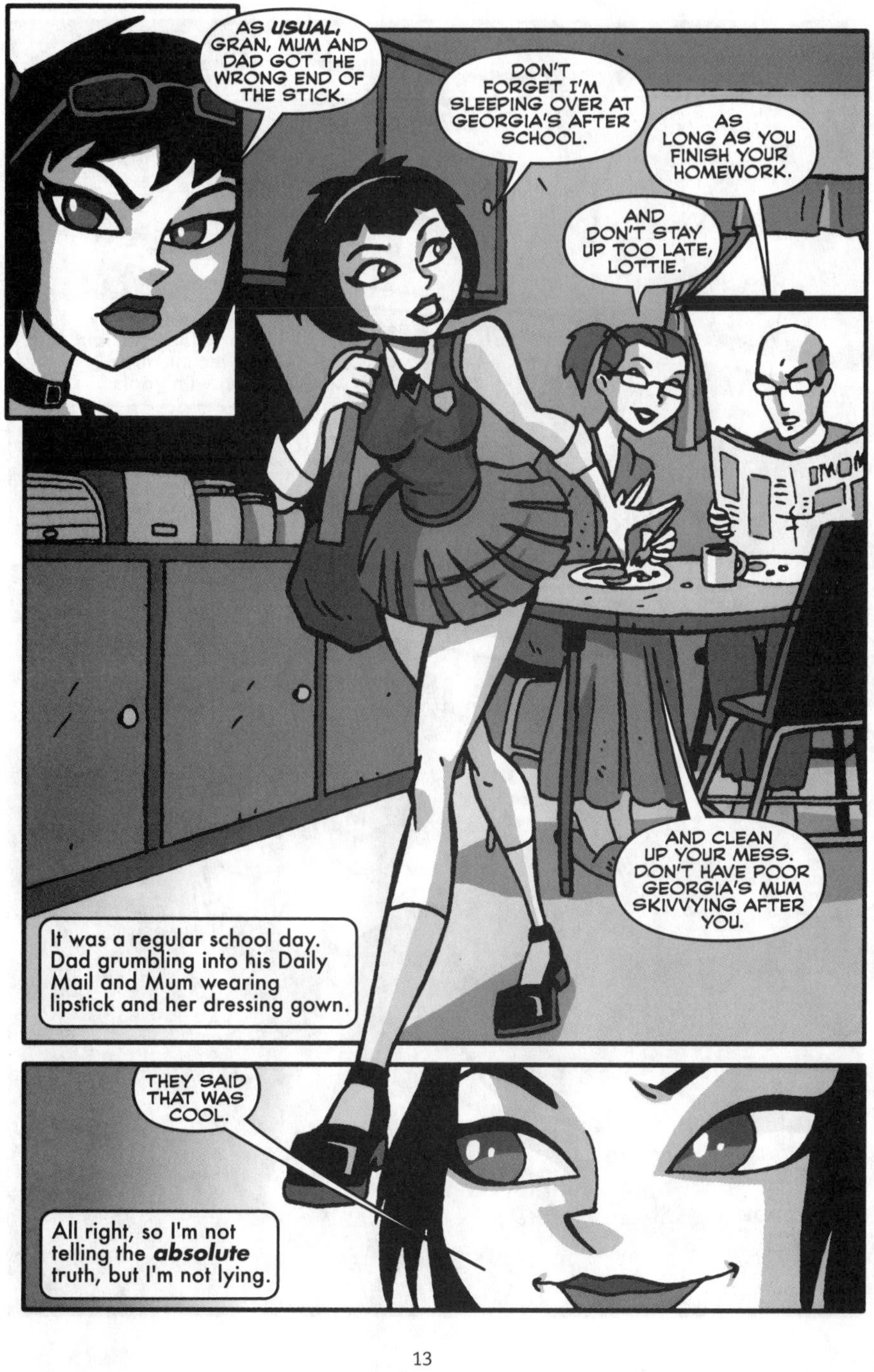
AS ***USUAL***, GRAN, MUM AND DAD GOT THE WRONG END OF THE STICK.
DON'T FORGET I'M SLEEPING OVER AT GEORGIA'S AFTER SCHOOL.
AS LONG AS YOU FINISH YOUR HOMEWORK.
AND DON'T STAY UP TOO LATE, LOTTIE.
AND CLEAN UP YOUR MESS. DON'T HAVE POOR GEORGIA'S MUM SKIVVYING AFTER YOU.
It was a regular school day. Dad grumbling into his Daily Mail and Mum wearing lipstick and her dressing gown.
THEY SAID THAT WAS COOL.
All right, so I'm not telling the ***absolute*** truth, but I'm not lying.

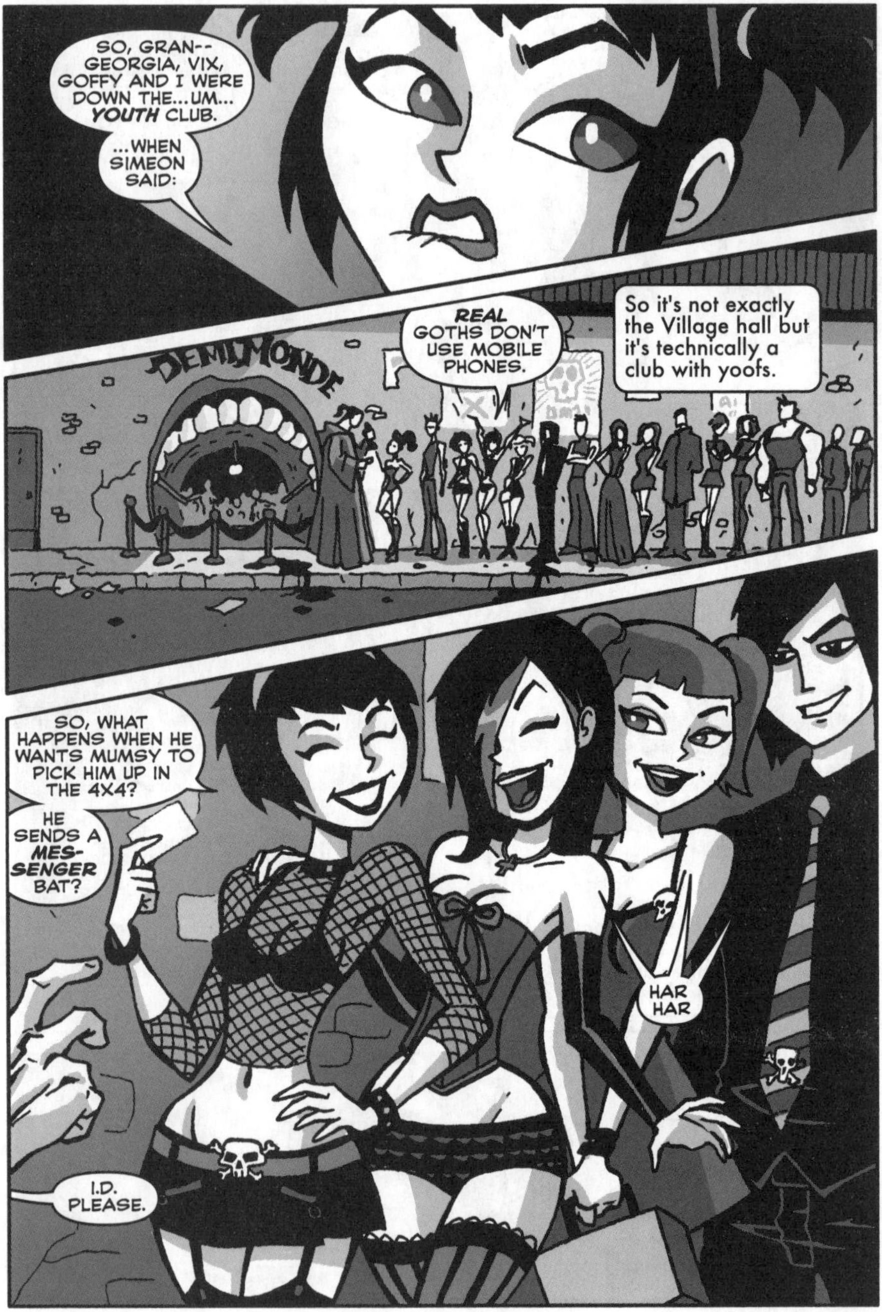
SO, GRAN--GEORGIA, VIX, GOFFY AND I WERE DOWN THE...UM... YOUTH CLUB.
...WHEN SIMEON SAID:
REAL GOTHS DON'T USE MOBILE PHONES.
So it's not exactly the Village hall but it's technically a club with yoofs.
DEMIMONDE
SO, WHAT HAPPENS WHEN HE WANTS MUMSY TO PICK HIM UP IN THE 4X4?
HE SENDS A MES-SENGER BAT?
HAR HAR
I.D. PLEASE.

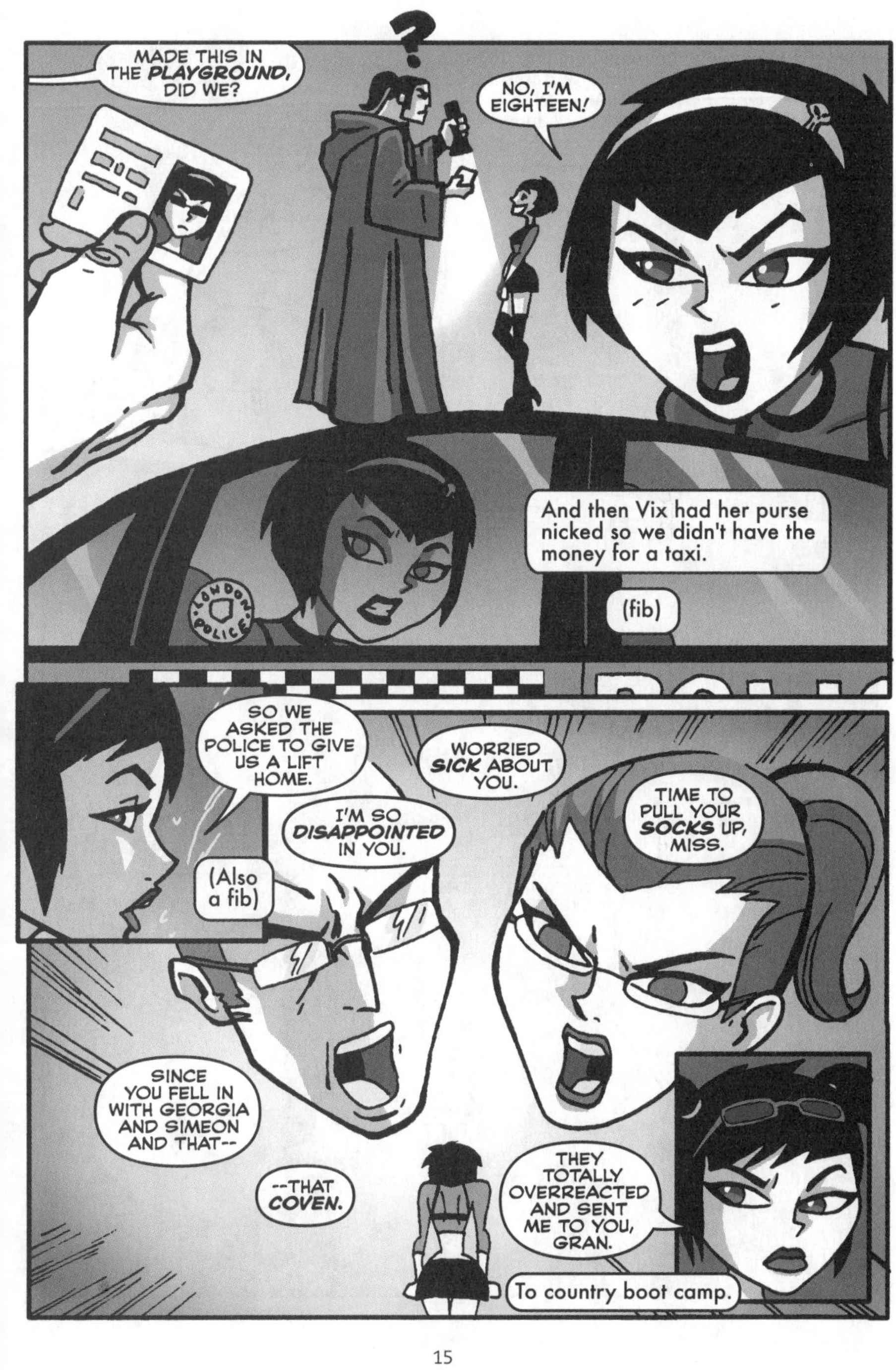
MADE THIS IN THE **PLAYGROUND,** DID WE?
NO, I'M EIGHTEEN!
And then Vix had her purse nicked so we didn't have the money for a taxi.
(fib)
SO WE ASKED THE POLICE TO GIVE US A LIFT HOME.
(Also a fib)
WORRIED **SICK** ABOUT YOU.
I'M SO **DISAPPOINTED** IN YOU.
TIME TO PULL YOUR **SOCKS** UP, MISS.
SINCE YOU FELL IN WITH GEORGIA AND SIMEON AND THAT--
--THAT **COVEN.**
THEY TOTALLY OVERREACTED AND SENT ME TO YOU, GRAN.
To country boot camp.

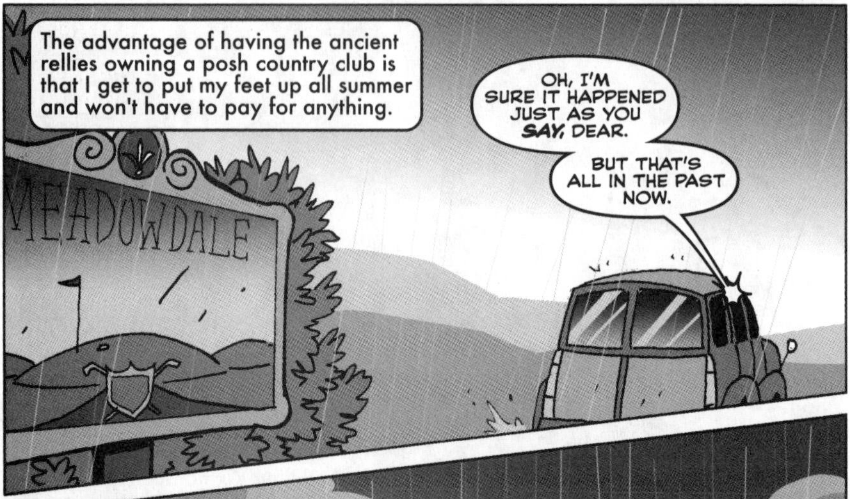
The advantage of having the ancient rellies owning a posh country club is that I get to put my feet up all summer and won't have to pay for anything.
MEADOWDALE
OH, I'M SURE IT HAPPENED JUST AS YOU *SAY,* DEAR.
BUT THAT'S ALL IN THE PAST NOW.

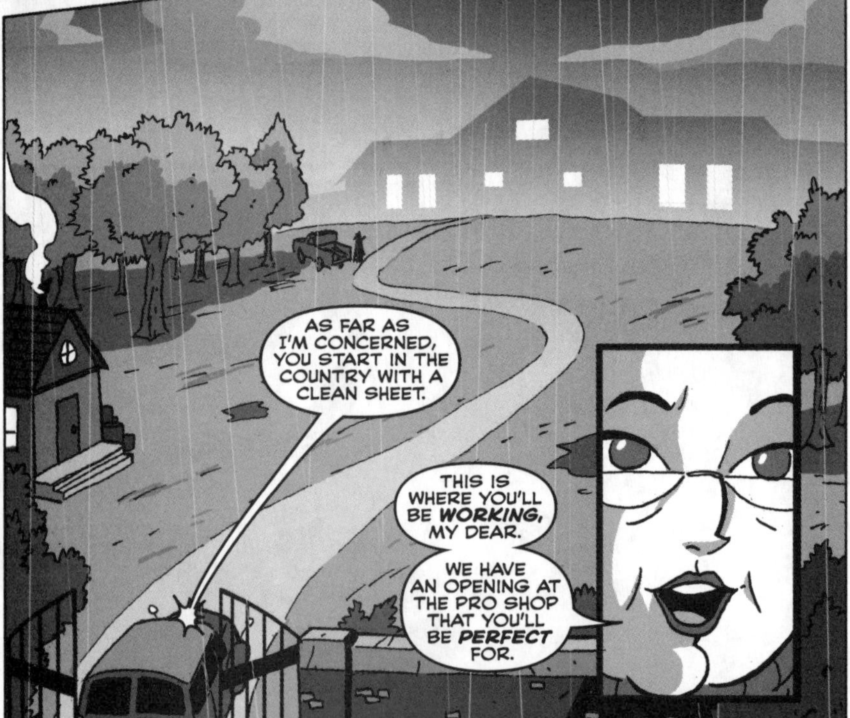
AS FAR AS I'M CONCERNED, YOU START IN THE COUNTRY WITH A CLEAN SHEET.
THIS IS WHERE YOU'LL BE *WORKING,* MY DEAR.
WE HAVE AN OPENING AT THE PRO SHOP THAT YOU'LL BE *PERFECT* FOR.

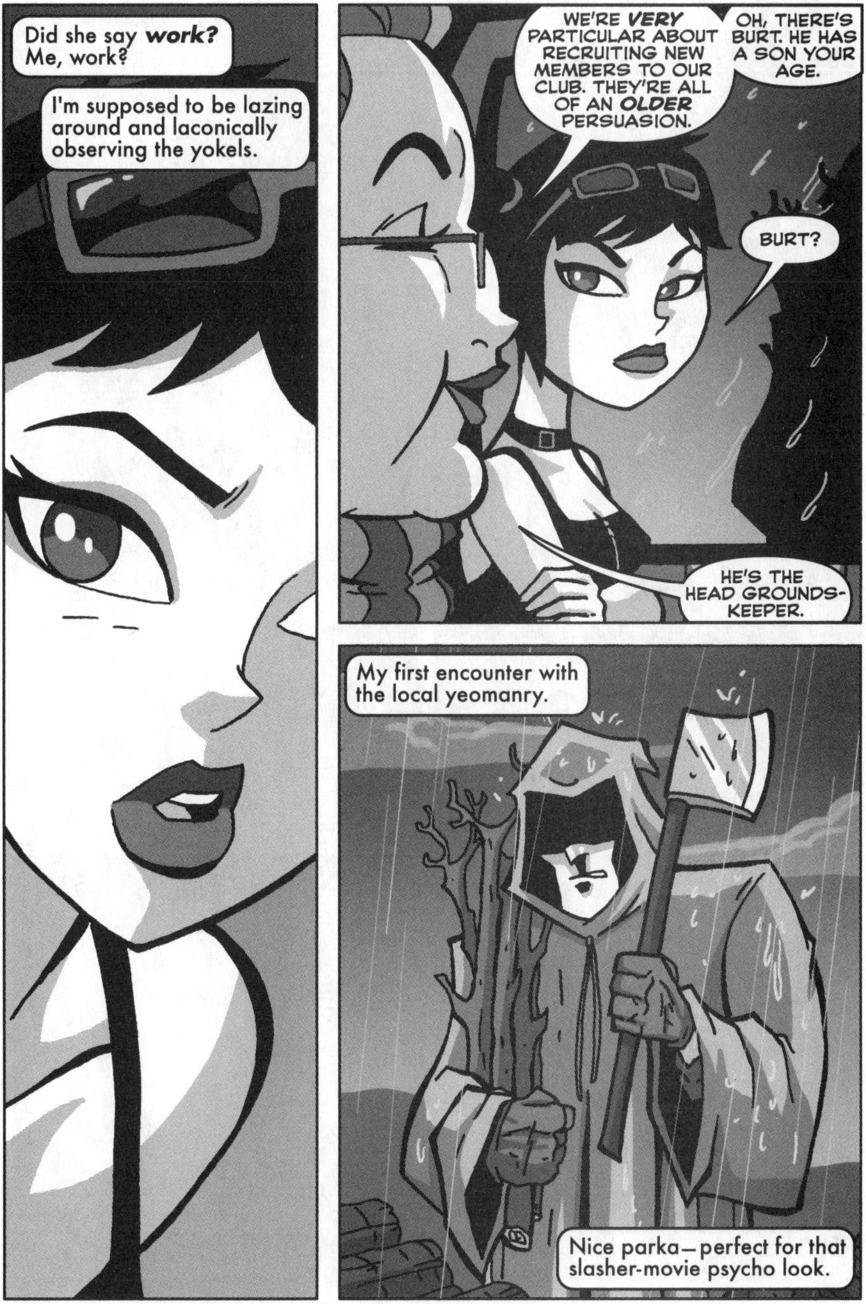
Did she say ***work?*** Me, work?
I'm supposed to be lazing around and laconically observing the yokels.
WE'RE ***VERY*** PARTICULAR ABOUT RECRUITING NEW MEMBERS TO OUR CLUB. THEY'RE ALL OF AN ***OLDER*** PERSUASION.
OH, THERE'S BURT. HE HAS A SON YOUR AGE.
BURT?
HE'S THE HEAD GROUNDS-KEEPER.
My first encounter with the local yeomanry.
Nice parka—perfect for that slasher-movie psycho look.

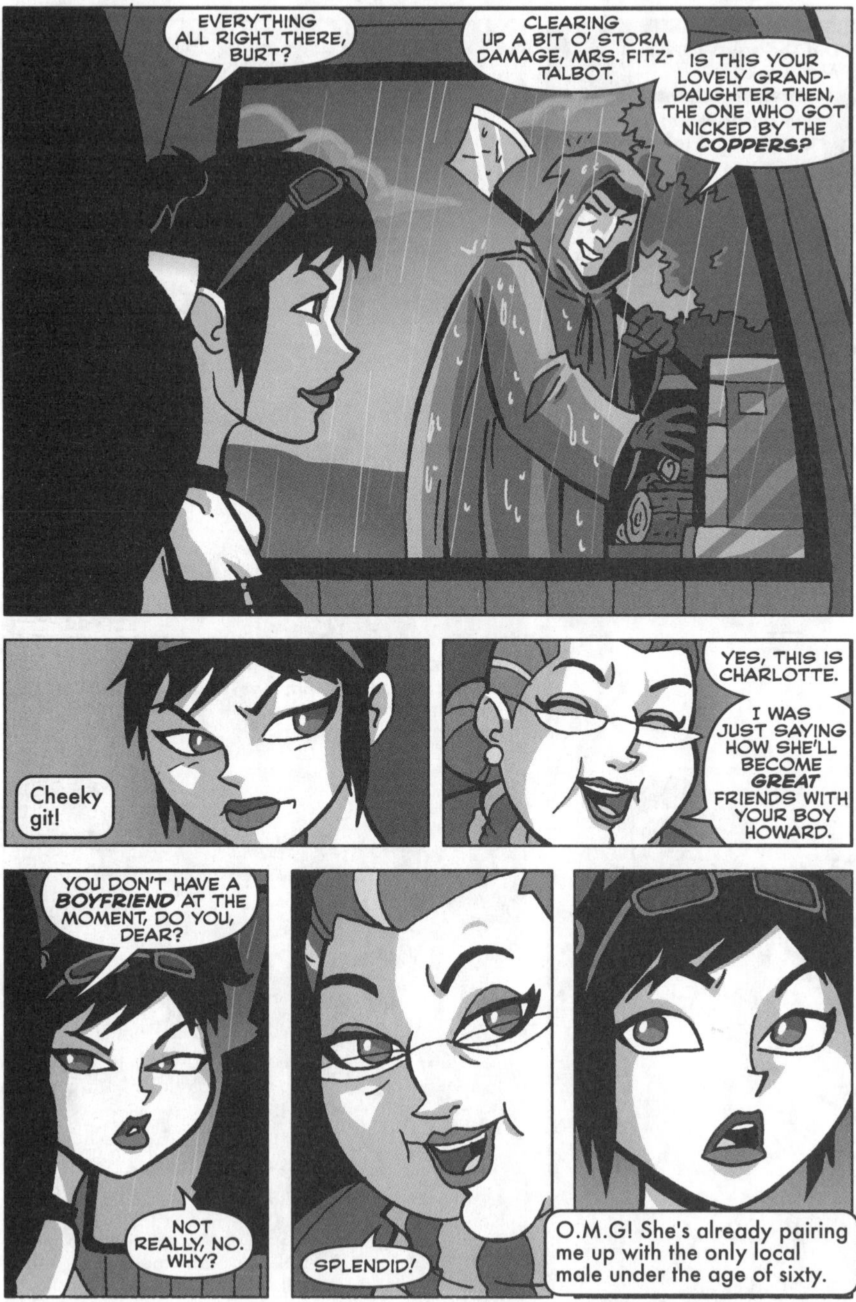
EVERYTHING ALL RIGHT THERE, BURT?
CLEARING UP A BIT O' STORM DAMAGE, MRS. FITZ-TALBOT.
IS THIS YOUR LOVELY GRAND-DAUGHTER THEN, THE ONE WHO GOT NICKED BY THE ***COPPERS?***
Cheeky git!
YES, THIS IS CHARLOTTE.
I WAS JUST SAYING HOW SHE'LL BECOME ***GREAT*** FRIENDS WITH YOUR BOY HOWARD.
YOU DON'T HAVE A ***BOYFRIEND*** AT THE MOMENT, DO YOU, DEAR?
NOT REALLY, NO. WHY?
SPLENDID!
O.M.G! She's already pairing me up with the only local male under the age of sixty.

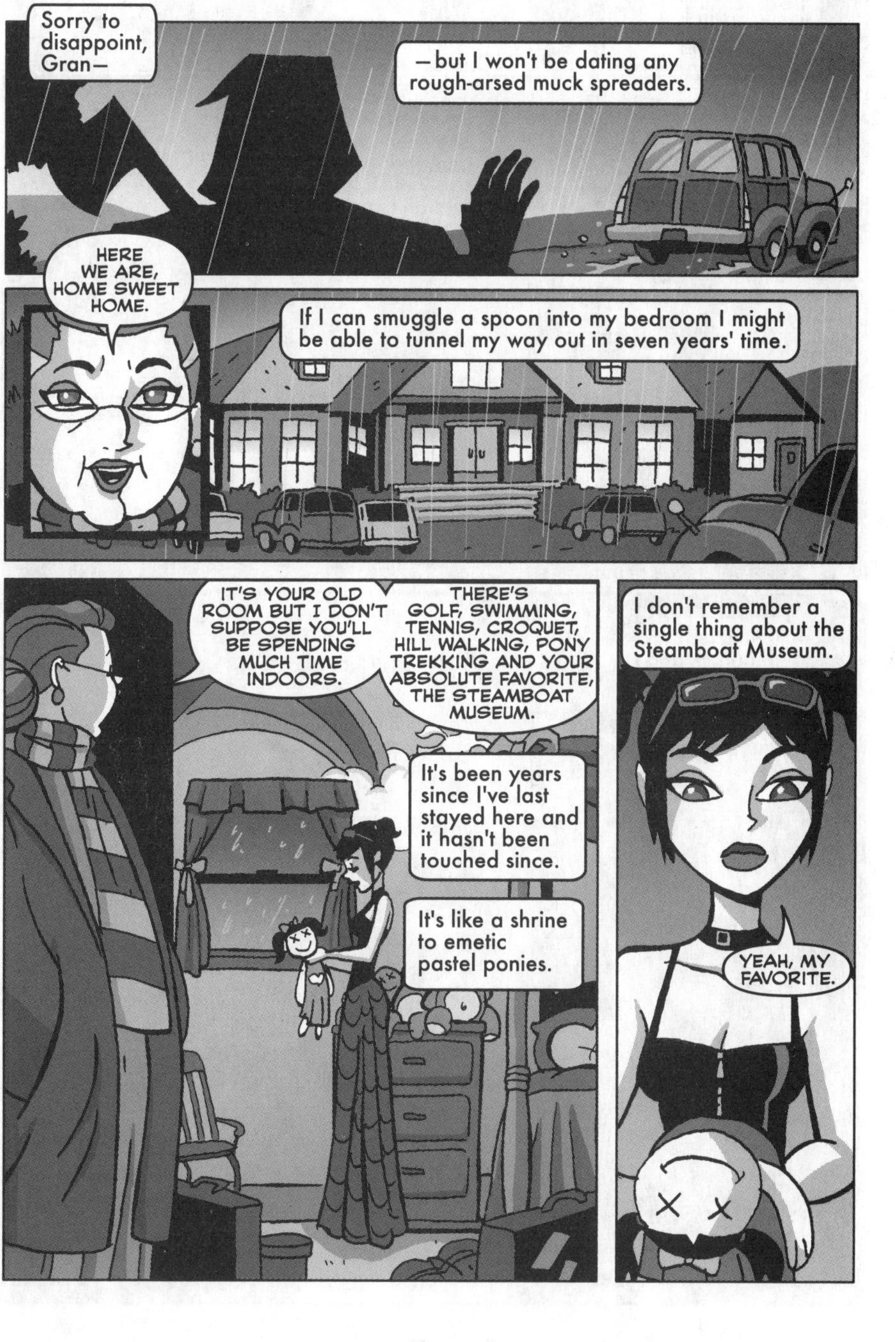
Sorry to disappoint, Gran—
—but I won't be dating any rough-arsed muck spreaders.
HERE WE ARE, HOME SWEET HOME.
If I can smuggle a spoon into my bedroom I might be able to tunnel my way out in seven years' time.
IT'S YOUR OLD ROOM BUT I DON'T SUPPOSE YOU'LL BE SPENDING MUCH TIME INDOORS.
THERE'S GOLF, SWIMMING, TENNIS, CROQUET, HILL WALKING, PONY TREKKING AND YOUR ABSOLUTE FAVORITE, THE STEAMBOAT MUSEUM.
It's been years since I've last stayed here and it hasn't been touched since.
It's like a shrine to emetic pastel ponies.
I don't remember a single thing about the Steamboat Museum.
YEAH, MY FAVORITE.

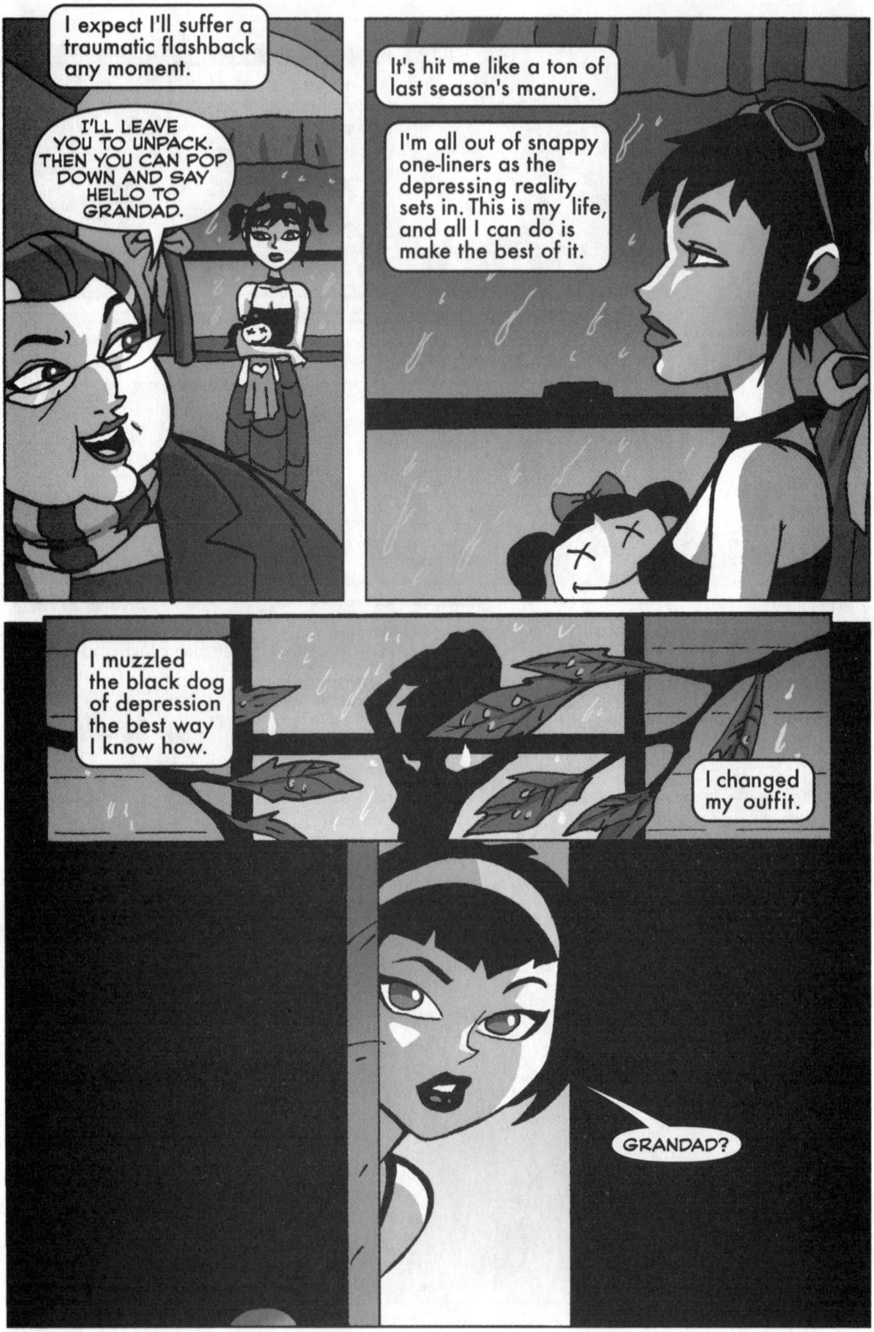
I expect I'll suffer a traumatic flashback any moment.
I'LL LEAVE YOU TO UNPACK. THEN YOU CAN POP DOWN AND SAY HELLO TO GRANDAD.
It's hit me like a ton of last season's manure.
I'm all out of snappy one-liners as the depressing reality sets in. This is my life, and all I can do is make the best of it.
I muzzled the black dog of depression the best way I know how.
I changed my outfit.
GRANDAD?

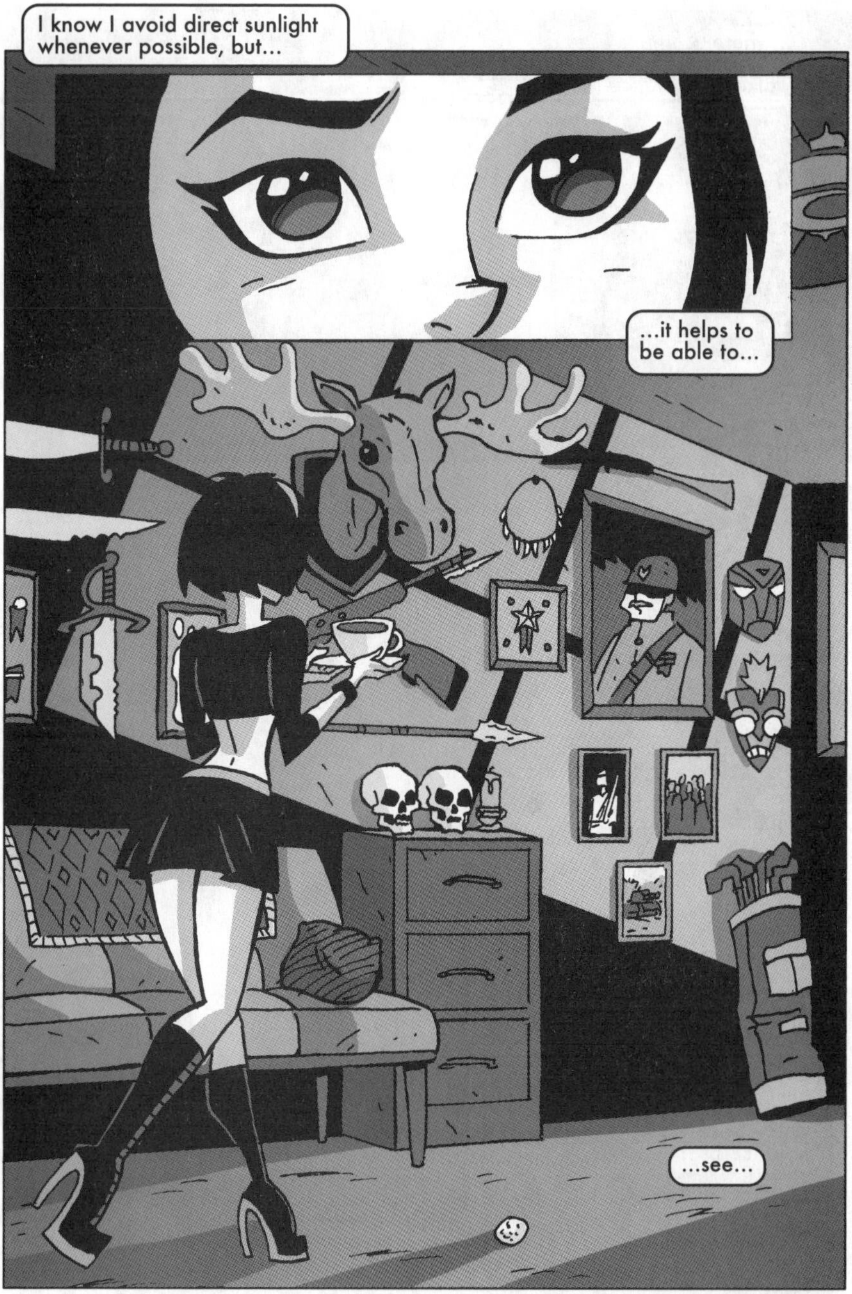
I know I avoid direct sunlight whenever possible, but...
...it helps to be able to...
...see...

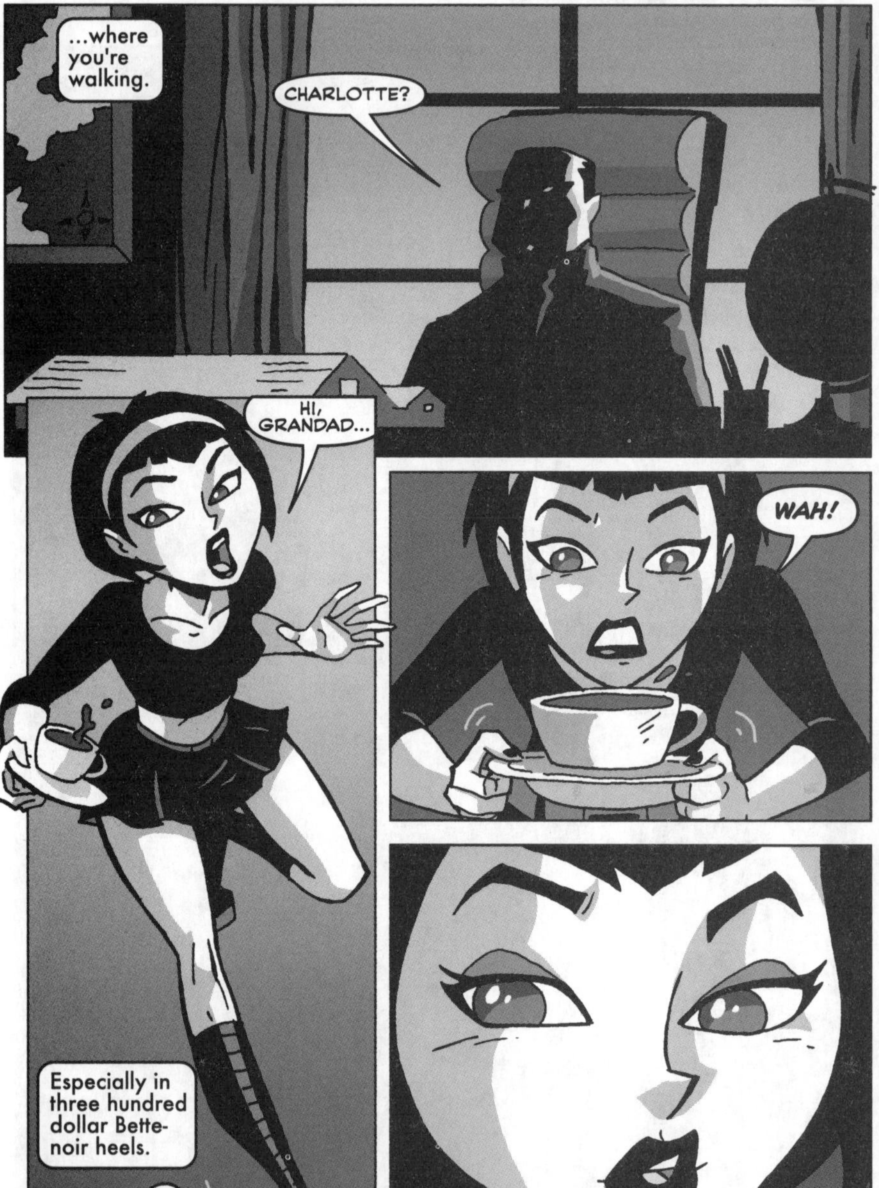
...where you're walking.
CHARLOTTE?
HI, GRANDAD...
Especially in three hundred dollar Bette-noir heels.
WAH!
GRANDAD. I BROUGHT YOU A CUP OF TEA.

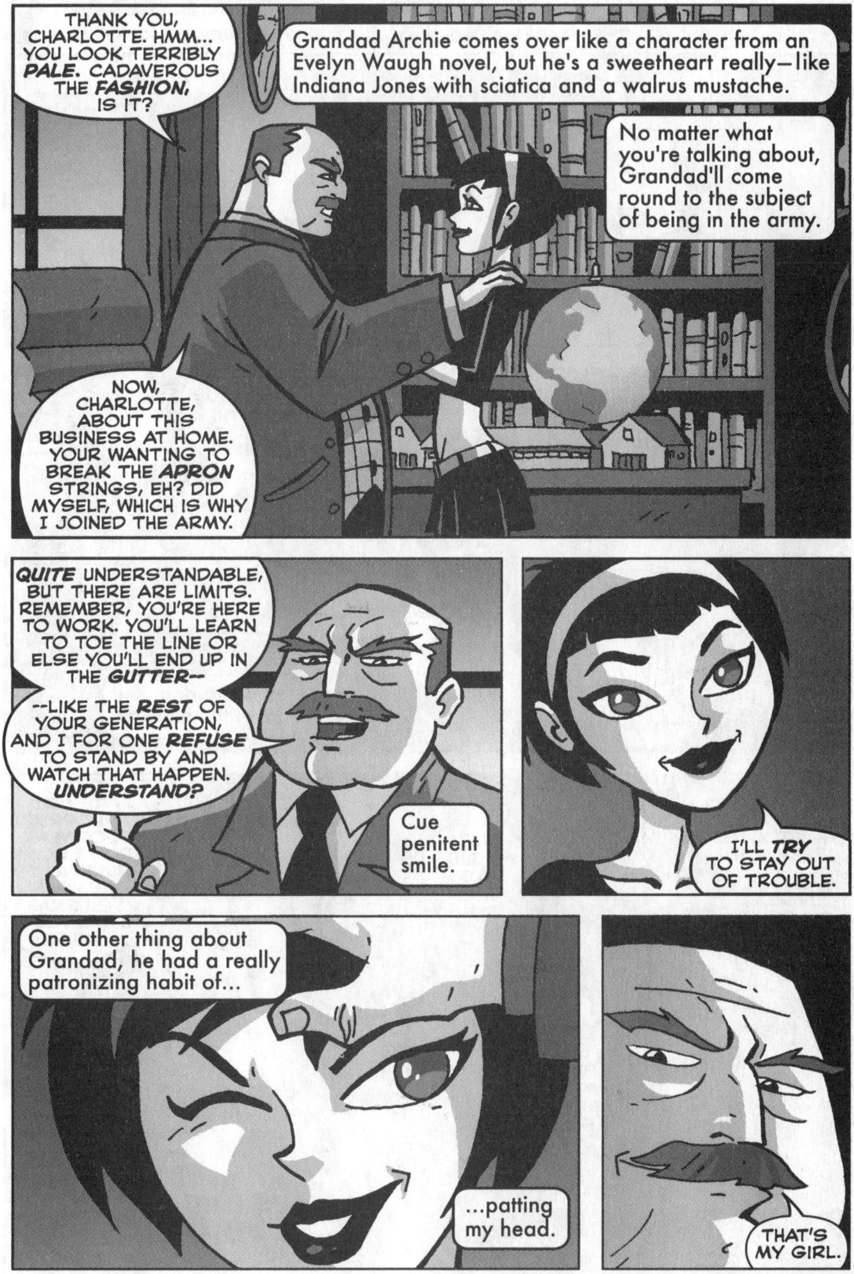
THANK YOU, CHARLOTTE. HMM... YOU LOOK TERRIBLY **PALE.** CADAVEROUS THE **FASHION,** IS IT?
Grandad Archie comes over like a character from an Evelyn Waugh novel, but he's a sweetheart really—like Indiana Jones with sciatica and a walrus mustache.
No matter what you're talking about, Grandad'll come round to the subject of being in the army.
NOW, CHARLOTTE, ABOUT THIS BUSINESS AT HOME. YOUR WANTING TO BREAK THE **APRON** STRINGS, EH? DID MYSELF, WHICH IS WHY I JOINED THE ARMY.
QUITE UNDERSTANDABLE, BUT THERE ARE LIMITS. REMEMBER, YOU'RE HERE TO WORK. YOU'LL LEARN TO TOE THE LINE OR ELSE YOU'LL END UP IN THE **GUTTER--**
--LIKE THE **REST** OF YOUR GENERATION, AND I FOR ONE **REFUSE** TO STAND BY AND WATCH THAT HAPPEN. **UNDERSTAND?**
Cue penitent smile.
I'LL **TRY** TO STAY OUT OF TROUBLE.
One other thing about Grandad, he had a really patronizing habit of...
...patting my head.
THAT'S MY GIRL.

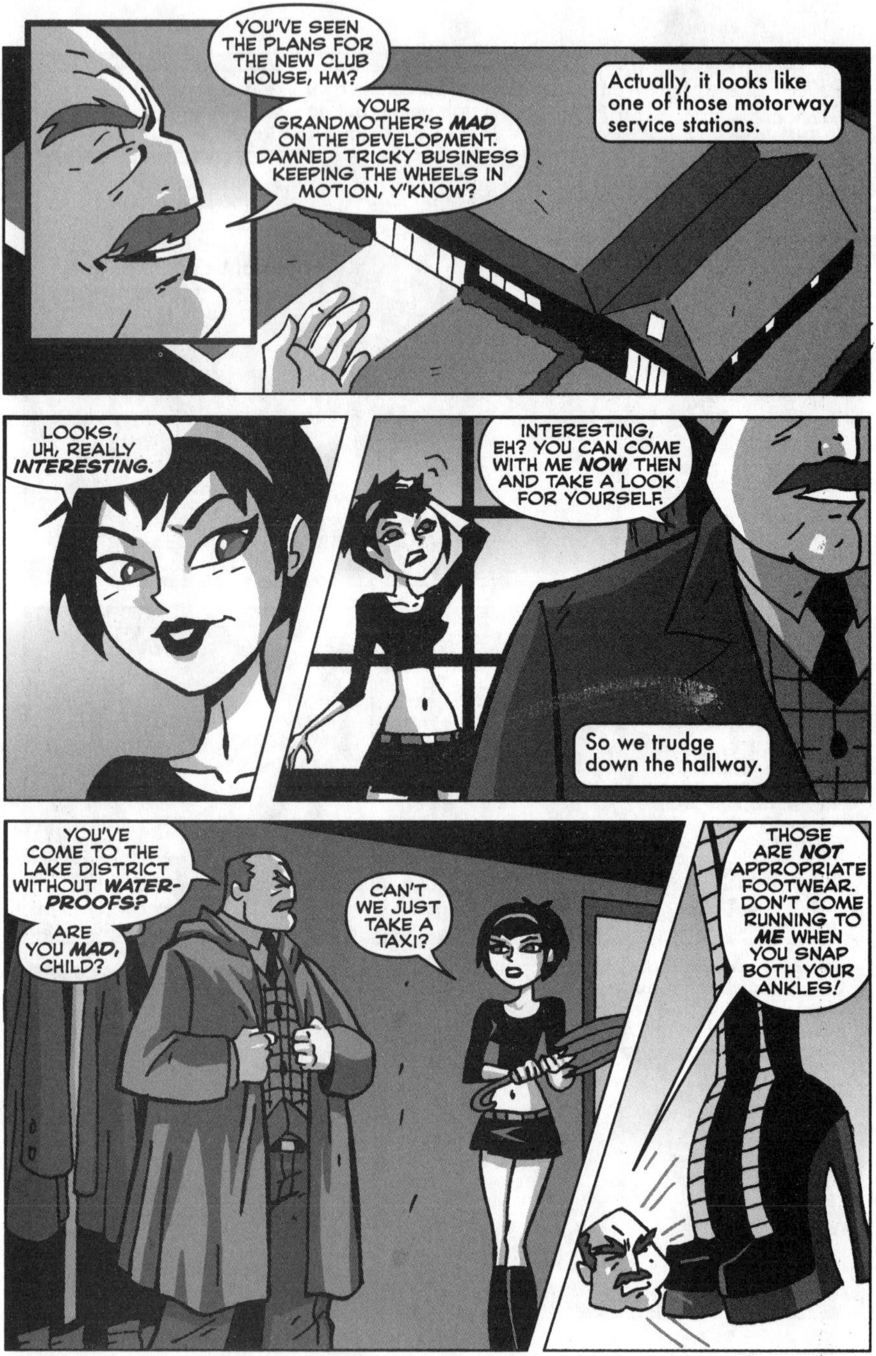
YOU'VE SEEN THE PLANS FOR THE NEW CLUB HOUSE, HM?
YOUR GRANDMOTHER'S MAD ON THE DEVELOPMENT. DAMNED TRICKY BUSINESS KEEPING THE WHEELS IN MOTION, Y'KNOW?
Actually, it looks like one of those motorway service stations.
LOOKS, UH, REALLY INTERESTING.
INTERESTING, EH? YOU CAN COME WITH ME NOW THEN AND TAKE A LOOK FOR YOURSELF.
So we trudge down the hallway.
YOU'VE COME TO THE LAKE DISTRICT WITHOUT WATER-PROOFS?
ARE YOU MAD, CHILD?
CAN'T WE JUST TAKE A TAXI?
THOSE ARE NOT APPROPRIATE FOOTWEAR. DON'T COME RUNNING TO ME WHEN YOU SNAP BOTH YOUR ANKLES!

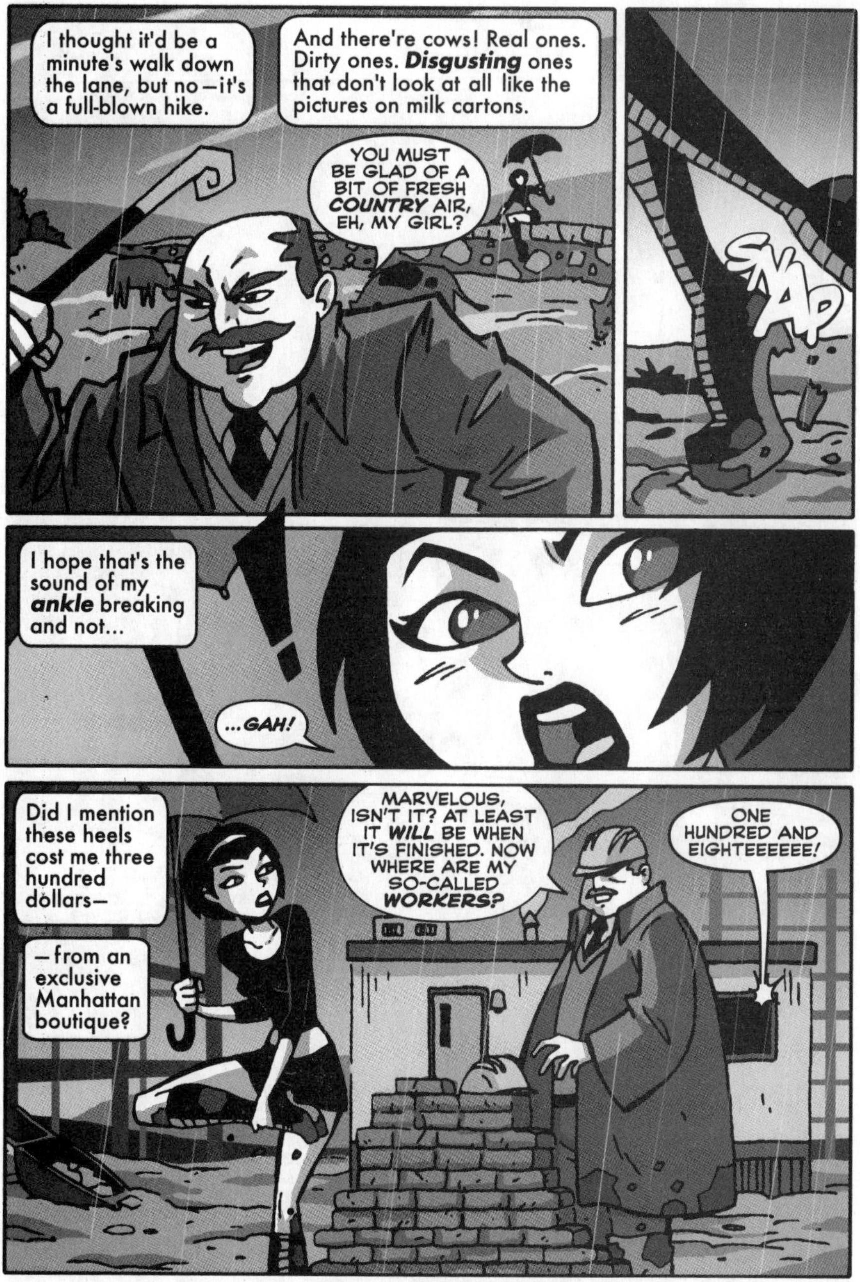
I thought it'd be a minute's walk down the lane, but no—it's a full-blown hike.
And there're cows! Real ones. Dirty ones. **Disgusting** ones that don't look at all like the pictures on milk cartons.
YOU MUST BE GLAD OF A BIT OF FRESH **COUNTRY** AIR, EH, MY GIRL?
SNAP
I hope that's the sound of my **ankle** breaking and not...
...GAH!
Did I mention these heels cost me three hundred dollars—
—from an exclusive Manhattan boutique?
MARVELOUS, ISN'T IT? AT LEAST IT **WILL** BE WHEN IT'S FINISHED. NOW WHERE ARE MY SO-CALLED **WORKERS?**
ONE HUNDRED AND EIGHTEEEEEEE!

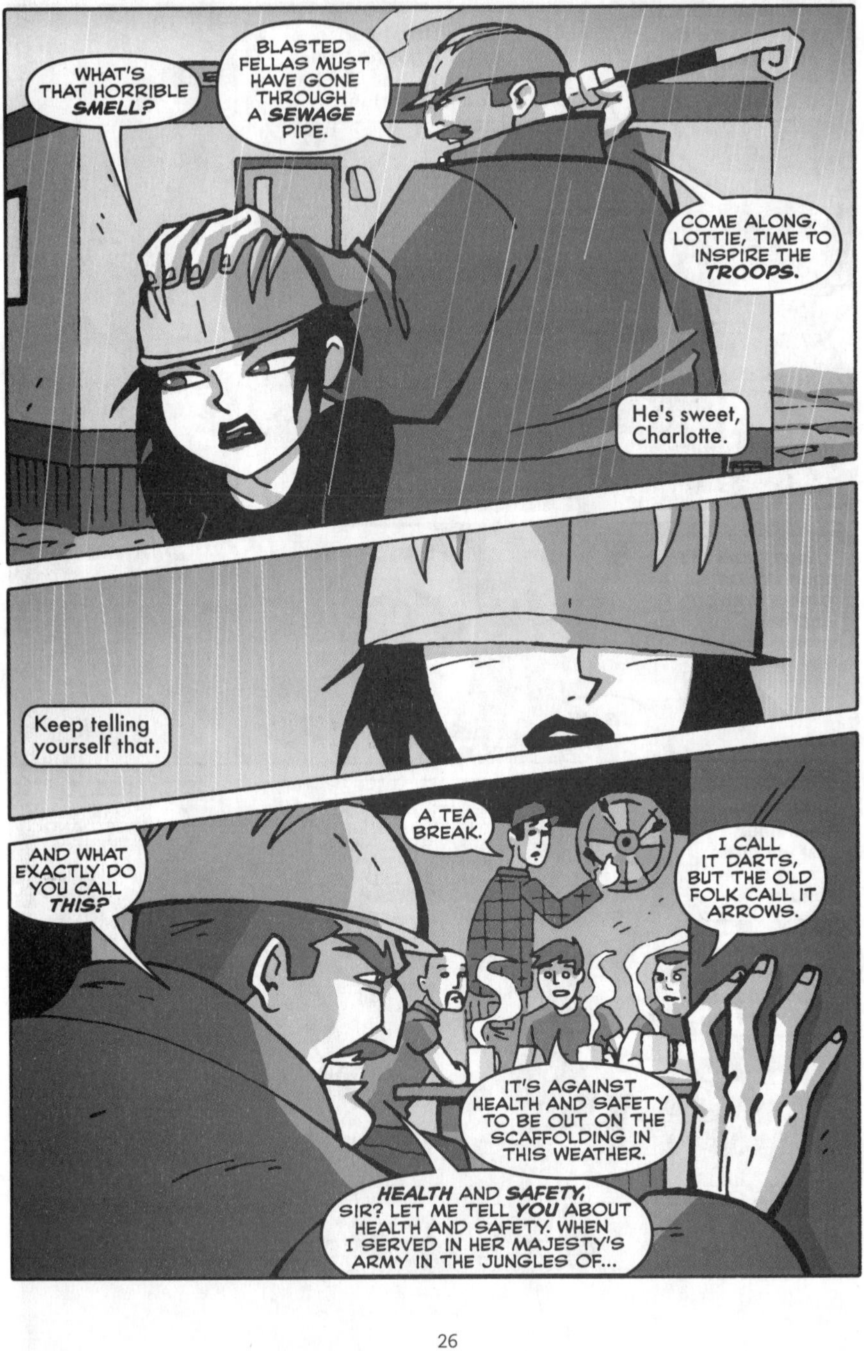
WHAT'S THAT HORRIBLE *SMELL?*
BLASTED FELLAS MUST HAVE GONE THROUGH A *SEWAGE* PIPE.
COME ALONG, LOTTIE, TIME TO INSPIRE THE *TROOPS.*
He's sweet, Charlotte.
Keep telling yourself that.
AND WHAT EXACTLY DO YOU CALL *THIS?*
A TEA BREAK.
I CALL IT DARTS, BUT THE OLD FOLK CALL IT ARROWS.
IT'S AGAINST HEALTH AND SAFETY TO BE OUT ON THE SCAFFOLDING IN THIS WEATHER.
HEALTH AND *SAFETY,* SIR? LET ME TELL *YOU* ABOUT HEALTH AND SAFETY. WHEN I SERVED IN HER MAJESTY'S ARMY IN THE JUNGLES OF...

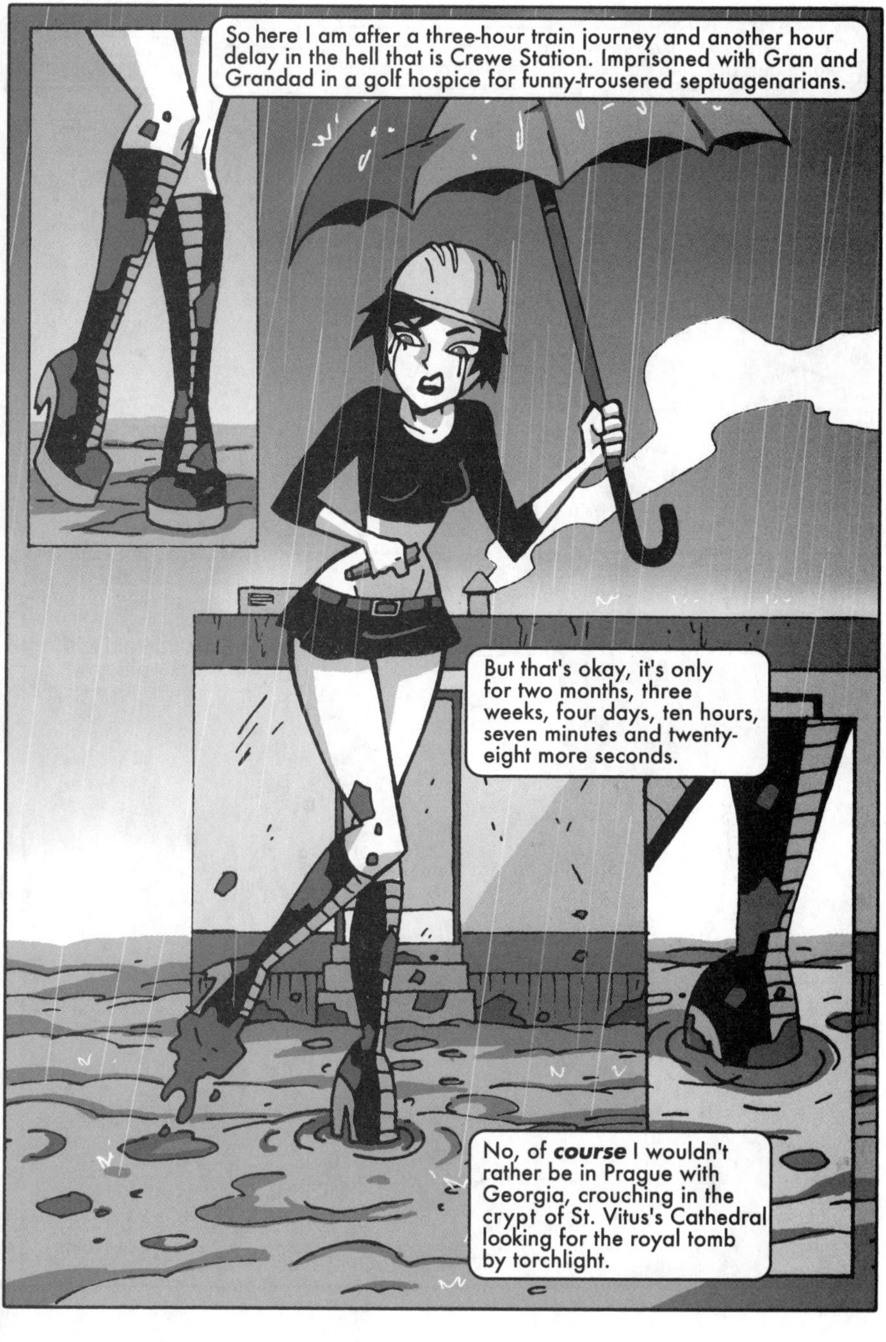
So here I am after a three-hour train journey and another hour delay in the hell that is Crewe Station. Imprisoned with Gran and Grandad in a golf hospice for funny-trousered septuagenarians.
But that's okay, it's only for two months, three weeks, four days, ten hours, seven minutes and twenty-eight more seconds.
No, of ***course*** I wouldn't rather be in Prague with Georgia, crouching in the crypt of St. Vitus's Cathedral looking for the royal tomb by torchlight.

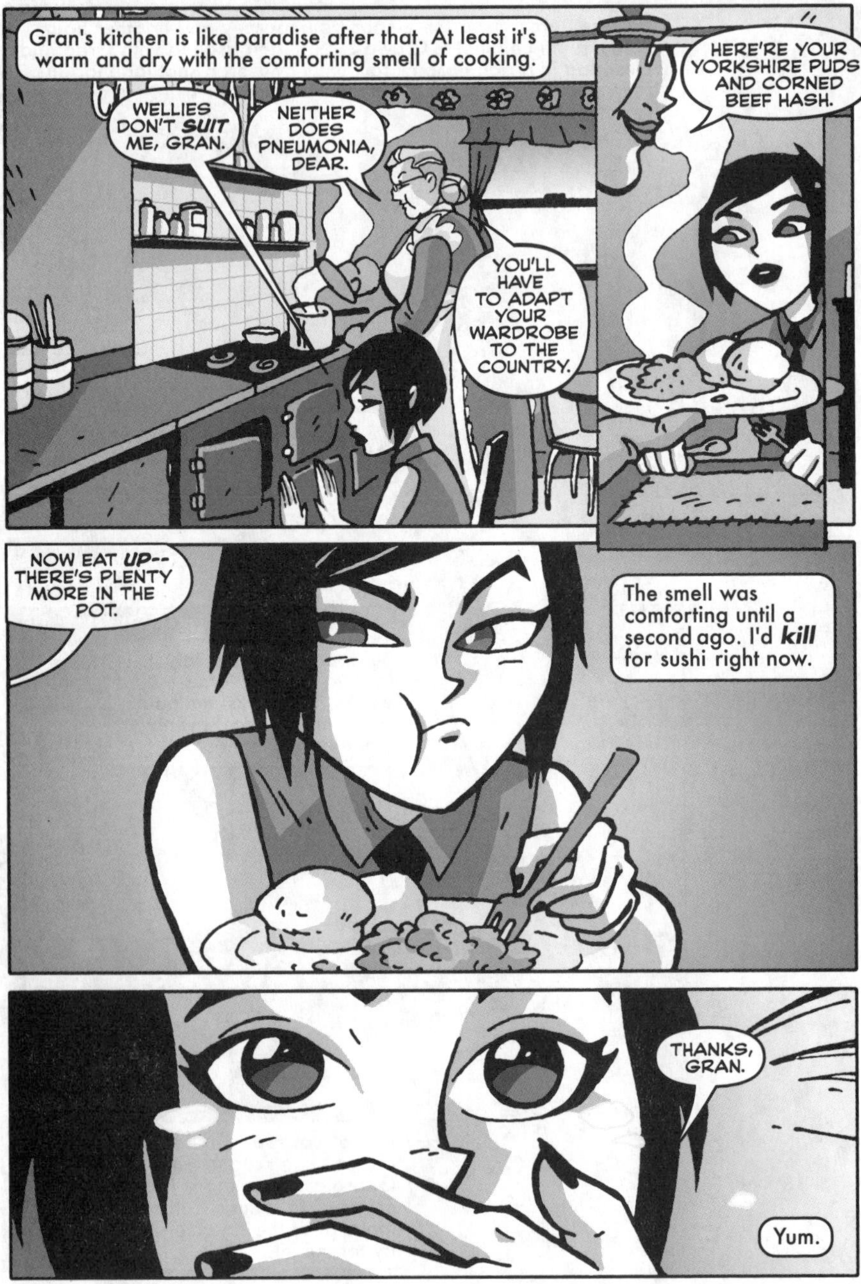

Gran's kitchen is like paradise after that. At least it's warm and dry with the comforting smell of cooking.
WELLIES DON'T SUIT ME, GRAN.
NEITHER DOES PNEUMONIA, DEAR.
YOU'LL HAVE TO ADAPT YOUR WARDROBE TO THE COUNTRY.
HERE'RE YOUR YORKSHIRE PUDS AND CORNED BEEF HASH.
NOW EAT UP-- THERE'S PLENTY MORE IN THE POT.
The smell was comforting until a second ago. I'd kill for sushi right now.
THANKS, GRAN.
Yum.

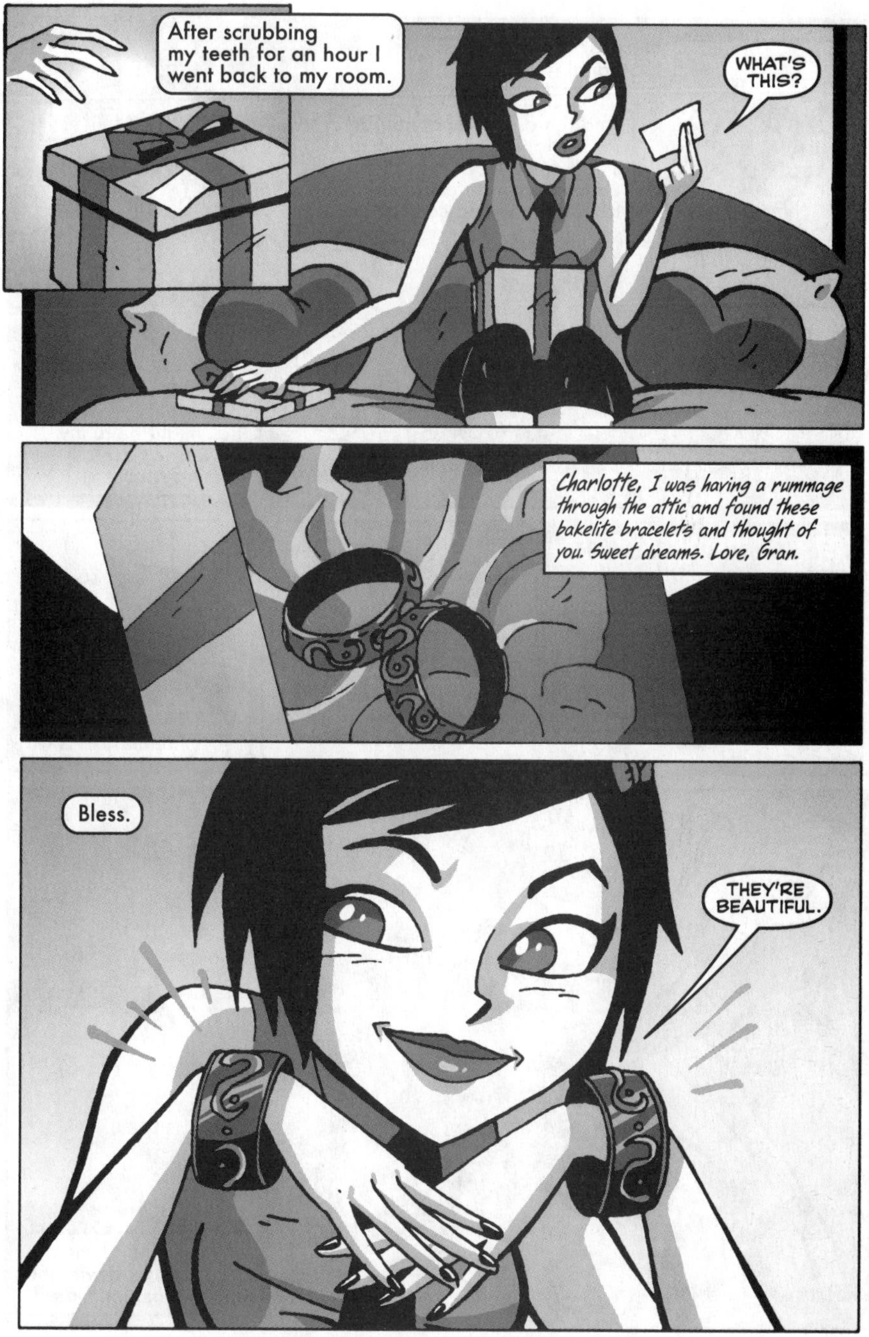
After scrubbing my teeth for an hour I went back to my room.
WHAT'S THIS?
Charlotte, I was having a rummage through the attic and found these bakelite bracelets and thought of you. Sweet dreams. Love, Gran.
Bless.
THEY'RE BEAUTIFUL.

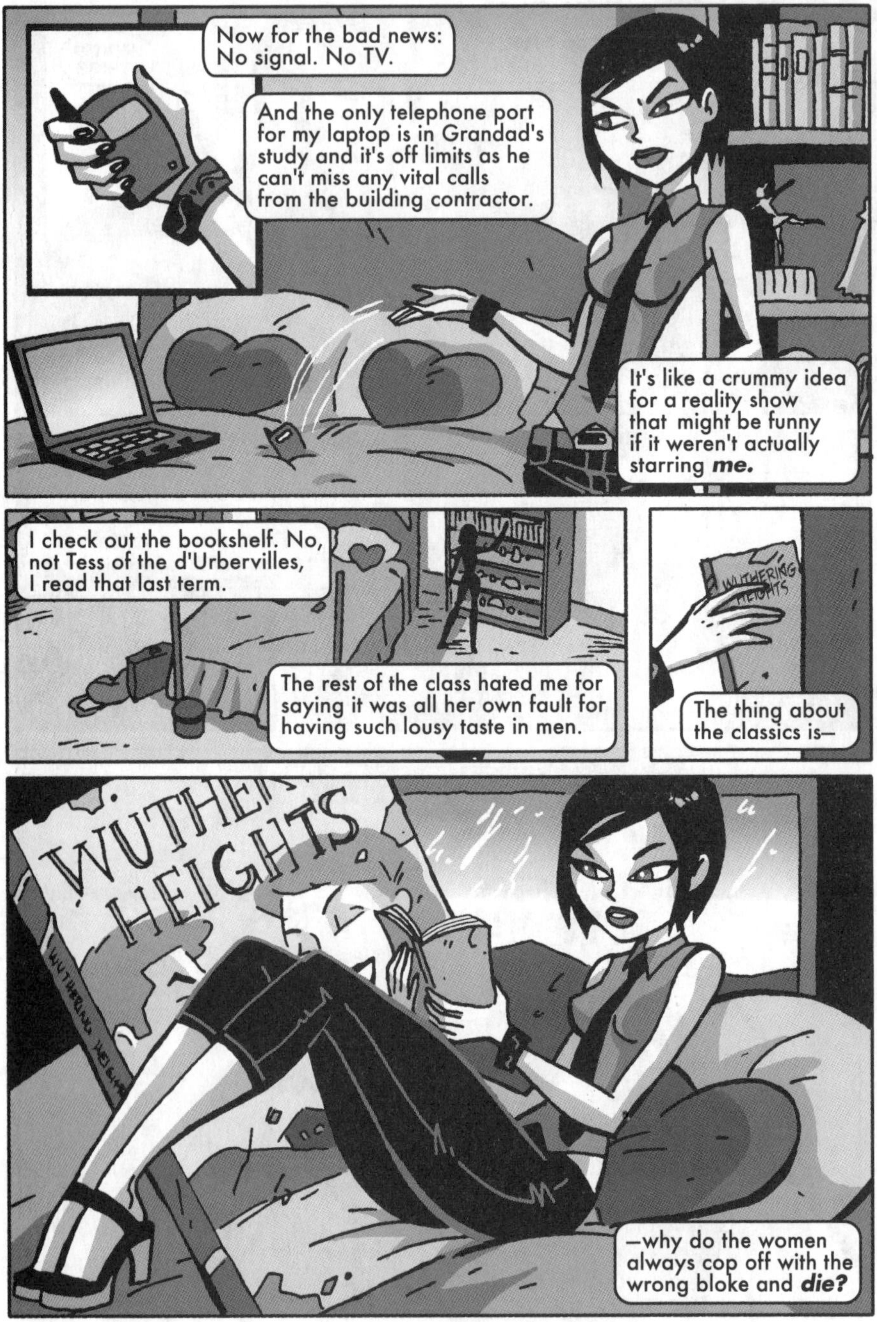
Now for the bad news: No signal. No TV.
And the only telephone port for my laptop is in Grandad's study and it's off limits as he can't miss any vital calls from the building contractor.
It's like a crummy idea for a reality show that might be funny if it weren't actually starring ***me.***
I check out the bookshelf. No, not Tess of the d'Urbervilles, I read that last term.
The rest of the class hated me for saying it was all her own fault for having such lousy taste in men.
WUTHERING HEIGHTS
The thing about the classics is—
—why do the women always cop off with the wrong bloke and ***die?***

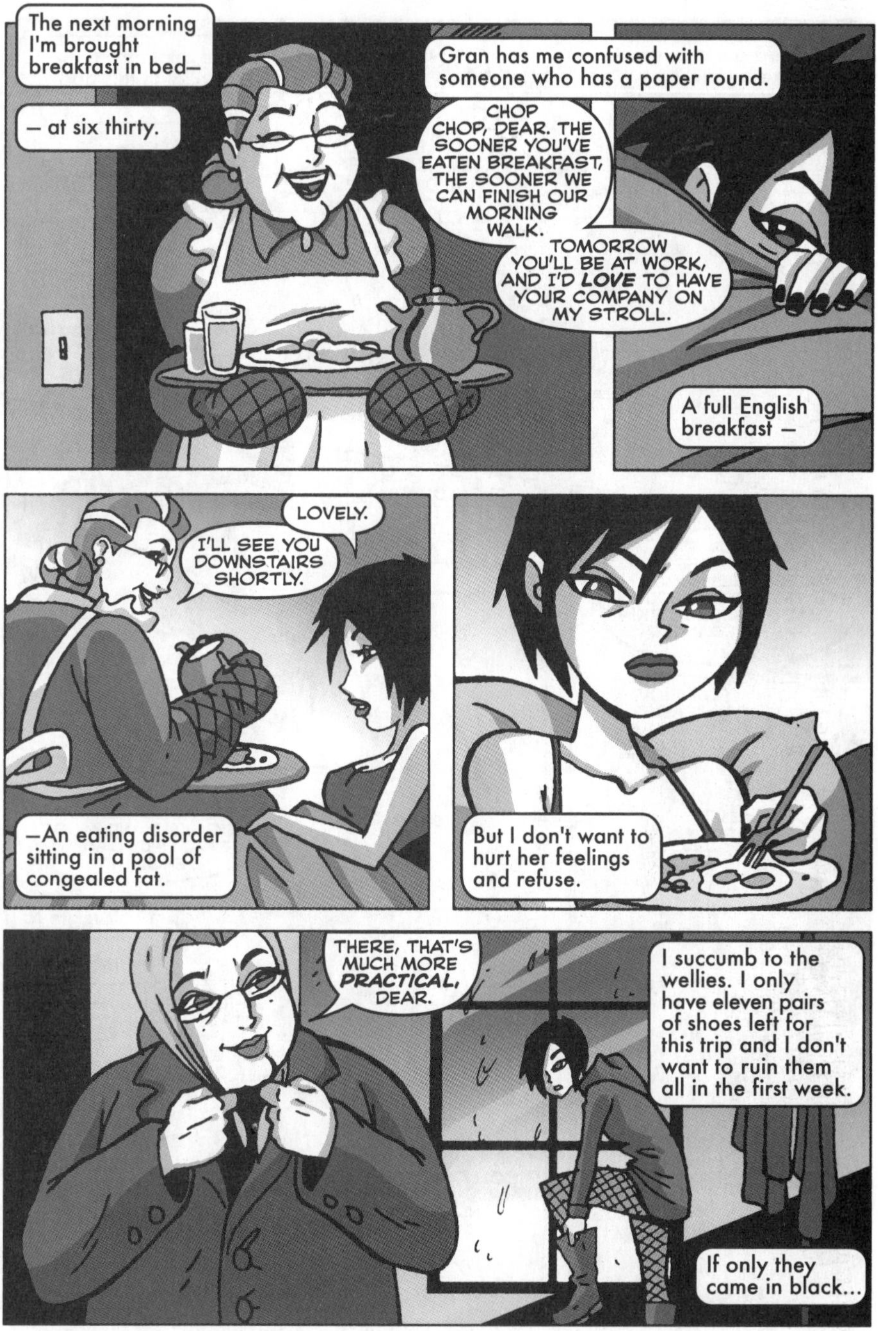
The next morning I'm brought breakfast in bed—
— at six thirty.
Gran has me confused with someone who has a paper round.
CHOP CHOP, DEAR. THE SOONER YOU'VE EATEN BREAKFAST, THE SOONER WE CAN FINISH OUR MORNING WALK.
TOMORROW YOU'LL BE AT WORK, AND I'D ***LOVE*** TO HAVE YOUR COMPANY ON MY STROLL.
A full English breakfast —
LOVELY.
I'LL SEE YOU DOWNSTAIRS SHORTLY.
—An eating disorder sitting in a pool of congealed fat.
But I don't want to hurt her feelings and refuse.
THERE, THAT'S MUCH MORE ***PRACTICAL,*** DEAR.
I succumb to the wellies. I only have eleven pairs of shoes left for this trip and I don't want to ruin them all in the first week.
If only they came in black...

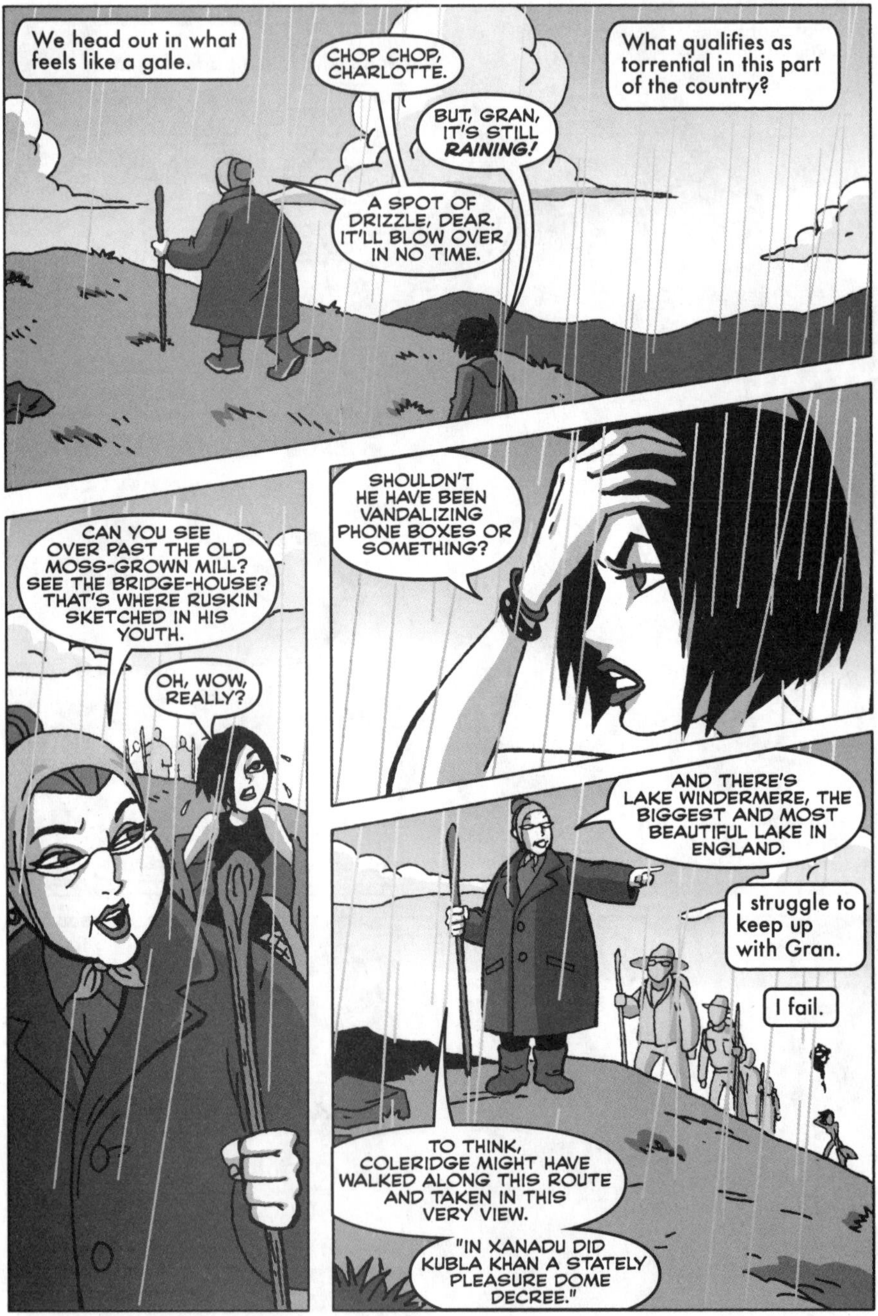
We head out in what feels like a gale.
CHOP CHOP, CHARLOTTE.
BUT, GRAN, IT'S STILL *RAINING!*
A SPOT OF DRIZZLE, DEAR. IT'LL BLOW OVER IN NO TIME.
What qualifies as torrential in this part of the country?
CAN YOU SEE OVER PAST THE OLD MOSS-GROWN MILL? SEE THE BRIDGE-HOUSE? THAT'S WHERE RUSKIN SKETCHED IN HIS YOUTH.
OH, WOW, REALLY?
SHOULDN'T HE HAVE BEEN VANDALIZING PHONE BOXES OR SOMETHING?
AND THERE'S LAKE WINDERMERE, THE BIGGEST AND MOST BEAUTIFUL LAKE IN ENGLAND.
I struggle to keep up with Gran.
I fail.
TO THINK, COLERIDGE MIGHT HAVE WALKED ALONG THIS ROUTE AND TAKEN IN THIS VERY VIEW.
"IN XANADU DID KUBLA KHAN A STATELY PLEASURE DOME DECREE."

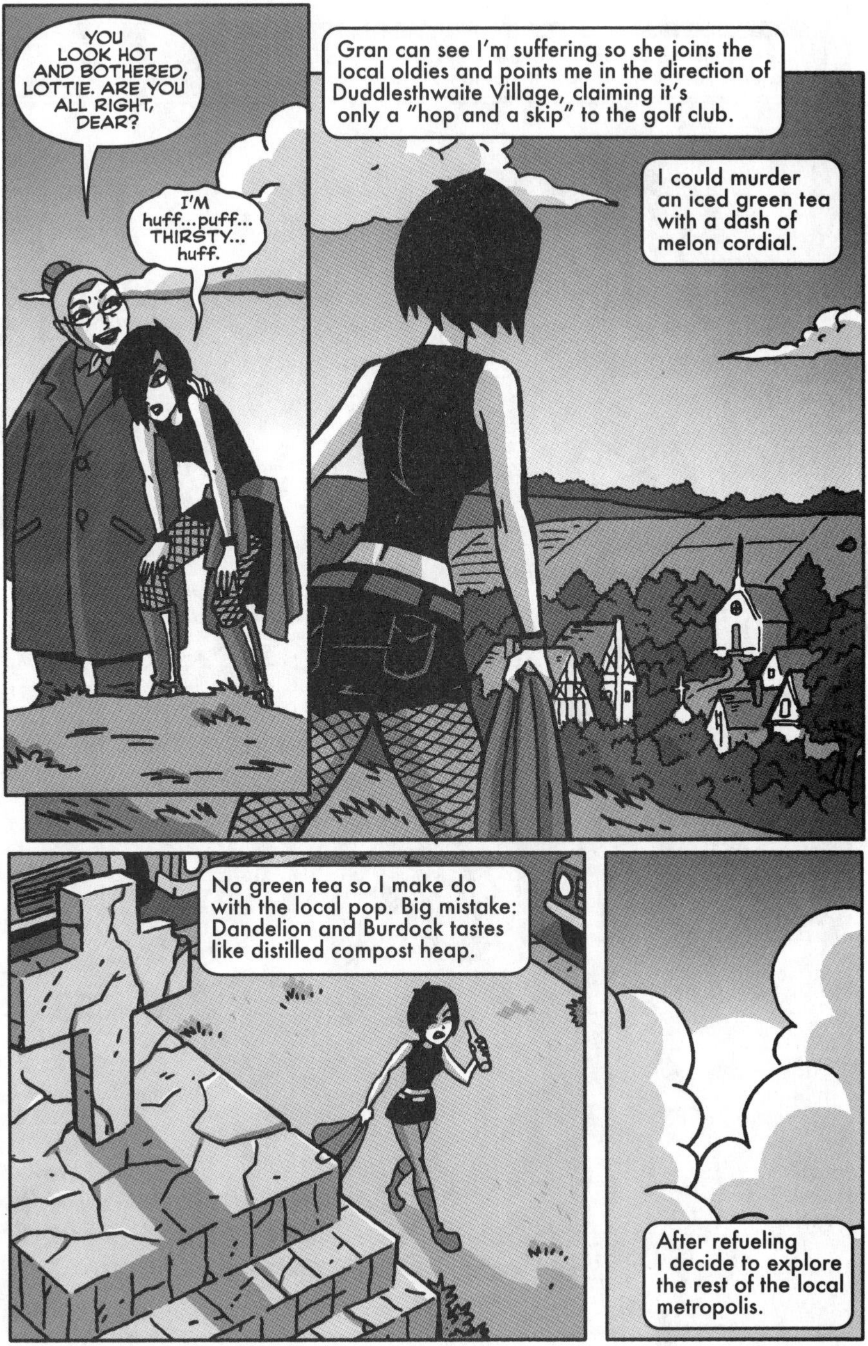
YOU LOOK HOT AND BOTHERED, LOTTIE. ARE YOU ALL RIGHT, DEAR?
I'M huff...puff... THIRSTY... huff.
Gran can see I'm suffering so she joins the local oldies and points me in the direction of Duddlesthwaite Village, claiming it's only a "hop and a skip" to the golf club.
I could murder an iced green tea with a dash of melon cordial.
No green tea so I make do with the local pop. Big mistake: Dandelion and Burdock tastes like distilled compost heap.
After refueling I decide to explore the rest of the local metropolis.

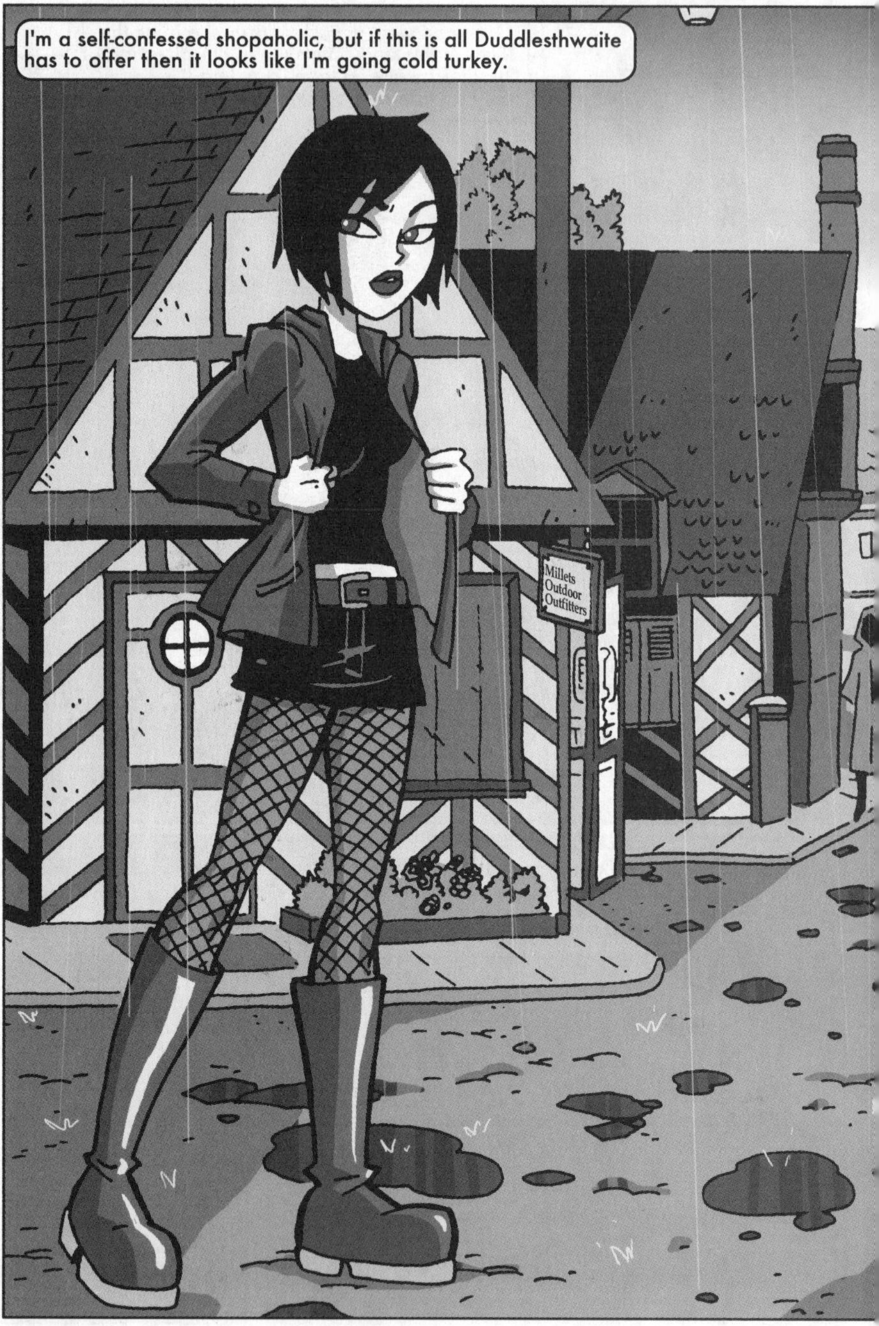
I'm a self-confessed shopaholic, but if this is all Duddlesthwaite has to offer then it looks like I'm going cold turkey.
Millets Outdoor Outfitters

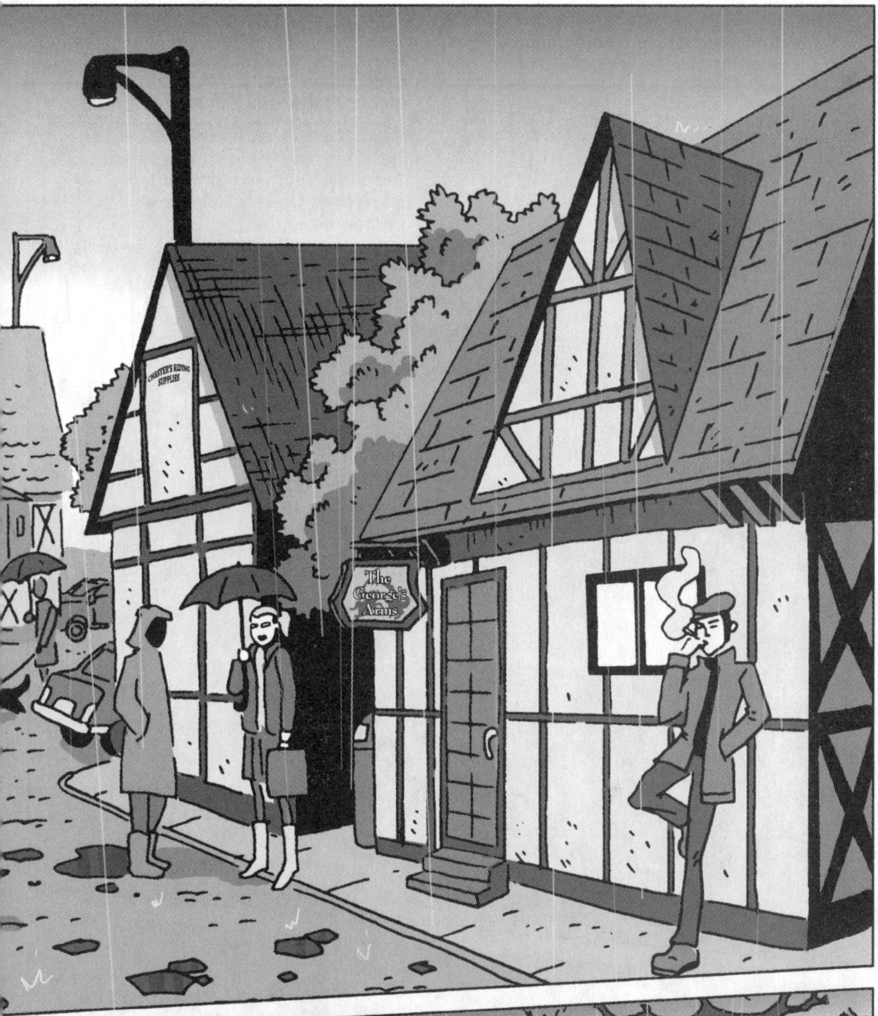
CHESTER'S RIDING SUPPLIES
The George's Arms

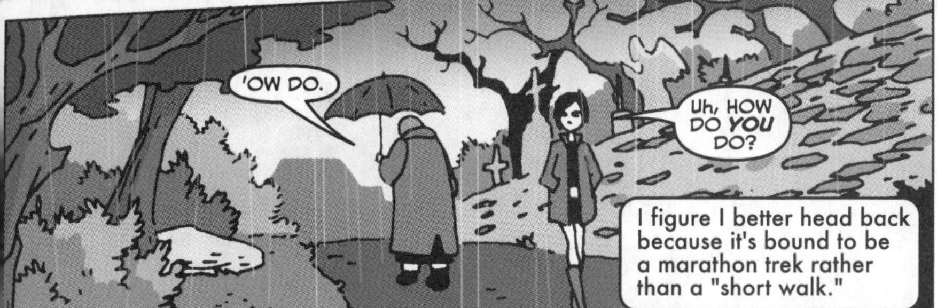
'OW DO.
Uh, HOW DO YOU DO?
I figure I better head back because it's bound to be a marathon trek rather than a "short walk."

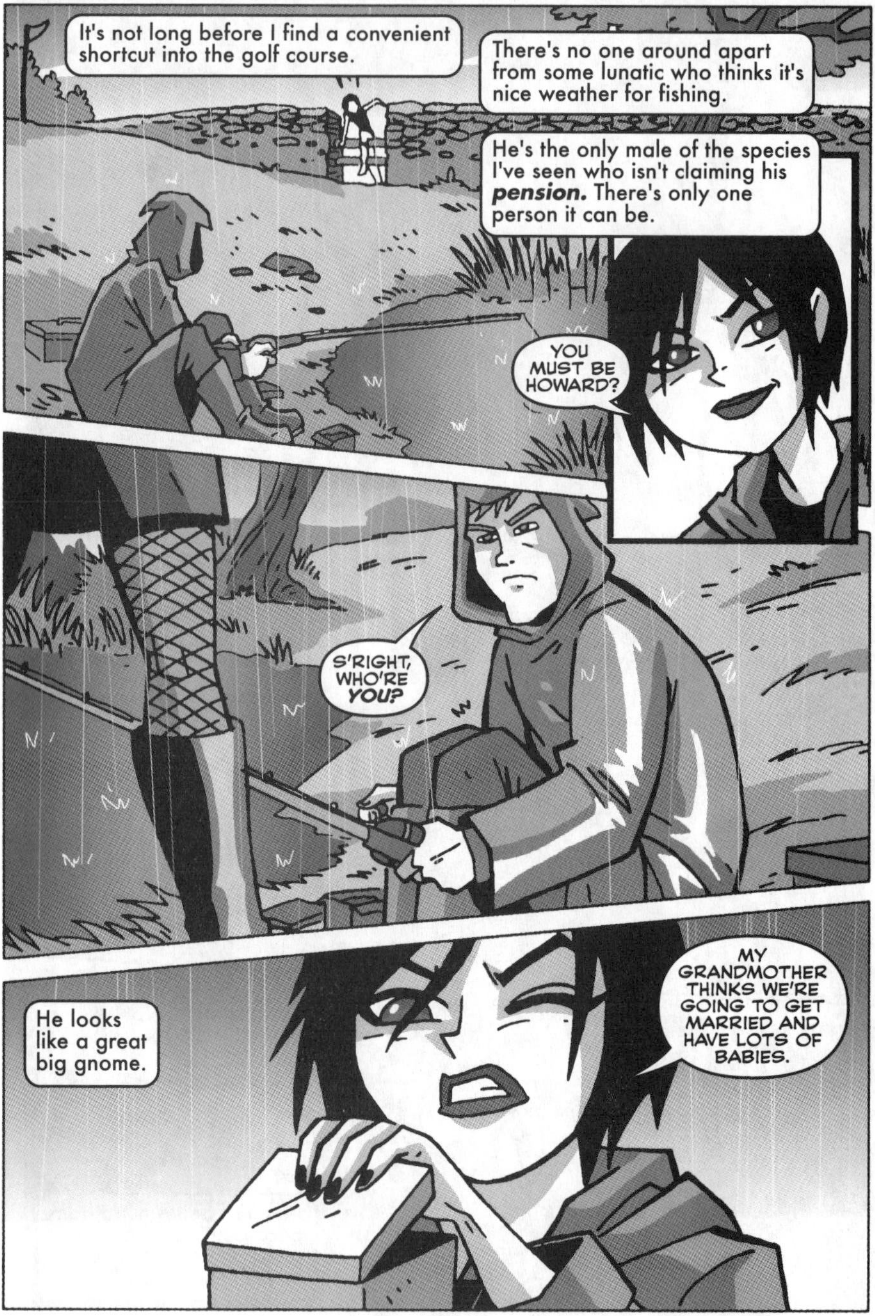
It's not long before I find a convenient shortcut into the golf course.
There's no one around apart from some lunatic who thinks it's nice weather for fishing.
He's the only male of the species I've seen who isn't claiming his ***pension.*** There's only one person it can be.
YOU MUST BE HOWARD?
S'RIGHT, WHO'RE ***YOU?***
He looks like a great big gnome.
MY GRANDMOTHER THINKS WE'RE GOING TO GET MARRIED AND HAVE LOTS OF BABIES.

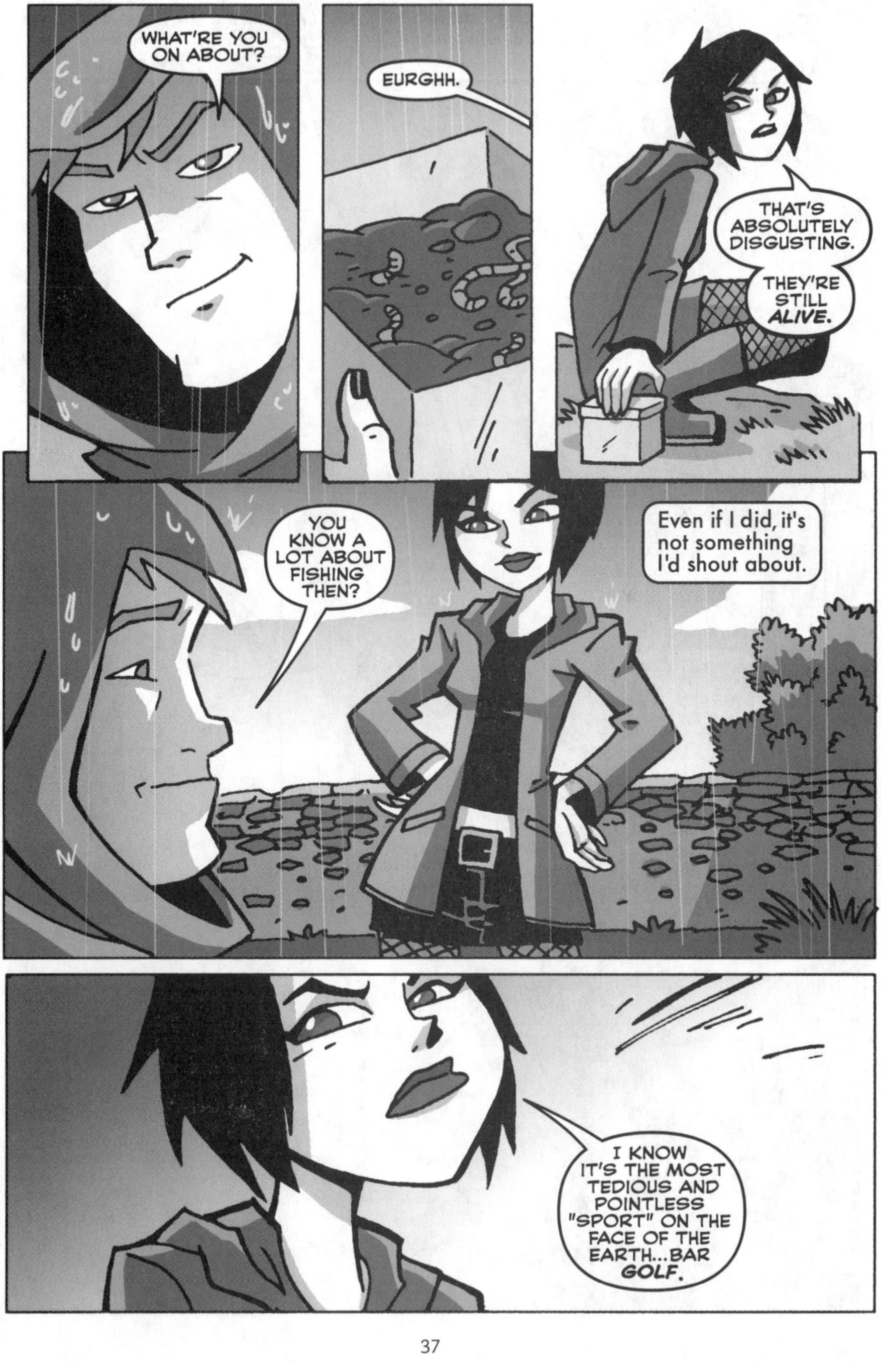
WHAT'RE YOU ON ABOUT?
EURGHH.
THAT'S ABSOLUTELY DISGUSTING.
THEY'RE STILL ***ALIVE***.
YOU KNOW A LOT ABOUT FISHING THEN?
Even if I did, it's not something I'd shout about.
I KNOW IT'S THE MOST TEDIOUS AND POINTLESS "SPORT" ON THE FACE OF THE EARTH...BAR ***GOLF***.

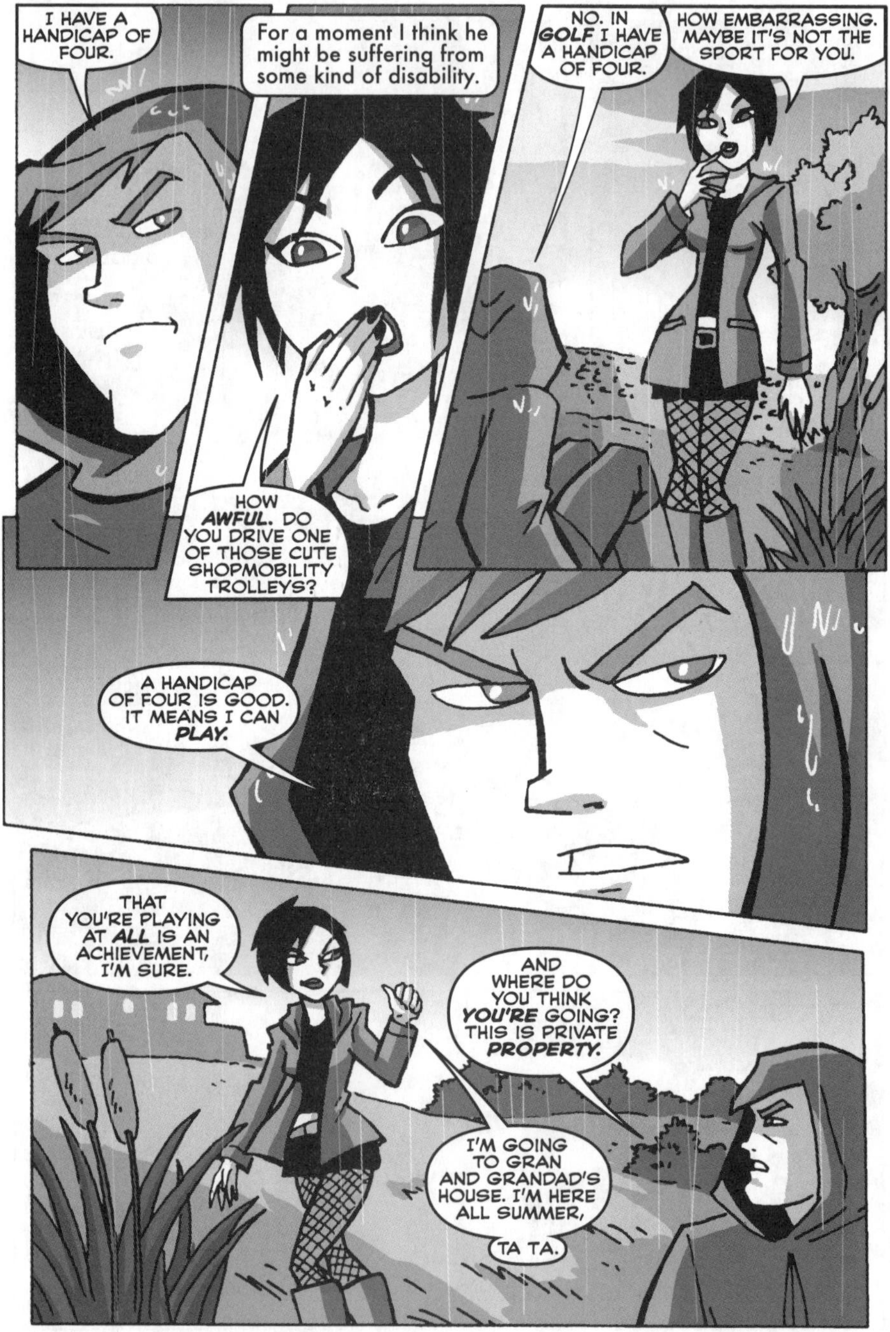
I HAVE A HANDICAP OF FOUR.
For a moment I think he might be suffering from some kind of disability.
HOW AWFUL. DO YOU DRIVE ONE OF THOSE CUTE SHOPMOBILITY TROLLEYS?
NO. IN GOLF I HAVE A HANDICAP OF FOUR.
HOW EMBARRASSING. MAYBE IT'S NOT THE SPORT FOR YOU.
A HANDICAP OF FOUR IS GOOD. IT MEANS I CAN PLAY.
THAT YOU'RE PLAYING AT ALL IS AN ACHIEVEMENT, I'M SURE.
AND WHERE DO YOU THINK YOU'RE GOING? THIS IS PRIVATE PROPERTY.
I'M GOING TO GRAN AND GRANDAD'S HOUSE. I'M HERE ALL SUMMER,
TA TA.

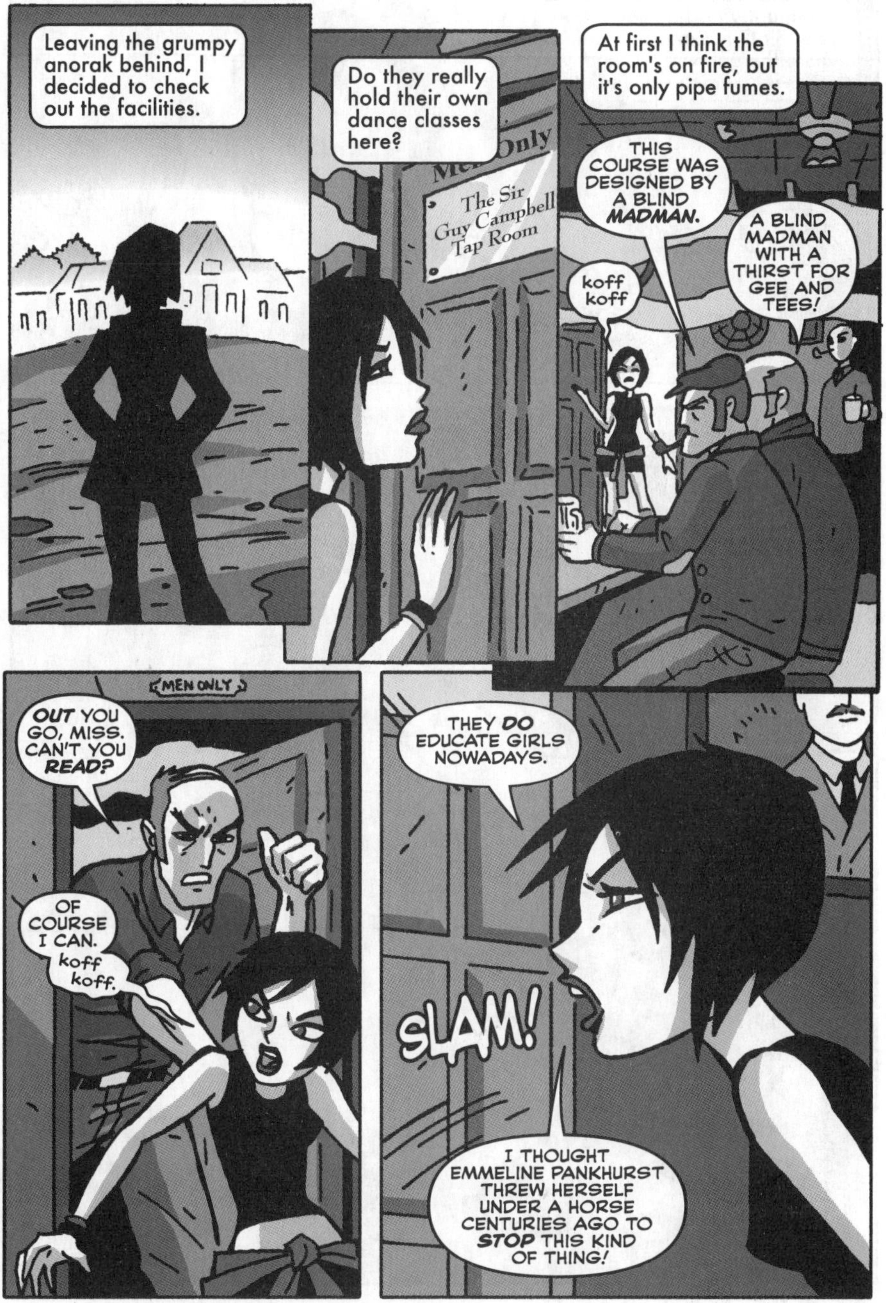
Leaving the grumpy anorak behind, I decided to check out the facilities.
Do they really hold their own dance classes here?
The Sir Guy Campbell Tap Room
At first I think the room's on fire, but it's only pipe fumes.
THIS COURSE WAS DESIGNED BY A BLIND *MADMAN.*
koff koff
A BLIND MADMAN WITH A THIRST FOR GEE AND TEES!
MEN ONLY
OUT YOU GO, MISS. CAN'T YOU *READ?*
OF COURSE I CAN.
koff koff.
THEY *DO* EDUCATE GIRLS NOWADAYS.
SLAM!
I THOUGHT EMMELINE PANKHURST THREW HERSELF UNDER A HORSE CENTURIES AGO TO *STOP* THIS KIND OF THING!

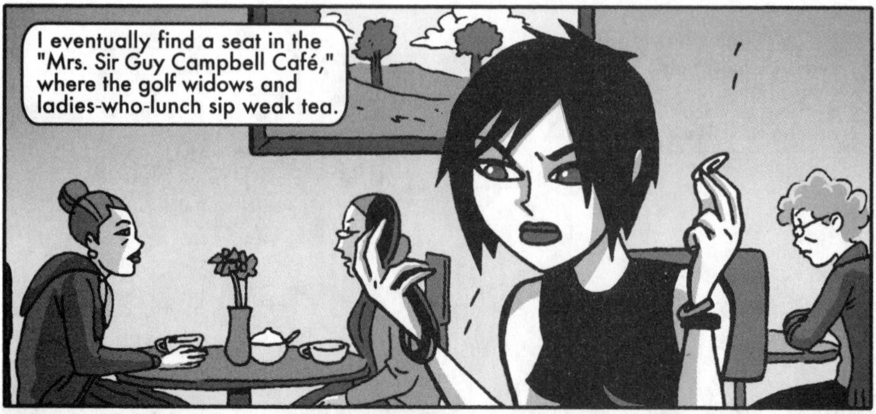
I eventually find a seat in the "Mrs. Sir Guy Campbell Café," where the golf widows and ladies-who-lunch sip weak tea.

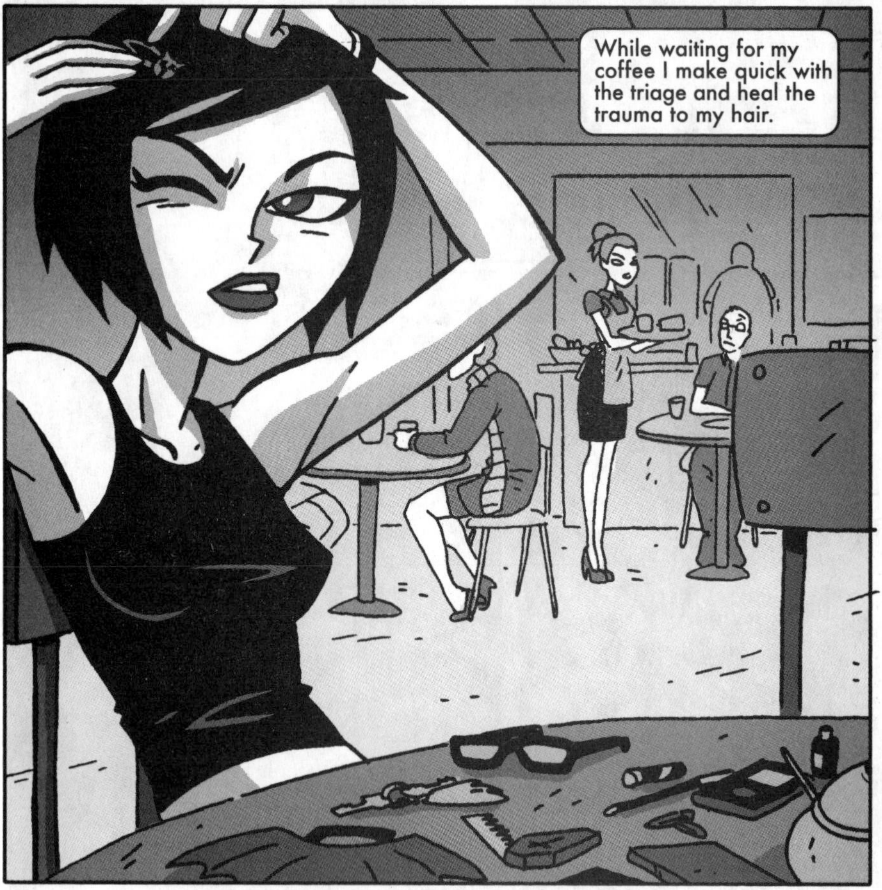
While waiting for my coffee I make quick with the triage and heal the trauma to my hair.

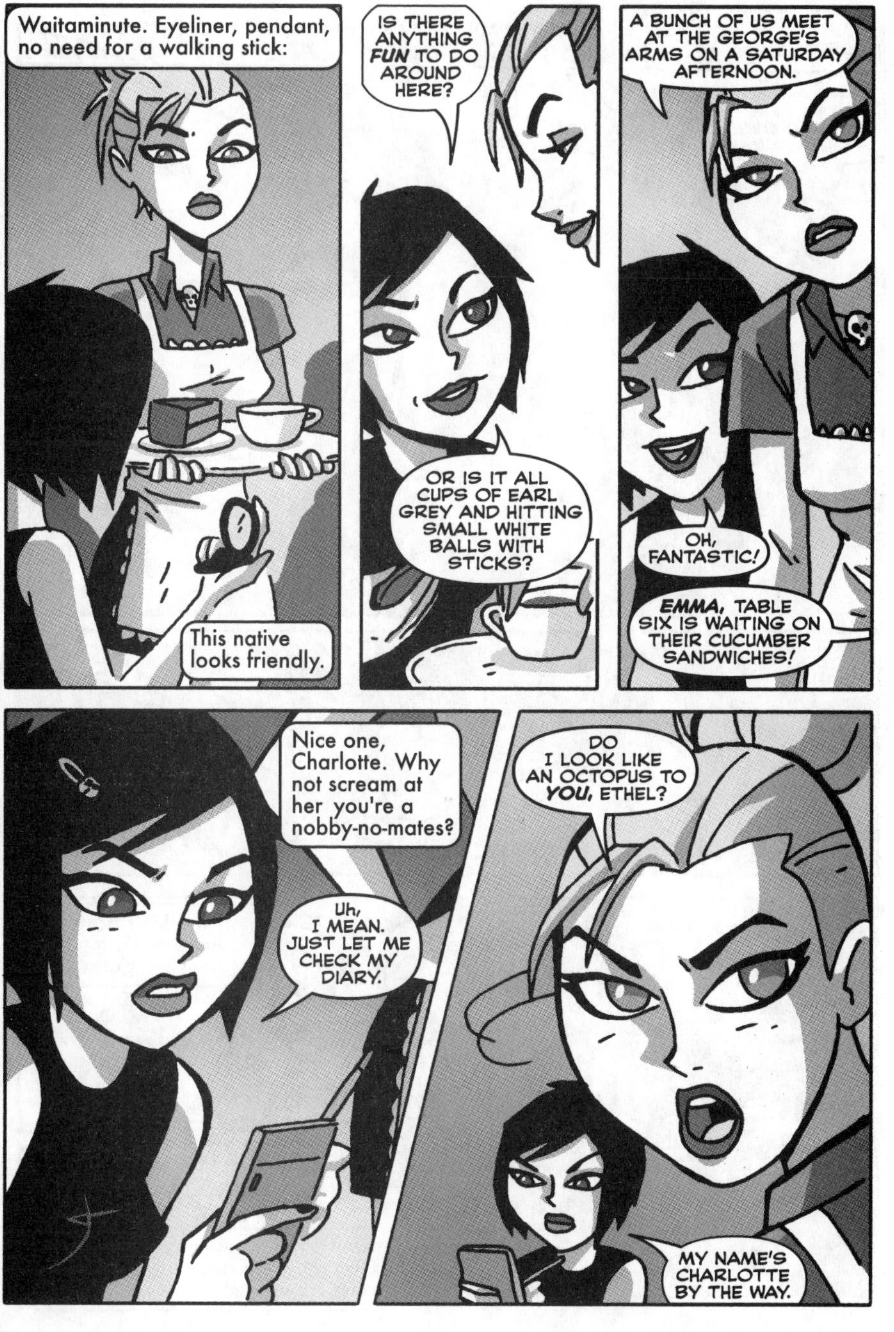
Waitaminute. Eyeliner, pendant, no need for a walking stick:
This native looks friendly.
IS THERE ANYTHING *FUN* TO DO AROUND HERE?
OR IS IT ALL CUPS OF EARL GREY AND HITTING SMALL WHITE BALLS WITH STICKS?
A BUNCH OF US MEET AT THE GEORGE'S ARMS ON A SATURDAY AFTERNOON.
OH, FANTASTIC!
EMMA, TABLE SIX IS WAITING ON THEIR CUCUMBER SANDWICHES!
Nice one, Charlotte. Why not scream at her you're a nobby-no-mates?
UH, I MEAN. JUST LET ME CHECK MY DIARY.
DO I LOOK LIKE AN OCTOPUS TO *YOU,* ETHEL?
MY NAME'S CHARLOTTE BY THE WAY.

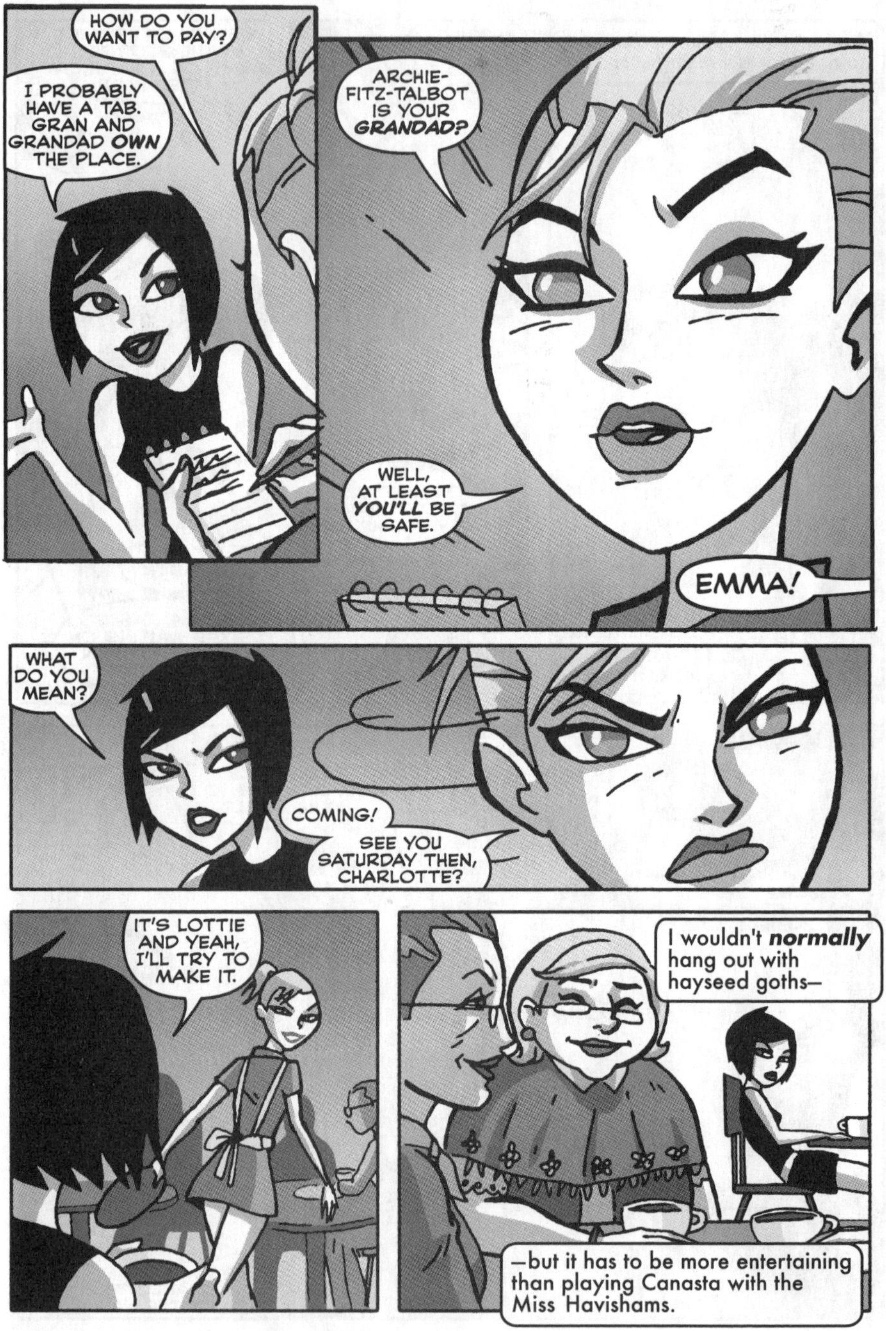
HOW DO YOU WANT TO PAY?
I PROBABLY HAVE A TAB. GRAN AND GRANDAD **OWN** THE PLACE.
ARCHIE-FITZ-TALBOT IS YOUR ***GRANDAD?***
WELL, AT LEAST ***YOU'LL*** BE SAFE.
EMMA!
WHAT DO YOU MEAN?
COMING!
SEE YOU SATURDAY THEN, CHARLOTTE?
IT'S LOTTIE AND YEAH, I'LL TRY TO MAKE IT.
I wouldn't ***normally*** hang out with hayseed goths–
–but it has to be more entertaining than playing Canasta with the Miss Havishams.

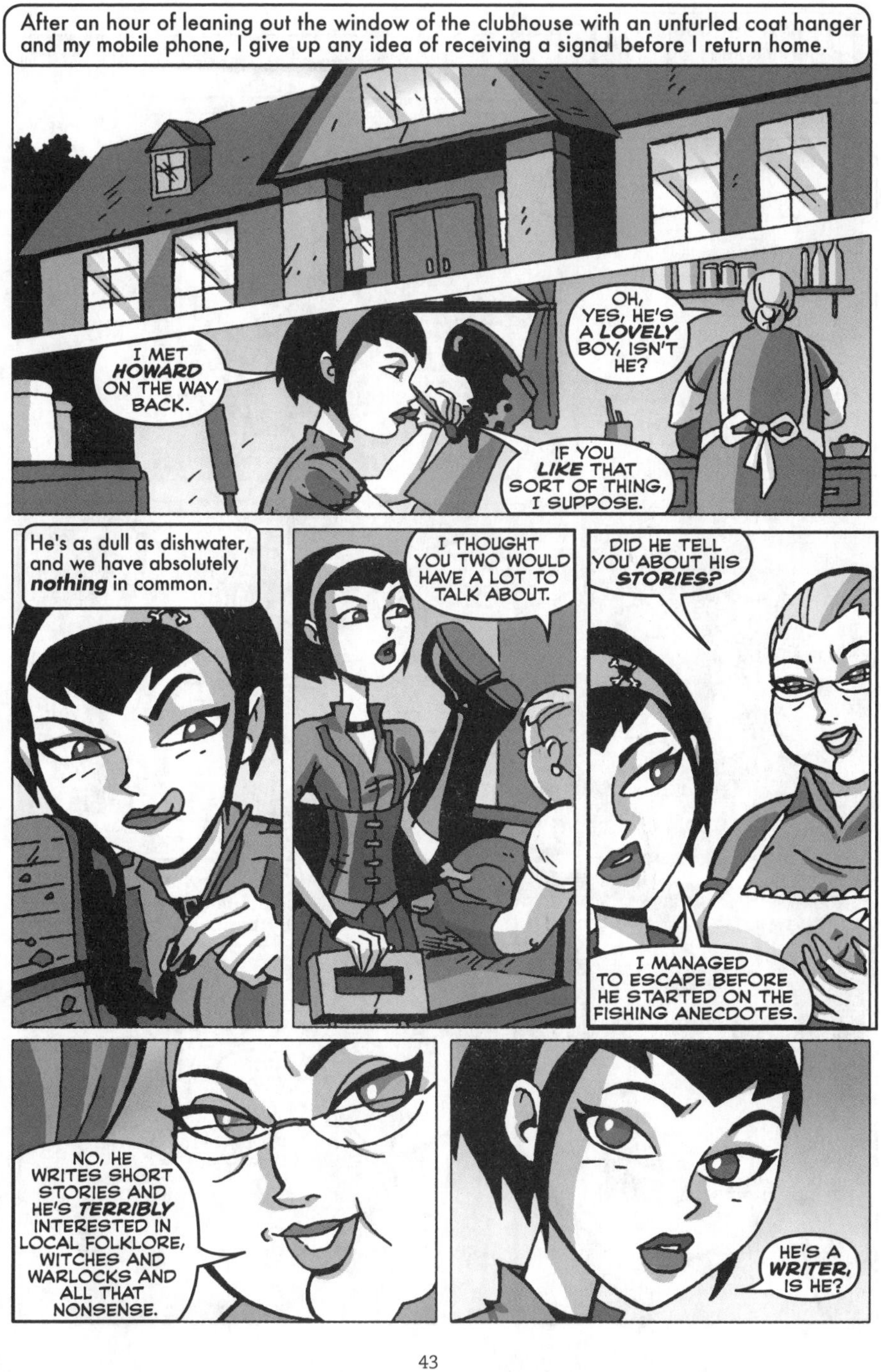
After an hour of leaning out the window of the clubhouse with an unfurled coat hanger and my mobile phone, I give up any idea of receiving a signal before I return home.
I MET HOWARD ON THE WAY BACK.
OH, YES, HE'S A LOVELY BOY, ISN'T HE?
IF YOU LIKE THAT SORT OF THING, I SUPPOSE.
He's as dull as dishwater, and we have absolutely nothing in common.
I THOUGHT YOU TWO WOULD HAVE A LOT TO TALK ABOUT.
DID HE TELL YOU ABOUT HIS STORIES?
I MANAGED TO ESCAPE BEFORE HE STARTED ON THE FISHING ANECDOTES.
NO, HE WRITES SHORT STORIES AND HE'S TERRIBLY INTERESTED IN LOCAL FOLKLORE, WITCHES AND WARLOCKS AND ALL THAT NONSENSE.
HE'S A WRITER, IS HE?

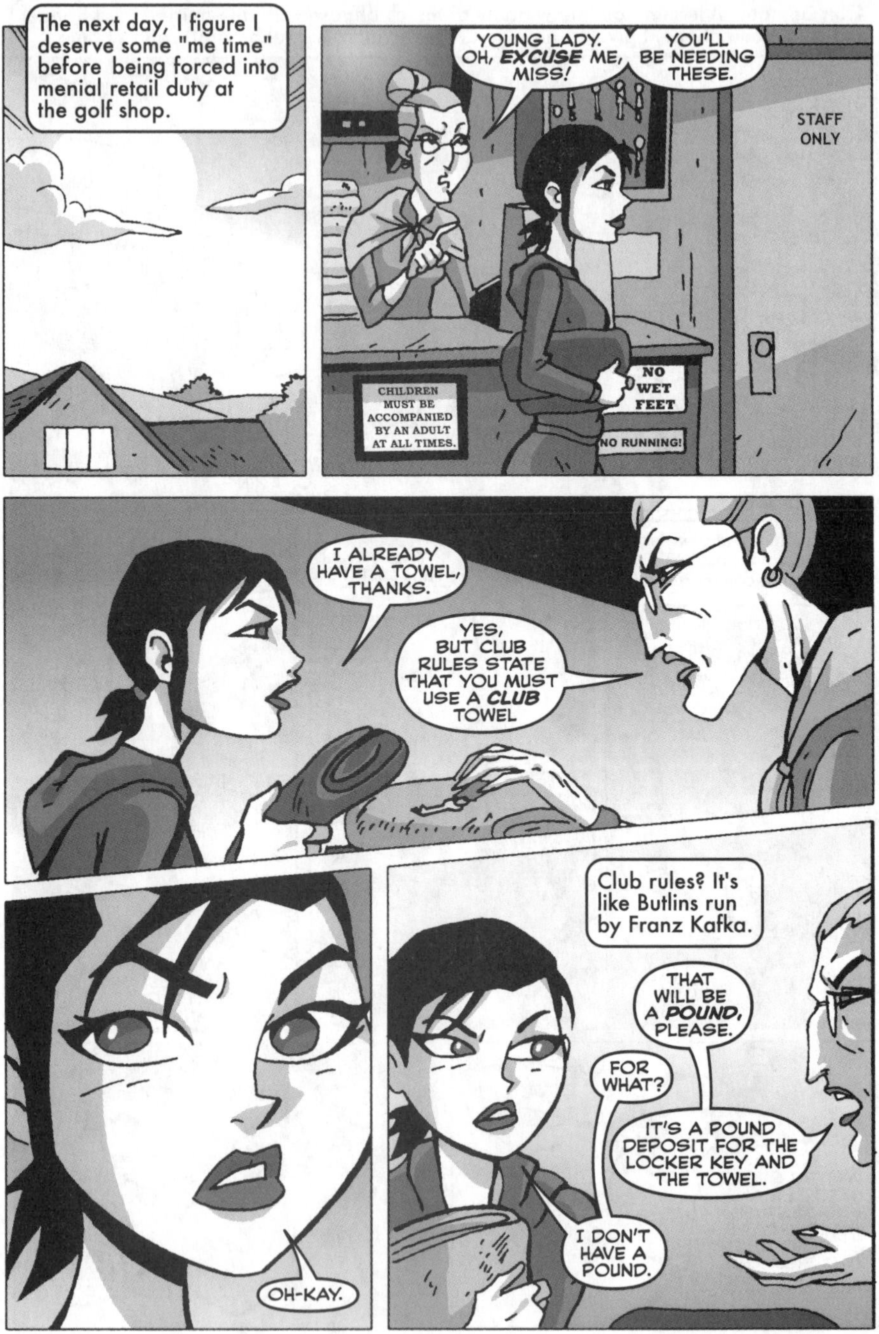
The next day, I figure I deserve some "me time" before being forced into menial retail duty at the golf shop.
YOUNG LADY. OH, EXCUSE ME, MISS!
YOU'LL BE NEEDING THESE.
STAFF ONLY
CHILDREN MUST BE ACCOMPANIED BY AN ADULT AT ALL TIMES.
NO WET FEET
NO RUNNING!
I ALREADY HAVE A TOWEL, THANKS.
YES, BUT CLUB RULES STATE THAT YOU MUST USE A CLUB TOWEL
OH-KAY.
Club rules? It's like Butlins run by Franz Kafka.
THAT WILL BE A POUND, PLEASE.
FOR WHAT?
IT'S A POUND DEPOSIT FOR THE LOCKER KEY AND THE TOWEL.
I DON'T HAVE A POUND.

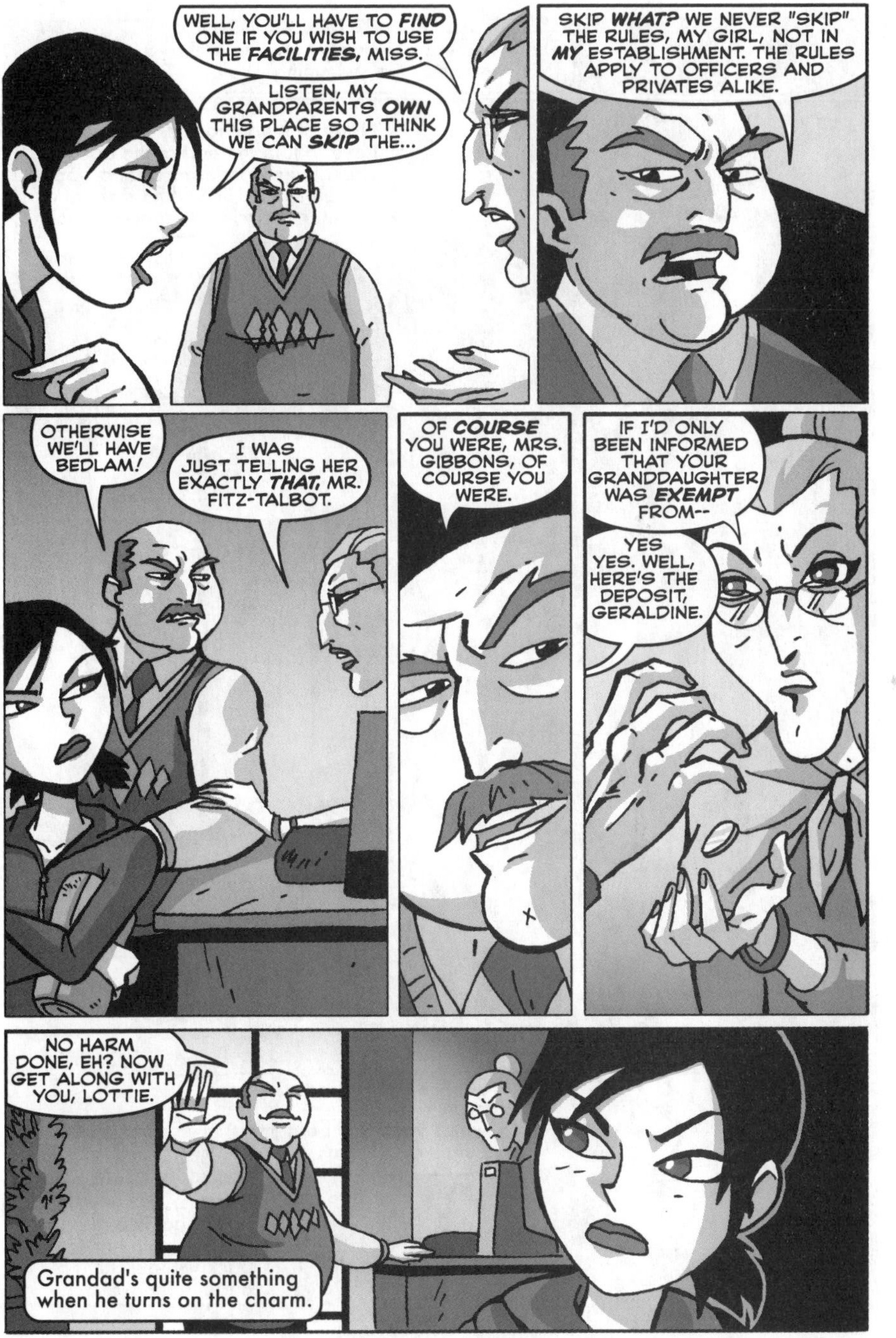
WELL, YOU'LL HAVE TO FIND ONE IF YOU WISH TO USE THE FACILITIES, MISS.
LISTEN, MY GRANDPARENTS OWN THIS PLACE SO I THINK WE CAN SKIP THE...
SKIP WHAT? WE NEVER "SKIP" THE RULES, MY GIRL, NOT IN MY ESTABLISHMENT. THE RULES APPLY TO OFFICERS AND PRIVATES ALIKE.
OTHERWISE WE'LL HAVE BEDLAM!
I WAS JUST TELLING HER EXACTLY THAT, MR. FITZ-TALBOT.
OF COURSE YOU WERE, MRS. GIBBONS, OF COURSE YOU WERE.
IF I'D ONLY BEEN INFORMED THAT YOUR GRANDDAUGHTER WAS EXEMPT FROM--
YES YES. WELL, HERE'S THE DEPOSIT, GERALDINE.
NO HARM DONE, EH? NOW GET ALONG WITH YOU, LOTTIE.
Grandad's quite something when he turns on the charm.

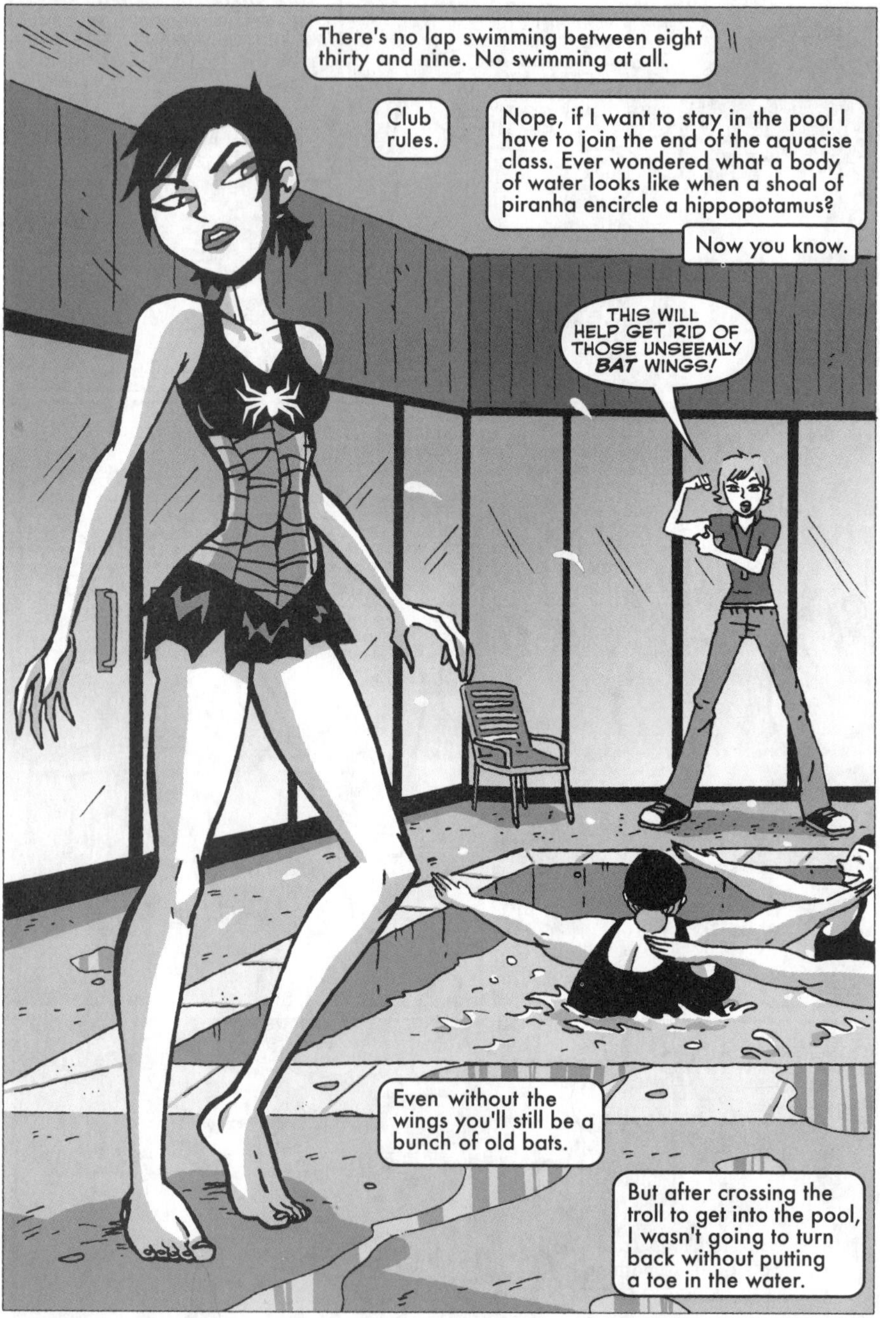
There's no lap swimming between eight thirty and nine. No swimming at all.
Club rules.
Nope, if I want to stay in the pool I have to join the end of the aquacise class. Ever wondered what a body of water looks like when a shoal of piranha encircle a hippopotamus?
Now you know.
THIS WILL HELP GET RID OF THOSE UNSEEMLY ***BAT*** WINGS!
Even without the wings you'll still be a bunch of old bats.
But after crossing the troll to get into the pool, I wasn't going to turn back without putting a toe in the water.

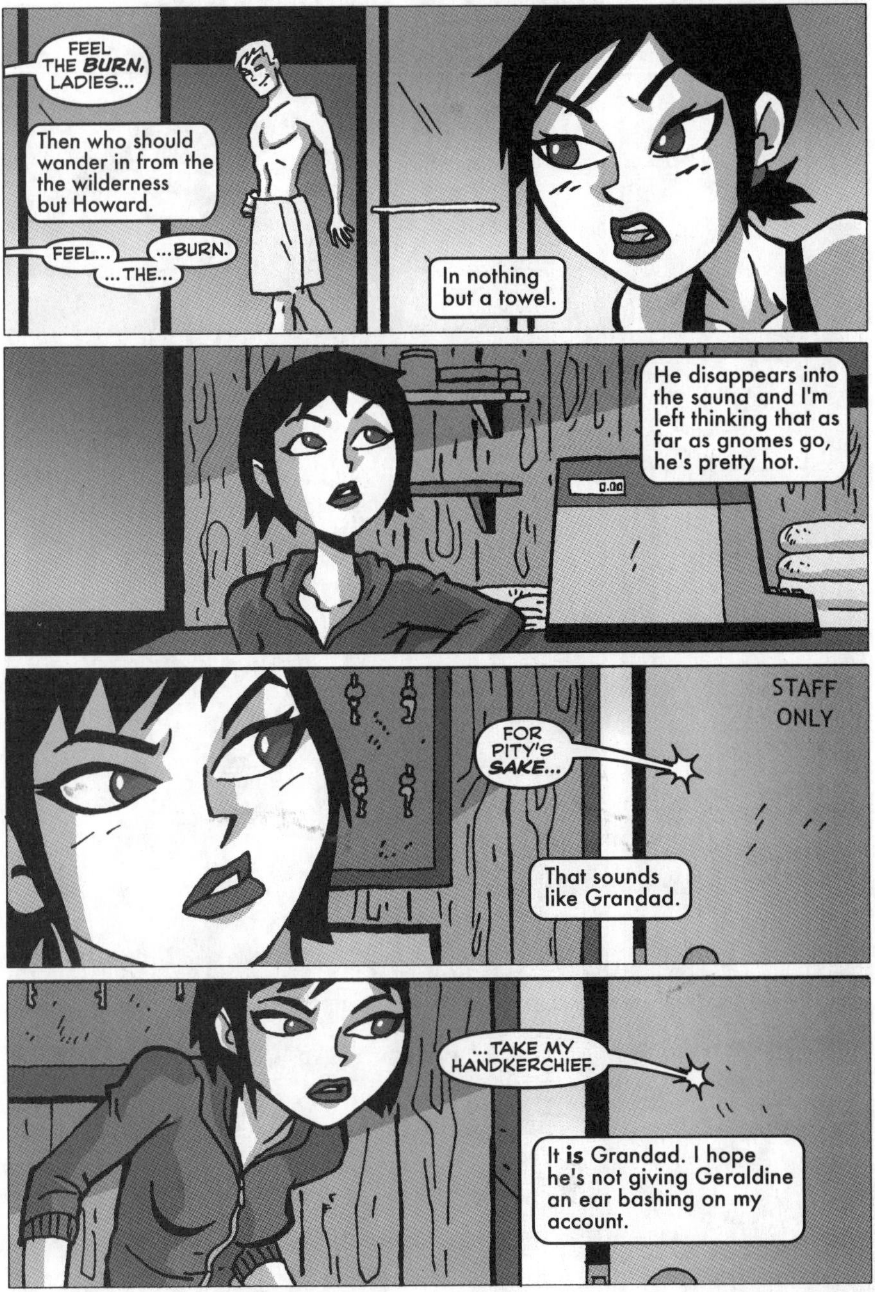
FEEL THE BURN, LADIES...
Then who should wander in from the the wilderness but Howard.
FEEL...
...THE...
...BURN.
In nothing but a towel.
He disappears into the sauna and I'm left thinking that as far as gnomes go, he's pretty hot.
0.00
STAFF ONLY
FOR PITY'S SAKE...
That sounds like Grandad.
...TAKE MY HANDKERCHIEF.
It is Grandad. I hope he's not giving Geraldine an ear bashing on my account.

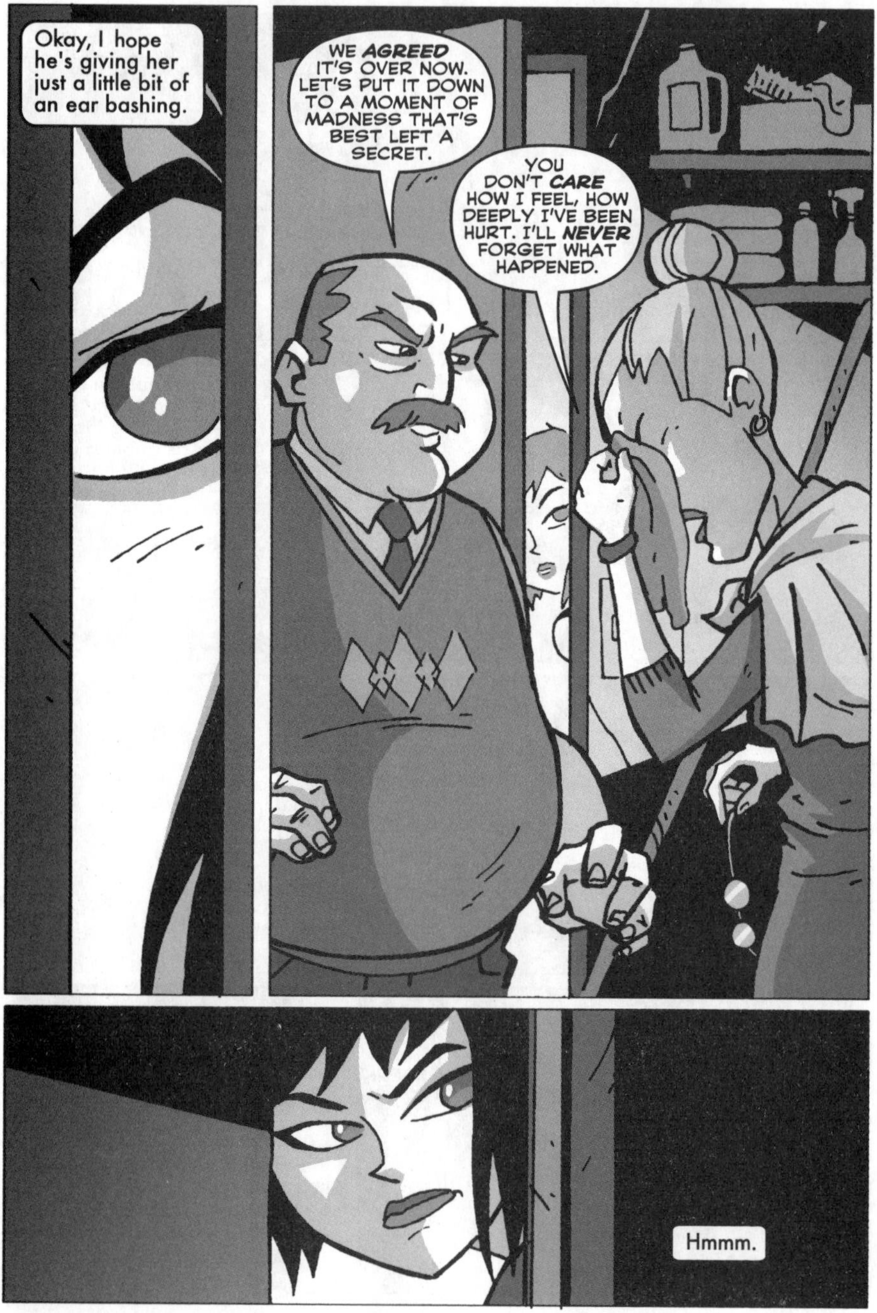

Okay, I hope he's giving her just a little bit of an ear bashing.
WE **AGREED** IT'S OVER NOW. LET'S PUT IT DOWN TO A MOMENT OF MADNESS THAT'S BEST LEFT A SECRET.
YOU DON'T **CARE** HOW I FEEL, HOW DEEPLY I'VE BEEN HURT. I'LL **NEVER** FORGET WHAT HAPPENED.
Hmmm.

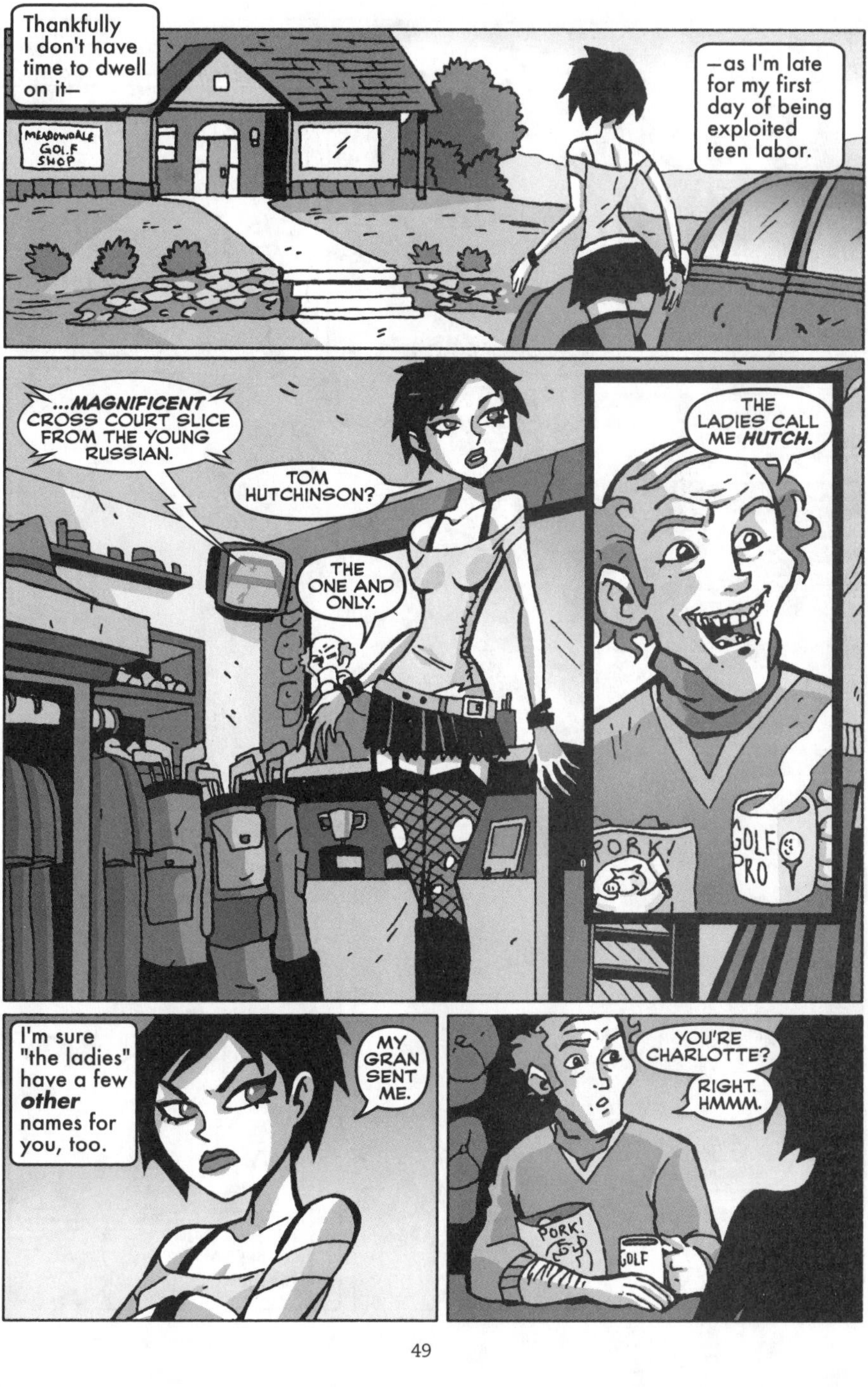
Thankfully I don't have time to dwell on it—
MEADOWDALE GOLF SHOP
—as I'm late for my first day of being exploited teen labor.
...MAGNIFICENT CROSS COURT SLICE FROM THE YOUNG RUSSIAN.
TOM HUTCHINSON?
THE ONE AND ONLY.
THE LADIES CALL ME HUTCH.
PORK!
GOLF PRO
I'm sure "the ladies" have a few other names for you, too.
MY GRAN SENT ME.
YOU'RE CHARLOTTE?
RIGHT. HMMM.
PORK!
GOLF

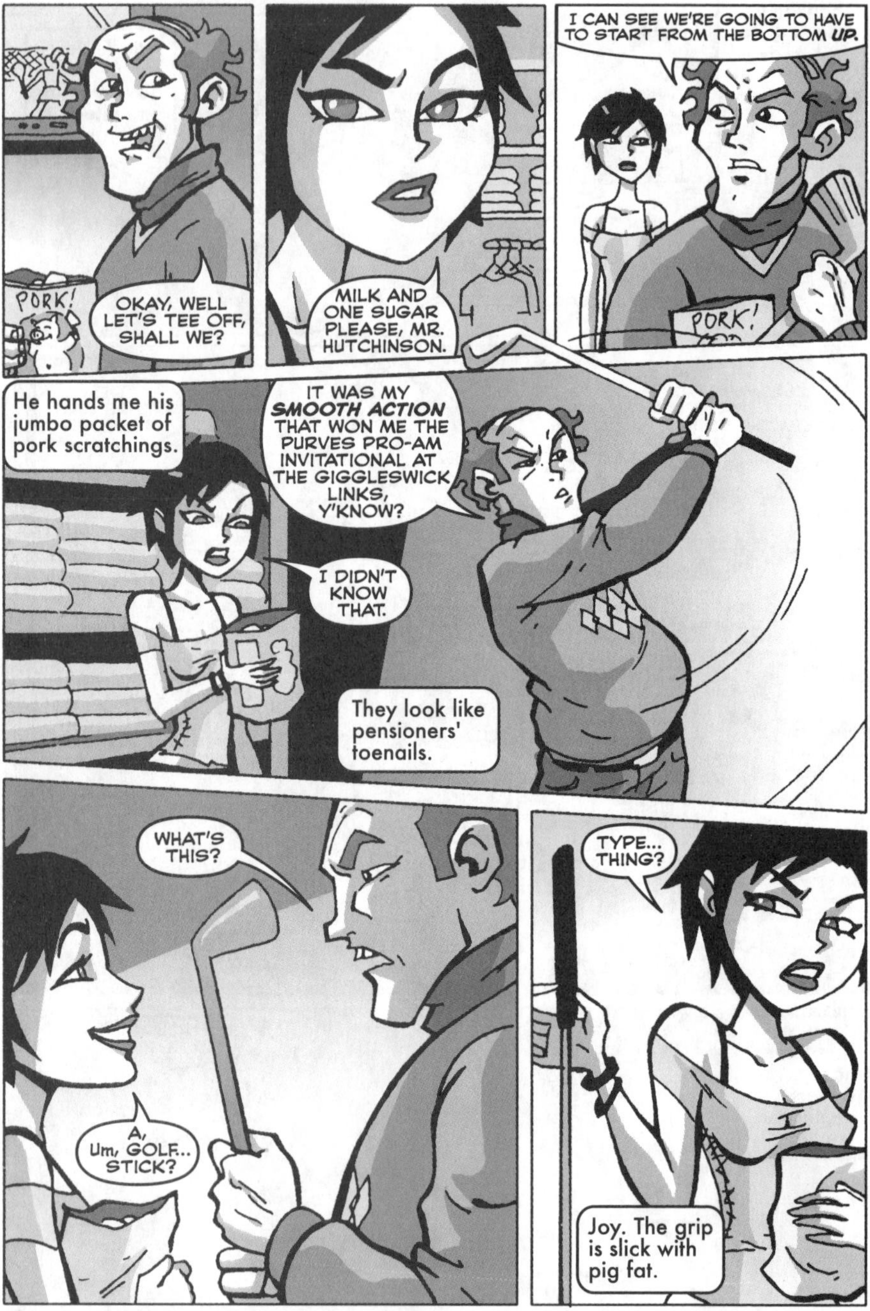
PORK!
OKAY, WELL LET'S TEE OFF, SHALL WE?
MILK AND ONE SUGAR PLEASE, MR. HUTCHINSON.
I CAN SEE WE'RE GOING TO HAVE TO START FROM THE BOTTOM UP.
PORK!
He hands me his jumbo packet of pork scratchings.
IT WAS MY SMOOTH ACTION THAT WON ME THE PURVES PRO-AM INVITATIONAL AT THE GIGGLESWICK LINKS, Y'KNOW?
I DIDN'T KNOW THAT.
They look like pensioners' toenails.
WHAT'S THIS?
A, Um, GOLF... STICK?
TYPE... THING?
Joy. The grip is slick with pig fat.

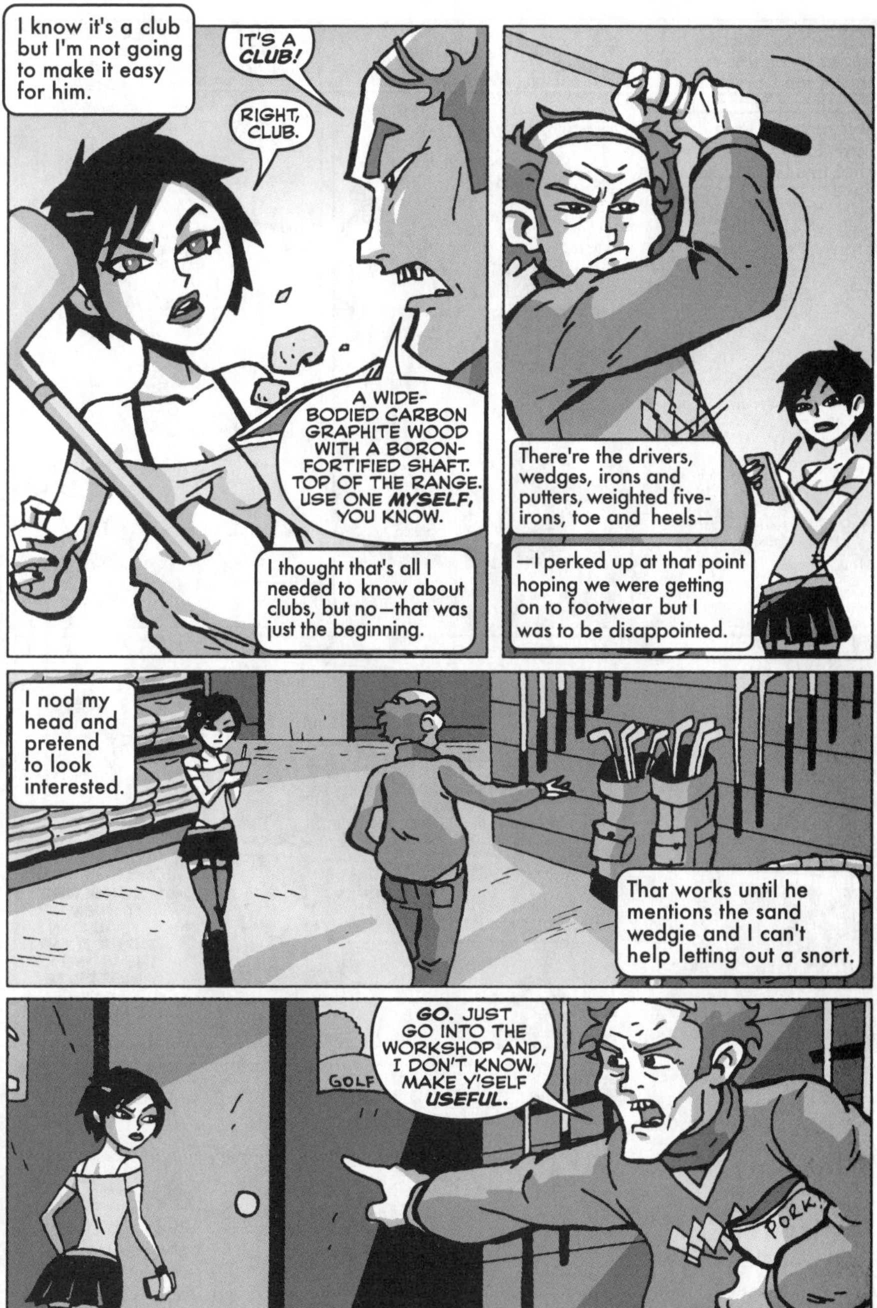
I know it's a club but I'm not going to make it easy for him.
IT'S A CLUB!
RIGHT, CLUB.
A WIDE-BODIED CARBON GRAPHITE WOOD WITH A BORON-FORTIFIED SHAFT. TOP OF THE RANGE. USE ONE MYSELF, YOU KNOW.
I thought that's all I needed to know about clubs, but no—that was just the beginning.
There're the drivers, wedges, irons and putters, weighted five-irons, toe and heels—
—I perked up at that point hoping we were getting on to footwear but I was to be disappointed.
I nod my head and pretend to look interested.
That works until he mentions the sand wedgie and I can't help letting out a snort.
GOLF
GO. JUST GO INTO THE WORKSHOP AND, I DON'T KNOW, MAKE Y'SELF USEFUL.
PORK.

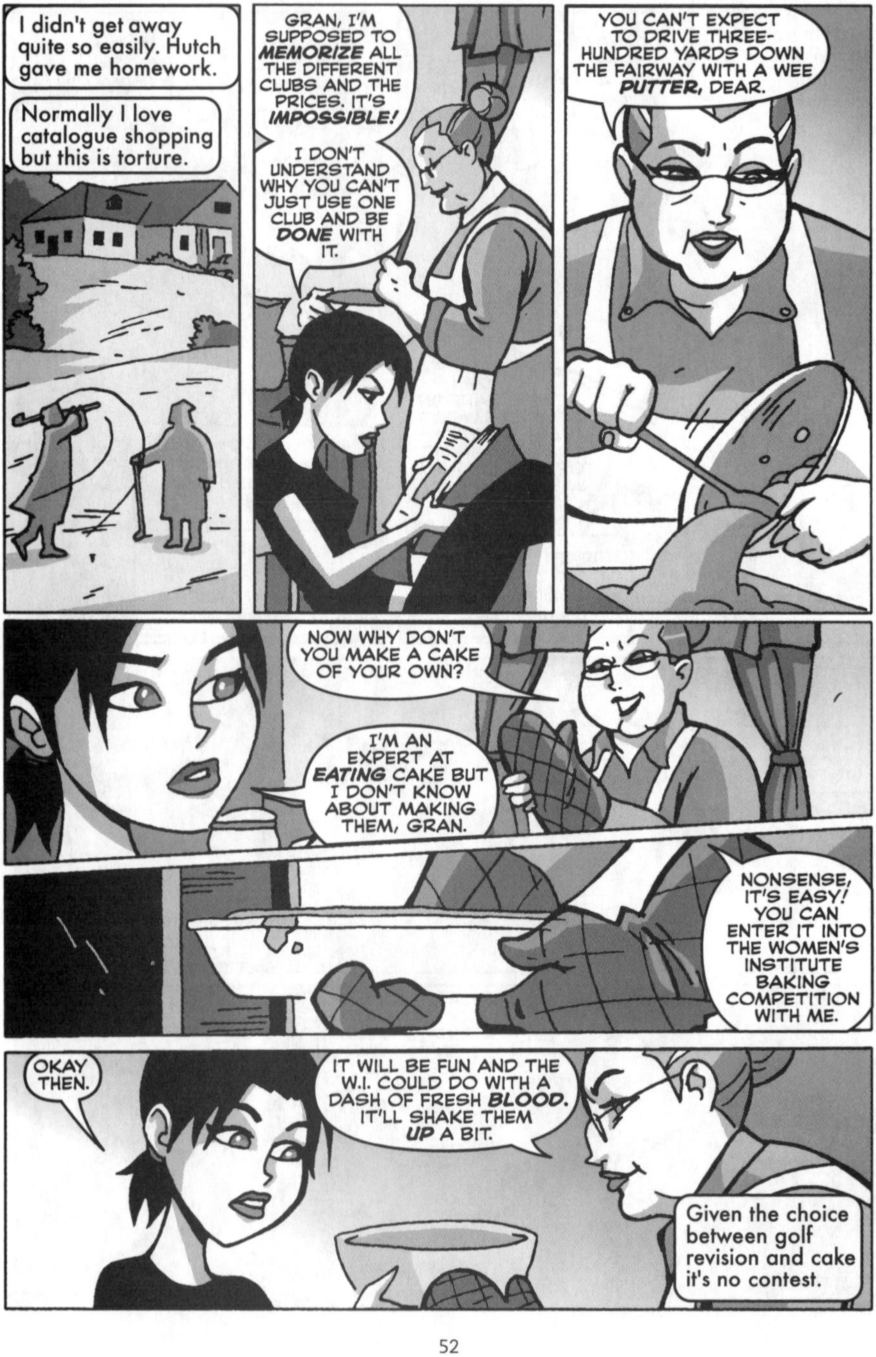
I didn't get away quite so easily. Hutch gave me homework.
Normally I love catalogue shopping but this is torture.
GRAN, I'M SUPPOSED TO MEMORIZE ALL THE DIFFERENT CLUBS AND THE PRICES. IT'S IMPOSSIBLE!
I DON'T UNDERSTAND WHY YOU CAN'T JUST USE ONE CLUB AND BE DONE WITH IT.
YOU CAN'T EXPECT TO DRIVE THREE-HUNDRED YARDS DOWN THE FAIRWAY WITH A WEE PUTTER, DEAR.
NOW WHY DON'T YOU MAKE A CAKE OF YOUR OWN?
I'M AN EXPERT AT EATING CAKE BUT I DON'T KNOW ABOUT MAKING THEM, GRAN.
NONSENSE, IT'S EASY! YOU CAN ENTER IT INTO THE WOMEN'S INSTITUTE BAKING COMPETITION WITH ME.
OKAY THEN.
IT WILL BE FUN AND THE W.I. COULD DO WITH A DASH OF FRESH BLOOD. IT'LL SHAKE THEM UP A BIT.
Given the choice between golf revision and cake it's no contest.

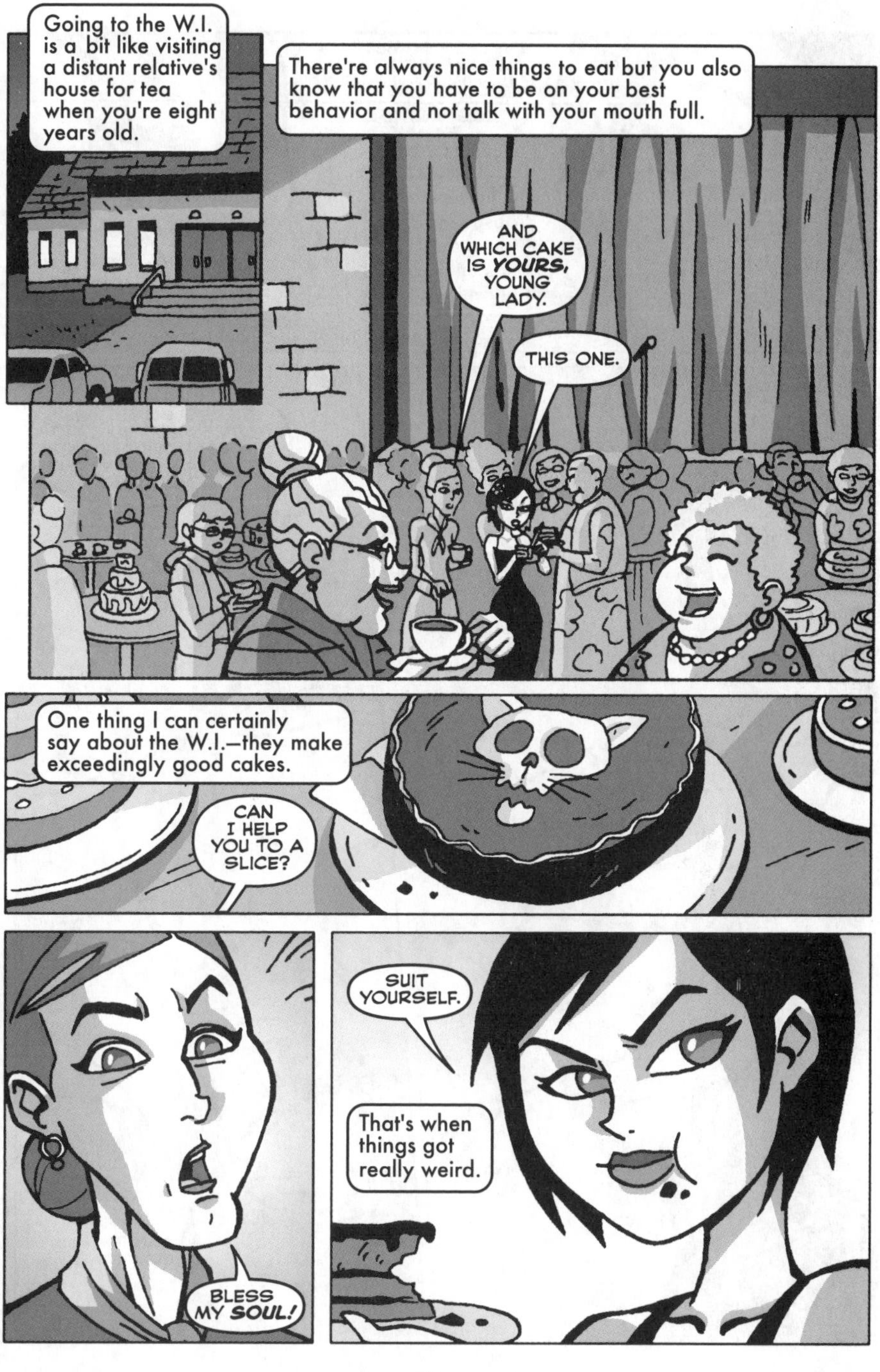
Going to the W.I. is a bit like visiting a distant relative's house for tea when you're eight years old.
There're always nice things to eat but you also know that you have to be on your best behavior and not talk with your mouth full.
AND WHICH CAKE IS YOURS, YOUNG LADY.
THIS ONE.
One thing I can certainly say about the W.I.—they make exceedingly good cakes.
CAN I HELP YOU TO A SLICE?
BLESS MY SOUL!
SUIT YOURSELF.
That's when things got really weird.

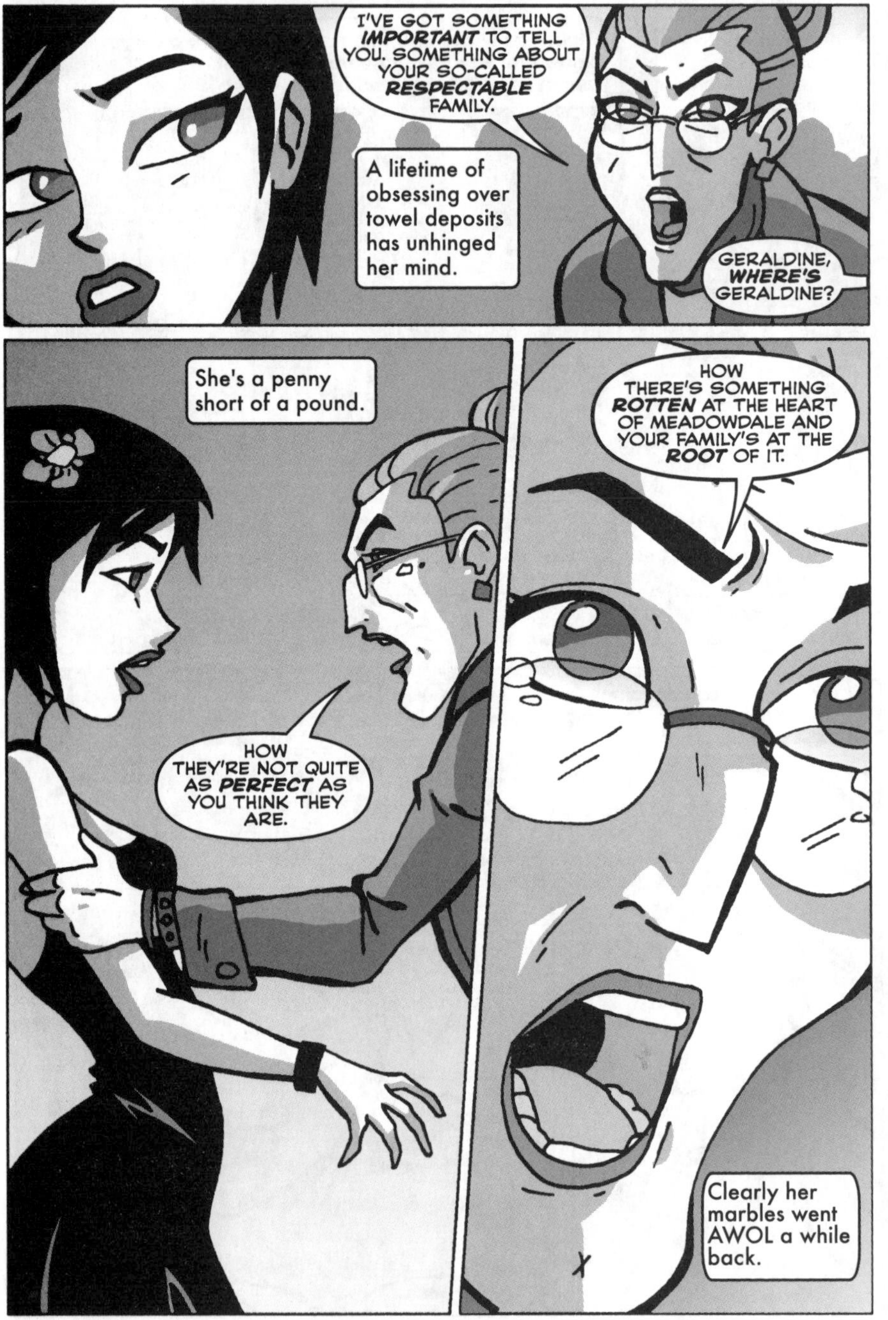
I'VE GOT SOMETHING IMPORTANT TO TELL YOU. SOMETHING ABOUT YOUR SO-CALLED RESPECTABLE FAMILY.
A lifetime of obsessing over towel deposits has unhinged her mind.
GERALDINE, WHERE'S GERALDINE?
She's a penny short of a pound.
HOW THEY'RE NOT QUITE AS PERFECT AS YOU THINK THEY ARE.
HOW THERE'S SOMETHING ROTTEN AT THE HEART OF MEADOWDALE AND YOUR FAMILY'S AT THE ROOT OF IT.
Clearly her marbles went AWOL a while back.

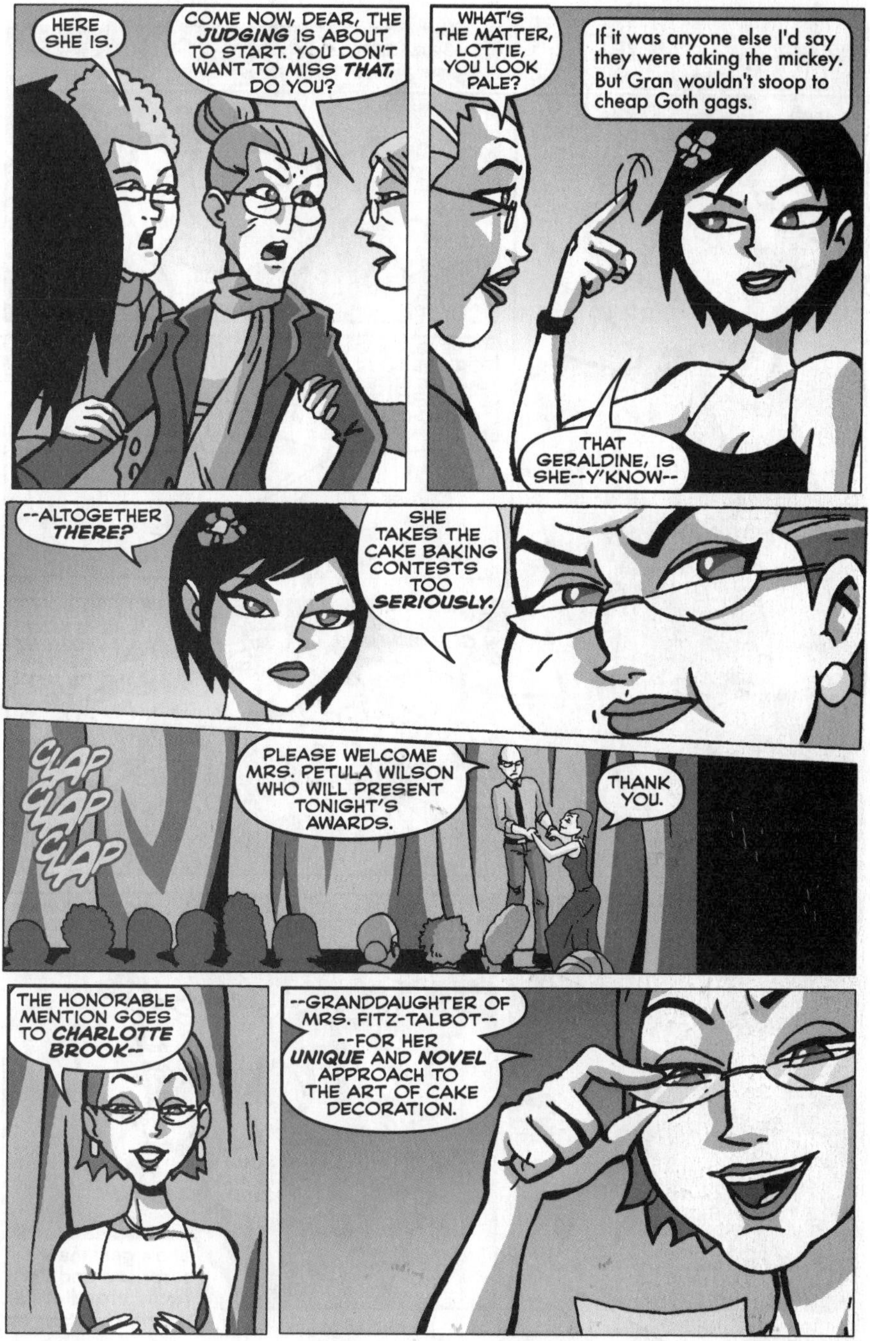
HERE SHE IS.
COME NOW, DEAR, THE *JUDGING* IS ABOUT TO START. YOU DON'T WANT TO MISS *THAT,* DO YOU?
WHAT'S THE MATTER, LOTTIE, YOU LOOK PALE?
If it was anyone else I'd say they were taking the mickey. But Gran wouldn't stoop to cheap Goth gags.
THAT GERALDINE, IS SHE--Y'KNOW--
--ALTOGETHER *THERE?*
SHE TAKES THE CAKE BAKING CONTESTS TOO *SERIOUSLY.*
CLAP CLAP CLAP
PLEASE WELCOME MRS. PETULA WILSON WHO WILL PRESENT TONIGHT'S AWARDS.
THANK YOU.
THE HONORABLE MENTION GOES TO *CHARLOTTE BROOK*--
--GRANDDAUGHTER OF MRS. FITZ-TALBOT--
--FOR HER *UNIQUE* AND *NOVEL* APPROACH TO THE ART OF CAKE DECORATION.

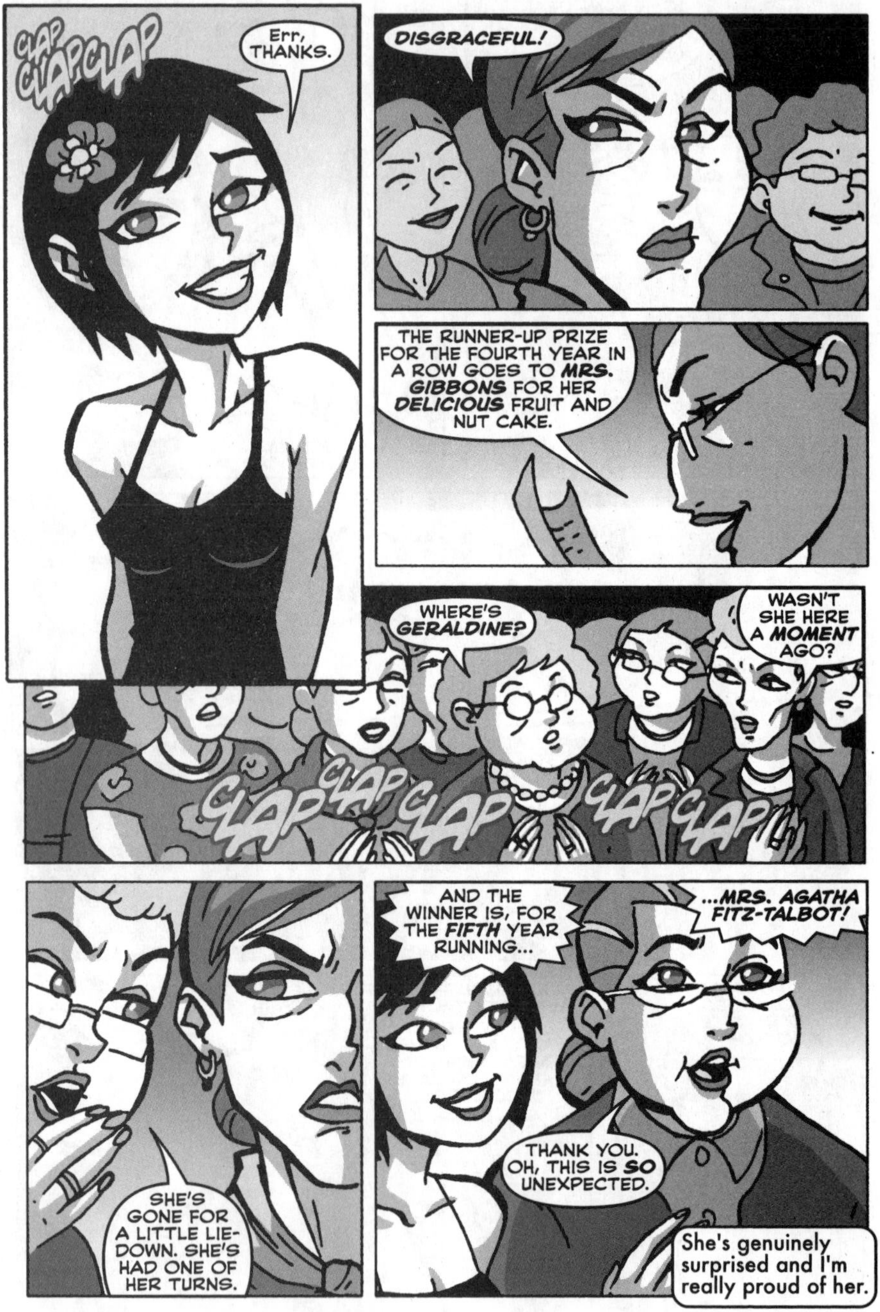
CLAP CLAP CLAP
Err, THANKS.
DISGRACEFUL!
THE RUNNER-UP PRIZE FOR THE FOURTH YEAR IN A ROW GOES TO MRS. GIBBONS FOR HER DELICIOUS FRUIT AND NUT CAKE.
WHERE'S GERALDINE?
WASN'T SHE HERE A MOMENT AGO?
CLAP CLAP CLAP CLAP CLAP
SHE'S GONE FOR A LITTLE LIE-DOWN. SHE'S HAD ONE OF HER TURNS.
AND THE WINNER IS, FOR THE FIFTH YEAR RUNNING...
...MRS. AGATHA FITZ-TALBOT!
THANK YOU. OH, THIS IS SO UNEXPECTED.
She's genuinely surprised and I'm really proud of her.

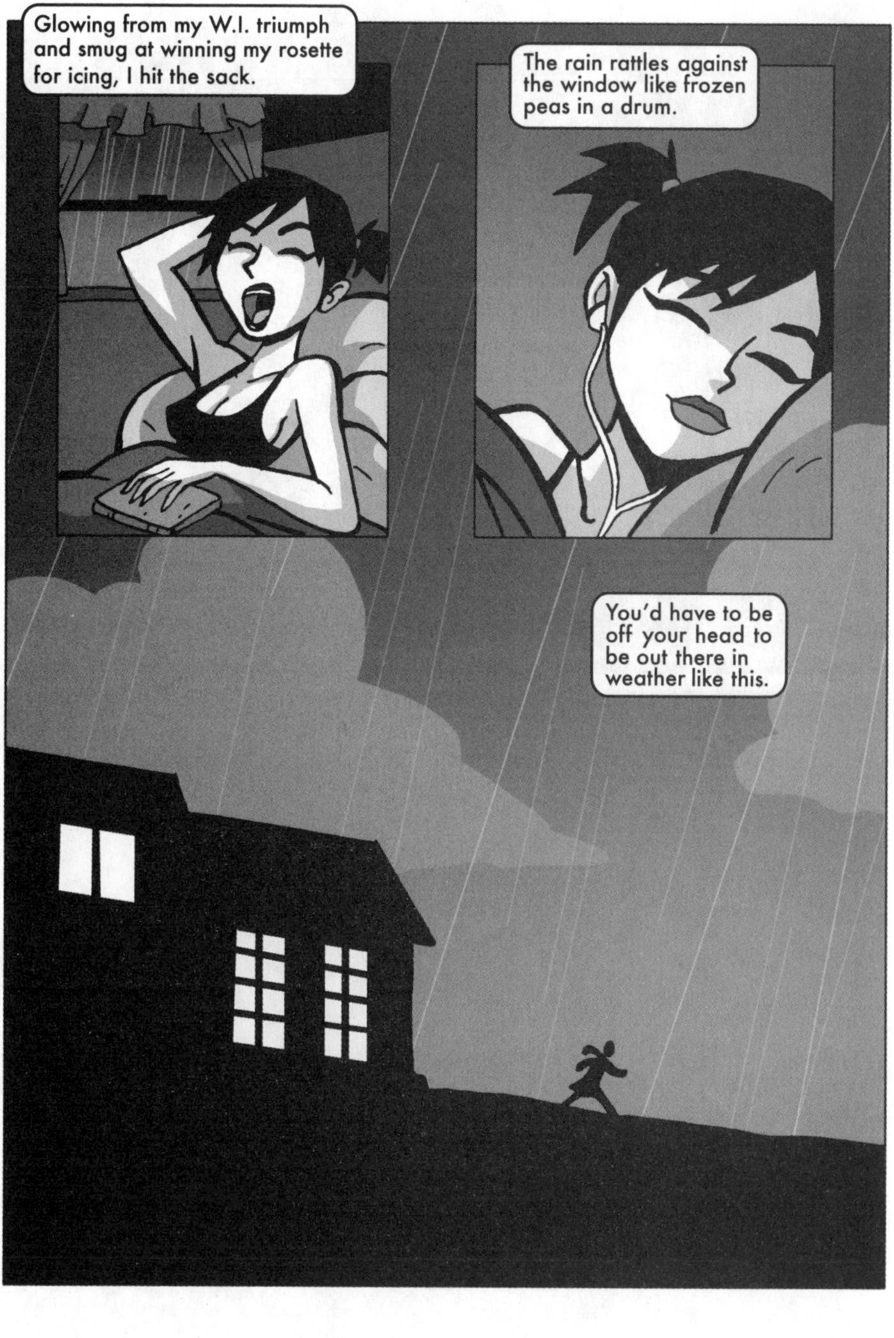
Glowing from my W.I. triumph and smug at winning my rosette for icing, I hit the sack.
The rain rattles against the window like frozen peas in a drum.
You'd have to be off your head to be out there in weather like this.

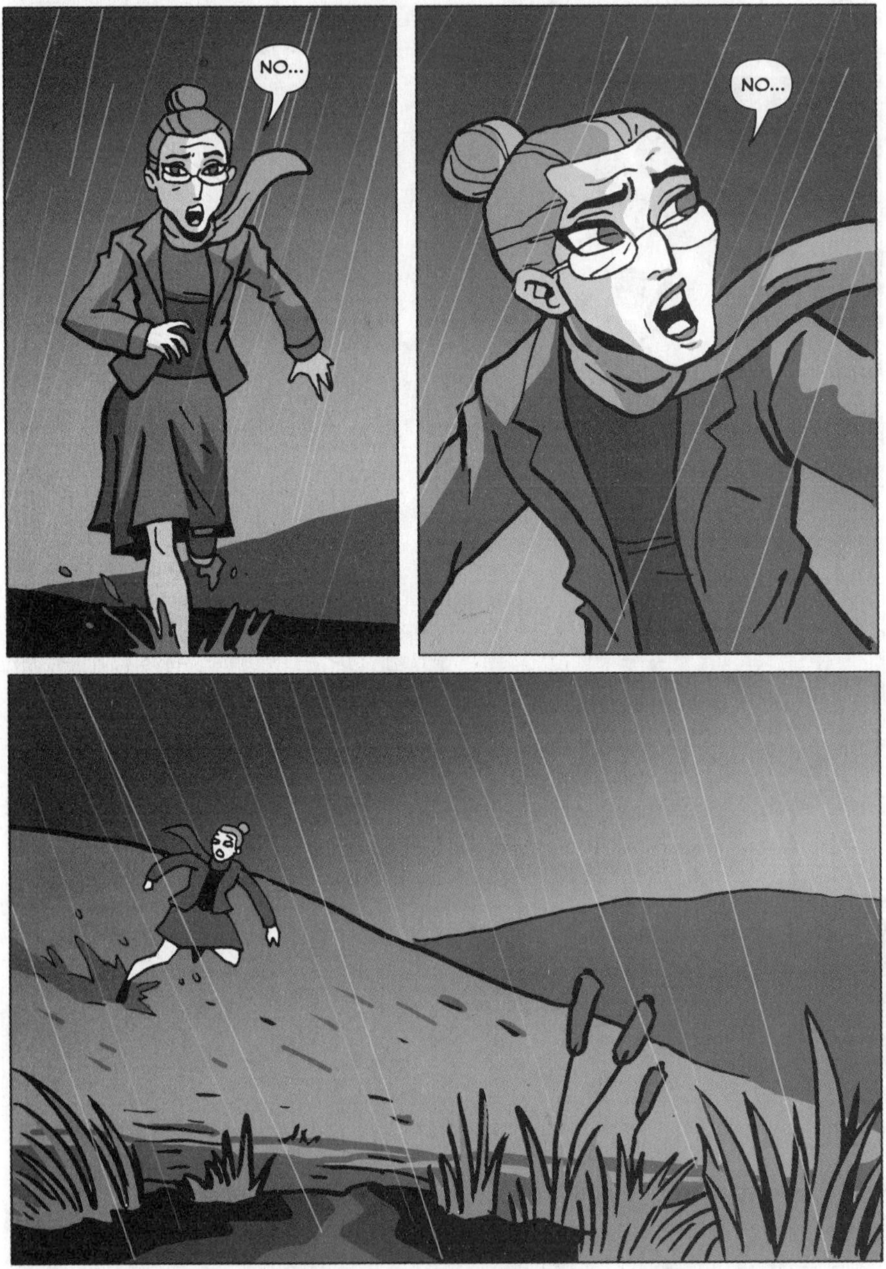
NO...
NO...

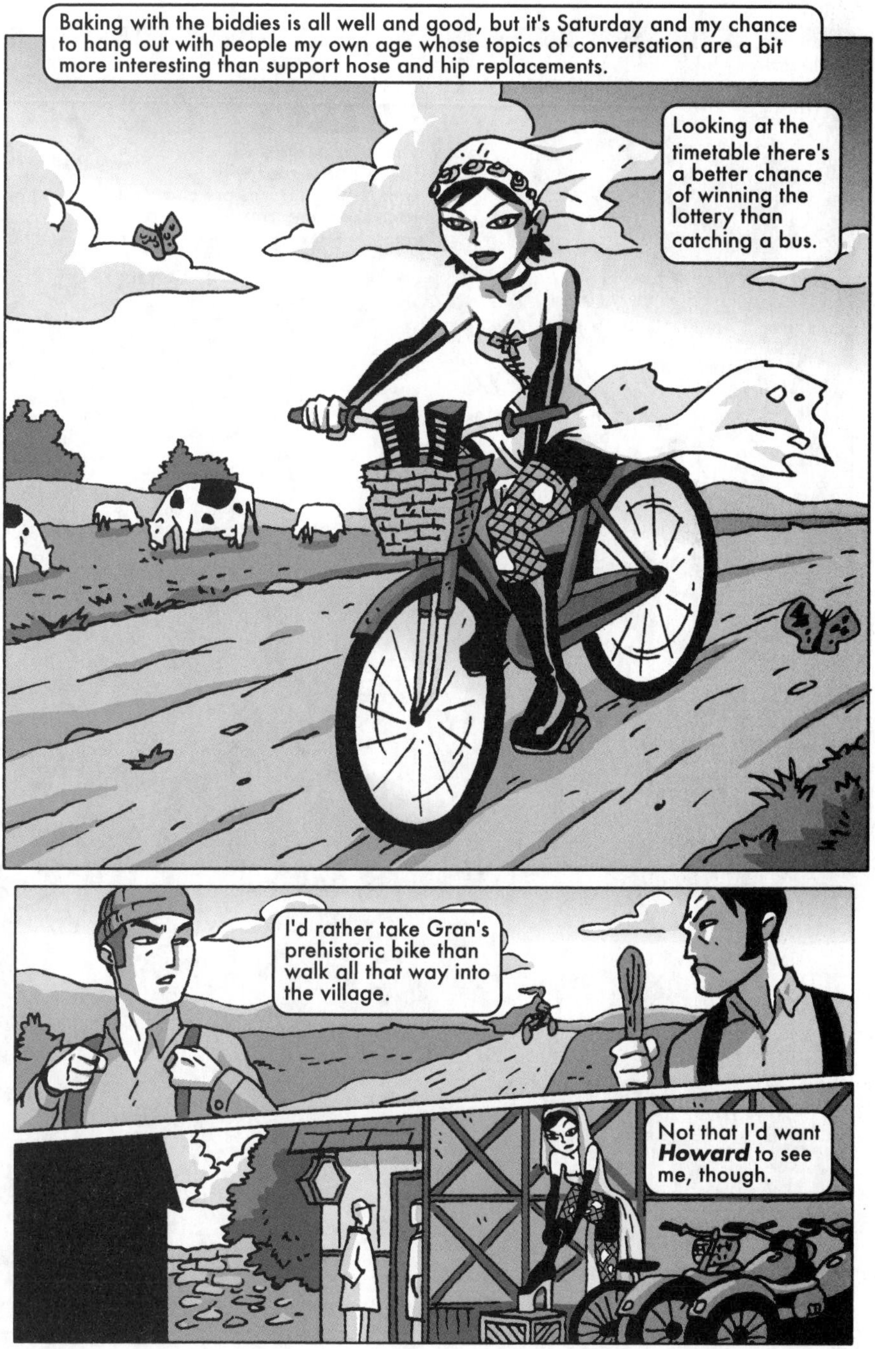
Baking with the biddies is all well and good, but it's Saturday and my chance to hang out with people my own age whose topics of conversation are a bit more interesting than support hose and hip replacements.
Looking at the timetable there's a better chance of winning the lottery than catching a bus.
I'd rather take Gran's prehistoric bike than walk all that way into the village.
Not that I'd want ***Howard*** to see me, though.

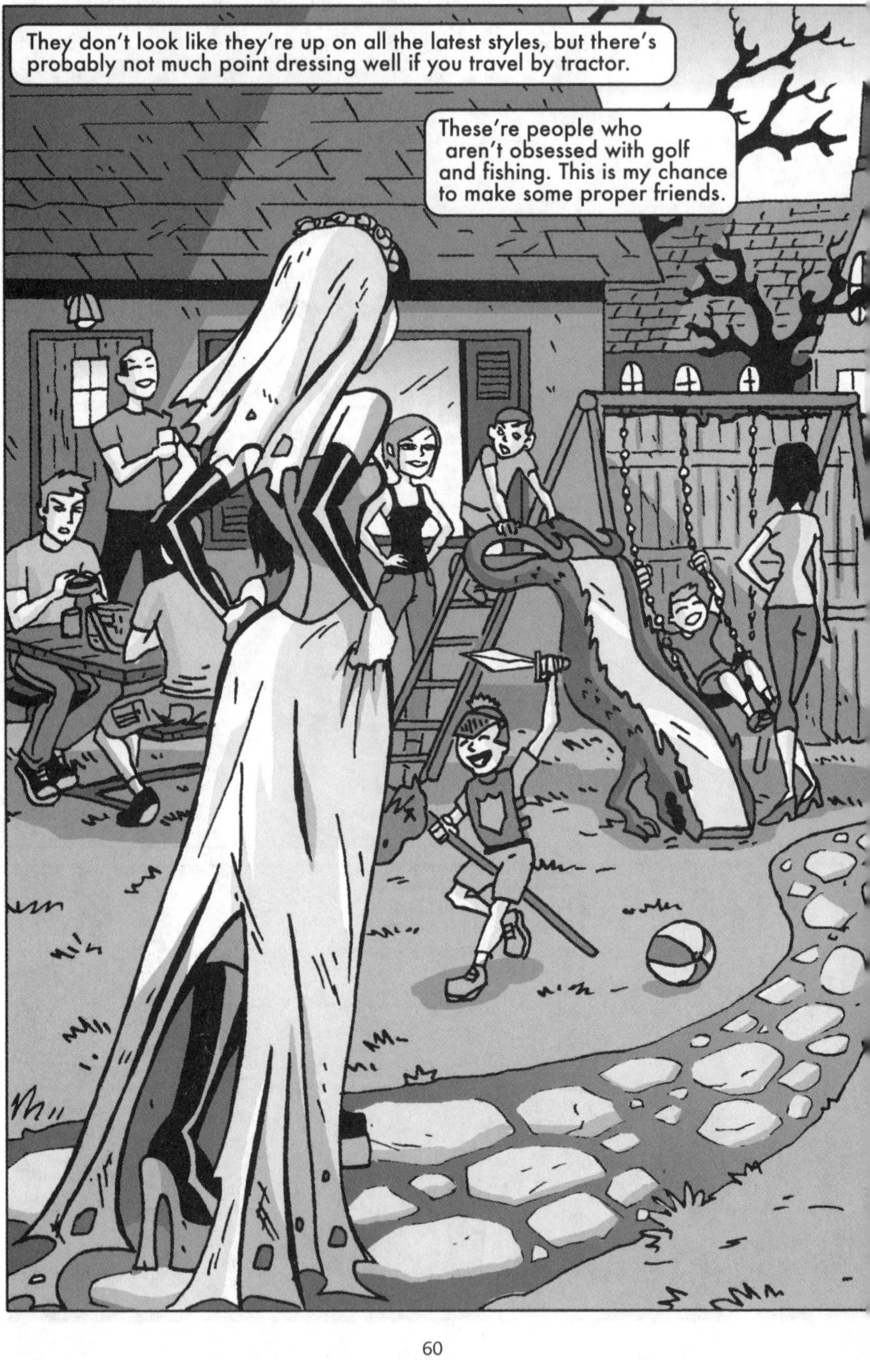
They don't look like they're up on all the latest styles, but there's probably not much point dressing well if you travel by tractor.
These're people who aren't obsessed with golf and fishing. This is my chance to make some proper friends.

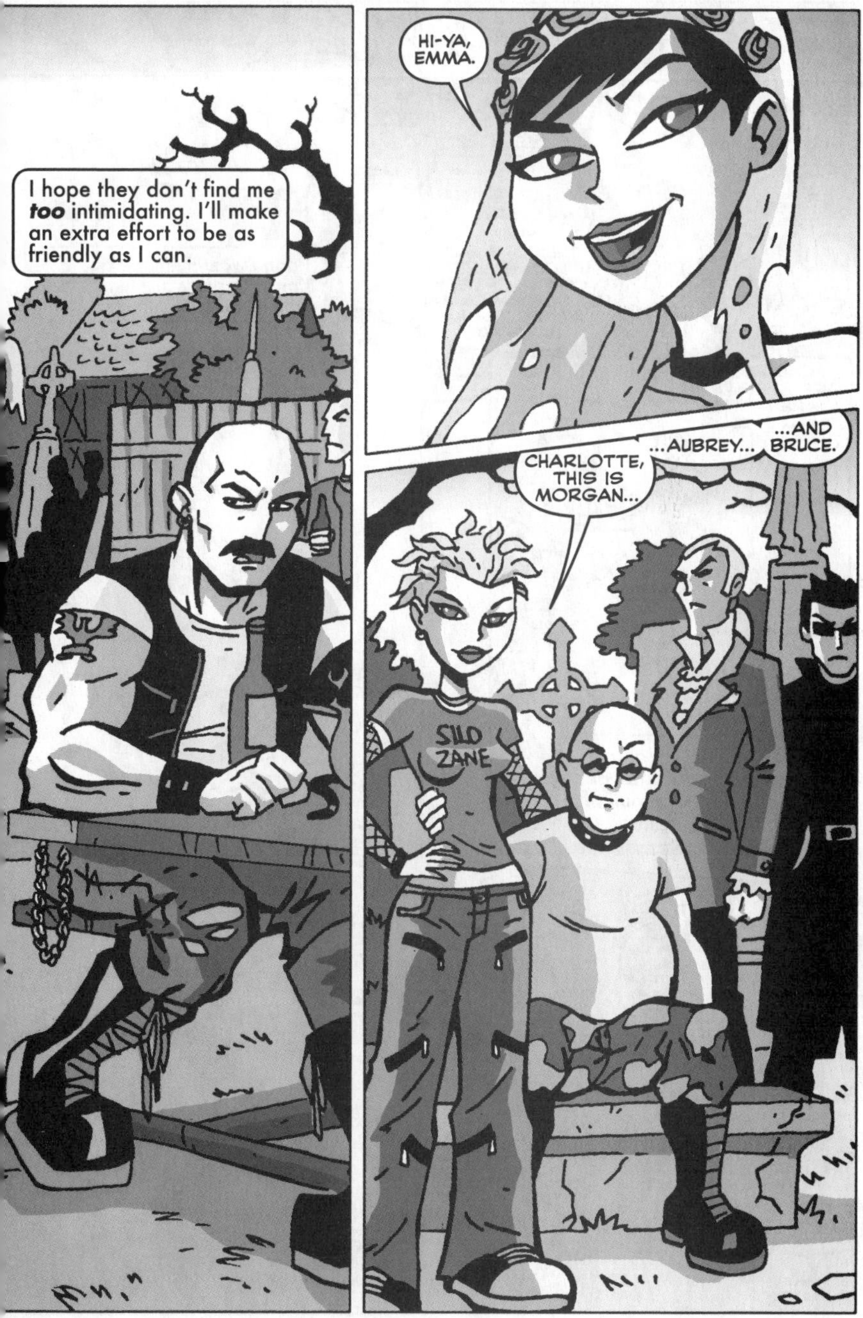
I hope they don't find me *too* intimidating. I'll make an extra effort to be as friendly as I can.
HI-YA, EMMA.
CHARLOTTE, THIS IS MORGAN...
...AUBREY...
...AND BRUCE.
SILO ZANE

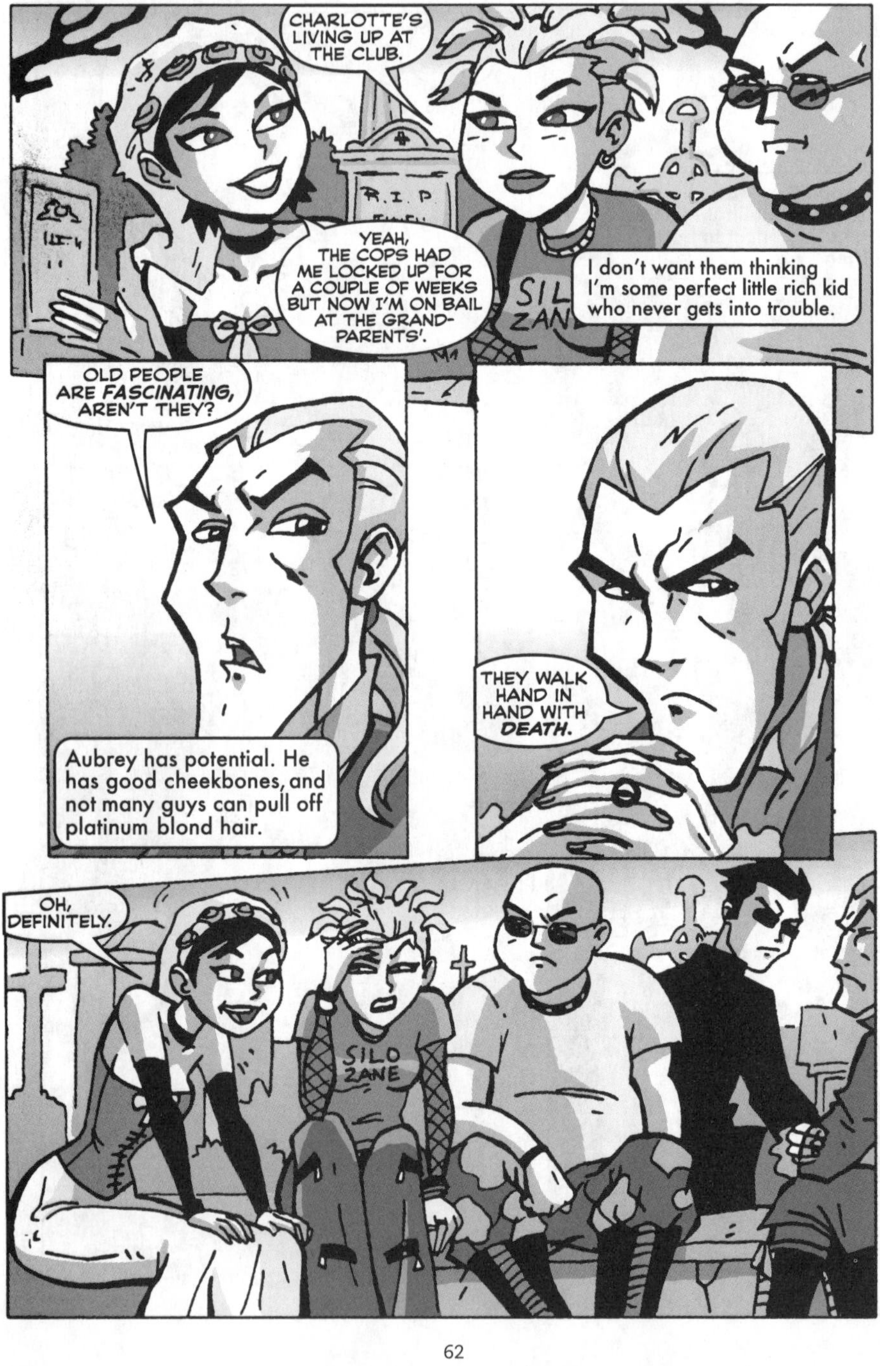

CHARLOTTE'S LIVING UP AT THE CLUB.
YEAH, THE COPS HAD ME LOCKED UP FOR A COUPLE OF WEEKS BUT NOW I'M ON BAIL AT THE GRAND-PARENTS'.
R.I.P
SILO ZANE
I don't want them thinking I'm some perfect little rich kid who never gets into trouble.
OLD PEOPLE ARE *FASCINATING,* AREN'T THEY?
Aubrey has potential. He has good cheekbones, and not many guys can pull off platinum blond hair.
THEY WALK HAND IN HAND WITH ***DEATH.***
OH, DEFINITELY.
SILO ZANE

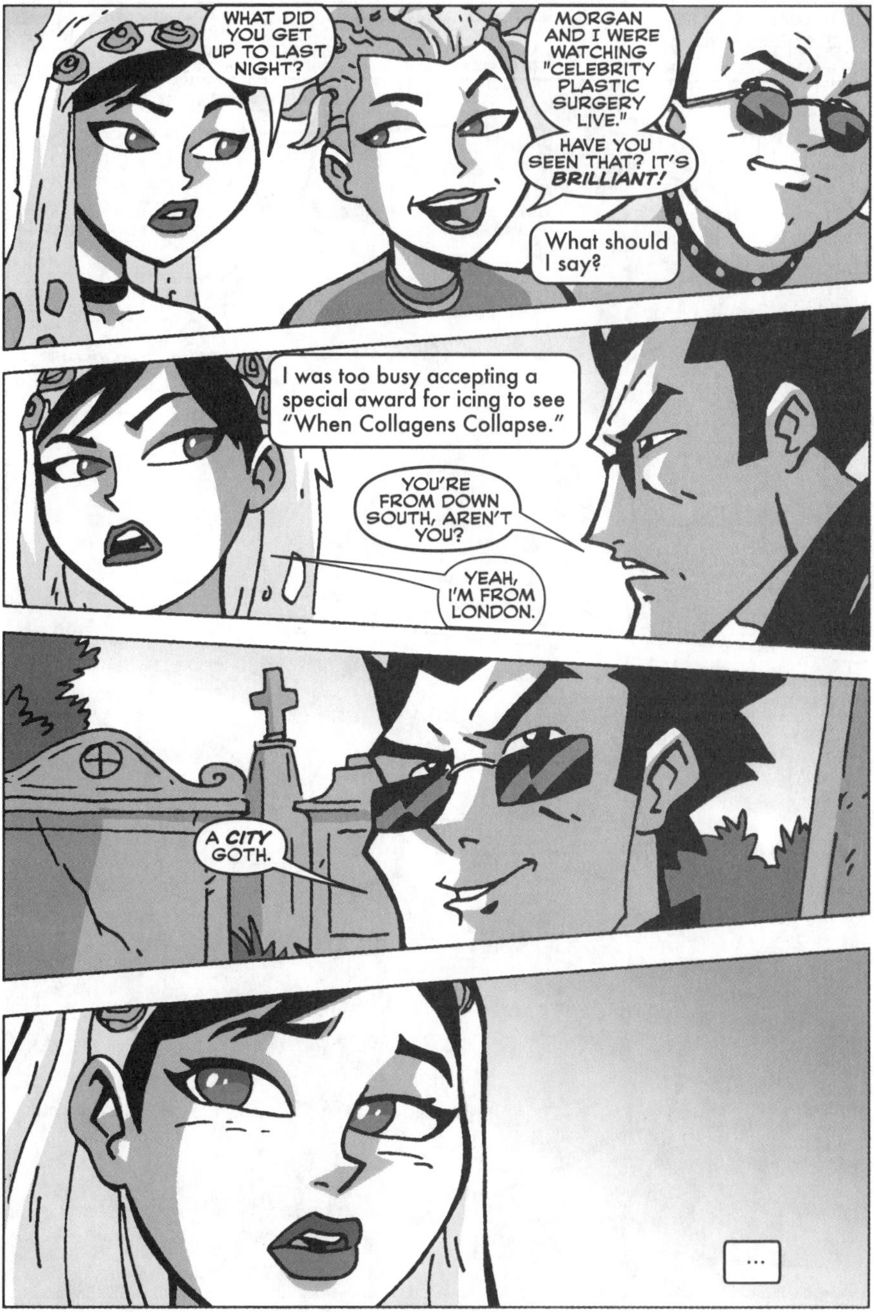
WHAT DID YOU GET UP TO LAST NIGHT?
MORGAN AND I WERE WATCHING "CELEBRITY PLASTIC SURGERY LIVE."
HAVE YOU SEEN THAT? IT'S ***BRILLIANT!***
What should I say?
I was too busy accepting a special award for icing to see "When Collagens Collapse."
YOU'RE FROM DOWN SOUTH, AREN'T YOU?
YEAH, I'M FROM LONDON.
A ***CITY*** GOTH.
...

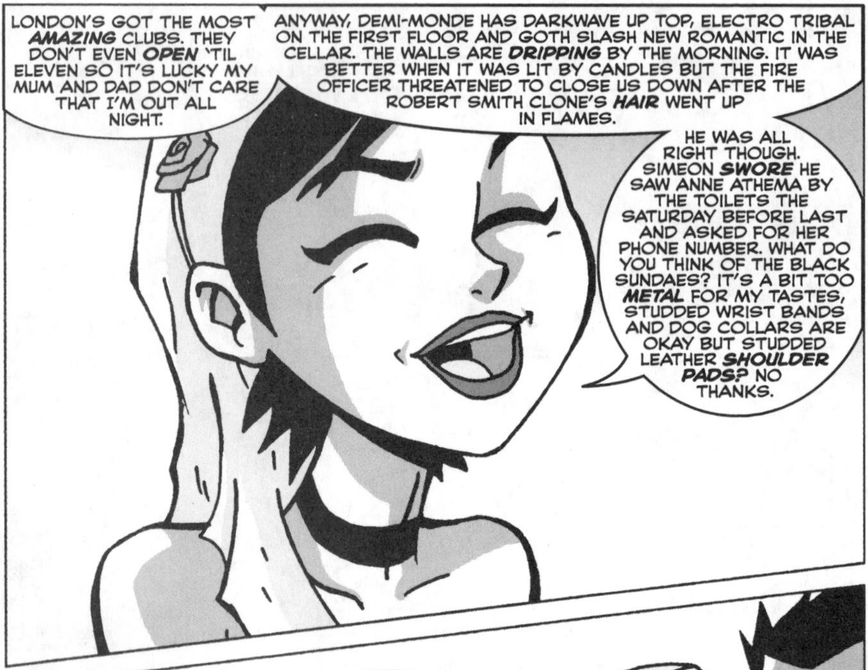
LONDON'S GOT THE MOST AMAZING CLUBS. THEY DON'T EVEN OPEN 'TIL ELEVEN SO IT'S LUCKY MY MUM AND DAD DON'T CARE THAT I'M OUT ALL NIGHT.
ANYWAY, DEMI-MONDE HAS DARKWAVE UP TOP, ELECTRO TRIBAL ON THE FIRST FLOOR AND GOTH SLASH NEW ROMANTIC IN THE CELLAR. THE WALLS ARE DRIPPING BY THE MORNING. IT WAS BETTER WHEN IT WAS LIT BY CANDLES BUT THE FIRE OFFICER THREATENED TO CLOSE US DOWN AFTER THE ROBERT SMITH CLONE'S HAIR WENT UP IN FLAMES.
HE WAS ALL RIGHT THOUGH. SIMEON SWORE HE SAW ANNE ATHEMA BY THE TOILETS THE SATURDAY BEFORE LAST AND ASKED FOR HER PHONE NUMBER. WHAT DO YOU THINK OF THE BLACK SUNDAES? IT'S A BIT TOO METAL FOR MY TASTES, STUDDED WRIST BANDS AND DOG COLLARS ARE OKAY BUT STUDDED LEATHER SHOULDER PADS? NO THANKS.
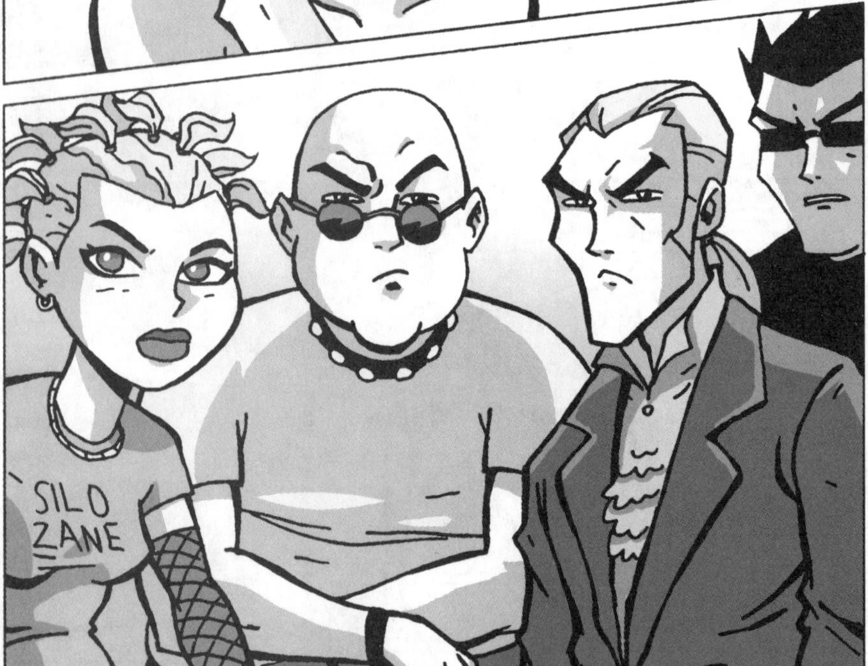
SILO ZANE

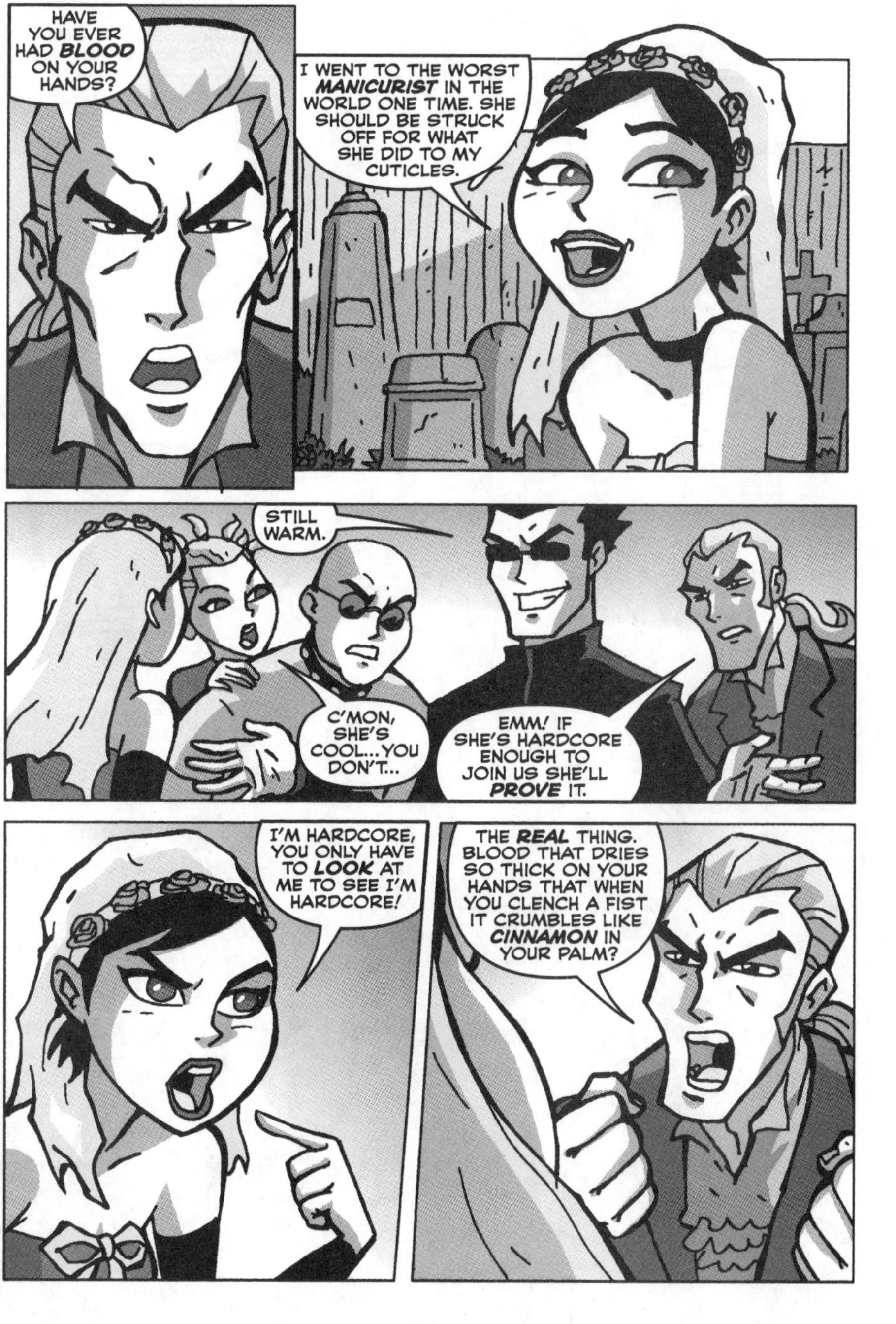

HAVE YOU EVER HAD **BLOOD** ON YOUR HANDS?
I WENT TO THE WORST **MANICURIST** IN THE WORLD ONE TIME. SHE SHOULD BE STRUCK OFF FOR WHAT SHE DID TO MY CUTICLES.
STILL WARM.
C'MON, SHE'S COOL...YOU DON'T...
EMM! IF SHE'S HARDCORE ENOUGH TO JOIN US SHE'LL **PROVE** IT.
I'M HARDCORE, YOU ONLY HAVE TO **LOOK** AT ME TO SEE I'M HARDCORE!
THE **REAL** THING. BLOOD THAT DRIES SO THICK ON YOUR HANDS THAT WHEN YOU CLENCH A FIST IT CRUMBLES LIKE **CINNAMON** IN YOUR PALM?

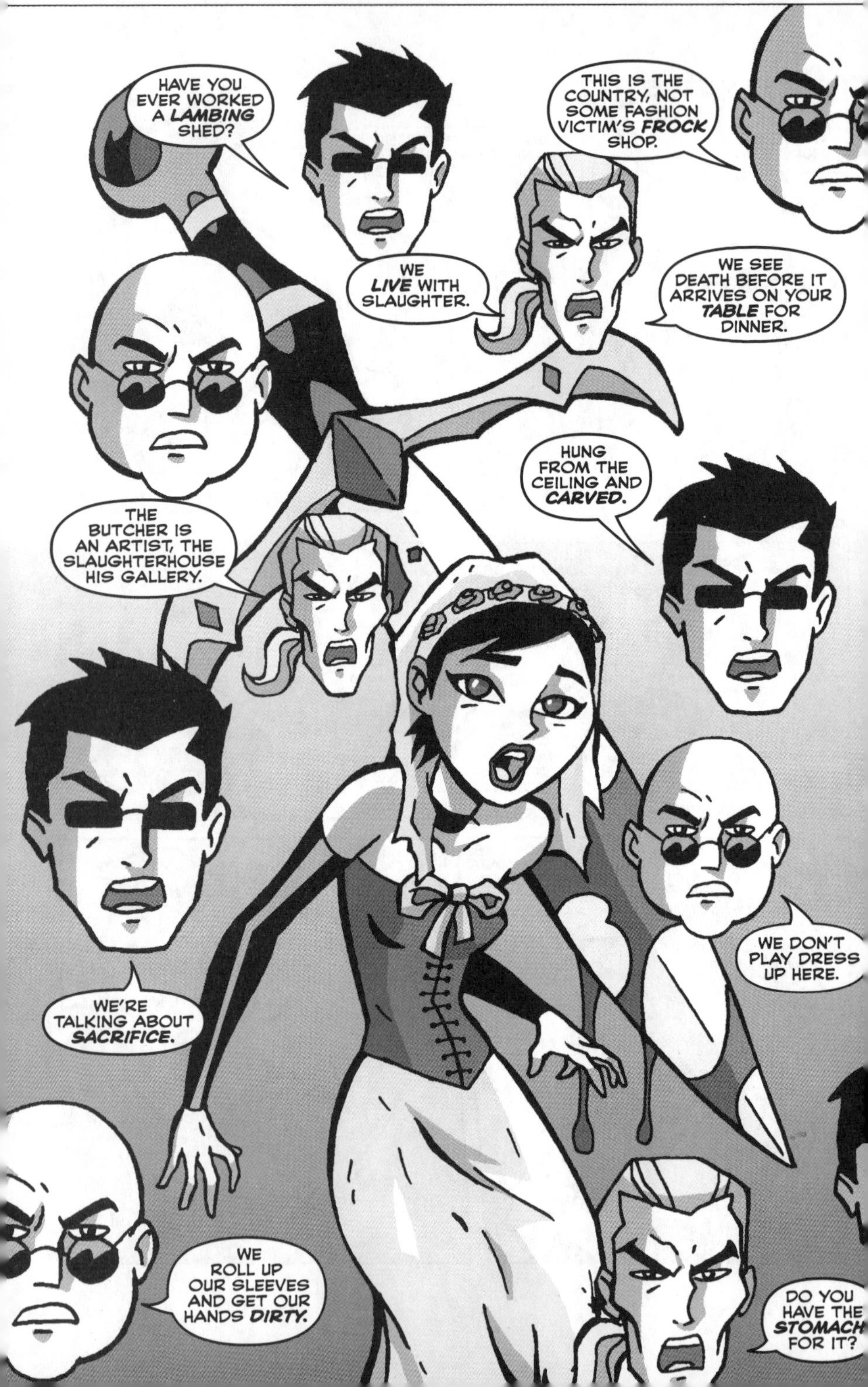
HAVE YOU EVER WORKED A LAMBING SHED?
THIS IS THE COUNTRY, NOT SOME FASHION VICTIM'S FROCK SHOP.
WE LIVE WITH SLAUGHTER.
WE SEE DEATH BEFORE IT ARRIVES ON YOUR TABLE FOR DINNER.
HUNG FROM THE CEILING AND CARVED.
THE BUTCHER IS AN ARTIST, THE SLAUGHTERHOUSE HIS GALLERY.
WE DON'T PLAY DRESS UP HERE.
WE'RE TALKING ABOUT SACRIFICE.
WE ROLL UP OUR SLEEVES AND GET OUR HANDS DIRTY.
DO YOU HAVE THE STOMACH FOR IT?

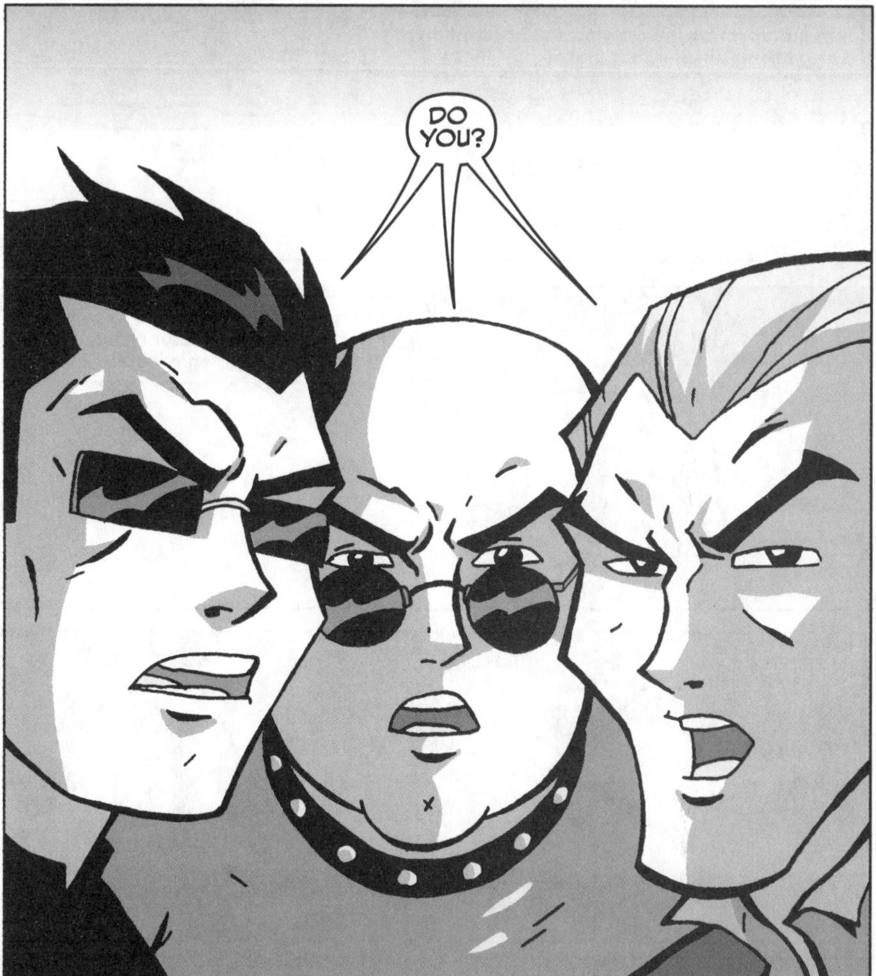
DO YOU?

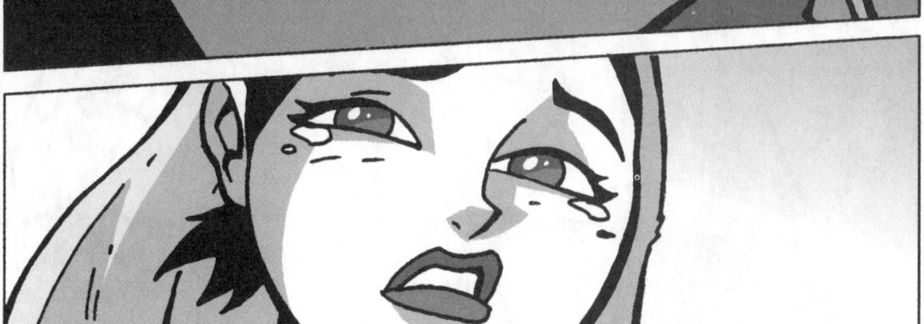

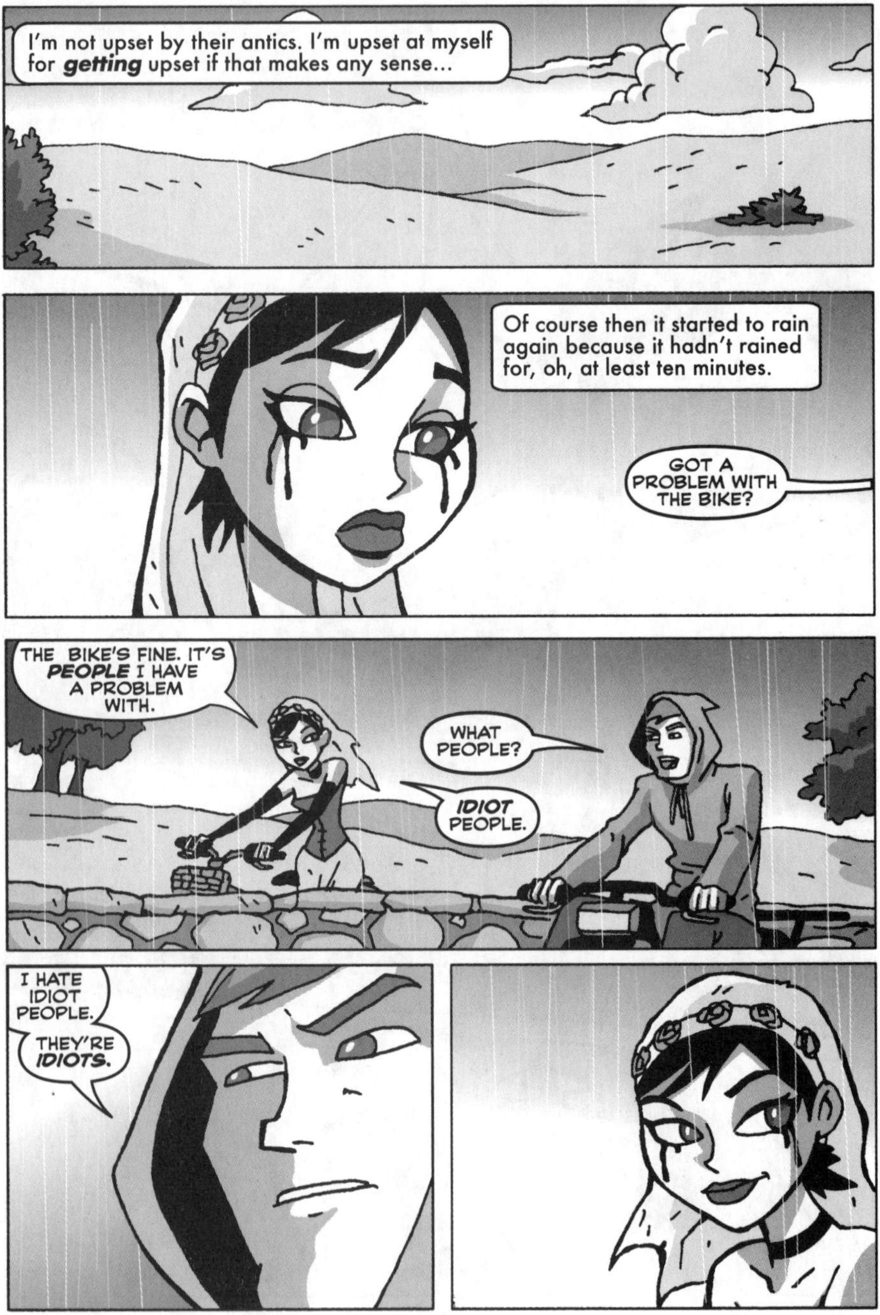
I'm not upset by their antics. I'm upset at myself for *getting* upset if that makes any sense...
Of course then it started to rain again because it hadn't rained for, oh, at least ten minutes.
GOT A PROBLEM WITH THE BIKE?
THE BIKE'S FINE. IT'S *PEOPLE* I HAVE A PROBLEM WITH.
WHAT PEOPLE?
IDIOT PEOPLE.
I HATE IDIOT PEOPLE.
THEY'RE *IDIOTS*.

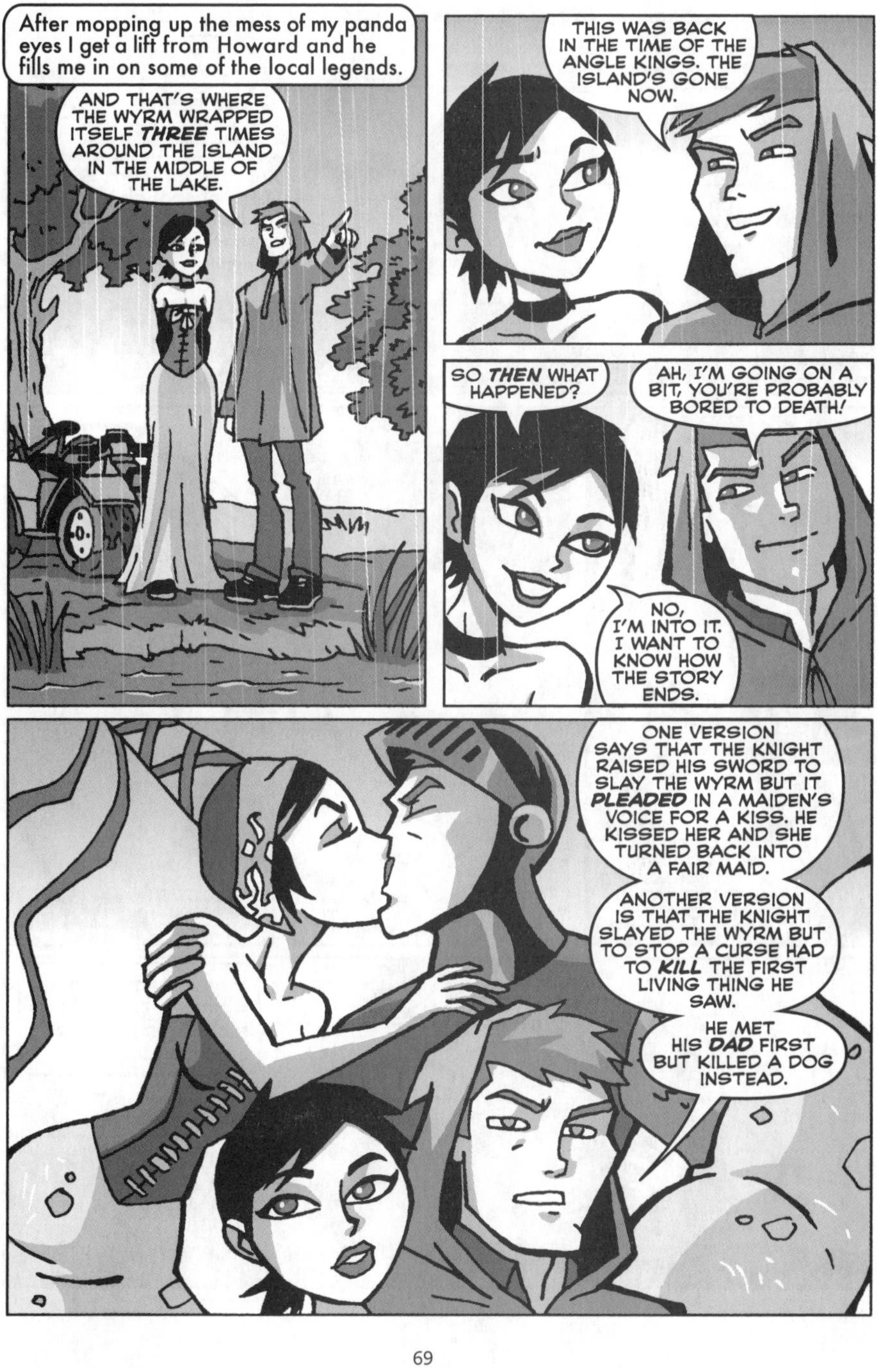
After mopping up the mess of my panda eyes I get a lift from Howard and he fills me in on some of the local legends.
AND THAT'S WHERE THE WYRM WRAPPED ITSELF ***THREE*** TIMES AROUND THE ISLAND IN THE MIDDLE OF THE LAKE.
THIS WAS BACK IN THE TIME OF THE ANGLE KINGS. THE ISLAND'S GONE NOW.
SO ***THEN*** WHAT HAPPENED?
AH, I'M GOING ON A BIT, YOU'RE PROBABLY BORED TO DEATH!
NO, I'M INTO IT. I WANT TO KNOW HOW THE STORY ENDS.
ONE VERSION SAYS THAT THE KNIGHT RAISED HIS SWORD TO SLAY THE WYRM BUT IT ***PLEADED*** IN A MAIDEN'S VOICE FOR A KISS. HE KISSED HER AND SHE TURNED BACK INTO A FAIR MAID.
ANOTHER VERSION IS THAT THE KNIGHT SLAYED THE WYRM BUT TO STOP A CURSE HAD TO ***KILL*** THE FIRST LIVING THING HE SAW.
HE MET HIS ***DAD*** FIRST BUT KILLED A DOG INSTEAD.

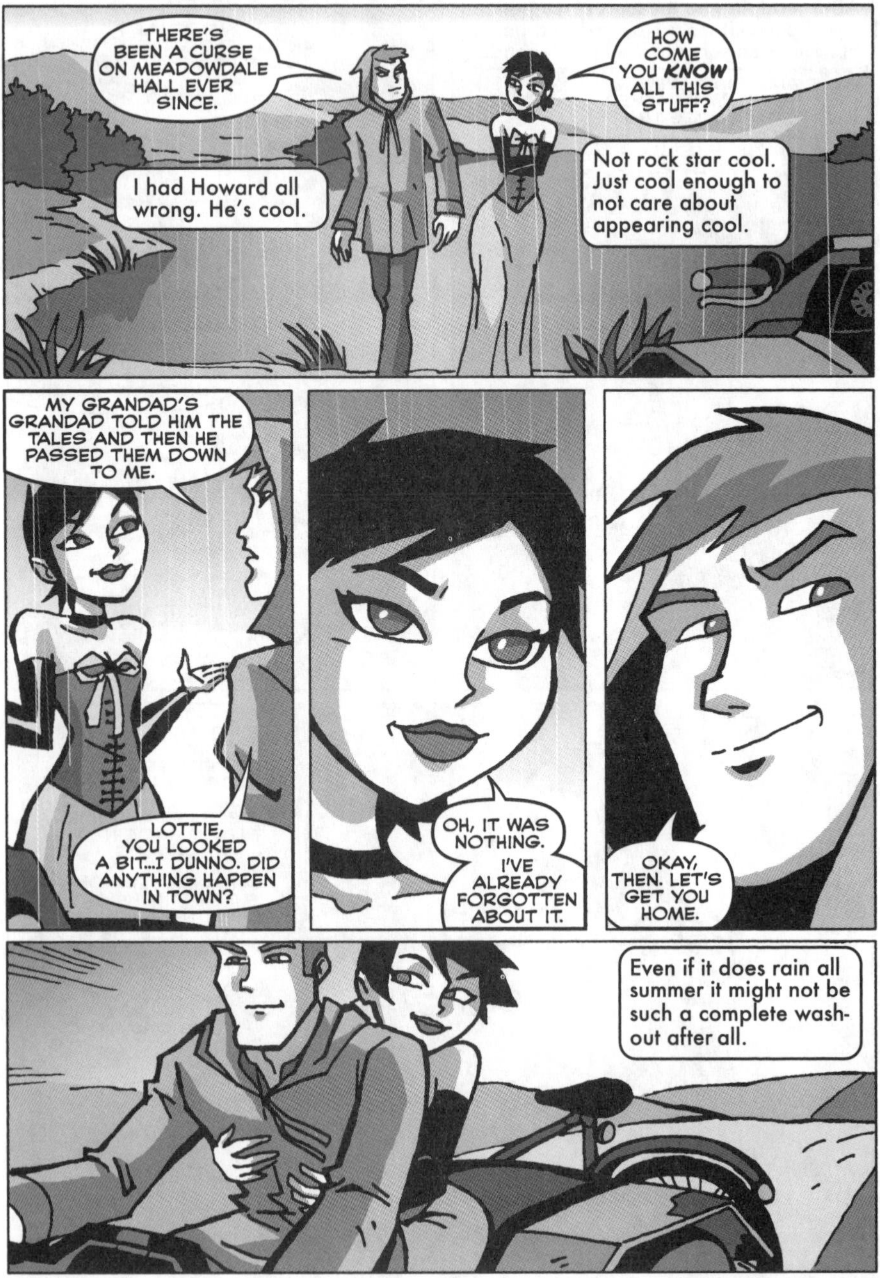
THERE'S BEEN A CURSE ON MEADOWDALE HALL EVER SINCE.
HOW COME YOU KNOW ALL THIS STUFF?
I had Howard all wrong. He's cool.
Not rock star cool. Just cool enough to not care about appearing cool.
MY GRANDAD'S GRANDAD TOLD HIM THE TALES AND THEN HE PASSED THEM DOWN TO ME.
LOTTIE, YOU LOOKED A BIT...I DUNNO. DID ANYTHING HAPPEN IN TOWN?
OH, IT WAS NOTHING.
I'VE ALREADY FORGOTTEN ABOUT IT.
OKAY, THEN. LET'S GET YOU HOME.
Even if it does rain all summer it might not be such a complete wash-out after all.

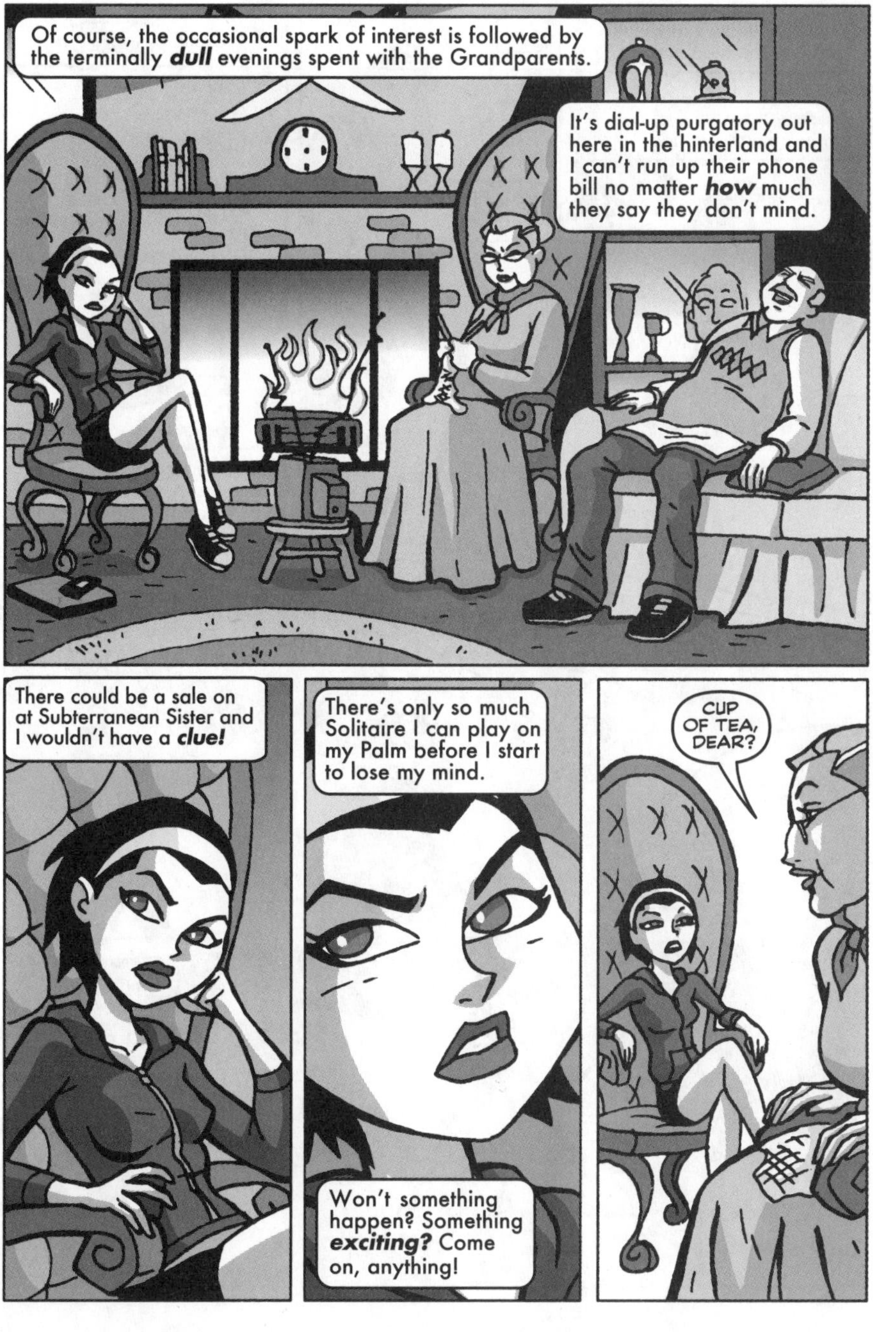

Of course, the occasional spark of interest is followed by the terminally **dull** evenings spent with the Grandparents.
It's dial-up purgatory out here in the hinterland and I can't run up their phone bill no matter **how** much they say they don't mind.
There could be a sale on at Subterranean Sister and I wouldn't have a **clue!**
There's only so much Solitaire I can play on my Palm before I start to lose my mind.
Won't something happen? Something **exciting?** Come on, anything!
CUP OF TEA, DEAR?

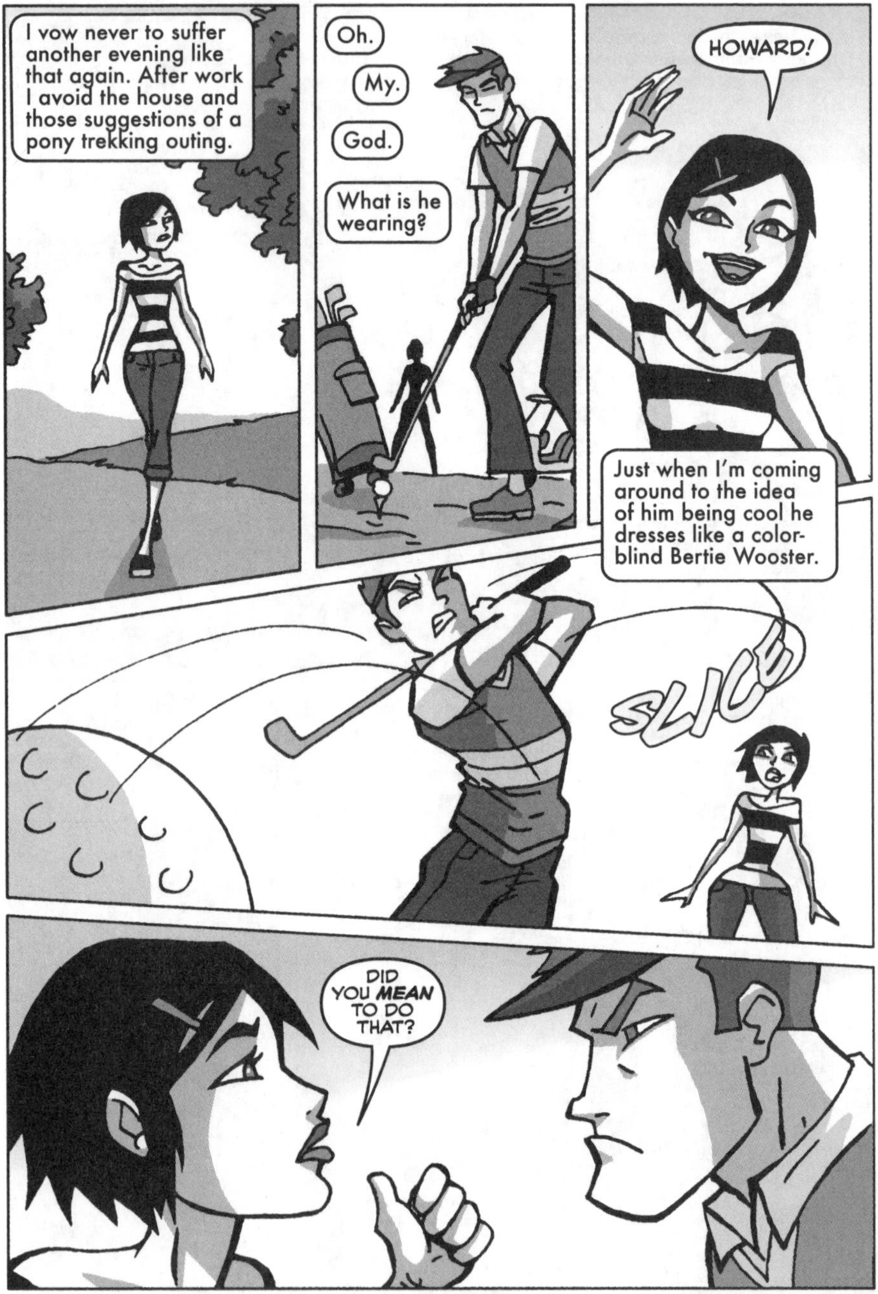
I vow never to suffer another evening like that again. After work I avoid the house and those suggestions of a pony trekking outing.
Oh.
My.
God.
What is he wearing?
HOWARD!
Just when I'm coming around to the idea of him being cool he dresses like a color-blind Bertie Wooster.
SLICE
DID YOU ***MEAN*** TO DO THAT?

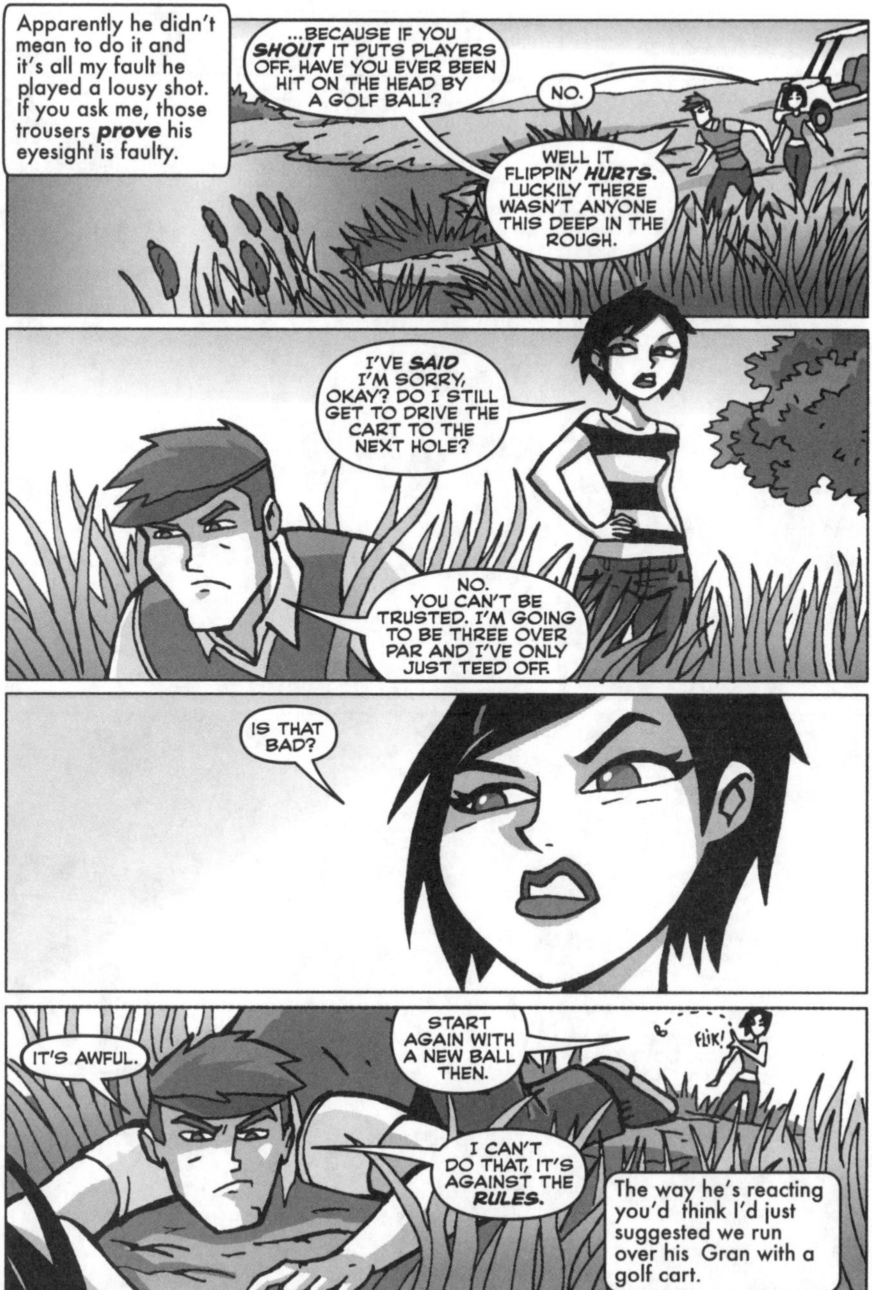

Apparently he didn't mean to do it and it's all my fault he played a lousy shot. If you ask me, those trousers **prove** his eyesight is faulty.
...BECAUSE IF YOU **SHOUT** IT PUTS PLAYERS OFF. HAVE YOU EVER BEEN HIT ON THE HEAD BY A GOLF BALL?
NO.
WELL IT FLIPPIN' **HURTS.** LUCKILY THERE WASN'T ANYONE THIS DEEP IN THE ROUGH.
I'VE **SAID** I'M SORRY, OKAY? DO I STILL GET TO DRIVE THE CART TO THE NEXT HOLE?
NO. YOU CAN'T BE TRUSTED. I'M GOING TO BE THREE OVER PAR AND I'VE ONLY JUST TEED OFF.
IS THAT BAD?
IT'S AWFUL.
START AGAIN WITH A NEW BALL THEN.
FLIK!
I CAN'T DO THAT, IT'S AGAINST THE **RULES.**
The way he's reacting you'd think I'd just suggested we run over his Gran with a golf cart.

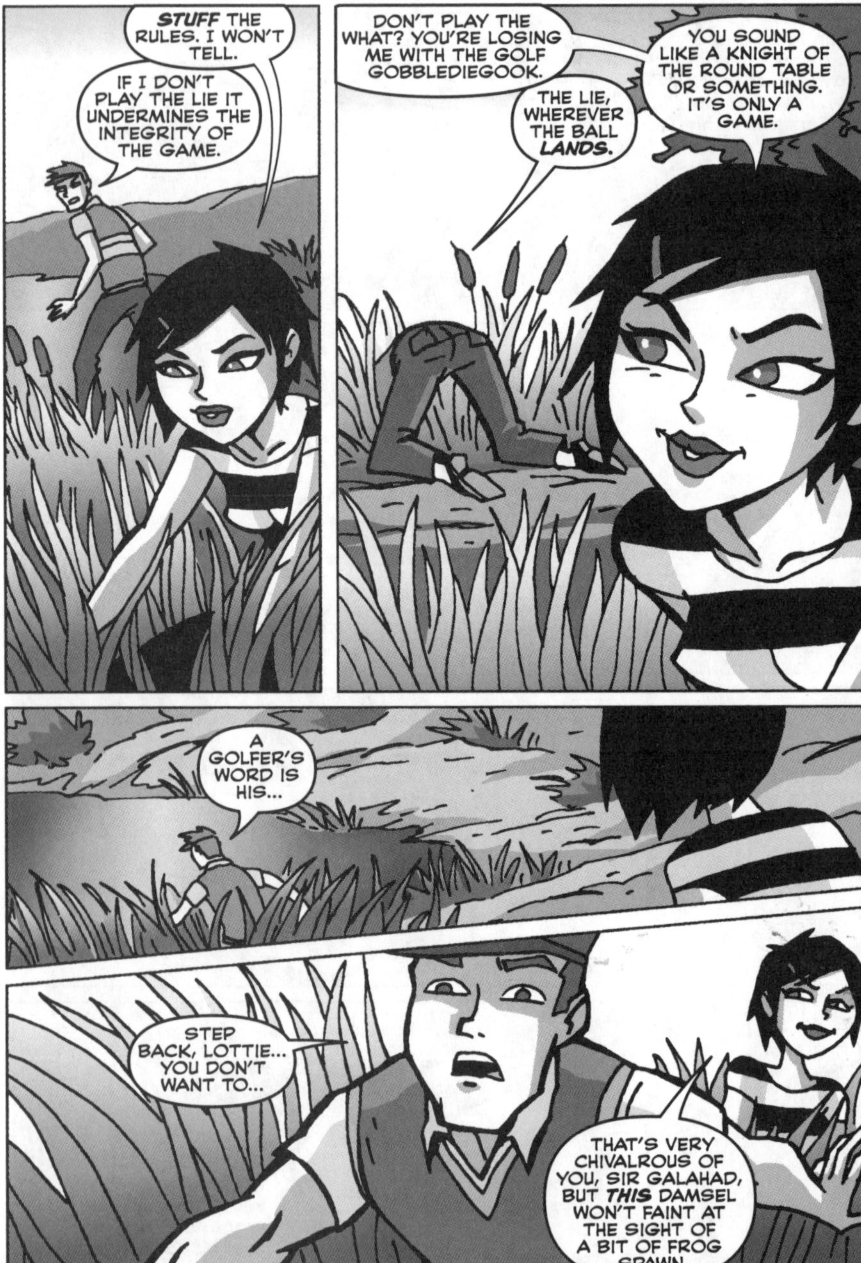
STUFF THE RULES. I WON'T TELL.
IF I DON'T PLAY THE LIE IT UNDERMINES THE INTEGRITY OF THE GAME.
DON'T PLAY THE WHAT? YOU'RE LOSING ME WITH THE GOLF GOBBLEDIEGOOK.
THE LIE, WHEREVER THE BALL LANDS.
YOU SOUND LIKE A KNIGHT OF THE ROUND TABLE OR SOMETHING. IT'S ONLY A GAME.
A GOLFER'S WORD IS HIS...
STEP BACK, LOTTIE... YOU DON'T WANT TO...
THAT'S VERY CHIVALROUS OF YOU, SIR GALAHAD, BUT THIS DAMSEL WON'T FAINT AT THE SIGHT OF A BIT OF FROG SPAWN.

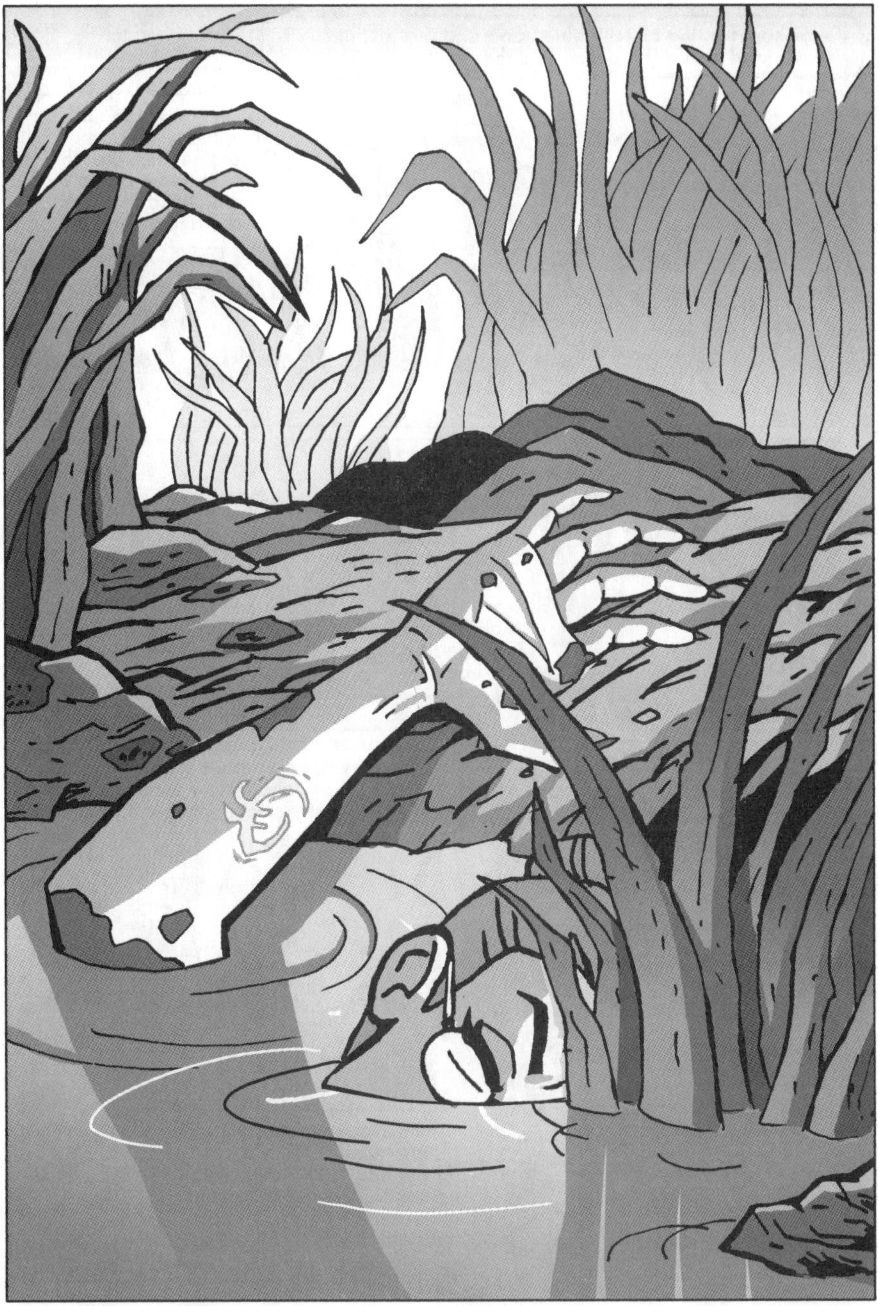

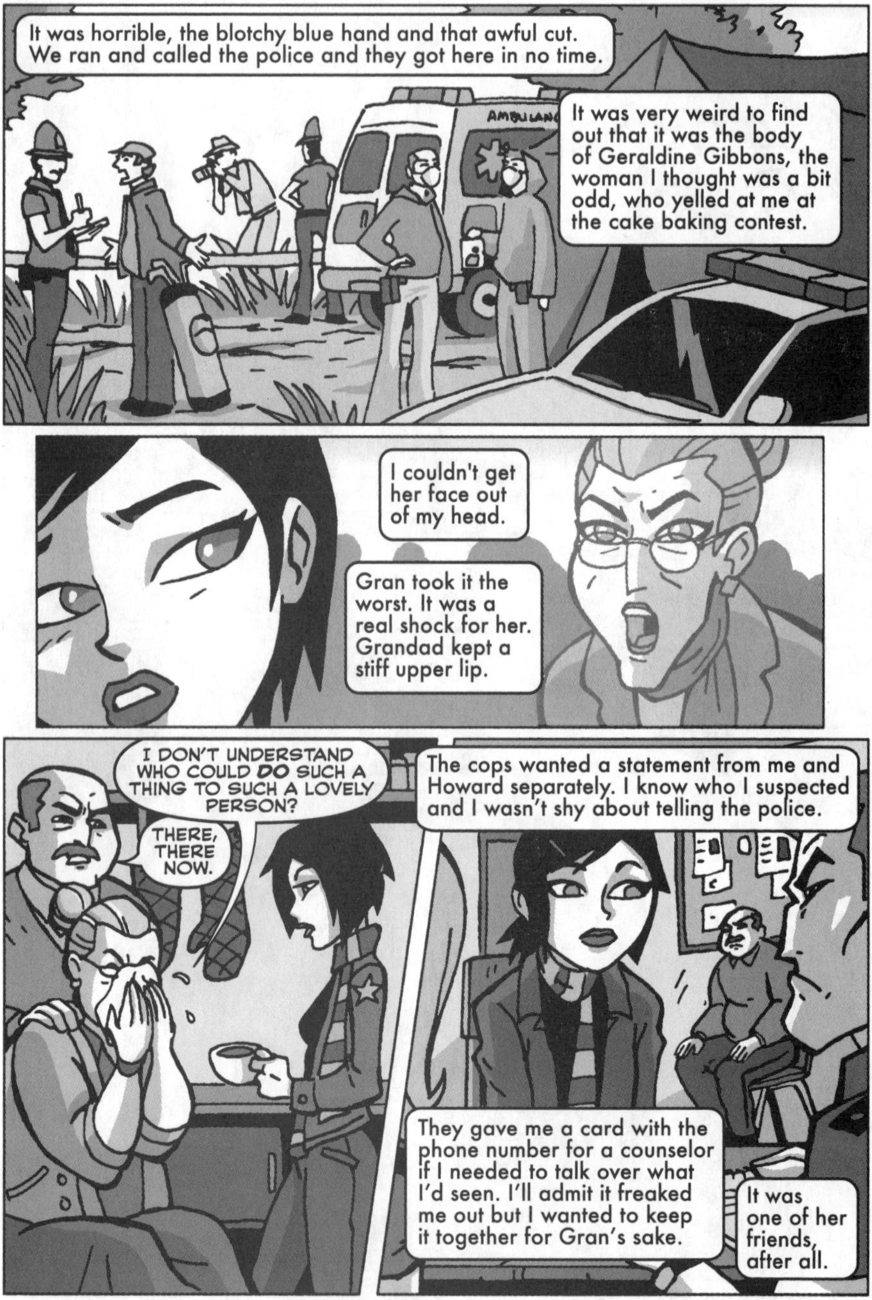

It was horrible, the blotchy blue hand and that awful cut. We ran and called the police and they got here in no time.
AMBULANC
It was very weird to find out that it was the body of Geraldine Gibbons, the woman I thought was a bit odd, who yelled at me at the cake baking contest.
I couldn't get her face out of my head.
Gran took it the worst. It was a real shock for her. Grandad kept a stiff upper lip.
I DON'T UNDERSTAND WHO COULD *DO* SUCH A THING TO SUCH A LOVELY PERSON?
THERE, THERE NOW.
The cops wanted a statement from me and Howard separately. I know who I suspected and I wasn't shy about telling the police.
They gave me a card with the phone number for a counselor if I needed to talk over what I'd seen. I'll admit it freaked me out but I wanted to keep it together for Gran's sake.
It was one of her friends, after all.

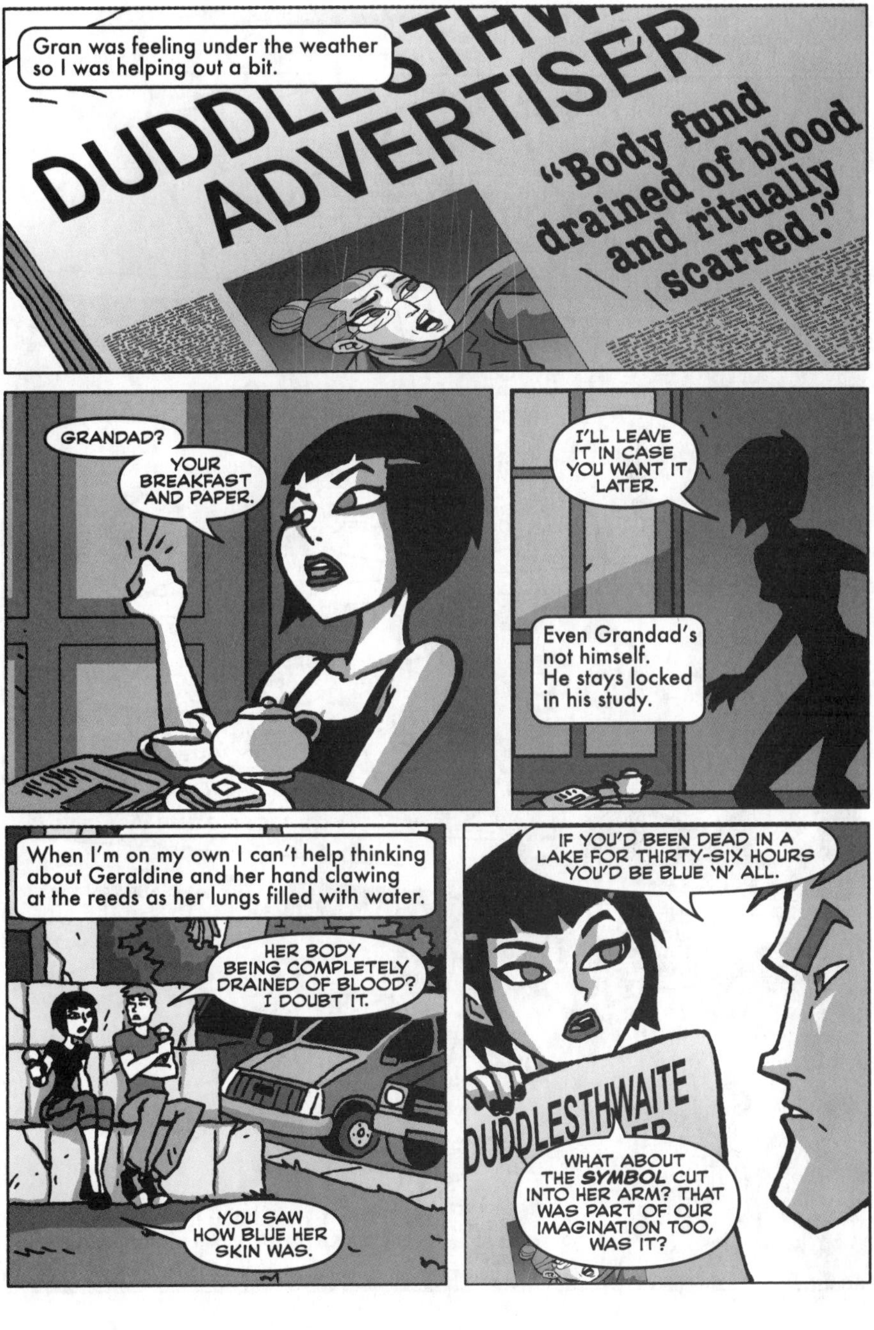
Gran was feeling under the weather so I was helping out a bit.
DUDDLESTHWAITE ADVERTISER
"Body fund drained of blood and ritually scarred."
GRANDAD?
YOUR BREAKFAST AND PAPER.
I'LL LEAVE IT IN CASE YOU WANT IT LATER.
Even Grandad's not himself. He stays locked in his study.
When I'm on my own I can't help thinking about Geraldine and her hand clawing at the reeds as her lungs filled with water.
HER BODY BEING COMPLETELY DRAINED OF BLOOD? I DOUBT IT.
YOU SAW HOW BLUE HER SKIN WAS.
IF YOU'D BEEN DEAD IN A LAKE FOR THIRTY-SIX HOURS YOU'D BE BLUE 'N' ALL.
DUDDLESTHWAITE
WHAT ABOUT THE *SYMBOL* CUT INTO HER ARM? THAT WAS PART OF OUR IMAGINATION TOO, WAS IT?

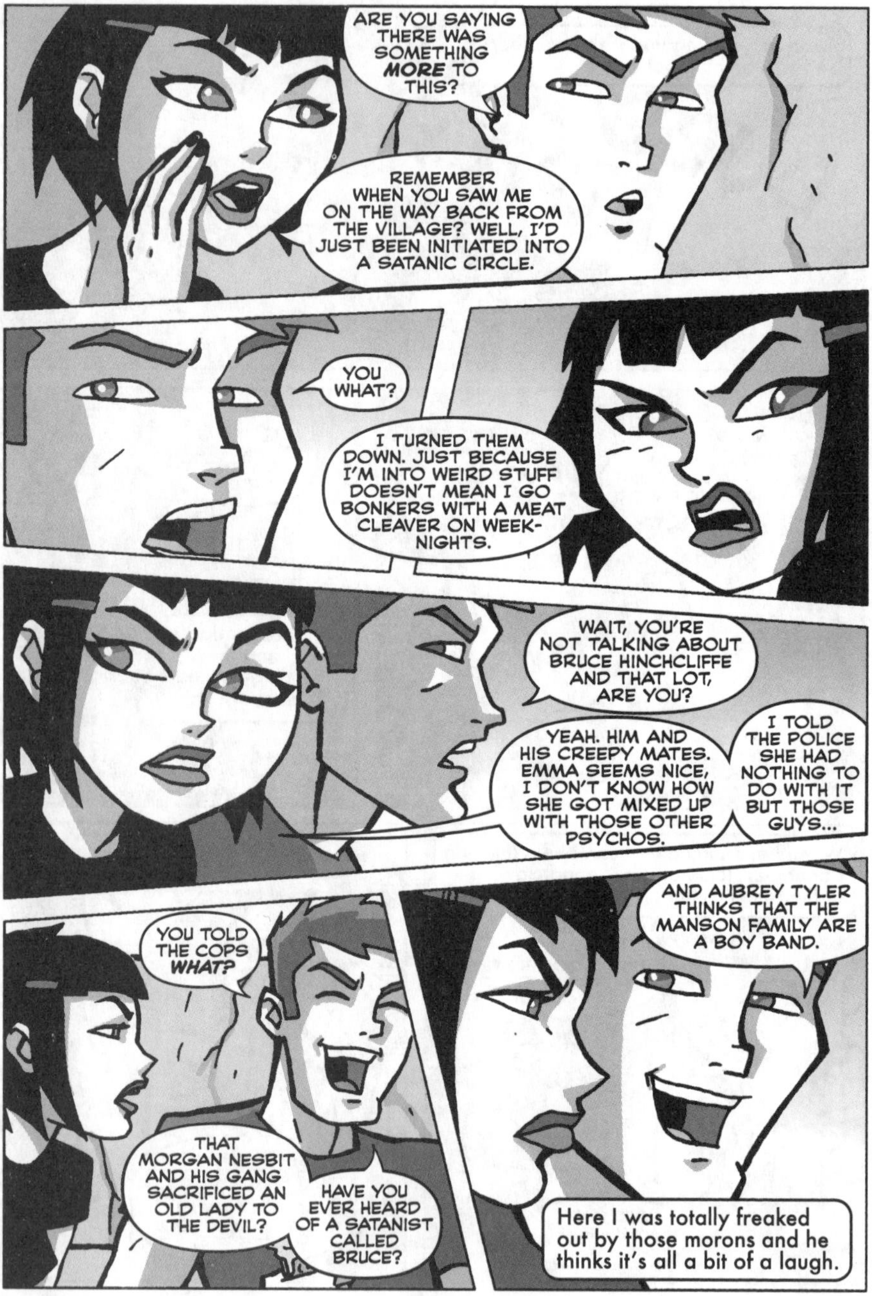
ARE YOU SAYING THERE WAS SOMETHING *MORE* TO THIS?
REMEMBER WHEN YOU SAW ME ON THE WAY BACK FROM THE VILLAGE? WELL, I'D JUST BEEN INITIATED INTO A SATANIC CIRCLE.
YOU WHAT?
I TURNED THEM DOWN. JUST BECAUSE I'M INTO WEIRD STUFF DOESN'T MEAN I GO BONKERS WITH A MEAT CLEAVER ON WEEK-NIGHTS.
WAIT, YOU'RE NOT TALKING ABOUT BRUCE HINCHCLIFFE AND THAT LOT, ARE YOU?
YEAH. HIM AND HIS CREEPY MATES. EMMA SEEMS NICE, I DON'T KNOW HOW SHE GOT MIXED UP WITH THOSE OTHER PSYCHOS.
I TOLD THE POLICE SHE HAD NOTHING TO DO WITH IT BUT THOSE GUYS...
YOU TOLD THE COPS *WHAT?*
THAT MORGAN NESBIT AND HIS GANG SACRIFICED AN OLD LADY TO THE DEVIL?
HAVE YOU EVER HEARD OF A SATANIST CALLED BRUCE?
AND AUBREY TYLER THINKS THAT THE MANSON FAMILY ARE A BOY BAND.
Here I was totally freaked out by those morons and he thinks it's all a bit of a laugh.

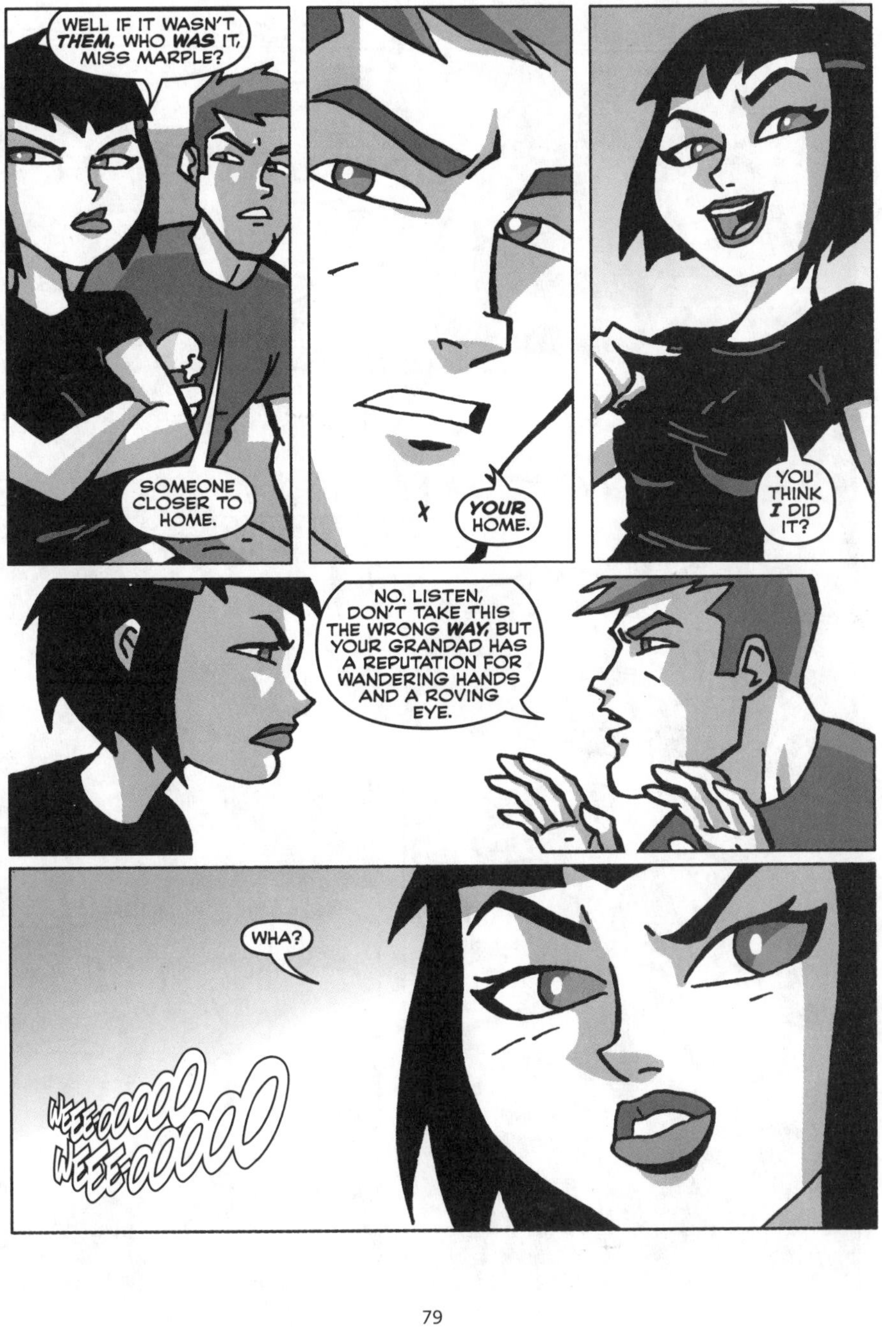
WELL IF IT WASN'T *THEM,* WHO *WAS* IT, MISS MARPLE?
SOMEONE CLOSER TO HOME.
YOUR HOME.
YOU THINK *I* DID IT?
NO. LISTEN, DON'T TAKE THIS THE WRONG *WAY,* BUT YOUR GRANDAD HAS A REPUTATION FOR WANDERING HANDS AND A ROVING EYE.
WHA?
WEEE-OOOOO
WEEE-OOOOO

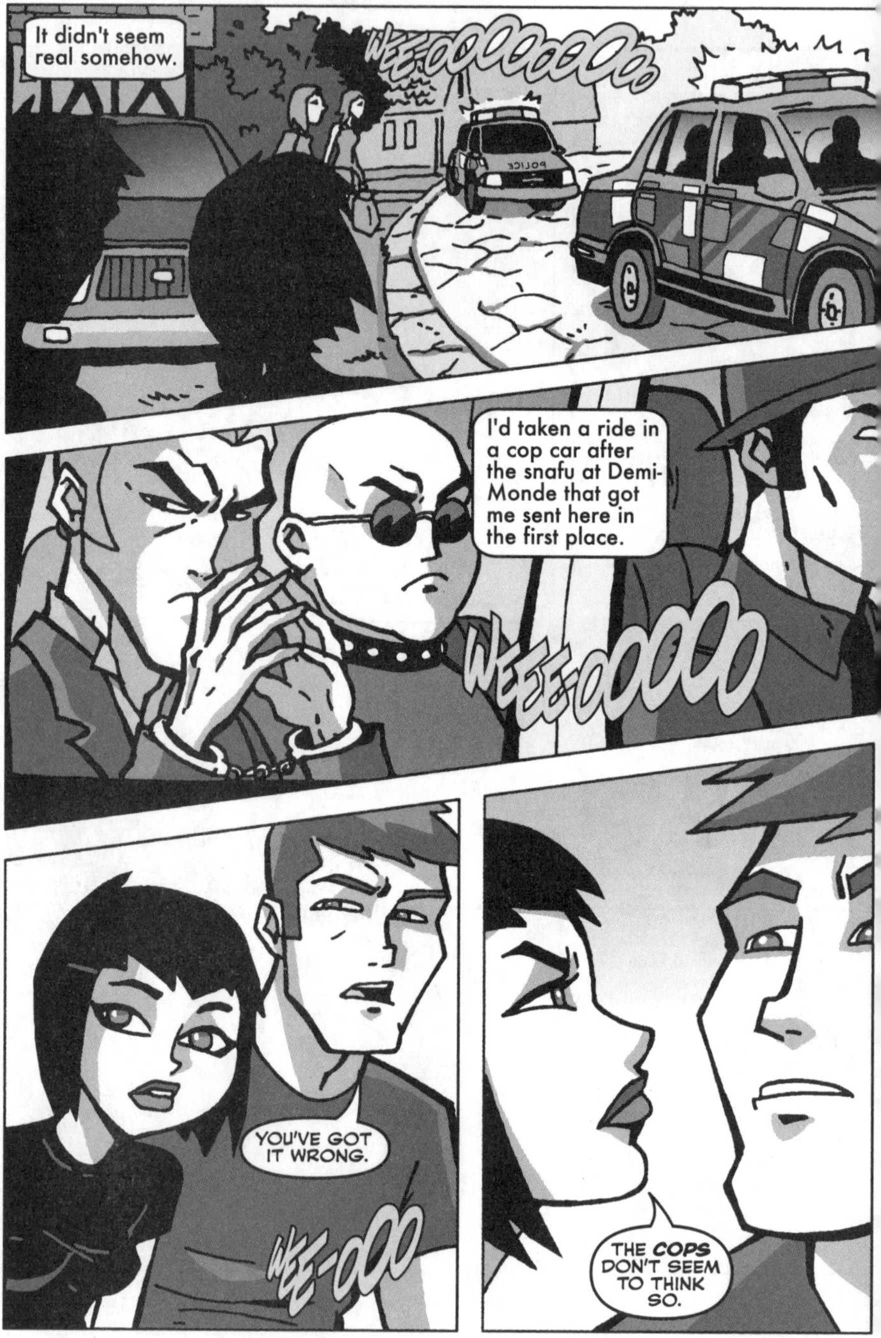

It didn't seem real somehow.
WEE-OOOOOOOOOOo
POLICE
I'd taken a ride in a cop car after the snafu at Demi-Monde that got me sent here in the first place.
WEEE-OOOOO
YOU'VE GOT IT WRONG.
WEE-OOO
THE **COPS** DON'T SEEM TO THINK SO.

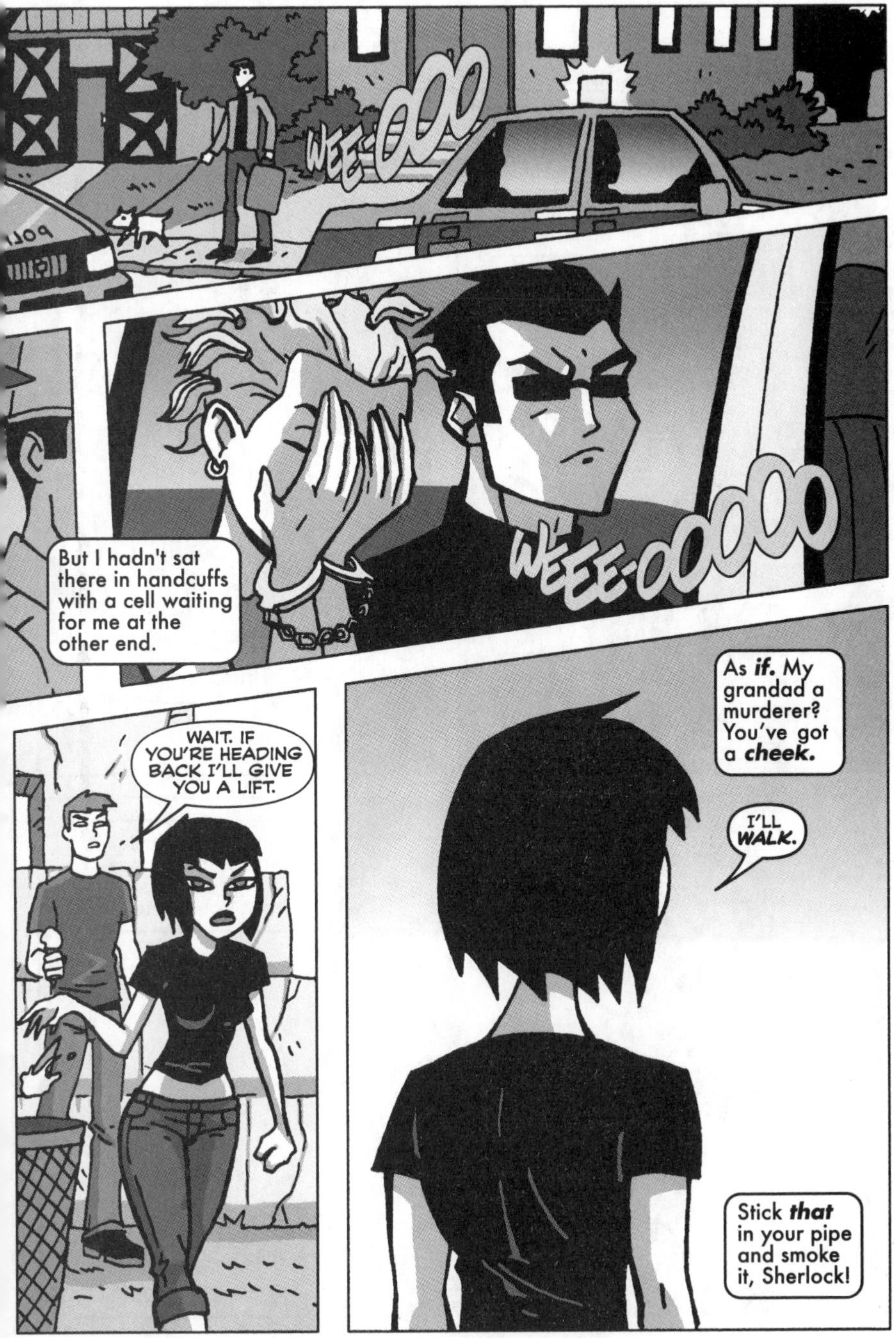
WEE-OOO
POL
WEEE-OOOOO
But I hadn't sat there in handcuffs with a cell waiting for me at the other end.
WAIT. IF YOU'RE HEADING BACK I'LL GIVE YOU A LIFT.
As *if.* My grandad a murderer? You've got a *cheek.*
I'LL *WALK.*
Stick *that* in your pipe and smoke it, Sherlock!

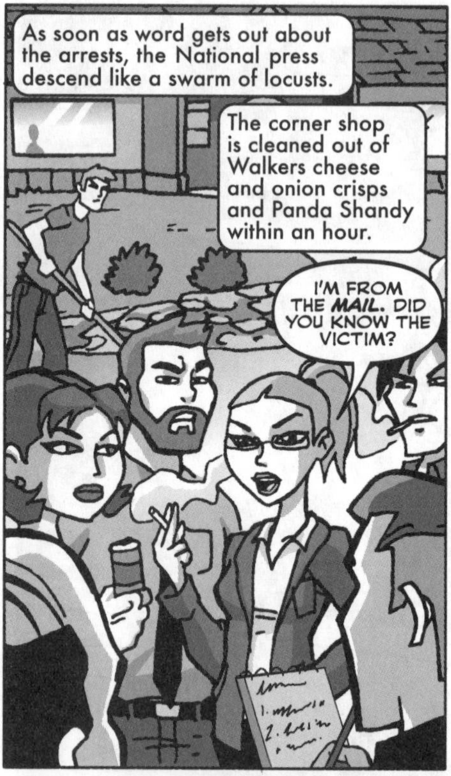
As soon as word gets out about the arrests, the National press descend like a swarm of locusts.
The corner shop is cleaned out of Walkers cheese and onion crisps and Panda Shandy within an hour.
I'M FROM THE MAIL. DID YOU KNOW THE VICTIM?

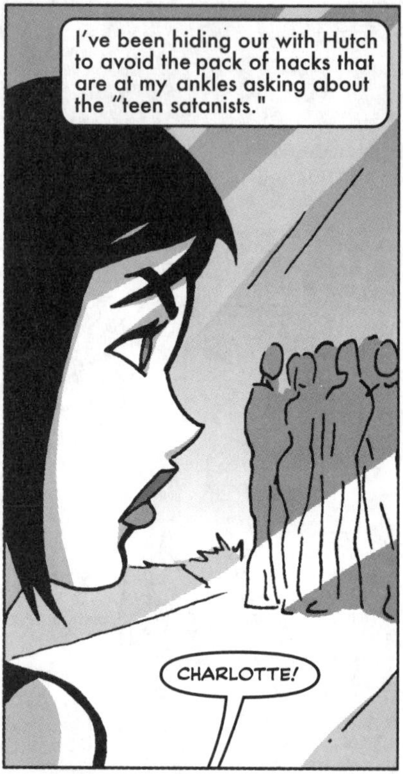
I've been hiding out with Hutch to avoid the pack of hacks that are at my ankles asking about the "teen satanists."
CHARLOTTE!

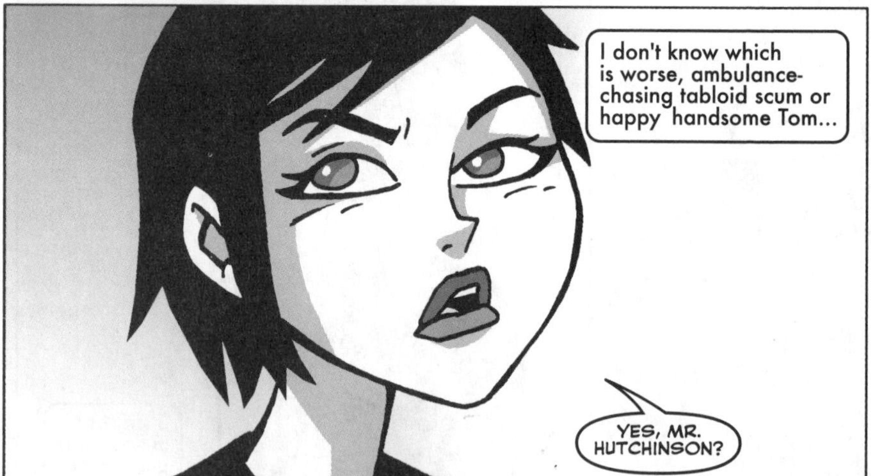
I don't know which is worse, ambulance-chasing tabloid scum or happy handsome Tom...
YES, MR. HUTCHINSON?

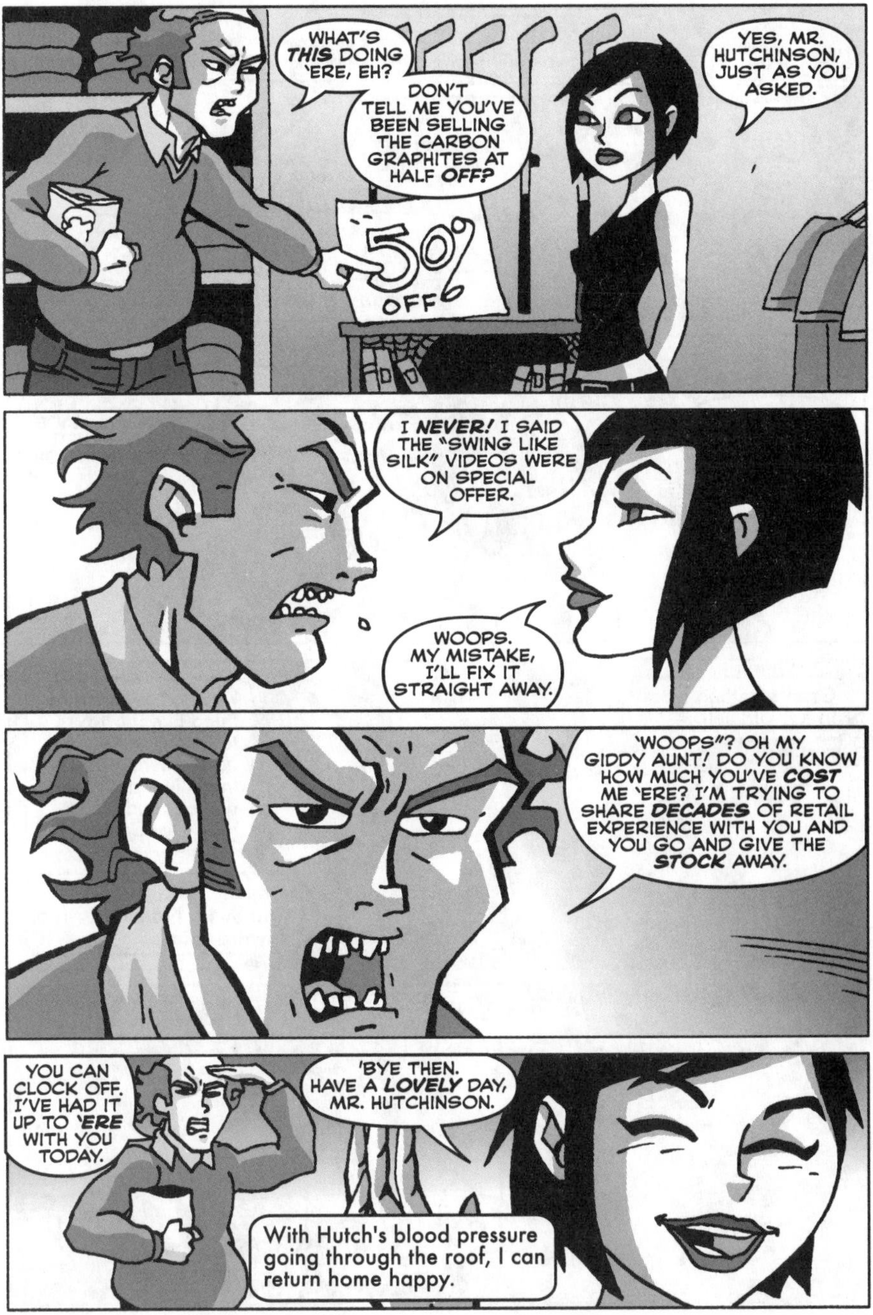
WHAT'S *THIS* DOING 'ERE, EH?
DON'T TELL ME YOU'VE BEEN SELLING THE CARBON GRAPHITES AT HALF *OFF?*
50% OFF
YES, MR. HUTCHINSON, JUST AS YOU ASKED.
I *NEVER!* I SAID THE "SWING LIKE SILK" VIDEOS WERE ON SPECIAL OFFER.
WOOPS. MY MISTAKE, I'LL FIX IT STRAIGHT AWAY.
'WOOPS"? OH MY GIDDY AUNT! DO YOU KNOW HOW MUCH YOU'VE *COST* ME 'ERE? I'M TRYING TO SHARE *DECADES* OF RETAIL EXPERIENCE WITH YOU AND YOU GO AND GIVE THE *STOCK* AWAY.
YOU CAN CLOCK OFF. I'VE HAD IT UP TO *'ERE* WITH YOU TODAY.
'BYE THEN. HAVE A *LOVELY* DAY, MR. HUTCHINSON.
With Hutch's blood pressure going through the roof, I can return home happy.

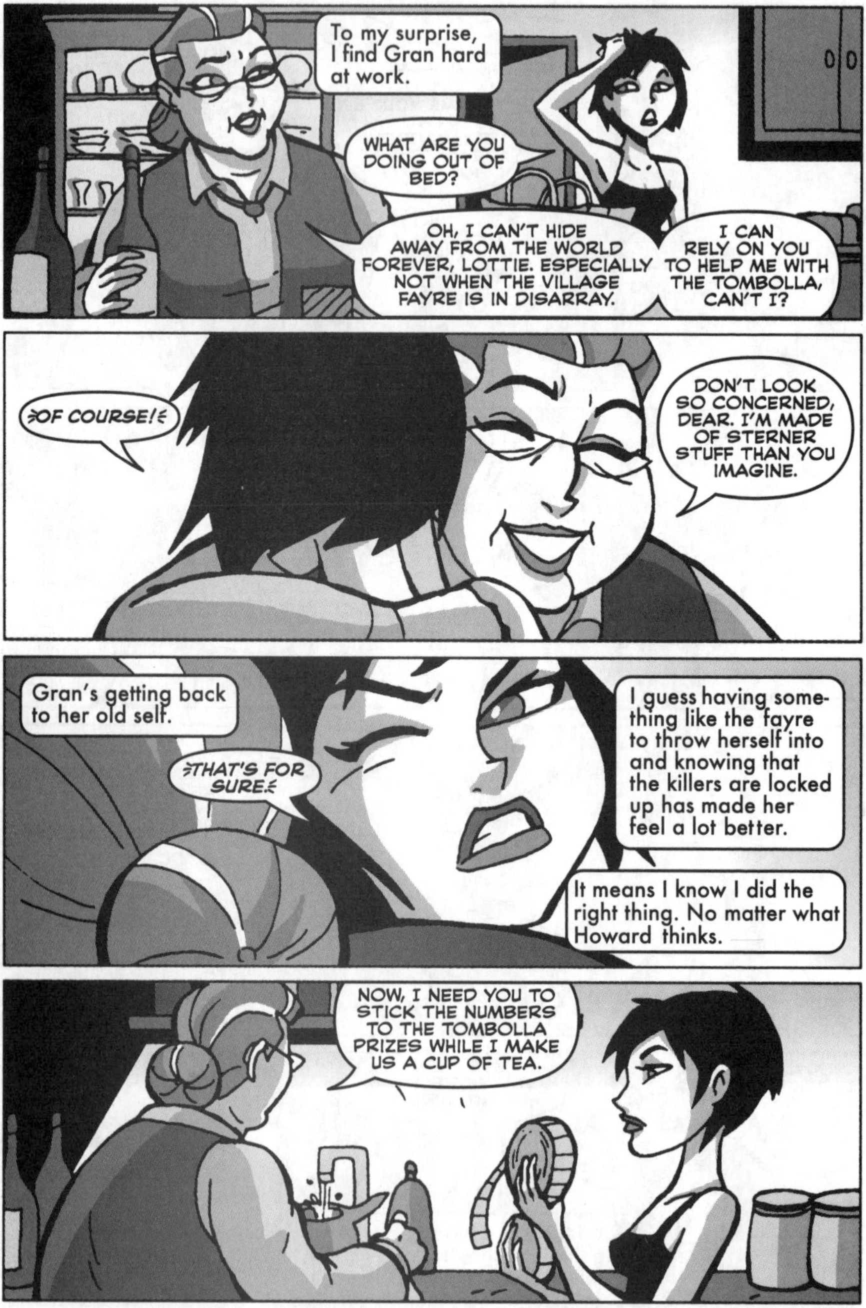
To my surprise, I find Gran hard at work.
WHAT ARE YOU DOING OUT OF BED?
OH, I CAN'T HIDE AWAY FROM THE WORLD FOREVER, LOTTIE. ESPECIALLY NOT WHEN THE VILLAGE FAYRE IS IN DISARRAY.
I CAN RELY ON YOU TO HELP ME WITH THE TOMBOLLA, CAN'T I?
OF COURSE!
DON'T LOOK SO CONCERNED, DEAR. I'M MADE OF STERNER STUFF THAN YOU IMAGINE.
Gran's getting back to her old self.
THAT'S FOR SURE.
I guess having something like the fayre to throw herself into and knowing that the killers are locked up has made her feel a lot better.
It means I know I did the right thing. No matter what Howard thinks.
NOW, I NEED YOU TO STICK THE NUMBERS TO THE TOMBOLLA PRIZES WHILE I MAKE US A CUP OF TEA.

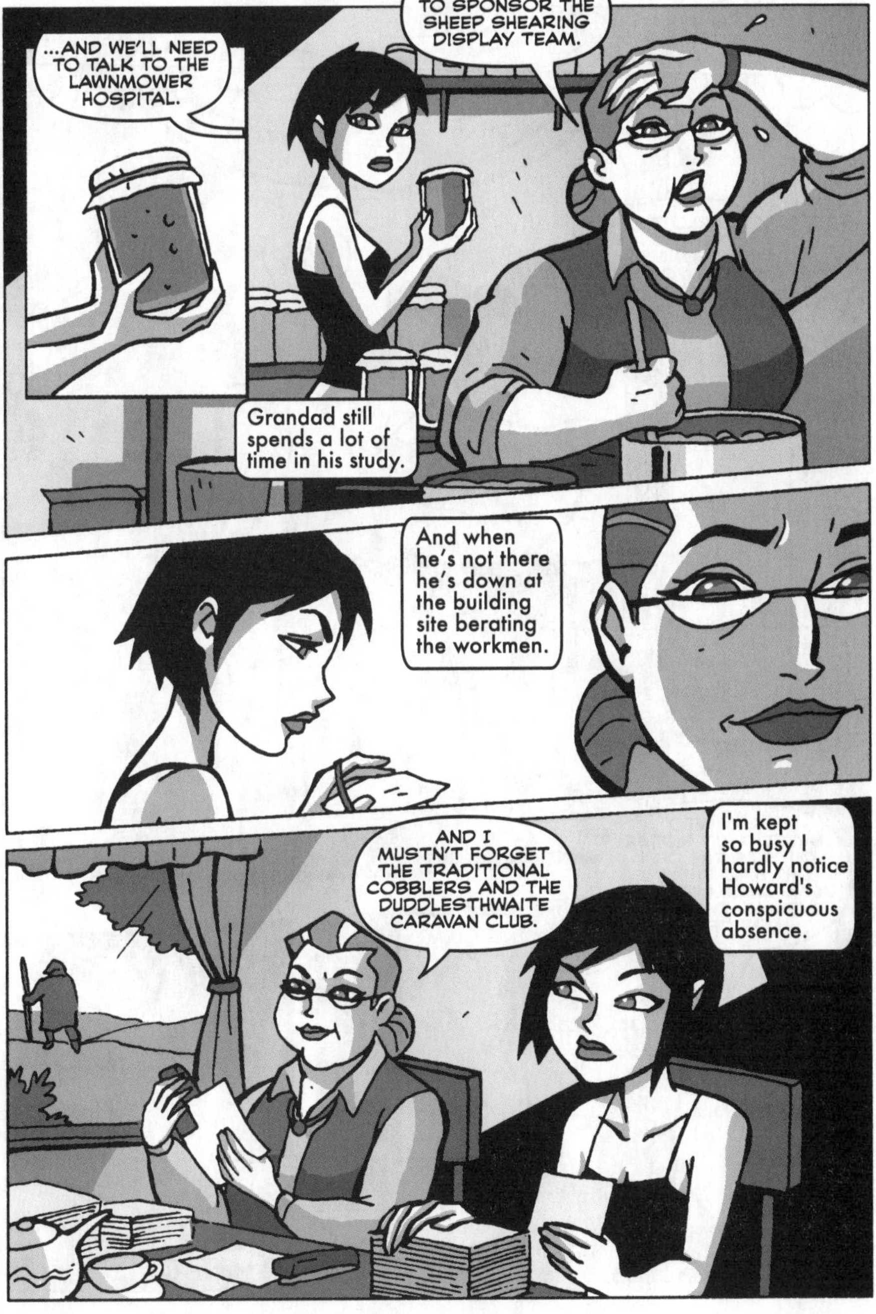
...AND WE'LL NEED TO TALK TO THE LAWNMOWER HOSPITAL.
THEY PROMISED TO SPONSOR THE SHEEP SHEARING DISPLAY TEAM.
Grandad still spends a lot of time in his study.
And when he's not there he's down at the building site berating the workmen.
AND I MUSTN'T FORGET THE TRADITIONAL COBBLERS AND THE DUDDLESTHWAITE CARAVAN CLUB.
I'm kept so busy I hardly notice Howard's conspicuous absence.

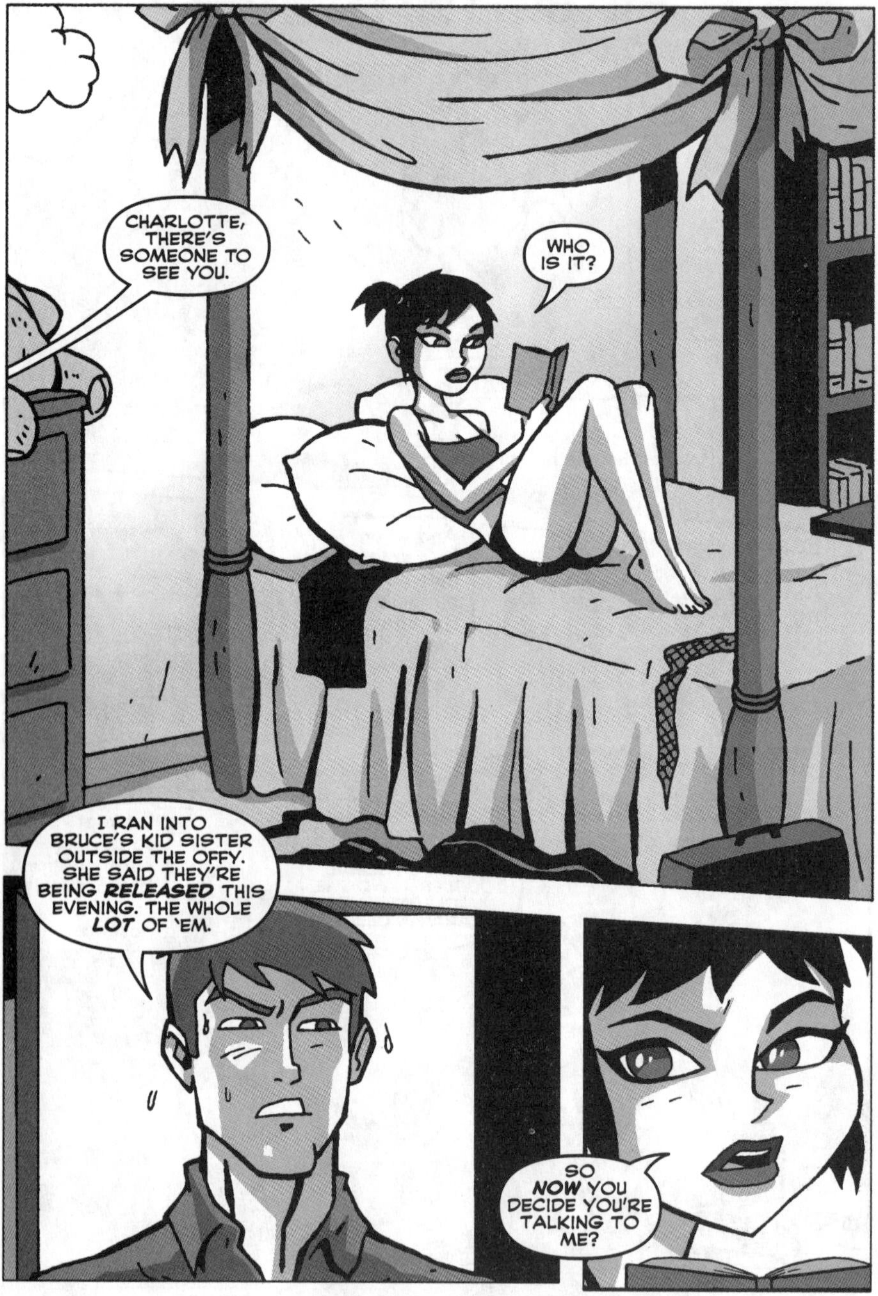
CHARLOTTE, THERE'S SOMEONE TO SEE YOU.
WHO IS IT?
I RAN INTO BRUCE'S KID SISTER OUTSIDE THE OFFY. SHE SAID THEY'RE BEING **RELEASED** THIS EVENING. THE WHOLE **LOT** OF 'EM.
SO **NOW** YOU DECIDE YOU'RE TALKING TO ME?

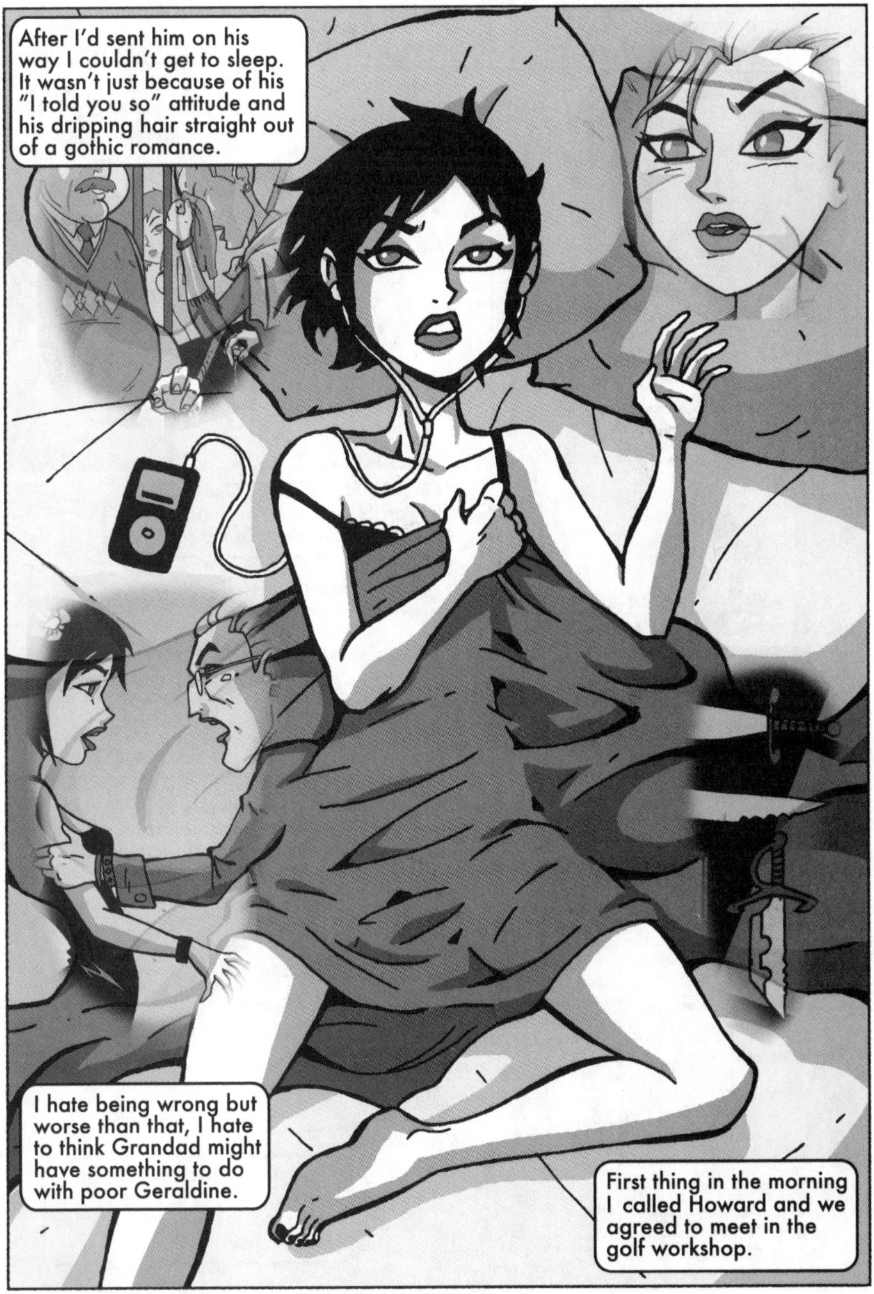
After I'd sent him on his way I couldn't get to sleep. It wasn't just because of his "I told you so" attitude and his dripping hair straight out of a gothic romance.
I hate being wrong but worse than that, I hate to think Grandad might have something to do with poor Geraldine.
First thing in the morning I called Howard and we agreed to meet in the golf workshop.

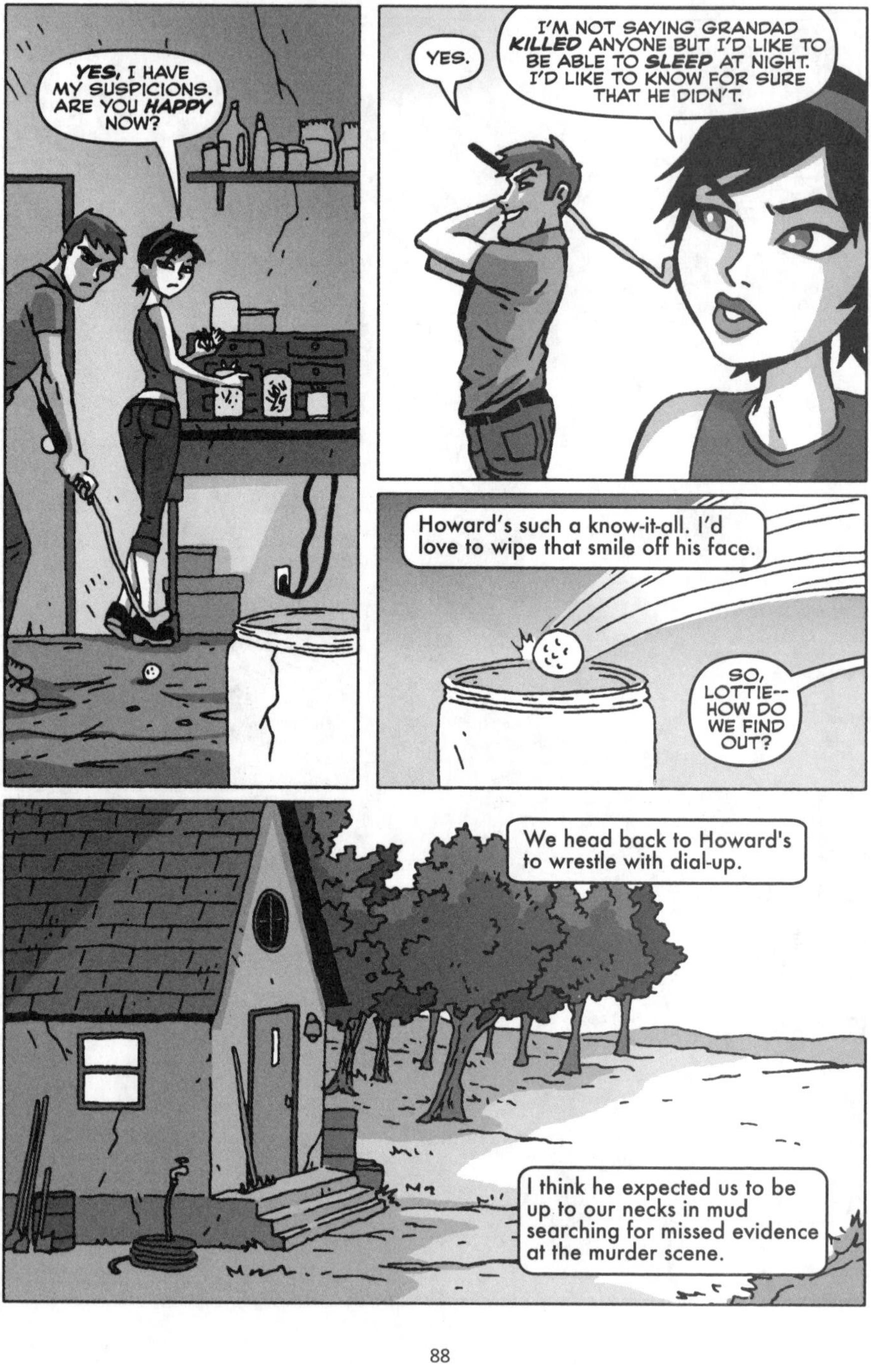
YES, I HAVE MY SUSPICIONS. ARE YOU HAPPY NOW?
YES.
I'M NOT SAYING GRANDAD KILLED ANYONE BUT I'D LIKE TO BE ABLE TO SLEEP AT NIGHT. I'D LIKE TO KNOW FOR SURE THAT HE DIDN'T.
Howard's such a know-it-all. I'd love to wipe that smile off his face.
SO, LOTTIE-- HOW DO WE FIND OUT?
We head back to Howard's to wrestle with dial-up.
I think he expected us to be up to our necks in mud searching for missed evidence at the murder scene.

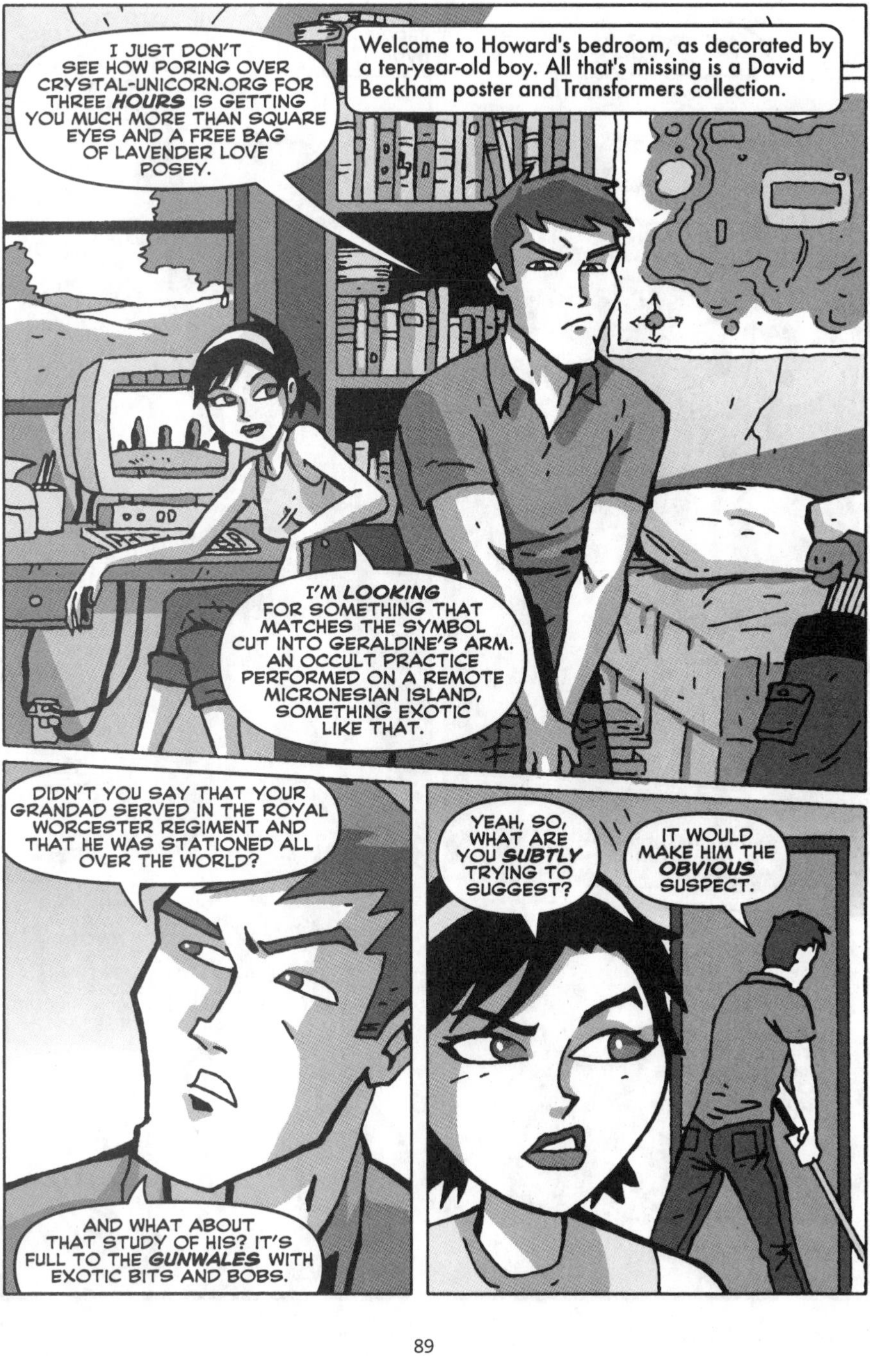
I JUST DON'T SEE HOW PORING OVER CRYSTAL-UNICORN.ORG FOR THREE **HOURS** IS GETTING YOU MUCH MORE THAN SQUARE EYES AND A FREE BAG OF LAVENDER LOVE POSEY.
Welcome to Howard's bedroom, as decorated by a ten-year-old boy. All that's missing is a David Beckham poster and Transformers collection.
I'M **LOOKING** FOR SOMETHING THAT MATCHES THE SYMBOL CUT INTO GERALDINE'S ARM. AN OCCULT PRACTICE PERFORMED ON A REMOTE MICRONESIAN ISLAND, SOMETHING EXOTIC LIKE THAT.
DIDN'T YOU SAY THAT YOUR GRANDAD SERVED IN THE ROYAL WORCESTER REGIMENT AND THAT HE WAS STATIONED ALL OVER THE WORLD?
AND WHAT ABOUT THAT STUDY OF HIS? IT'S FULL TO THE **GUNWALES** WITH EXOTIC BITS AND BOBS.
YEAH, SO, WHAT ARE YOU **SUBTLY** TRYING TO SUGGEST?
IT WOULD MAKE HIM THE **OBVIOUS** SUSPECT.

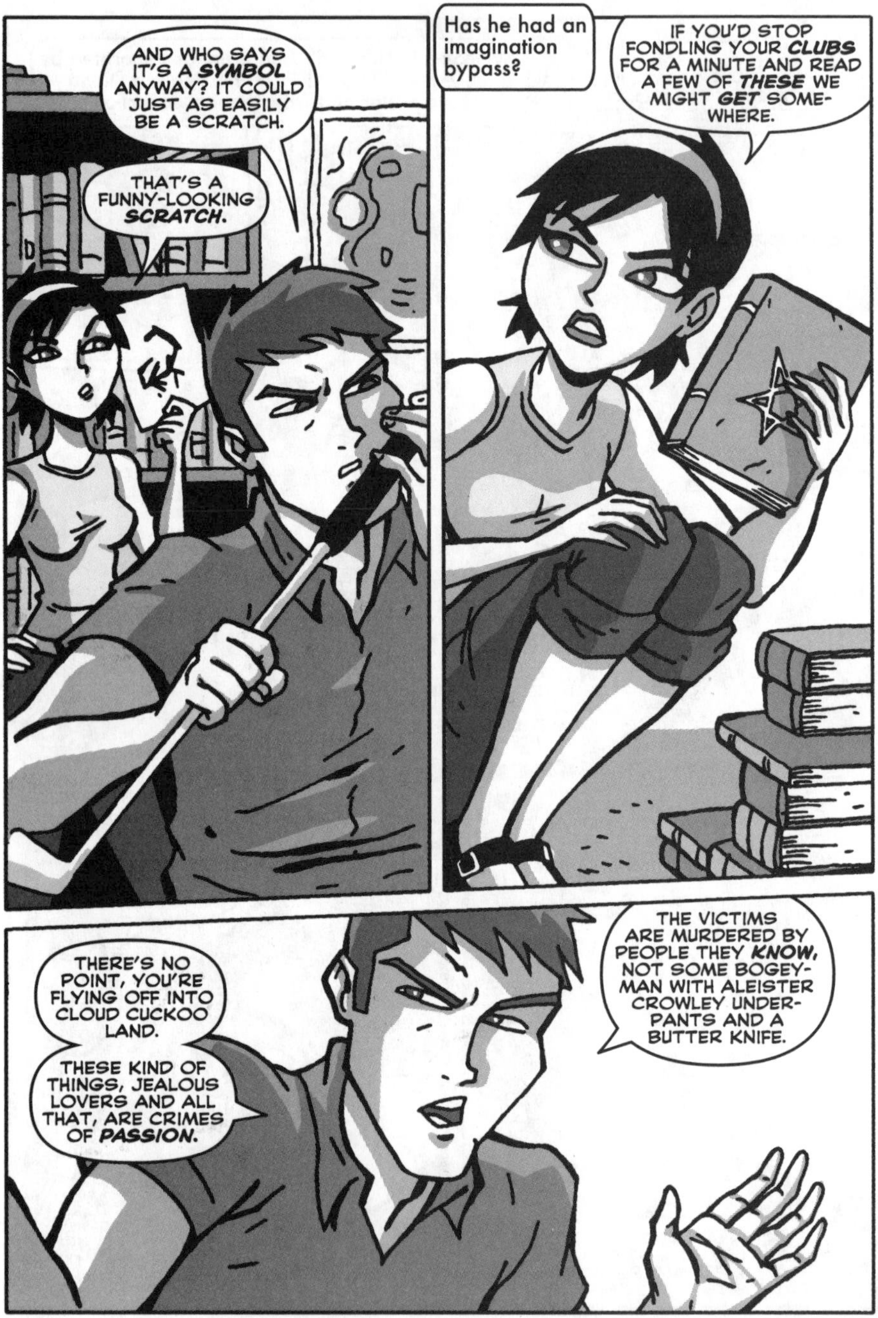
AND WHO SAYS IT'S A SYMBOL ANYWAY? IT COULD JUST AS EASILY BE A SCRATCH.
THAT'S A FUNNY-LOOKING SCRATCH.
Has he had an imagination bypass?
IF YOU'D STOP FONDLING YOUR CLUBS FOR A MINUTE AND READ A FEW OF THESE WE MIGHT GET SOME-WHERE.
THERE'S NO POINT, YOU'RE FLYING OFF INTO CLOUD CUCKOO LAND.
THESE KIND OF THINGS, JEALOUS LOVERS AND ALL THAT, ARE CRIMES OF PASSION.
THE VICTIMS ARE MURDERED BY PEOPLE THEY KNOW, NOT SOME BOGEY-MAN WITH ALEISTER CROWLEY UNDER-PANTS AND A BUTTER KNIFE.

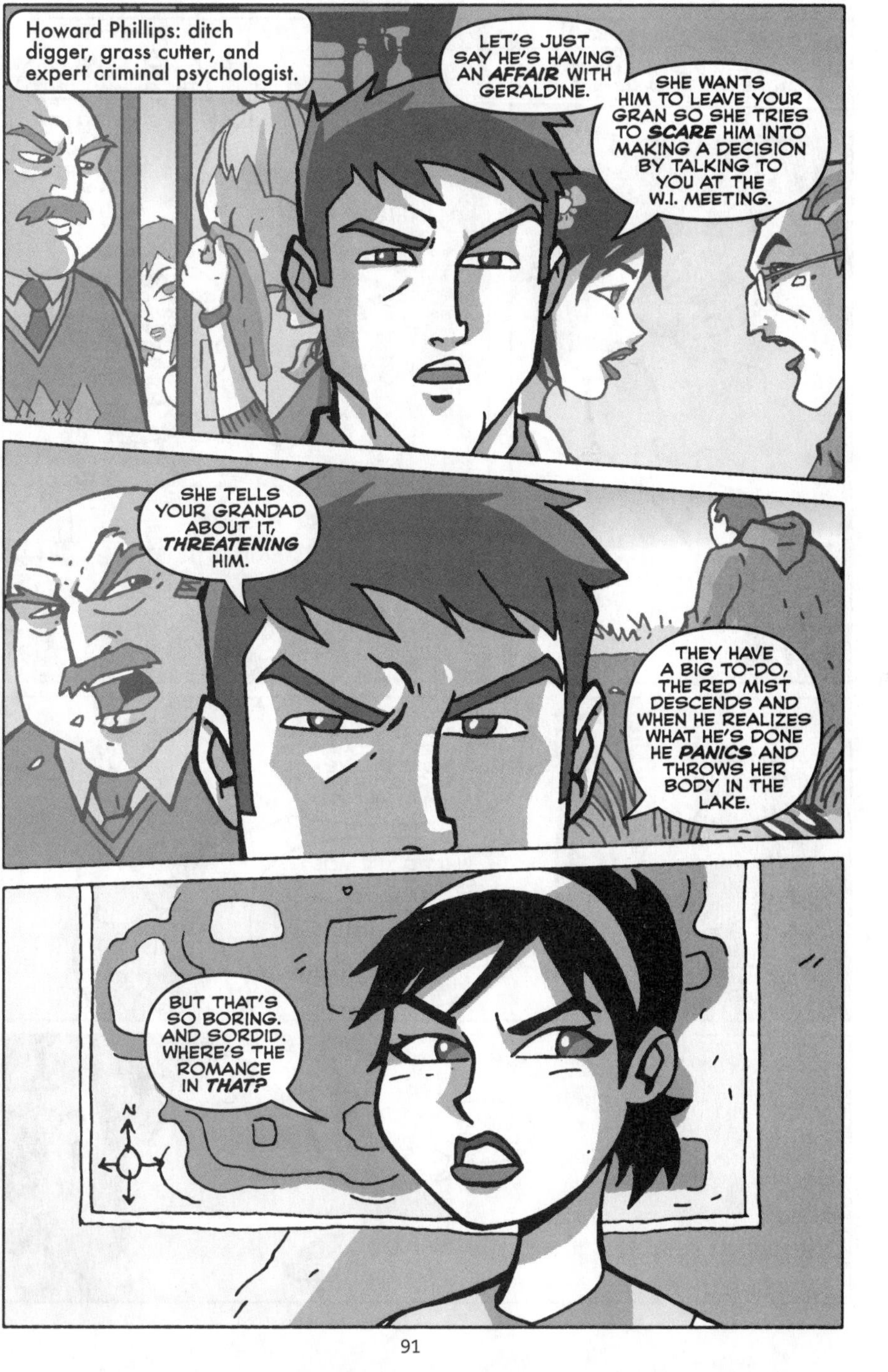
Howard Phillips: ditch digger, grass cutter, and expert criminal psychologist.
LET'S JUST SAY HE'S HAVING AN AFFAIR WITH GERALDINE.
SHE WANTS HIM TO LEAVE YOUR GRAN SO SHE TRIES TO SCARE HIM INTO MAKING A DECISION BY TALKING TO YOU AT THE W.I. MEETING.
SHE TELLS YOUR GRANDAD ABOUT IT, THREATENING HIM.
THEY HAVE A BIG TO-DO, THE RED MIST DESCENDS AND WHEN HE REALIZES WHAT HE'S DONE HE PANICS AND THROWS HER BODY IN THE LAKE.
BUT THAT'S SO BORING. AND SORDID. WHERE'S THE ROMANCE IN THAT?
N

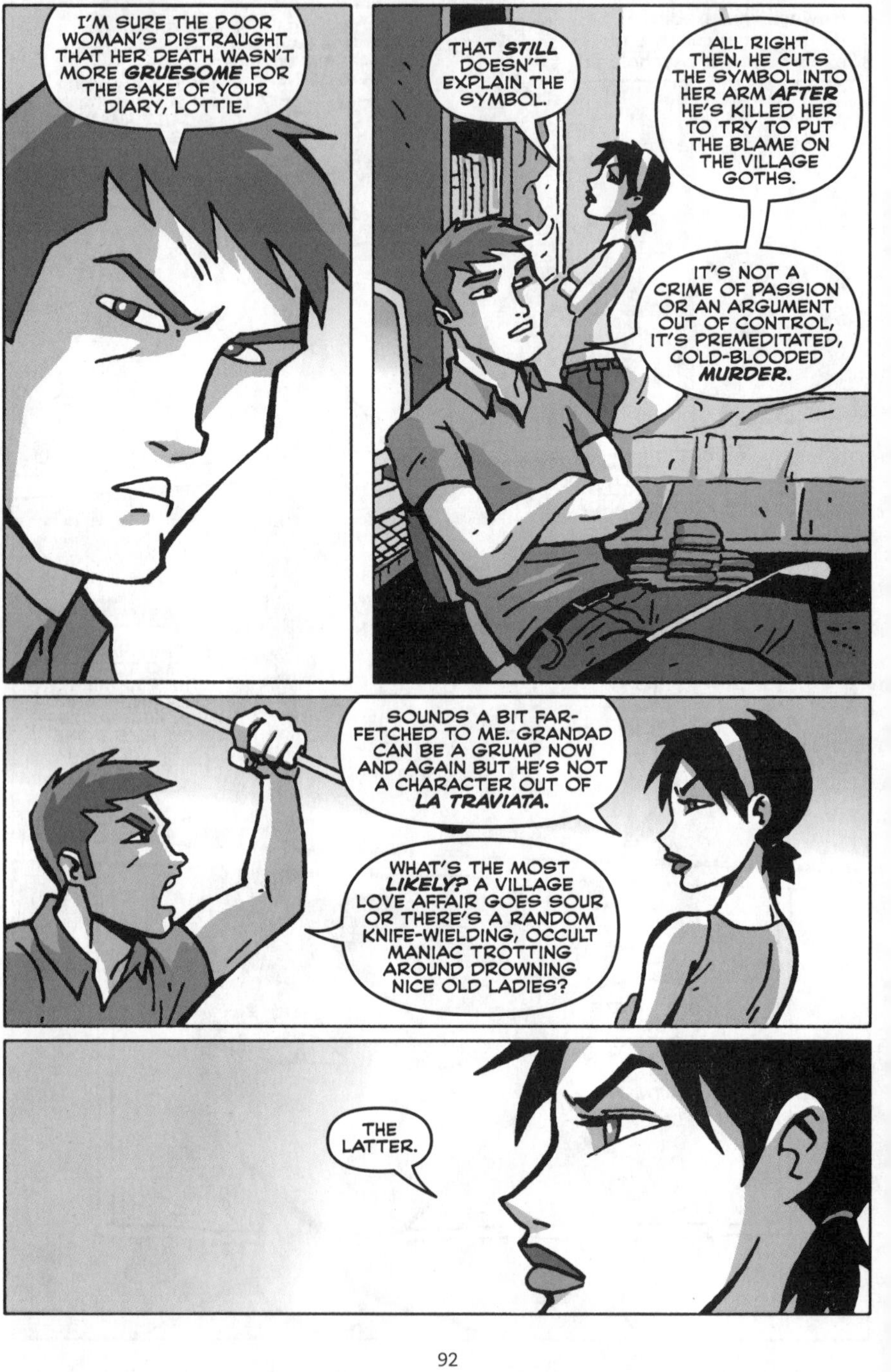
I'M SURE THE POOR WOMAN'S DISTRAUGHT THAT HER DEATH WASN'T MORE GRUESOME FOR THE SAKE OF YOUR DIARY, LOTTIE.
THAT STILL DOESN'T EXPLAIN THE SYMBOL.
ALL RIGHT THEN, HE CUTS THE SYMBOL INTO HER ARM AFTER HE'S KILLED HER TO TRY TO PUT THE BLAME ON THE VILLAGE GOTHS.
IT'S NOT A CRIME OF PASSION OR AN ARGUMENT OUT OF CONTROL, IT'S PREMEDITATED, COLD-BLOODED MURDER.
SOUNDS A BIT FAR-FETCHED TO ME. GRANDAD CAN BE A GRUMP NOW AND AGAIN BUT HE'S NOT A CHARACTER OUT OF LA TRAVIATA.
WHAT'S THE MOST LIKELY? A VILLAGE LOVE AFFAIR GOES SOUR OR THERE'S A RANDOM KNIFE-WIELDING, OCCULT MANIAC TROTTING AROUND DROWNING NICE OLD LADIES?
THE LATTER.

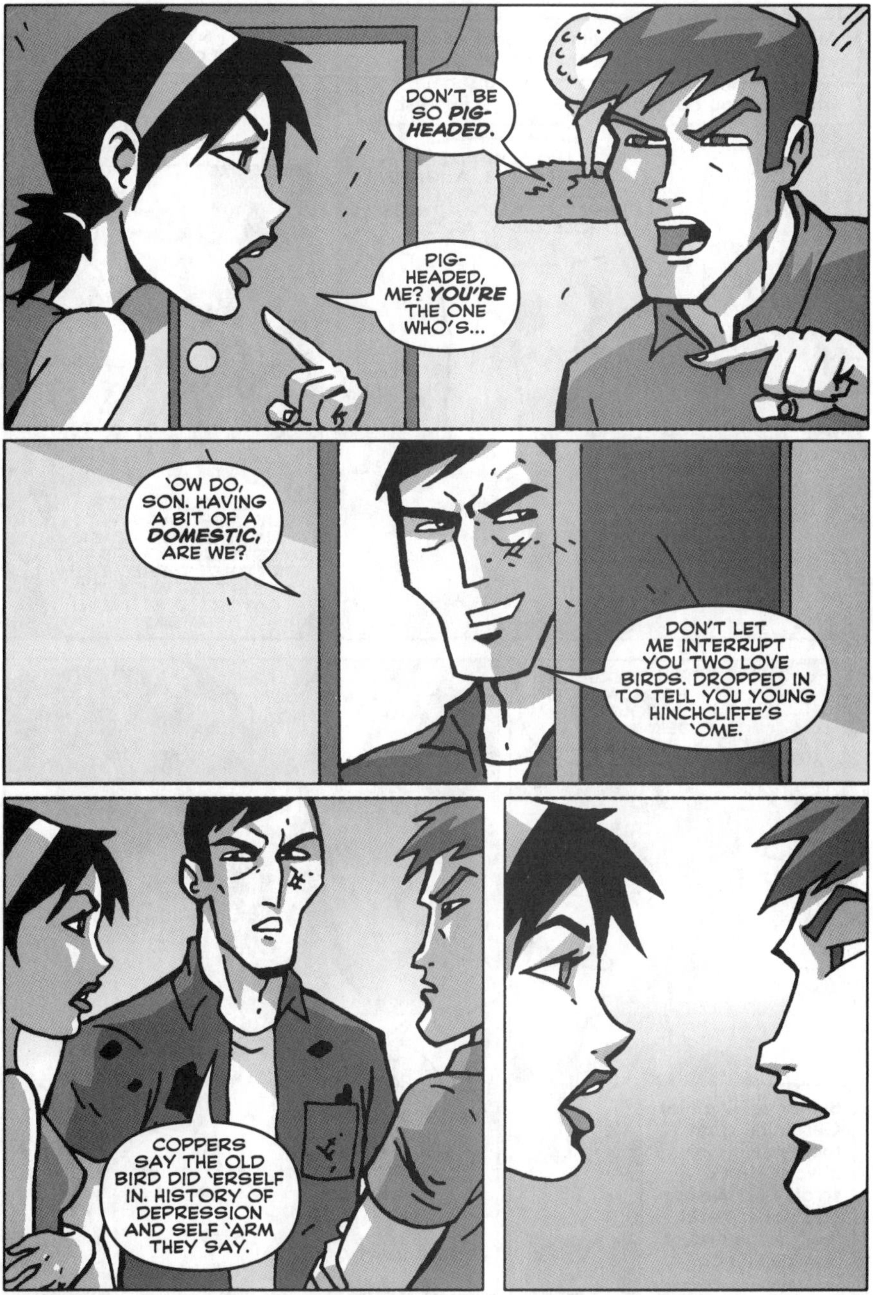
DON'T BE SO PIG-HEADED.
PIG-HEADED, ME? YOU'RE THE ONE WHO'S...
'OW DO, SON. HAVING A BIT OF A DOMESTIC, ARE WE?
DON'T LET ME INTERRUPT YOU TWO LOVE BIRDS. DROPPED IN TO TELL YOU YOUNG HINCHCLIFFE'S 'OME.
COPPERS SAY THE OLD BIRD DID 'ERSELF IN. HISTORY OF DEPRESSION AND SELF 'ARM THEY SAY.

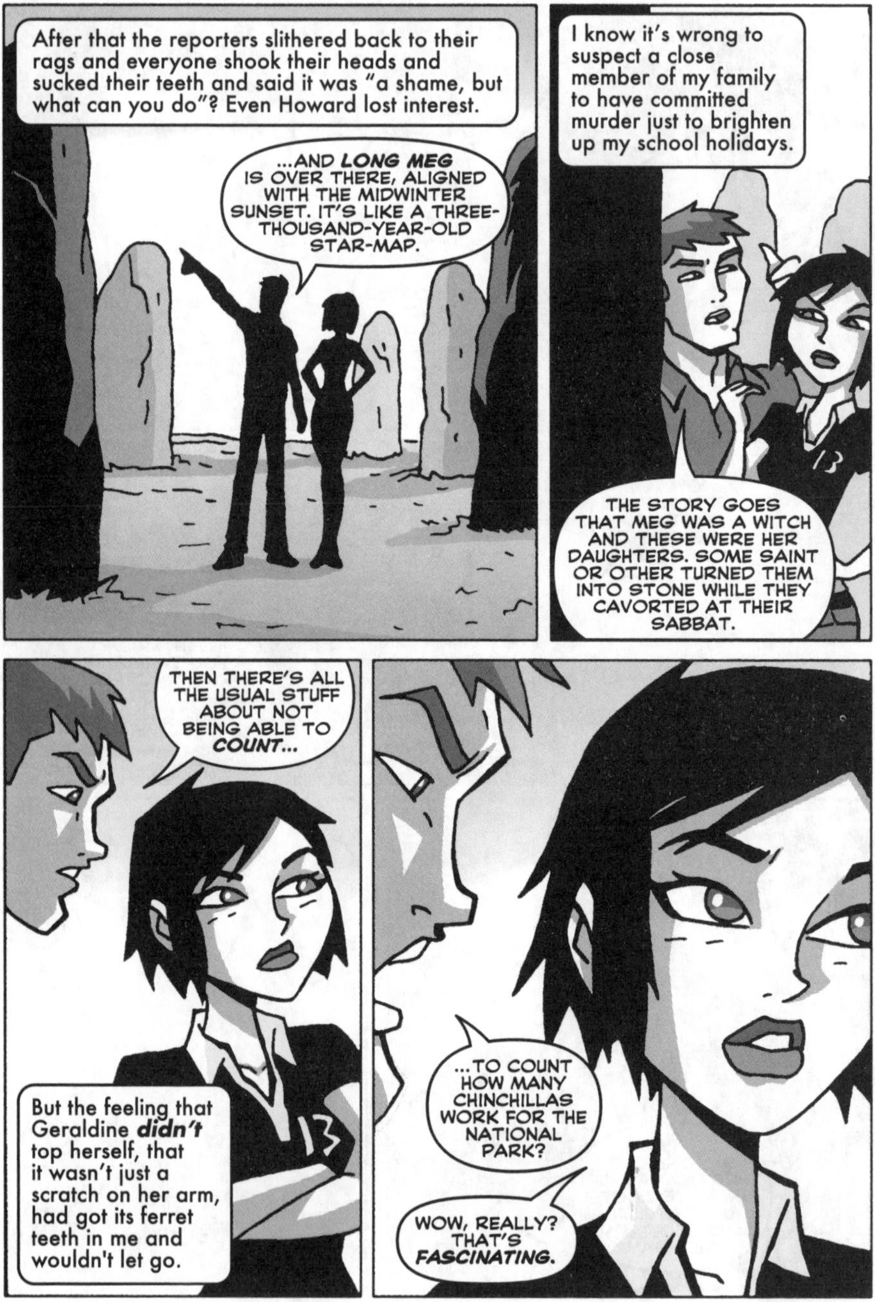

After that the reporters slithered back to their rags and everyone shook their heads and sucked their teeth and said it was "a shame, but what can you do"? Even Howard lost interest.
...AND **LONG MEG** IS OVER THERE, ALIGNED WITH THE MIDWINTER SUNSET. IT'S LIKE A THREE-THOUSAND-YEAR-OLD STAR-MAP.
I know it's wrong to suspect a close member of my family to have committed murder just to brighten up my school holidays.
THE STORY GOES THAT MEG WAS A WITCH AND THESE WERE HER DAUGHTERS. SOME SAINT OR OTHER TURNED THEM INTO STONE WHILE THEY CAVORTED AT THEIR SABBAT.
THEN THERE'S ALL THE USUAL STUFF ABOUT NOT BEING ABLE TO **COUNT**...
But the feeling that Geraldine ***didn't*** top herself, that it wasn't just a scratch on her arm, had got its ferret teeth in me and wouldn't let go.
...TO COUNT HOW MANY CHINCHILLAS WORK FOR THE NATIONAL PARK?
WOW, REALLY? THAT'S ***FASCINATING***.

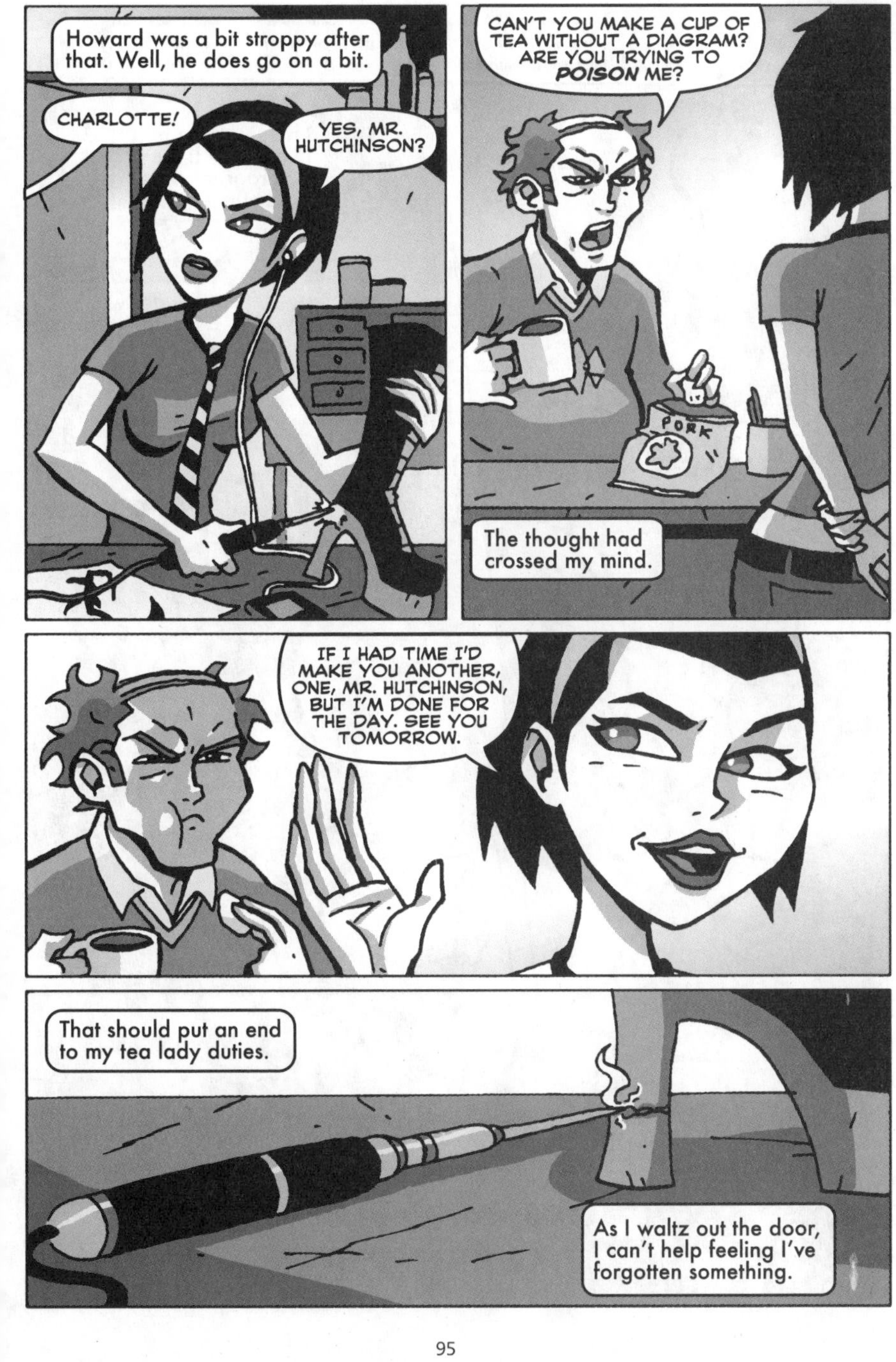

Howard was a bit stroppy after that. Well, he does go on a bit.
CHARLOTTE!
YES, MR. HUTCHINSON?
CAN'T YOU MAKE A CUP OF TEA WITHOUT A DIAGRAM? ARE YOU TRYING TO *POISON* ME?
PORK
The thought had crossed my mind.
IF I HAD TIME I'D MAKE YOU ANOTHER, ONE, MR. HUTCHINSON, BUT I'M DONE FOR THE DAY. SEE YOU TOMORROW.
That should put an end to my tea lady duties.
As I waltz out the door, I can't help feeling I've forgotten something.

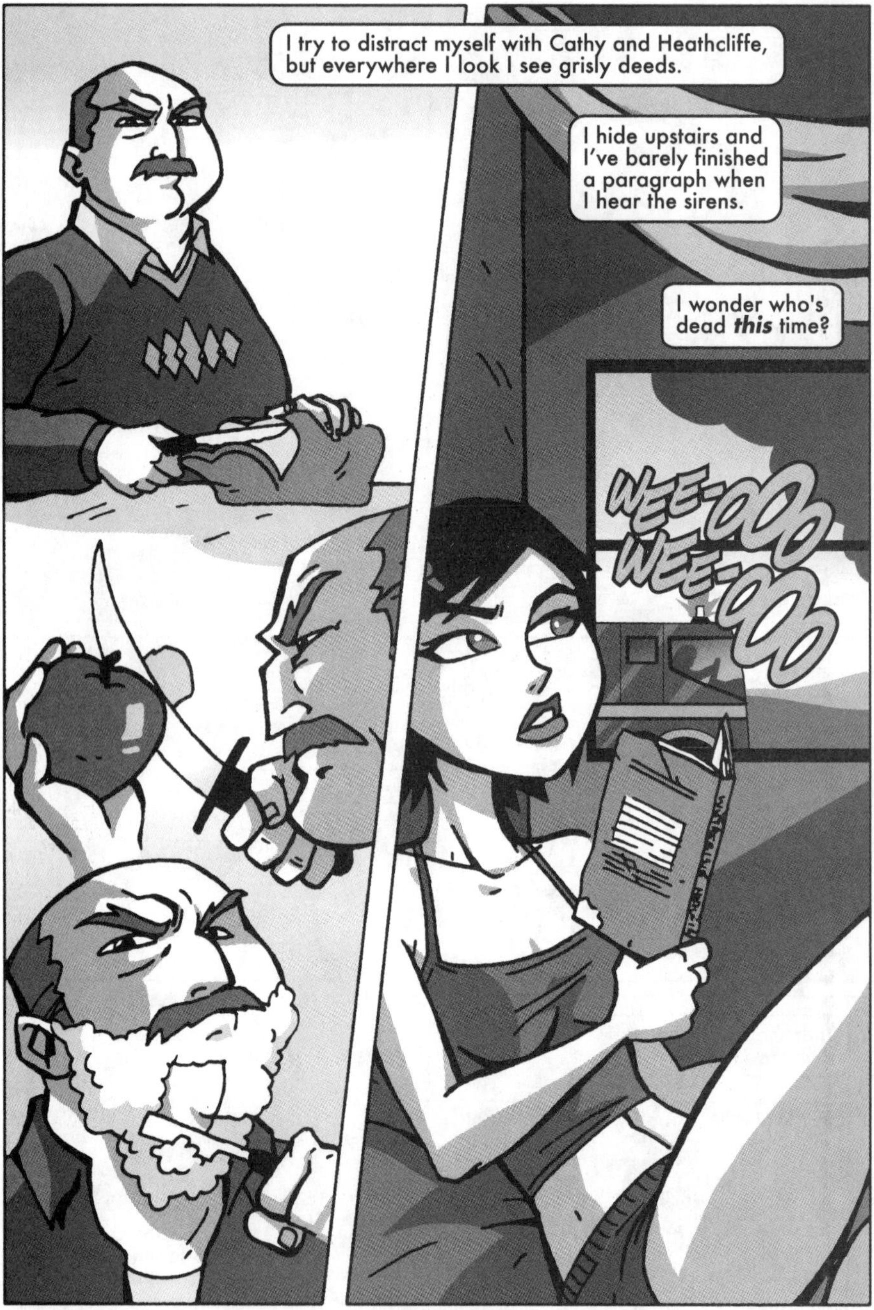
I try to distract myself with Cathy and Heathcliffe, but everywhere I look I see grisly deeds.
I hide upstairs and I've barely finished a paragraph when I hear the sirens.
I wonder who's dead ***this*** time?
WEE-OOO
WEE-OOO

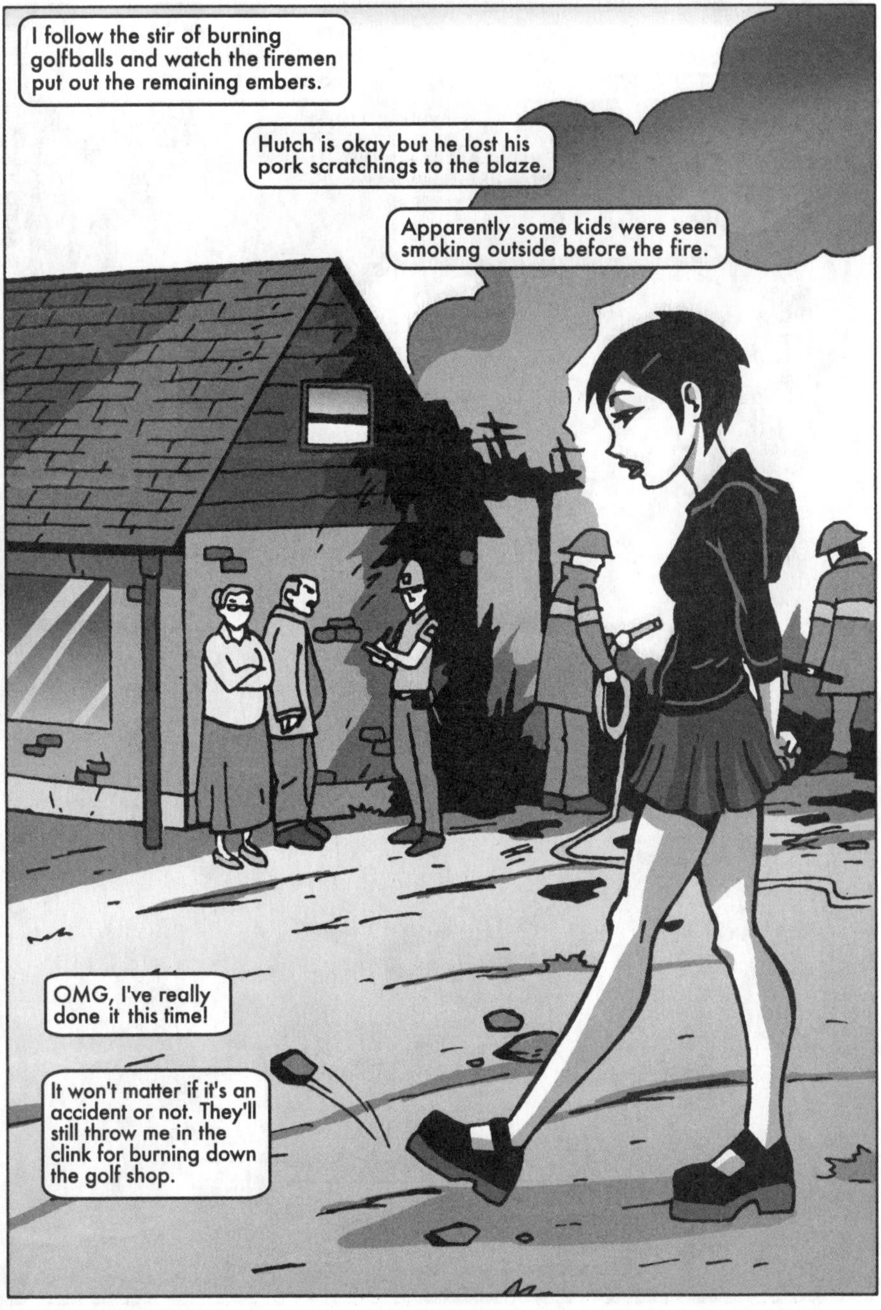
I follow the stir of burning golfballs and watch the firemen put out the remaining embers.
Hutch is okay but he lost his pork scratchings to the blaze.
Apparently some kids were seen smoking outside before the fire.
OMG, I've really done it this time!
It won't matter if it's an accident or not. They'll still throw me in the clink for burning down the golf shop.

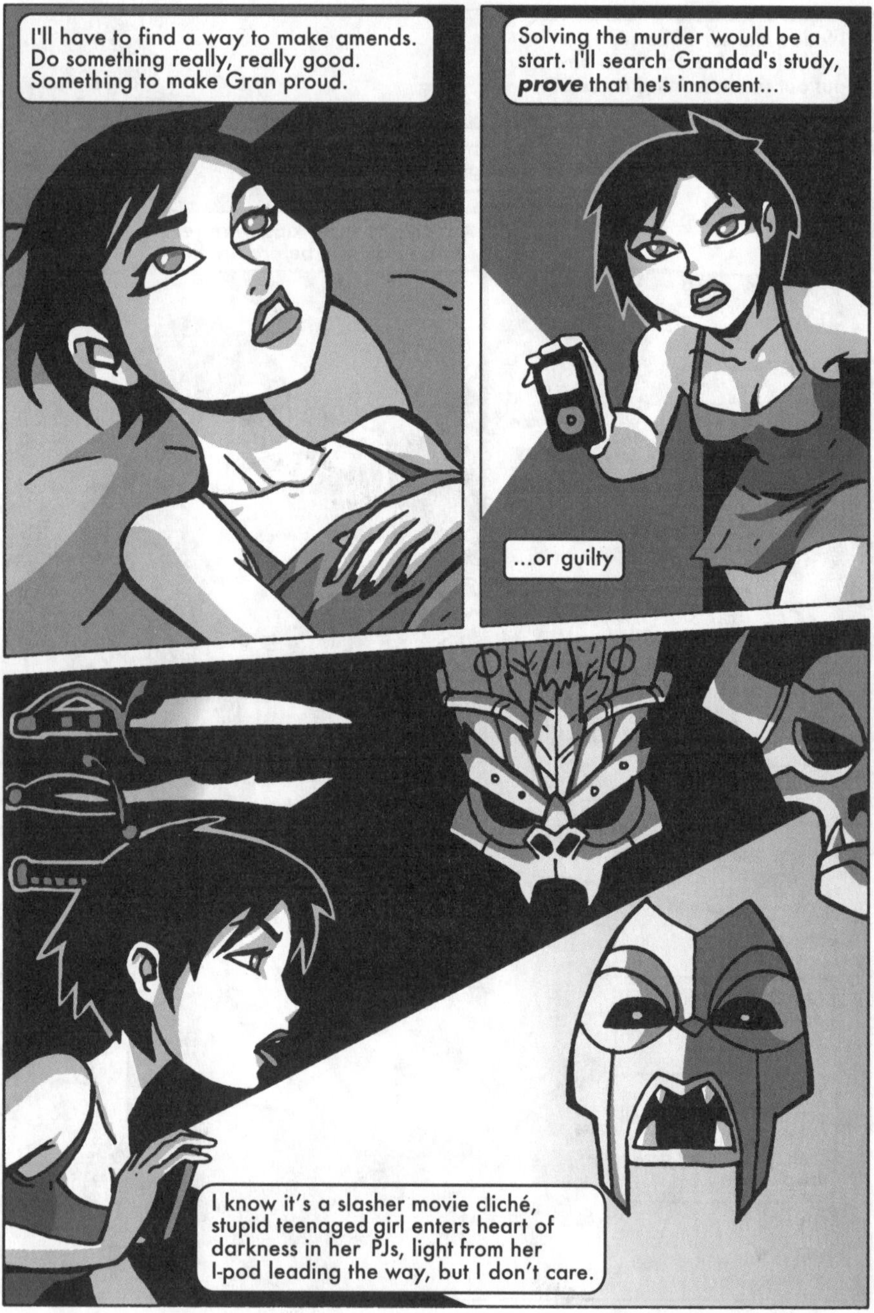
I'll have to find a way to make amends. Do something really, really good. Something to make Gran proud.
Solving the murder would be a start. I'll search Grandad's study, *prove* that he's innocent...
...or guilty
I know it's a slasher movie cliché, stupid teenaged girl enters heart of darkness in her PJs, light from her I-pod leading the way, but I don't care.

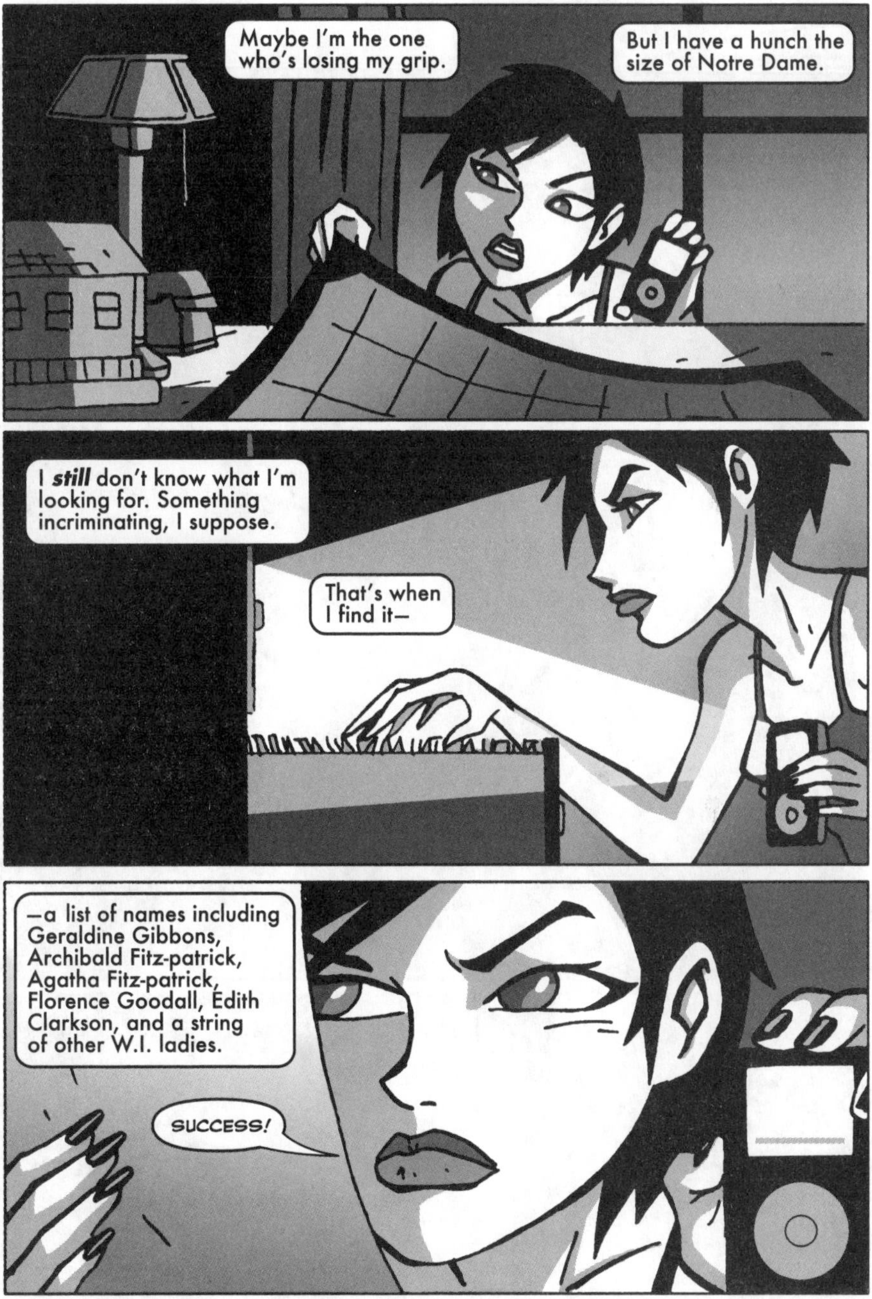

Maybe I'm the one who's losing my grip.
But I have a hunch the size of Notre Dame.
I ***still*** don't know what I'm looking for. Something incriminating, I suppose.
That's when I find it—
—a list of names including Geraldine Gibbons, Archibald Fitz-patrick, Agatha Fitz-patrick, Florence Goodall, Edith Clarkson, and a string of other W.I. ladies.
SUCCESS!

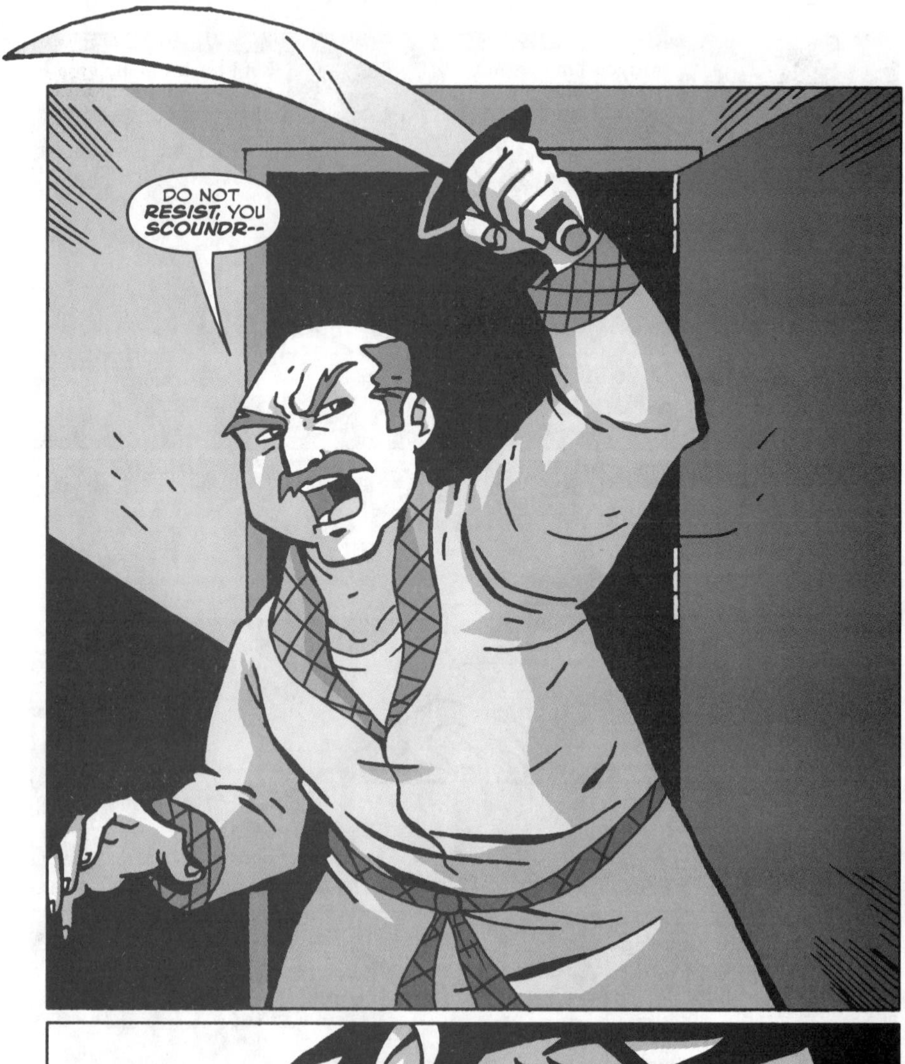
DO NOT RESIST, YOU SCOUNDR--

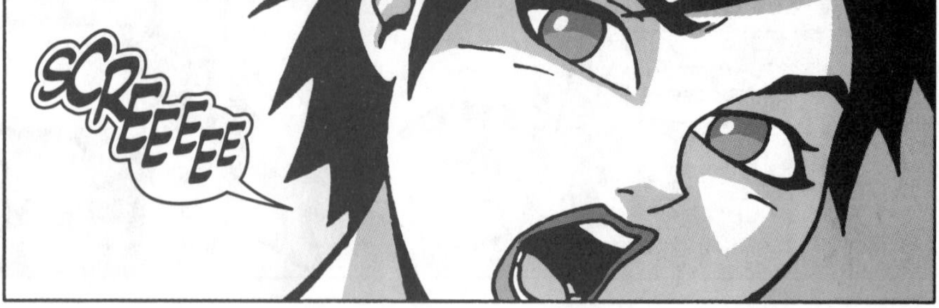
SCREEEEEEE

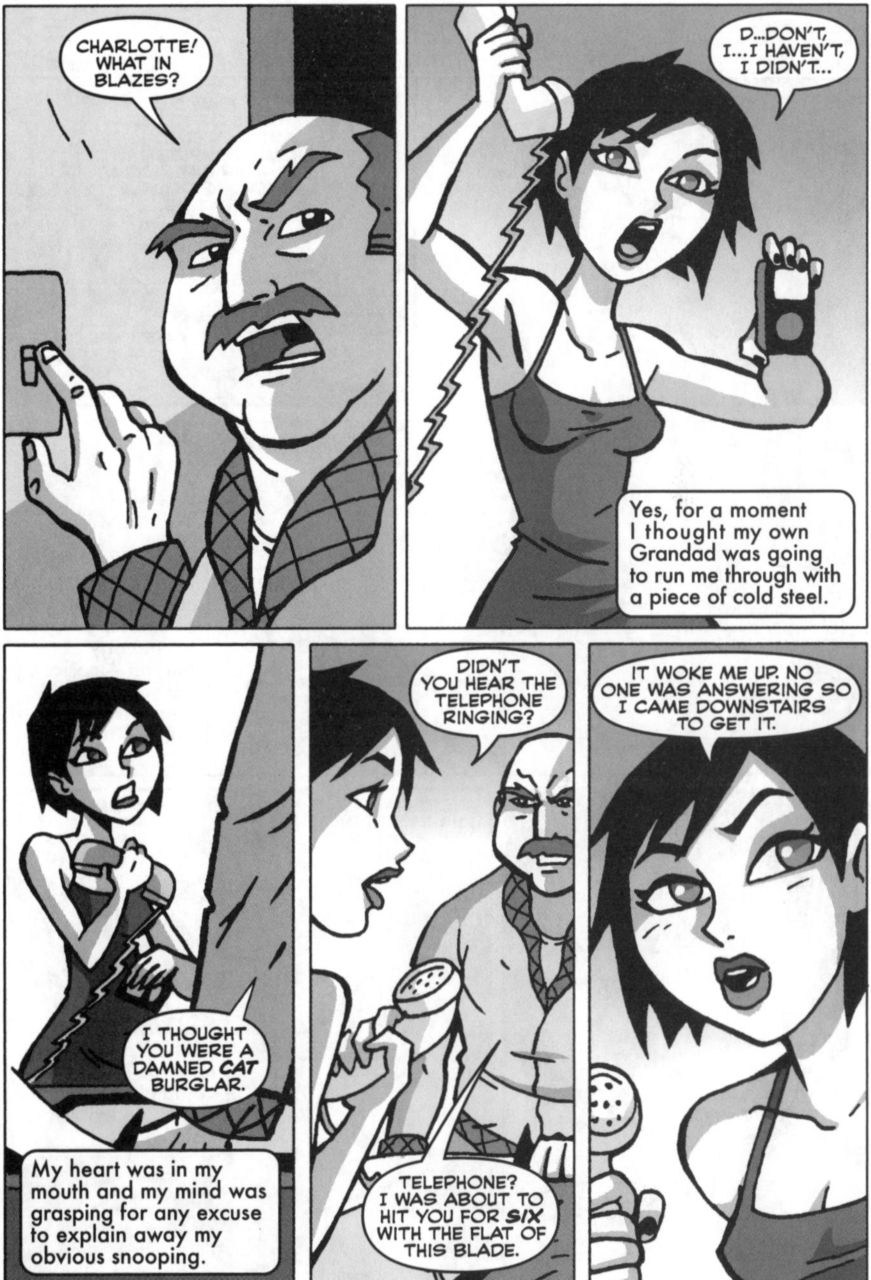
CHARLOTTE! WHAT IN BLAZES?
D...DON'T, I...I HAVEN'T, I DIDN'T...
Yes, for a moment I thought my own Grandad was going to run me through with a piece of cold steel.
I THOUGHT YOU WERE A DAMNED *CAT* BURGLAR.
My heart was in my mouth and my mind was grasping for any excuse to explain away my obvious snooping.
DIDN'T YOU HEAR THE TELEPHONE RINGING?
TELEPHONE? I WAS ABOUT TO HIT YOU FOR *SIX* WITH THE FLAT OF THIS BLADE.
IT WOKE ME UP. NO ONE WAS ANSWERING SO I CAME DOWNSTAIRS TO GET IT.

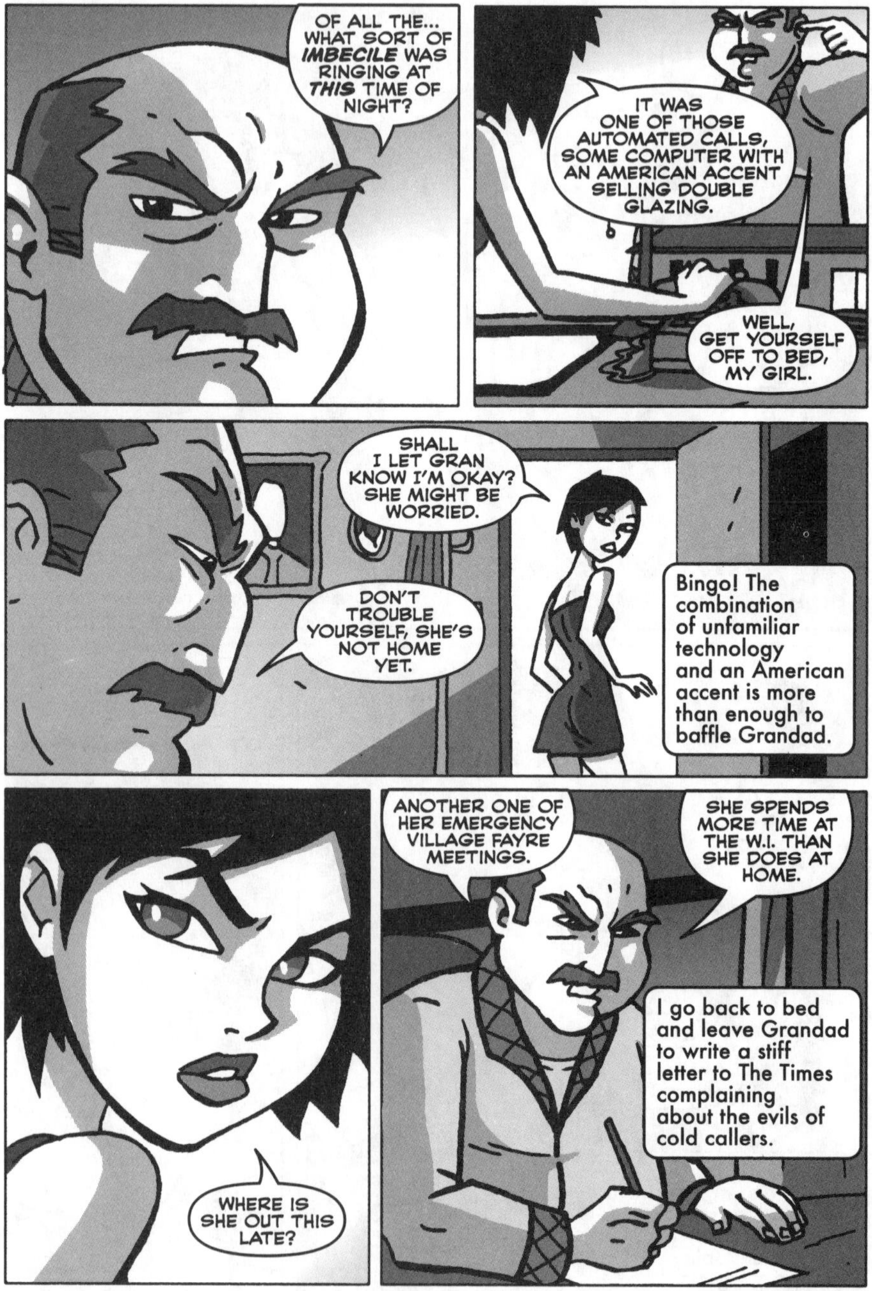
OF ALL THE... WHAT SORT OF IMBECILE WAS RINGING AT THIS TIME OF NIGHT?
IT WAS ONE OF THOSE AUTOMATED CALLS, SOME COMPUTER WITH AN AMERICAN ACCENT SELLING DOUBLE GLAZING.
WELL, GET YOURSELF OFF TO BED, MY GIRL.
SHALL I LET GRAN KNOW I'M OKAY? SHE MIGHT BE WORRIED.
DON'T TROUBLE YOURSELF, SHE'S NOT HOME YET.
Bingo! The combination of unfamiliar technology and an American accent is more than enough to baffle Grandad.
WHERE IS SHE OUT THIS LATE?
ANOTHER ONE OF HER EMERGENCY VILLAGE FAYRE MEETINGS.
SHE SPENDS MORE TIME AT THE W.I. THAN SHE DOES AT HOME.
I go back to bed and leave Grandad to write a stiff letter to The Times complaining about the evils of cold callers.

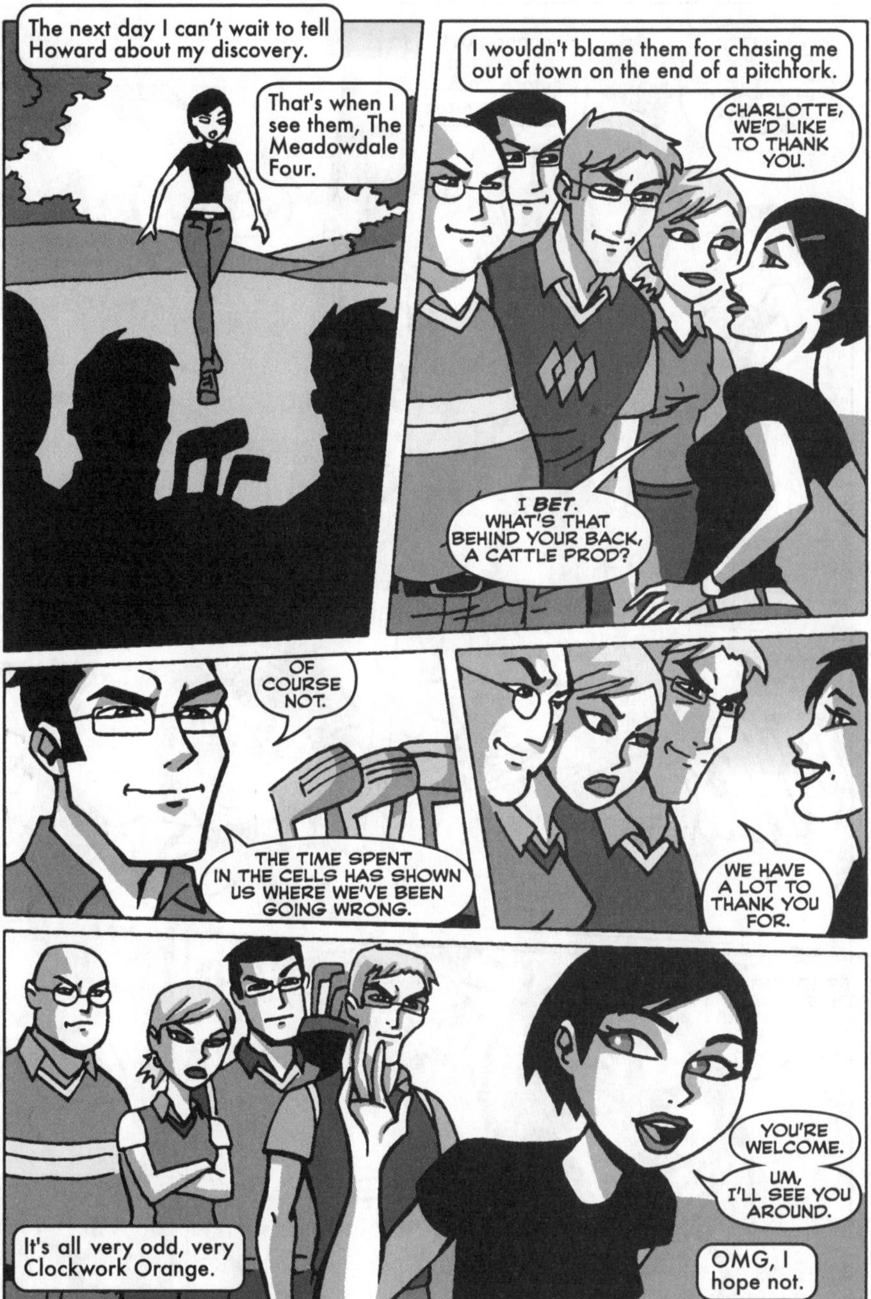
The next day I can't wait to tell Howard about my discovery.
That's when I see them, The Meadowdale Four.
I wouldn't blame them for chasing me out of town on the end of a pitchfork.
CHARLOTTE, WE'D LIKE TO THANK YOU.
I *BET*. WHAT'S THAT BEHIND YOUR BACK, A CATTLE PROD?
OF COURSE NOT.
THE TIME SPENT IN THE CELLS HAS SHOWN US WHERE WE'VE BEEN GOING WRONG.
WE HAVE A LOT TO THANK YOU FOR.
YOU'RE WELCOME.
UM, I'LL SEE YOU AROUND.
It's all very odd, very Clockwork Orange.
OMG, I hope not.

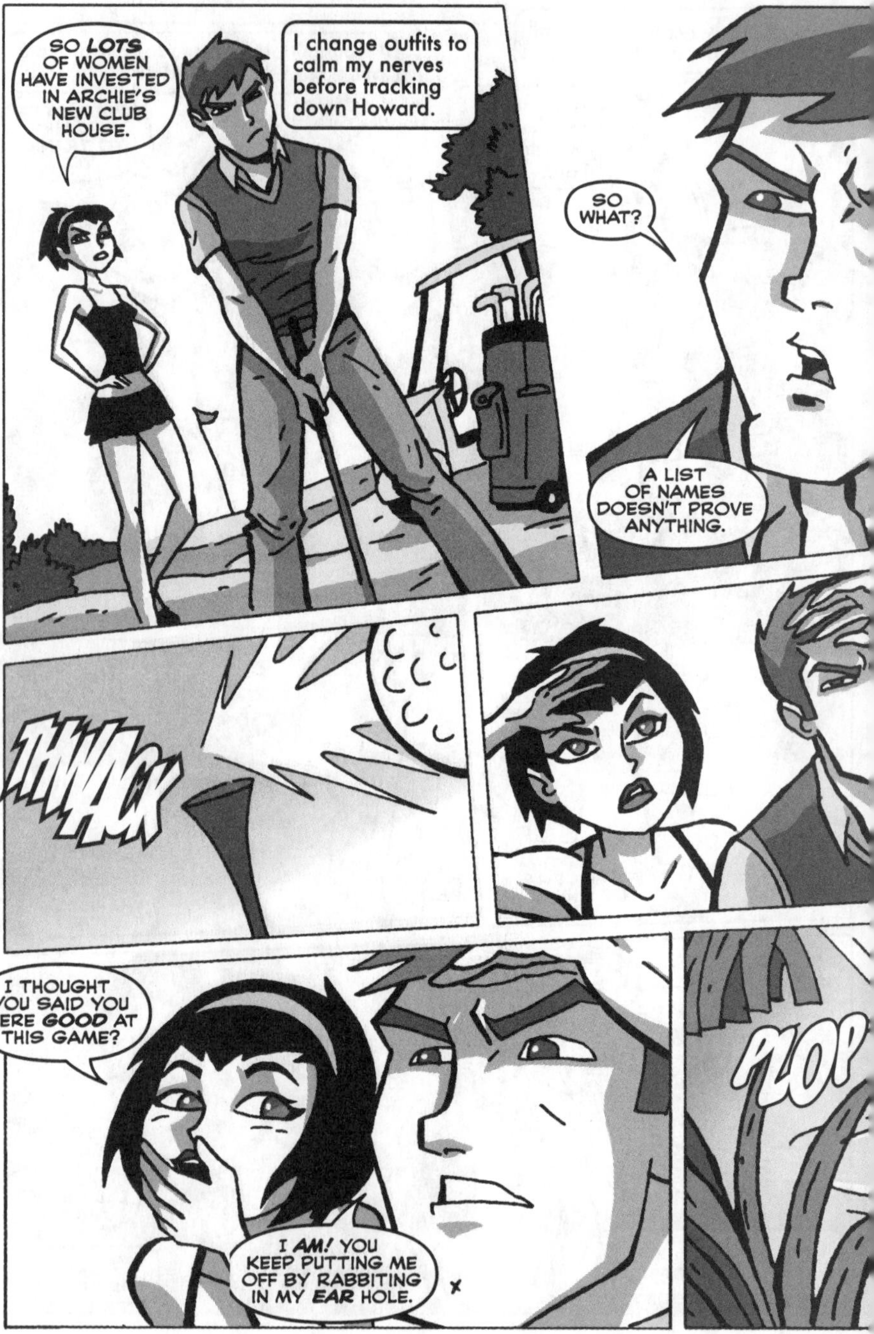
SO **LOTS** OF WOMEN HAVE INVESTED IN ARCHIE'S NEW CLUB HOUSE.
I change outfits to calm my nerves before tracking down Howard.
SO WHAT?
A LIST OF NAMES DOESN'T PROVE ANYTHING.
THWACK
I THOUGHT YOU SAID YOU WERE **GOOD** AT THIS GAME?
I **AM!** YOU KEEP PUTTING ME OFF BY RABBITING IN MY **EAR** HOLE.
PLOP

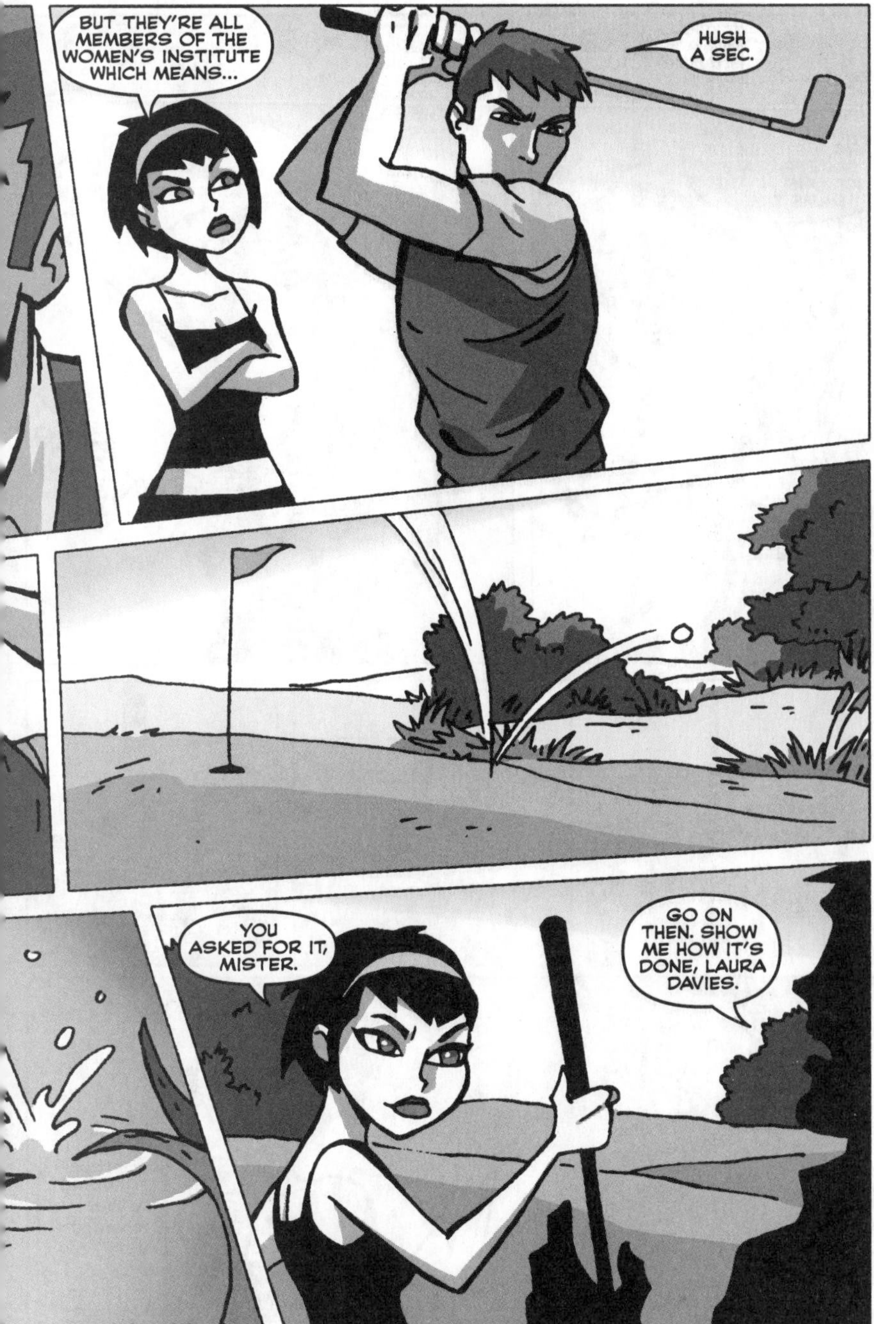
BUT THEY'RE ALL MEMBERS OF THE WOMEN'S INSTITUTE WHICH MEANS...
HUSH A SEC.
YOU ASKED FOR IT, MISTER.
GO ON THEN. SHOW ME HOW IT'S DONE, LAURA DAVIES.

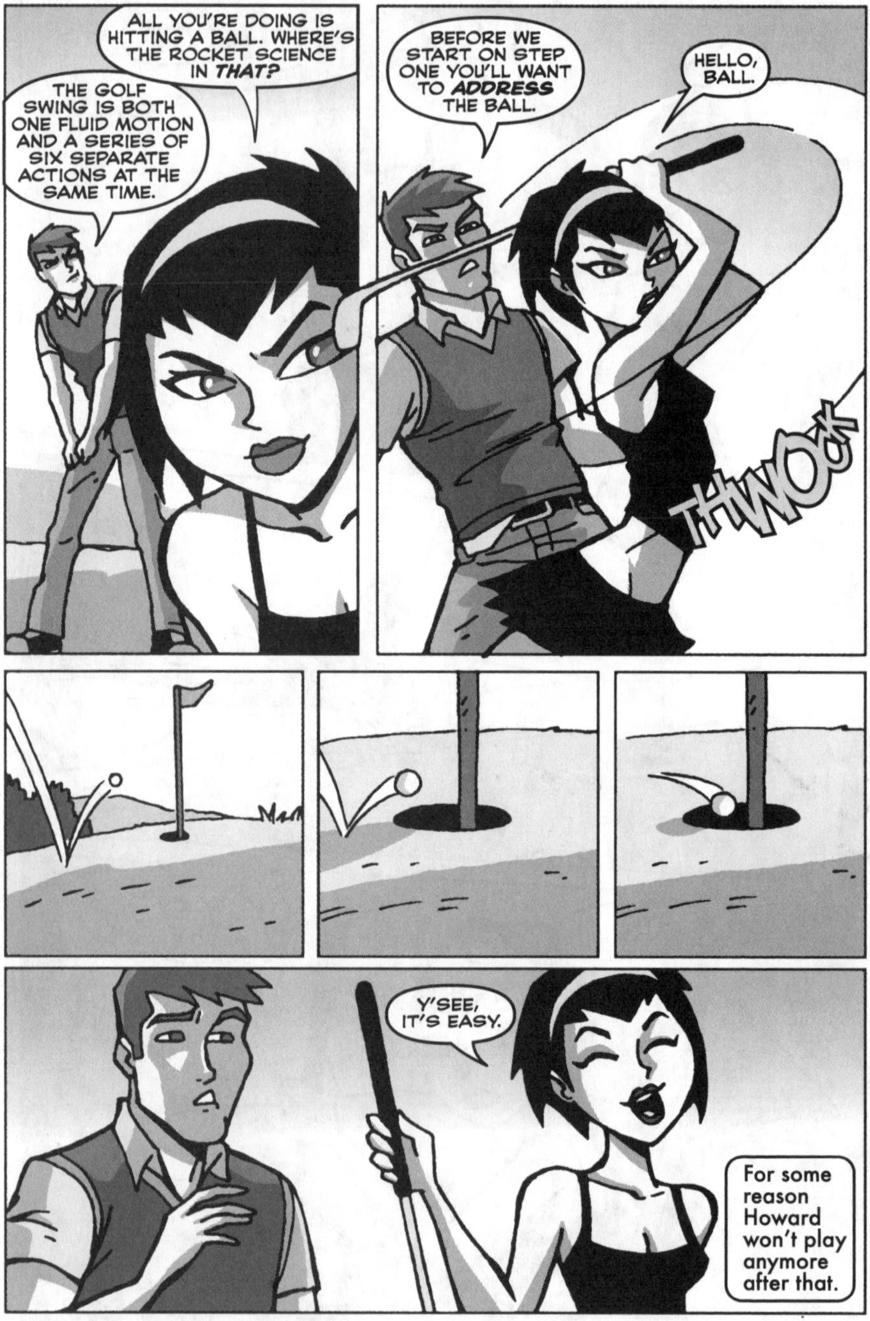
THE GOLF SWING IS BOTH ONE FLUID MOTION AND A SERIES OF SIX SEPARATE ACTIONS AT THE SAME TIME.
ALL YOU'RE DOING IS HITTING A BALL. WHERE'S THE ROCKET SCIENCE IN *THAT?*
BEFORE WE START ON STEP ONE YOU'LL WANT TO ***ADDRESS*** THE BALL.
HELLO, BALL.
THWOCK
Y'SEE, IT'S EASY.
For some reason Howard won't play anymore after that.

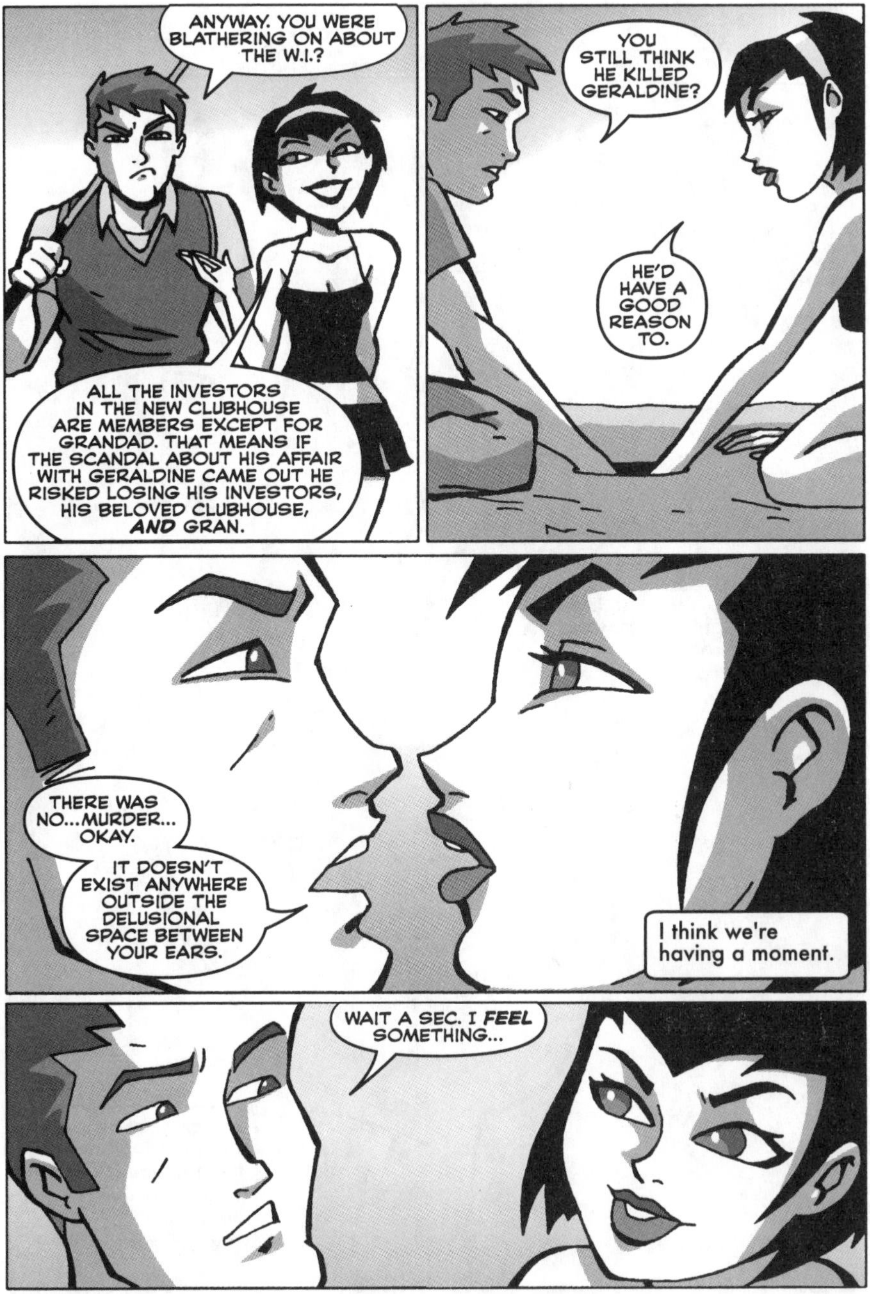
ANYWAY. YOU WERE BLATHERING ON ABOUT THE W.I.?
ALL THE INVESTORS IN THE NEW CLUBHOUSE ARE MEMBERS EXCEPT FOR GRANDAD. THAT MEANS IF THE SCANDAL ABOUT HIS AFFAIR WITH GERALDINE CAME OUT HE RISKED LOSING HIS INVESTORS, HIS BELOVED CLUBHOUSE, ***AND*** GRAN.
YOU STILL THINK HE KILLED GERALDINE?
HE'D HAVE A GOOD REASON TO.
THERE WAS NO...MURDER... OKAY.
IT DOESN'T EXIST ANYWHERE OUTSIDE THE DELUSIONAL SPACE BETWEEN YOUR EARS.
I think we're having a moment.
WAIT A SEC. I ***FEEL*** SOMETHING...

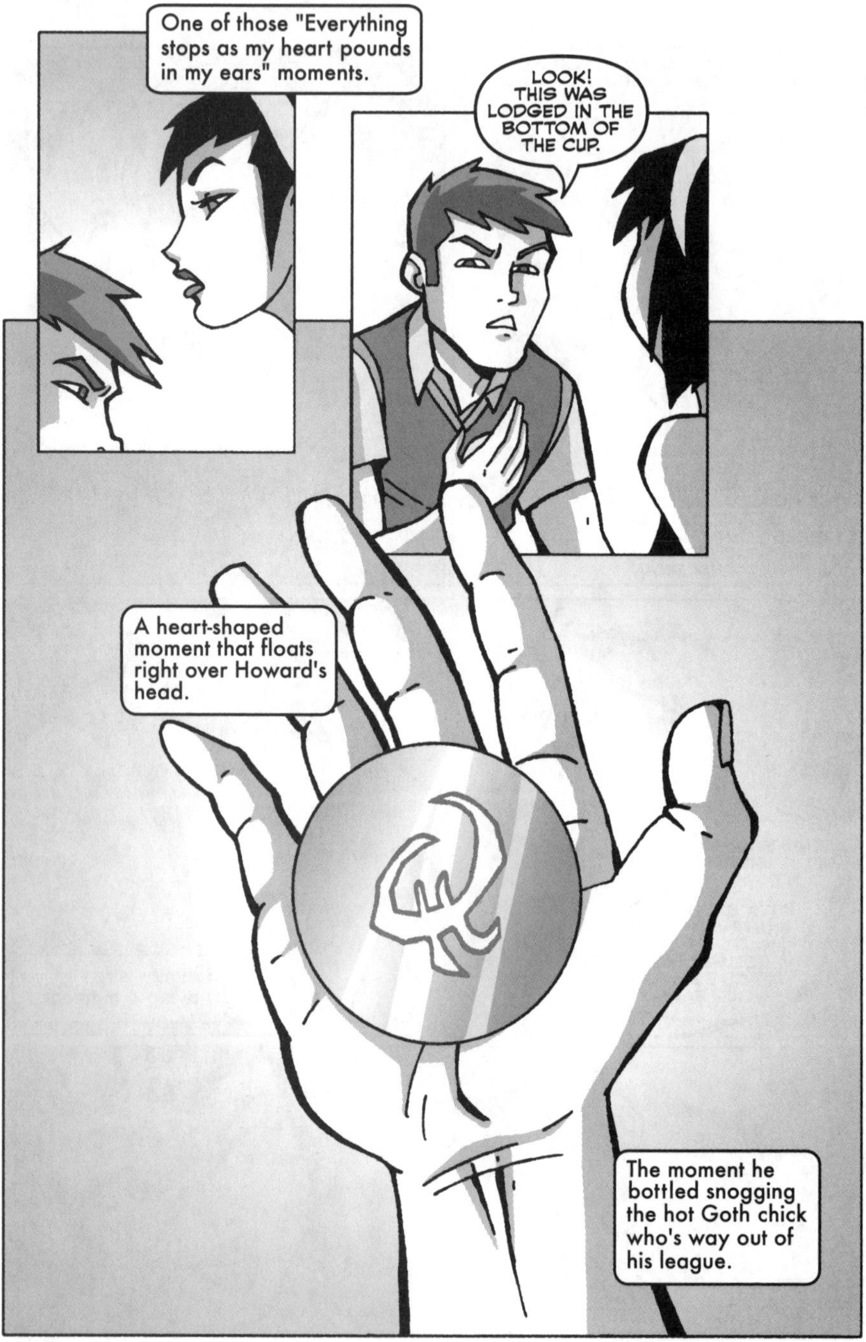
One of those "Everything stops as my heart pounds in my ears" moments.
LOOK! THIS WAS LODGED IN THE BOTTOM OF THE CUP.
A heart-shaped moment that floats right over Howard's head.
The moment he bottled snogging the hot Goth chick who's way out of his league.

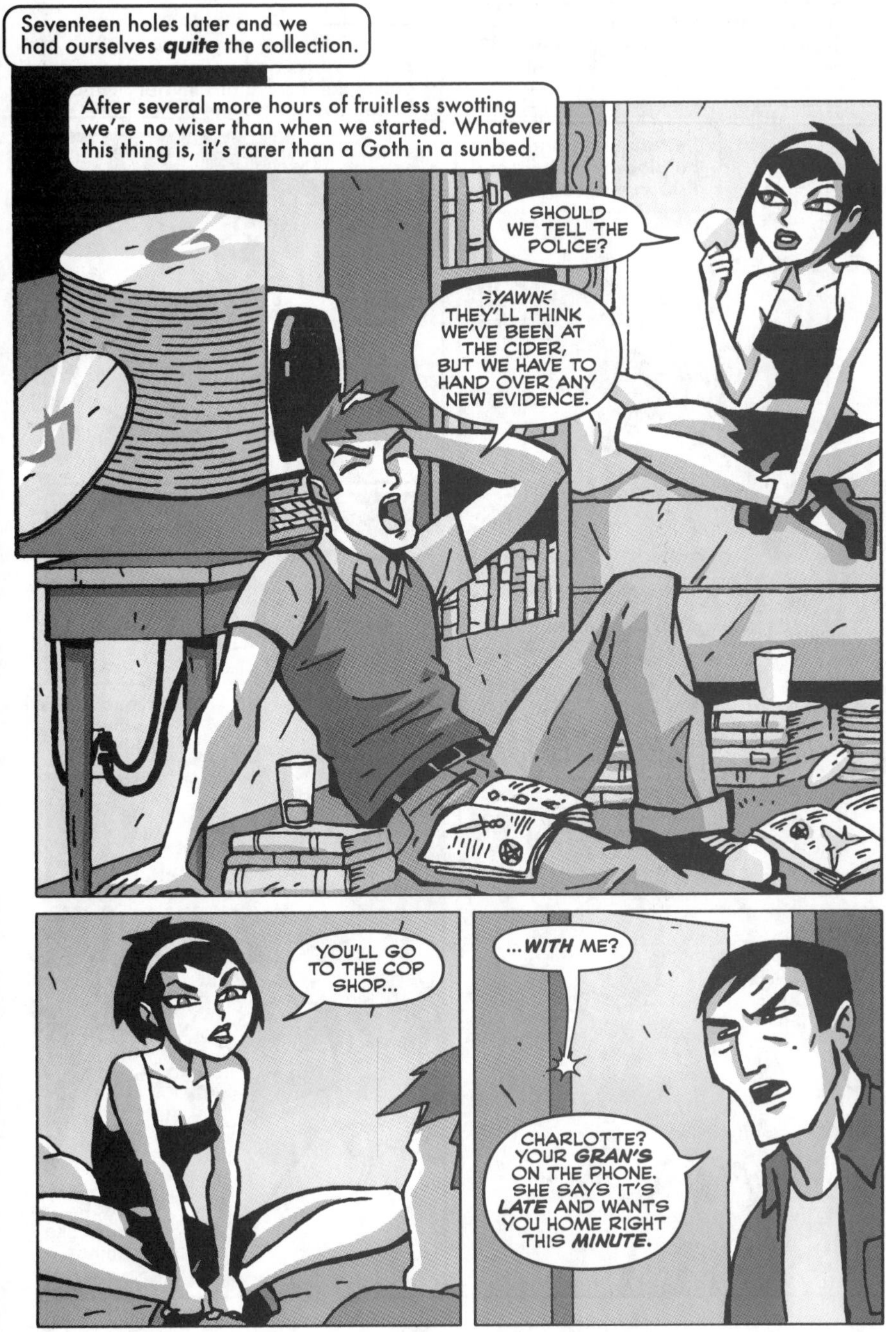
Seventeen holes later and we had ourselves *quite* the collection.
After several more hours of fruitless swotting we're no wiser than when we started. Whatever this thing is, it's rarer than a Goth in a sunbed.
SHOULD WE TELL THE POLICE?
≷YAWN≶ THEY'LL THINK WE'VE BEEN AT THE CIDER, BUT WE HAVE TO HAND OVER ANY NEW EVIDENCE.
YOU'LL GO TO THE COP SHOP...
...*WITH* ME?
CHARLOTTE? YOUR *GRAN'S* ON THE PHONE. SHE SAYS IT'S *LATE* AND WANTS YOU HOME RIGHT THIS *MINUTE*.

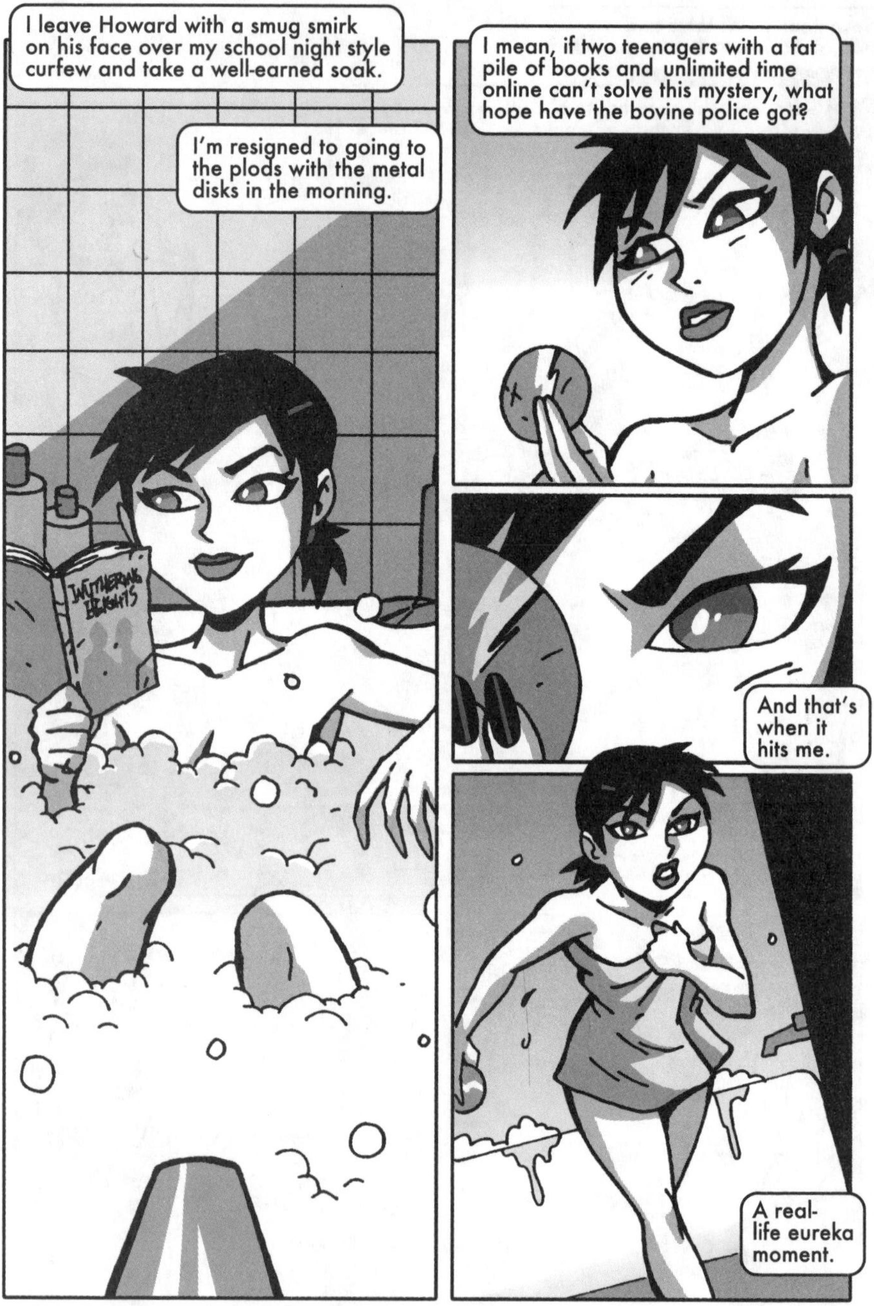
I leave Howard with a smug smirk on his face over my school night style curfew and take a well-earned soak.
I'm resigned to going to the plods with the metal disks in the morning.
WUTHERING HEIGHTS
I mean, if two teenagers with a fat pile of books and unlimited time online can't solve this mystery, what hope have the bovine police got?
And that's when it hits me.
A real-life eureka moment.

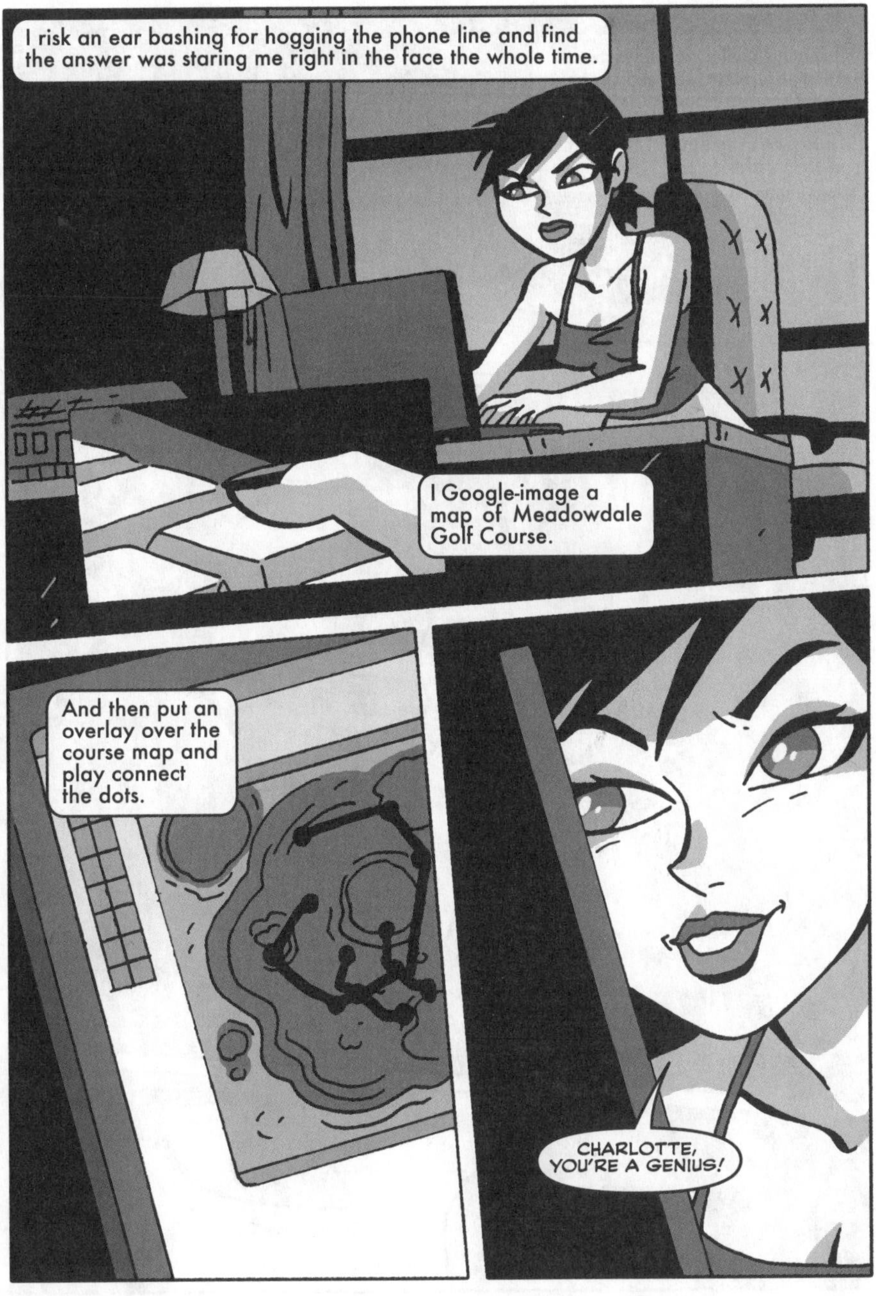
I risk an ear bashing for hogging the phone line and find the answer was staring me right in the face the whole time.
I Google-image a map of Meadowdale Golf Course.
And then put an overlay over the course map and play connect the dots.
CHARLOTTE, YOU'RE A GENIUS!

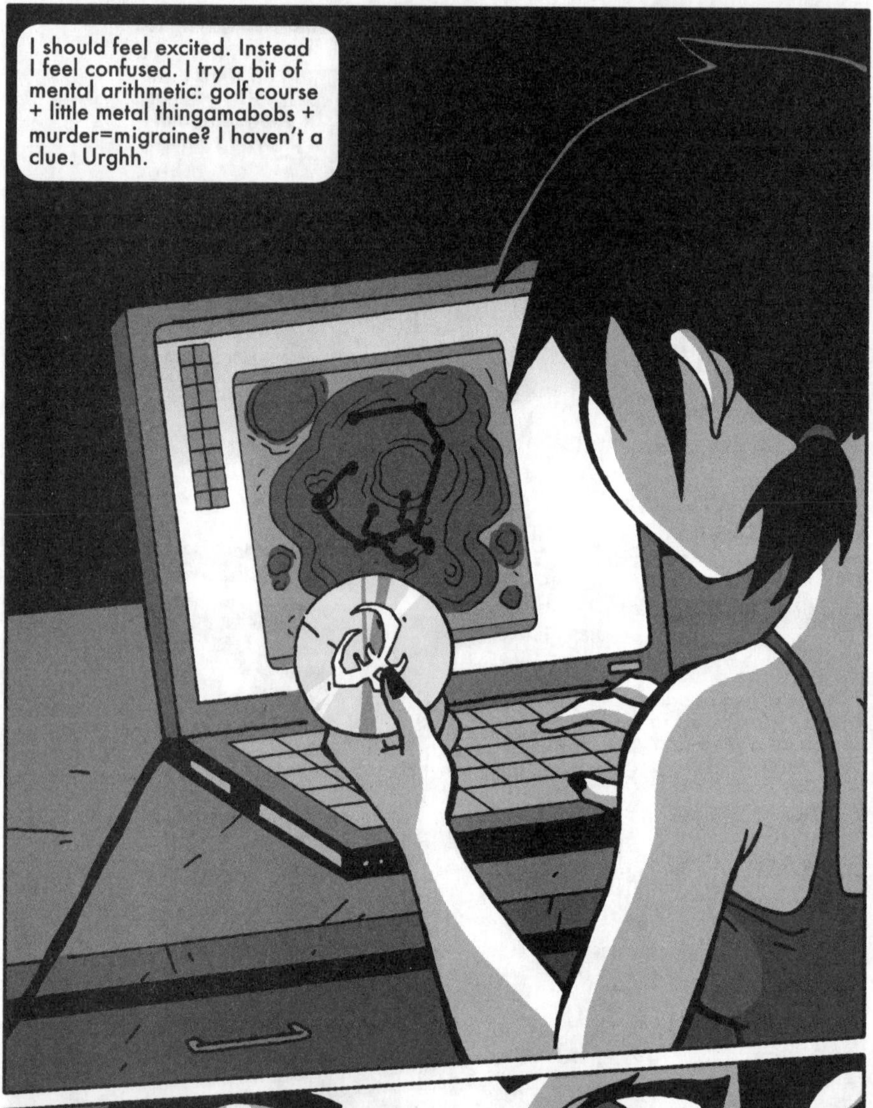
I should feel excited. Instead I feel confused. I try a bit of mental arithmetic: golf course + little metal thingamabobs + murder=migraine? I haven't a clue. Urghh.

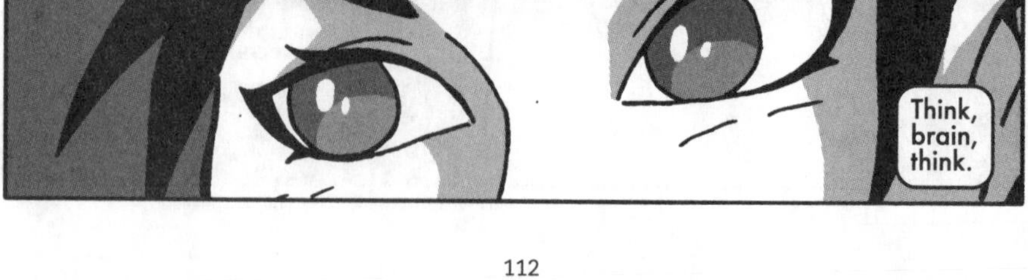
Think, brain, think.

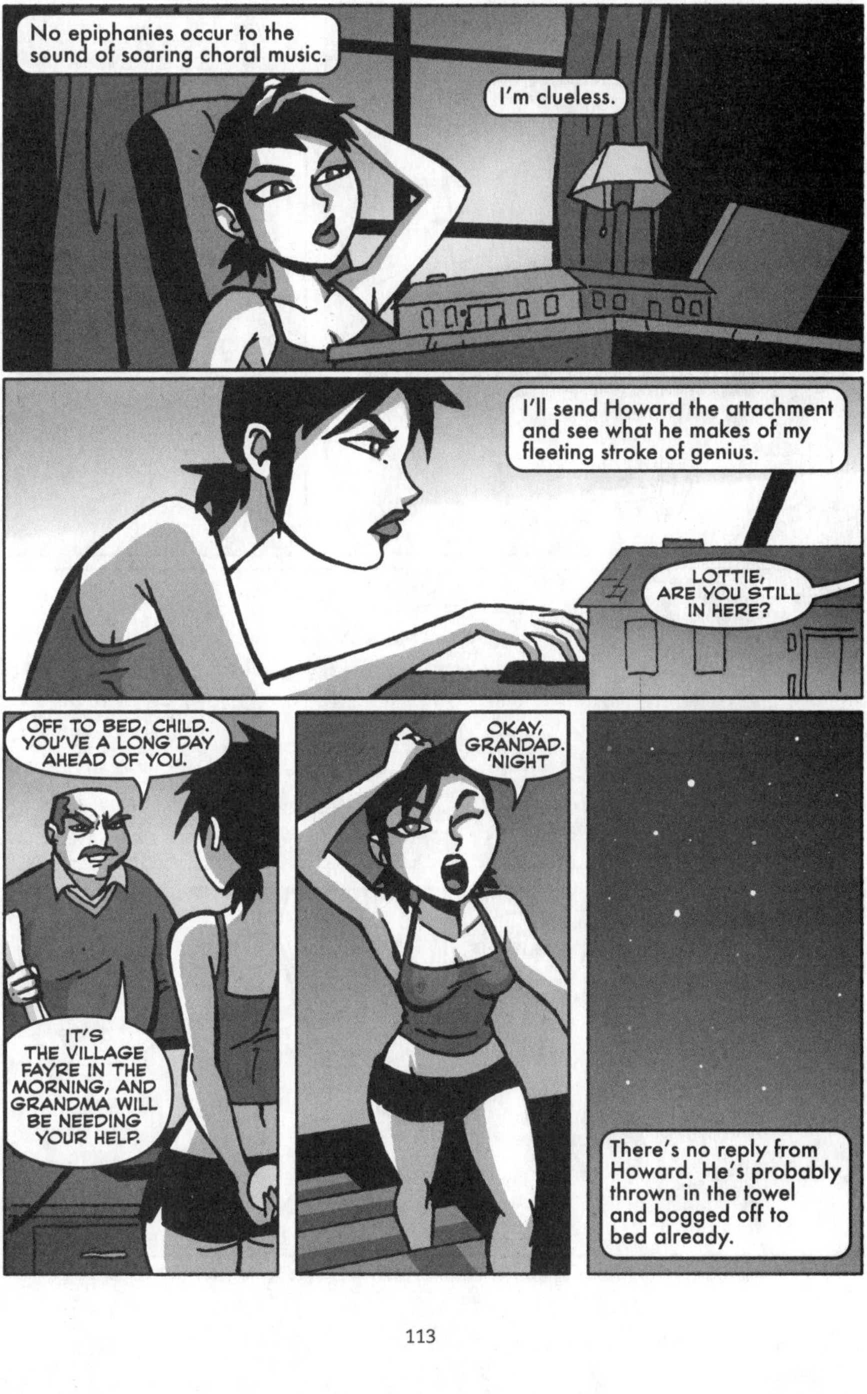
No epiphanies occur to the sound of soaring choral music.
I'm clueless.
I'll send Howard the attachment and see what he makes of my fleeting stroke of genius.
LOTTIE, ARE YOU STILL IN HERE?
OFF TO BED, CHILD. YOU'VE A LONG DAY AHEAD OF YOU.
IT'S THE VILLAGE FAYRE IN THE MORNING, AND GRANDMA WILL BE NEEDING YOUR HELP.
OKAY, GRANDAD. 'NIGHT
There's no reply from Howard. He's probably thrown in the towel and bogged off to bed already.

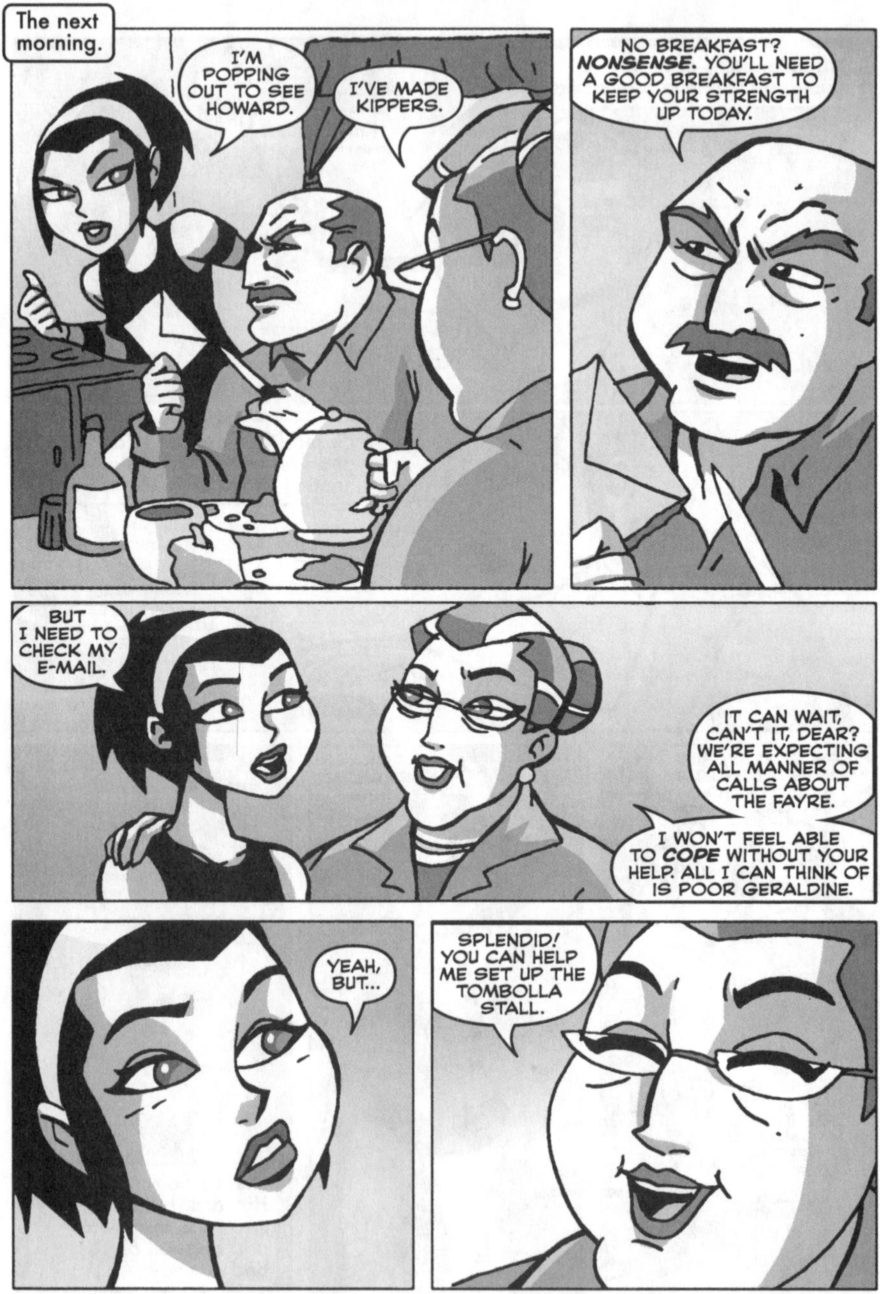
The next morning.
I'M POPPING OUT TO SEE HOWARD.
I'VE MADE KIPPERS.
NO BREAKFAST? NONSENSE. YOU'LL NEED A GOOD BREAKFAST TO KEEP YOUR STRENGTH UP TODAY.
BUT I NEED TO CHECK MY E-MAIL.
IT CAN WAIT, CAN'T IT, DEAR? WE'RE EXPECTING ALL MANNER OF CALLS ABOUT THE FAYRE.
I WON'T FEEL ABLE TO COPE WITHOUT YOUR HELP. ALL I CAN THINK OF IS POOR GERALDINE.
YEAH, BUT...
SPLENDID! YOU CAN HELP ME SET UP THE TOMBOLLA STALL.

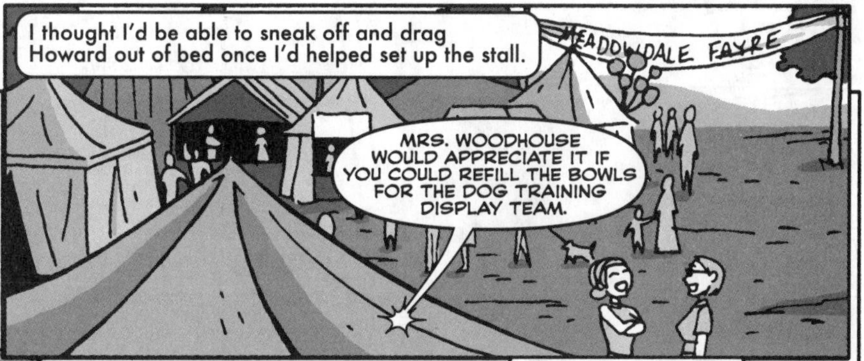

I thought I'd be able to sneak off and drag Howard out of bed once I'd helped set up the stall.
MEADOWDALE FAYRE
MRS. WOODHOUSE WOULD APPRECIATE IT IF YOU COULD REFILL THE BOWLS FOR THE DOG TRAINING DISPLAY TEAM.

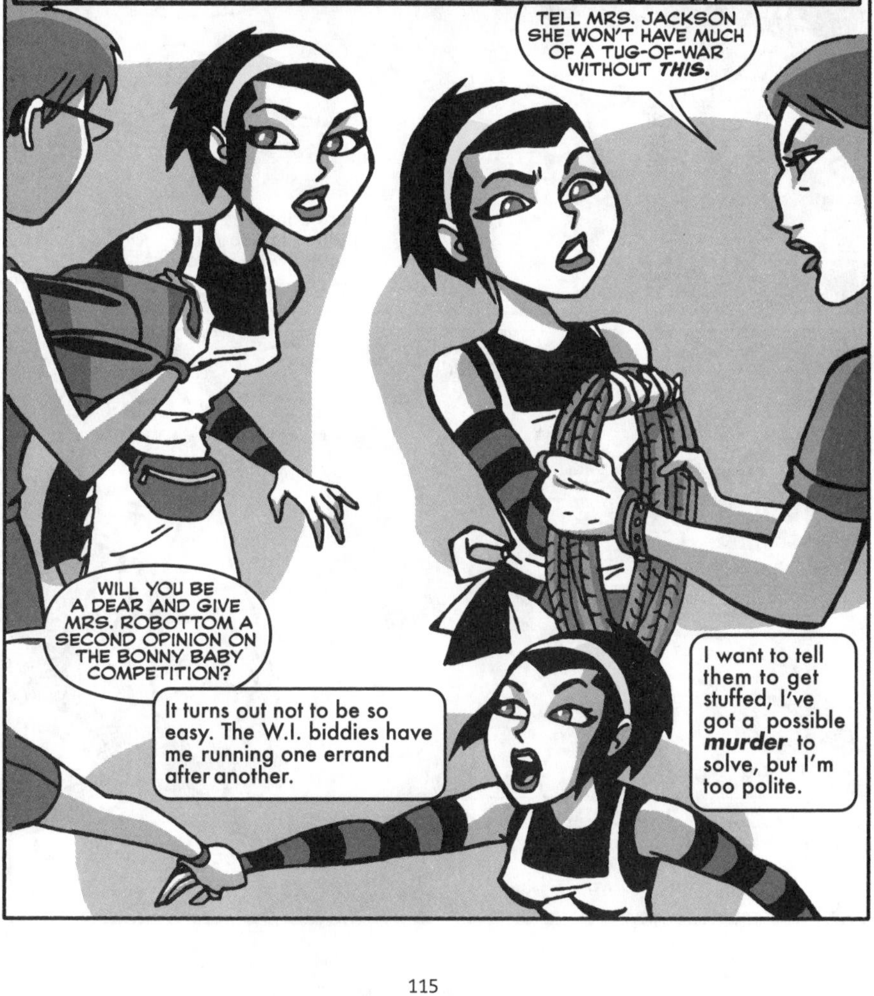

TELL MRS. JACKSON SHE WON'T HAVE MUCH OF A TUG-OF-WAR WITHOUT ***THIS***.
WILL YOU BE A DEAR AND GIVE MRS. ROBOTTOM A SECOND OPINION ON THE BONNY BABY COMPETITION?
It turns out not to be so easy. The W.I. biddies have me running one errand after another.
I want to tell them to get stuffed, I've got a possible ***murder*** to solve, but I'm too polite.

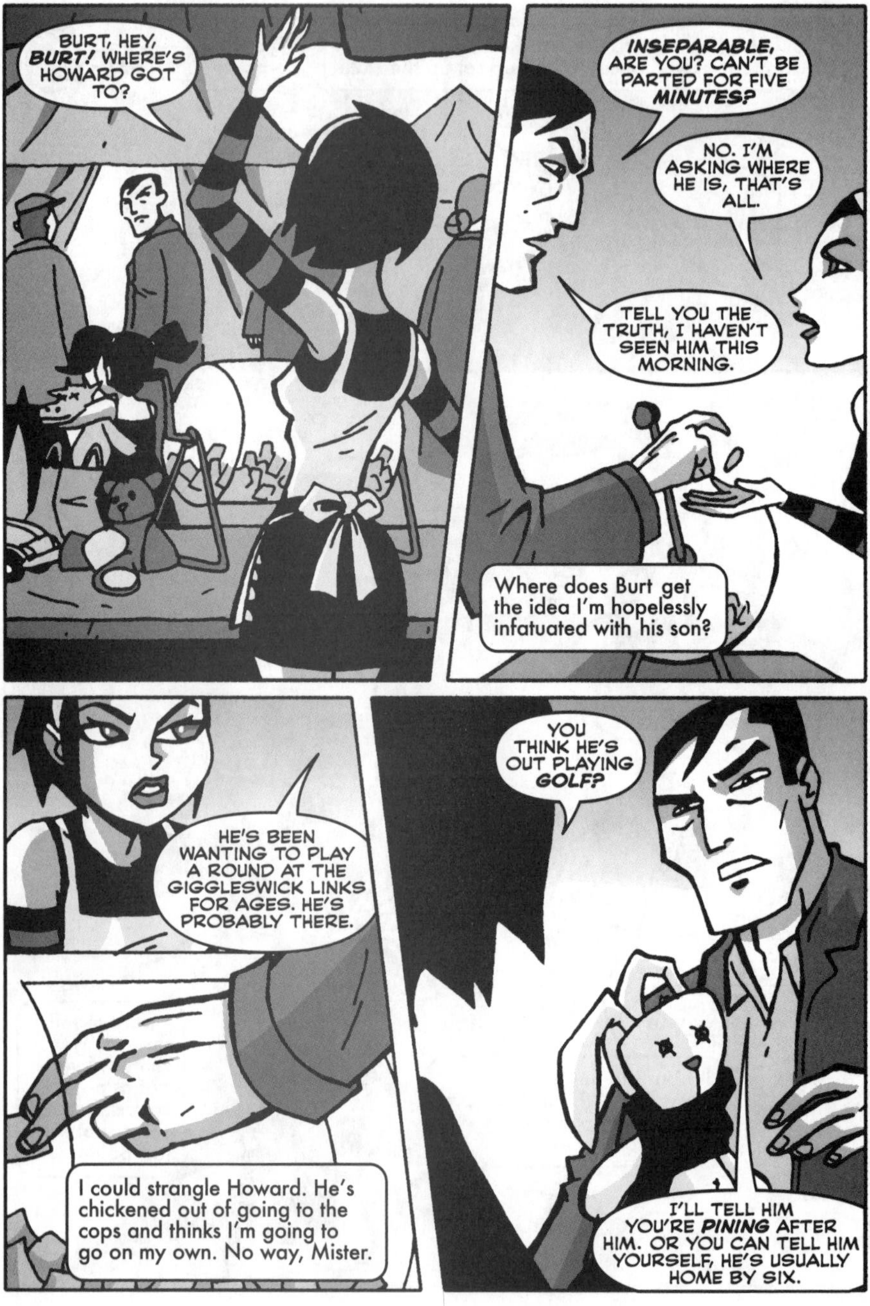
BURT, HEY, **BURT!** WHERE'S HOWARD GOT TO?
INSEPARABLE, ARE YOU? CAN'T BE PARTED FOR FIVE ***MINUTES?***
NO. I'M ASKING WHERE HE IS, THAT'S ALL.
TELL YOU THE TRUTH, I HAVEN'T SEEN HIM THIS MORNING.
Where does Burt get the idea I'm hopelessly infatuated with his son?
HE'S BEEN WANTING TO PLAY A ROUND AT THE GIGGLESWICK LINKS FOR AGES. HE'S PROBABLY THERE.
I could strangle Howard. He's chickened out of going to the cops and thinks I'm going to go on my own. No way, Mister.
YOU THINK HE'S OUT PLAYING ***GOLF?***
I'LL TELL HIM YOU'RE ***PINING*** AFTER HIM. OR YOU CAN TELL HIM YOURSELF, HE'S USUALLY HOME BY SIX.

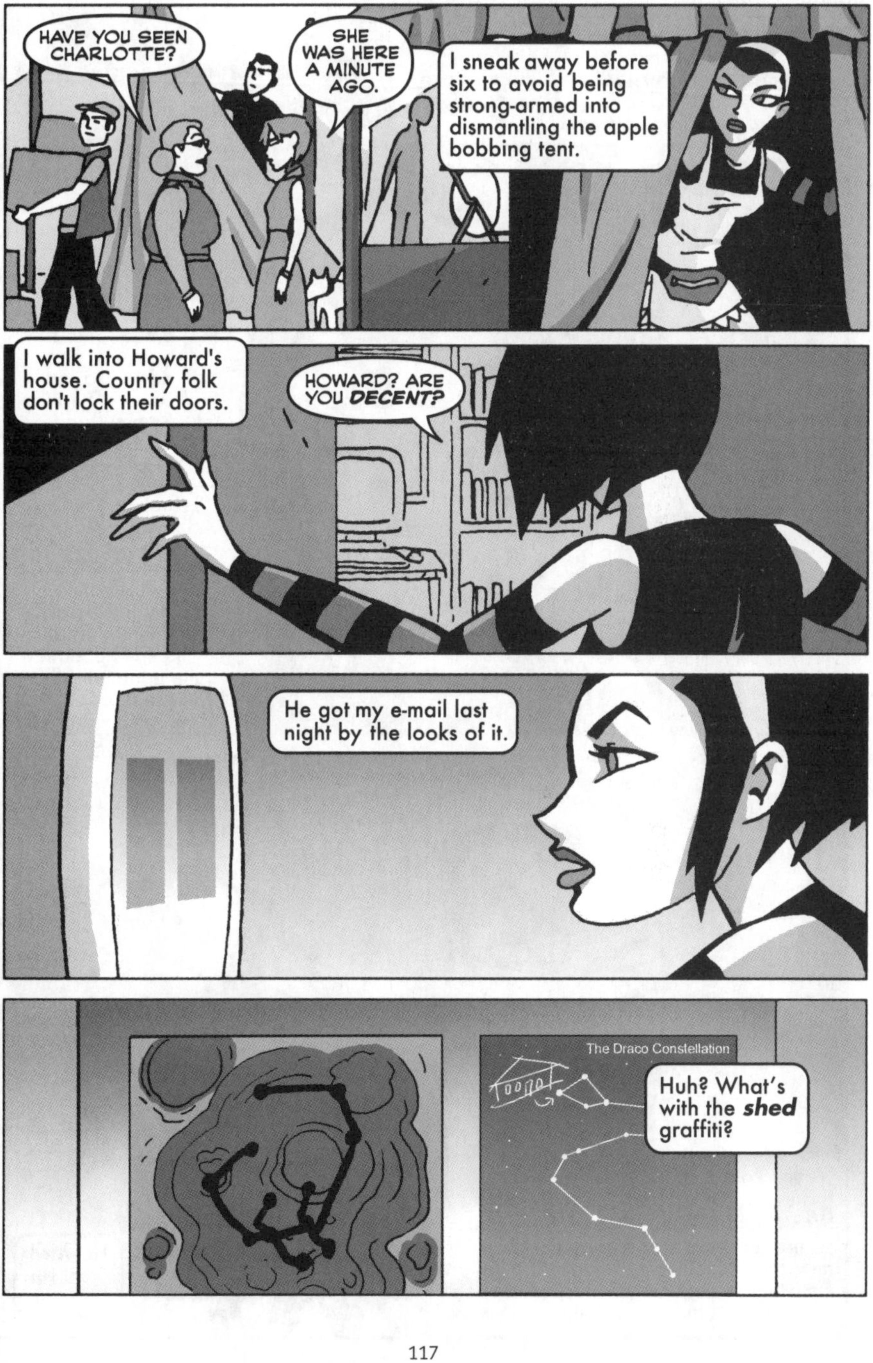
HAVE YOU SEEN CHARLOTTE?
SHE WAS HERE A MINUTE AGO.
I sneak away before six to avoid being strong-armed into dismantling the apple bobbing tent.
I walk into Howard's house. Country folk don't lock their doors.
HOWARD? ARE YOU ***DECENT?***
He got my e-mail last night by the looks of it.
The Draco Constellation
Huh? What's with the ***shed*** graffiti?

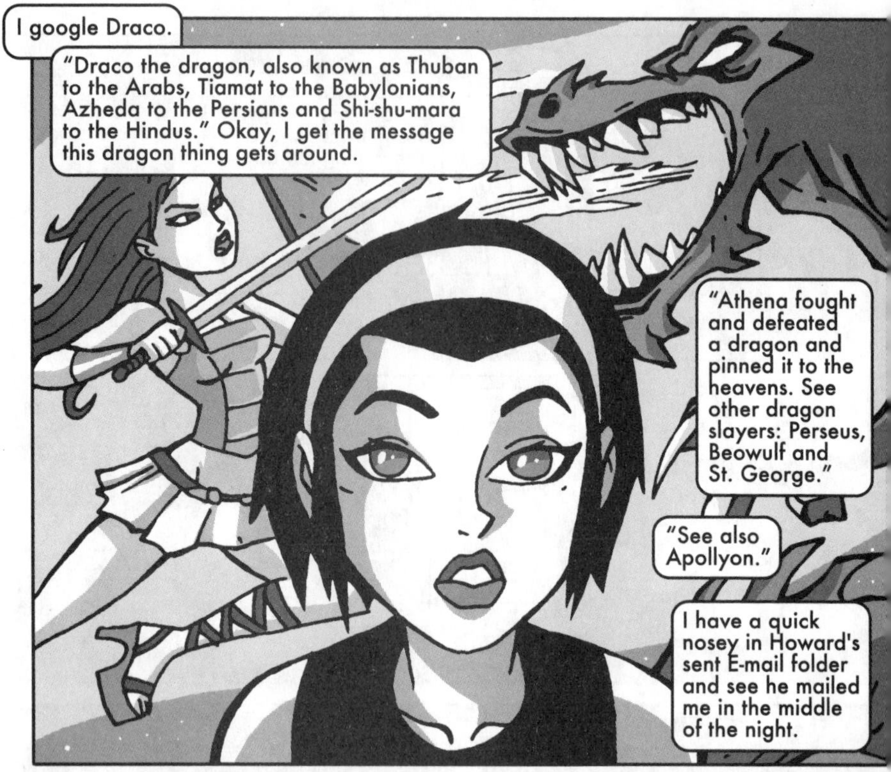

I google Draco.
"Draco the dragon, also known as Thuban to the Arabs, Tiamat to the Babylonians, Azheda to the Persians and Shi-shu-mara to the Hindus." Okay, I get the message this dragon thing gets around.
"Athena fought and defeated a dragon and pinned it to the heavens. See other dragon slayers: Perseus, Beowulf and St. George."
"See also Apollyon."
I have a quick nosey in Howard's sent E-mail folder and see he mailed me in the middle of the night.

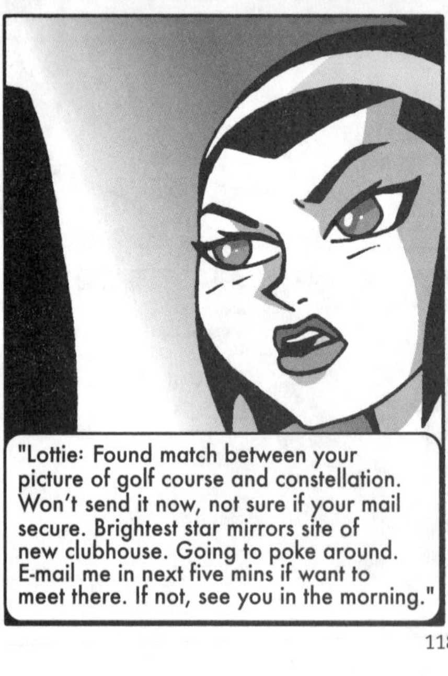

"Lottie: Found match between your picture of golf course and constellation. Won't send it now, not sure if your mail secure. Brightest star mirrors site of new clubhouse. Going to poke around. E-mail me in next five mins if want to meet there. If not, see you in the morning."

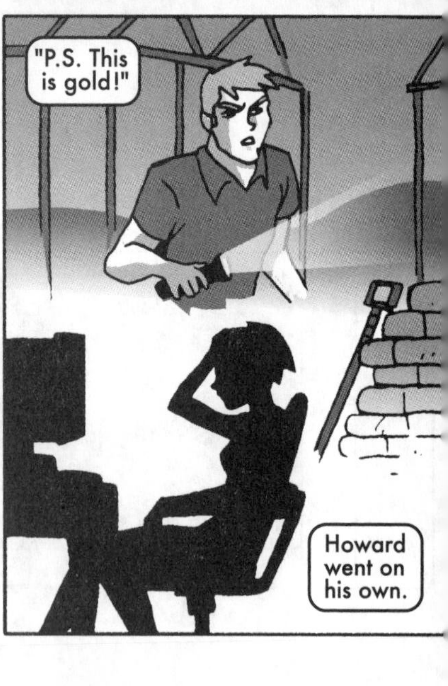

"P.S. This is gold!"
Howard went on his own.

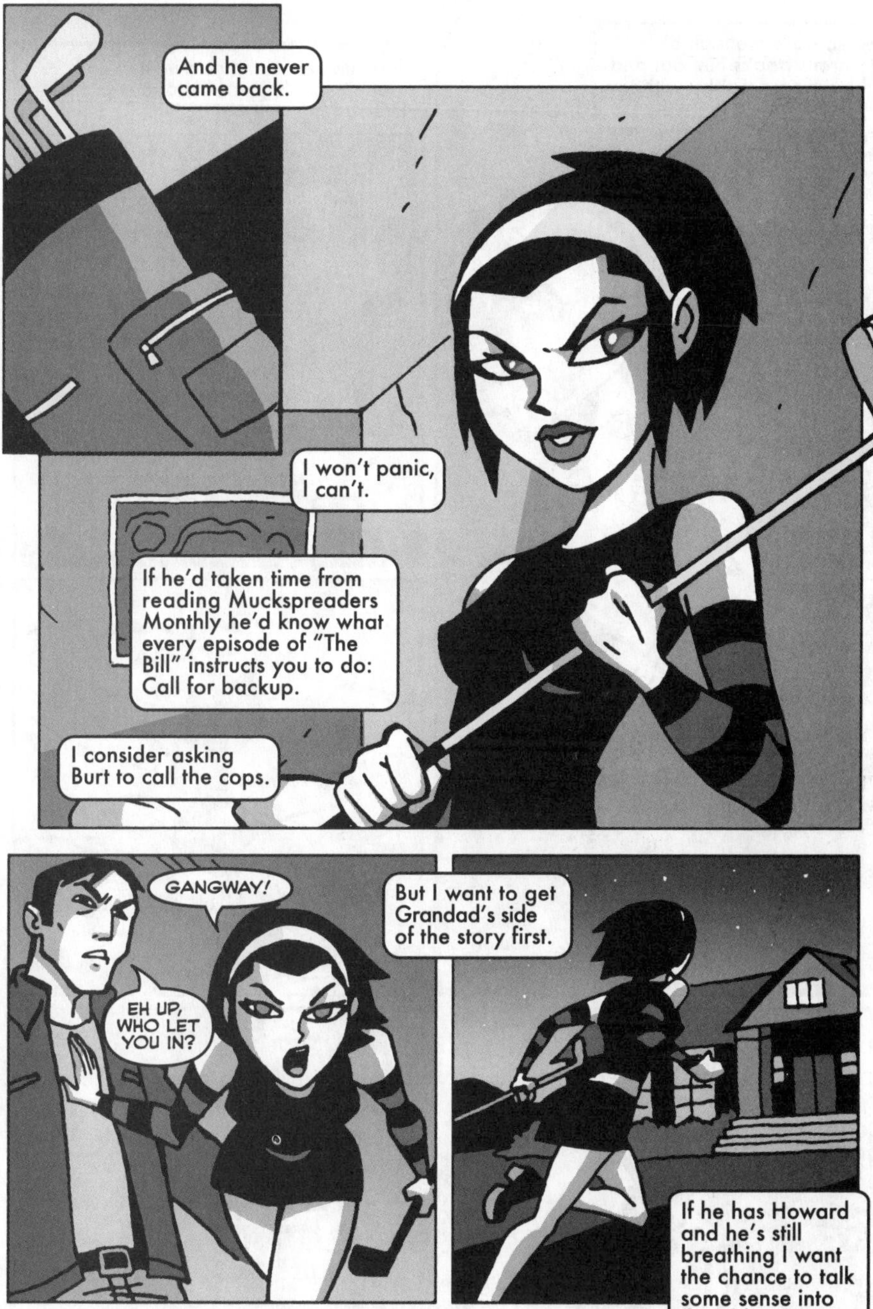

And he never came back.
I won't panic, I can't.
If he'd taken time from reading Muckspreaders Monthly he'd know what every episode of "The Bill" instructs you to do: Call for backup.
I consider asking Burt to call the cops.
GANGWAY!
EH UP, WHO LET YOU IN?
But I want to get Grandad's side of the story first.
If he has Howard and he's still breathing I want the chance to talk some sense into the old maniac—

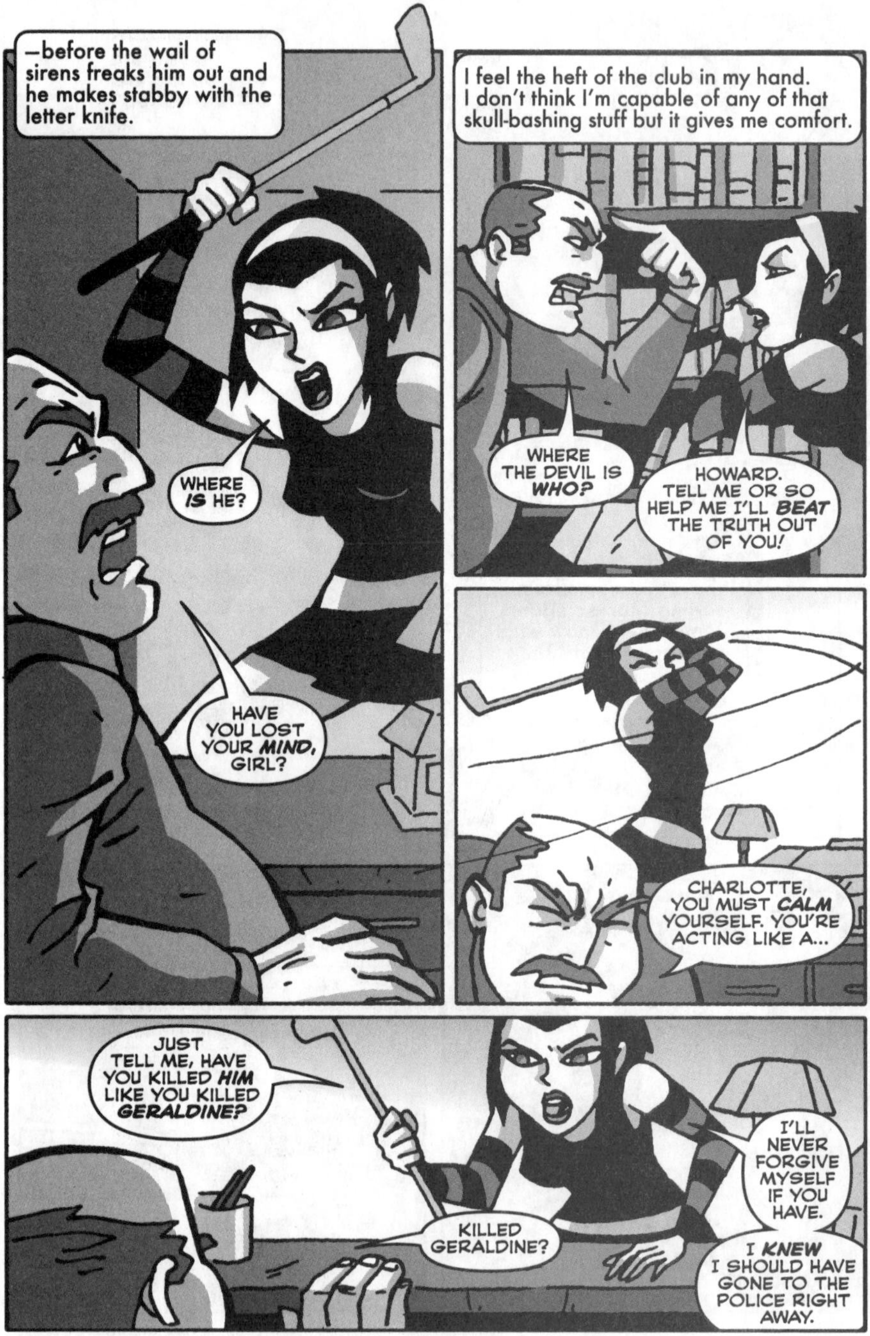
—before the wail of sirens freaks him out and he makes stabby with the letter knife.
WHERE IS HE?
HAVE YOU LOST YOUR MIND, GIRL?
I feel the heft of the club in my hand. I don't think I'm capable of any of that skull-bashing stuff but it gives me comfort.
WHERE THE DEVIL IS WHO?
HOWARD. TELL ME OR SO HELP ME I'LL BEAT THE TRUTH OUT OF YOU!
CHARLOTTE, YOU MUST CALM YOURSELF. YOU'RE ACTING LIKE A...
JUST TELL ME, HAVE YOU KILLED HIM LIKE YOU KILLED GERALDINE?
KILLED GERALDINE?
I'LL NEVER FORGIVE MYSELF IF YOU HAVE.
I KNEW I SHOULD HAVE GONE TO THE POLICE RIGHT AWAY.

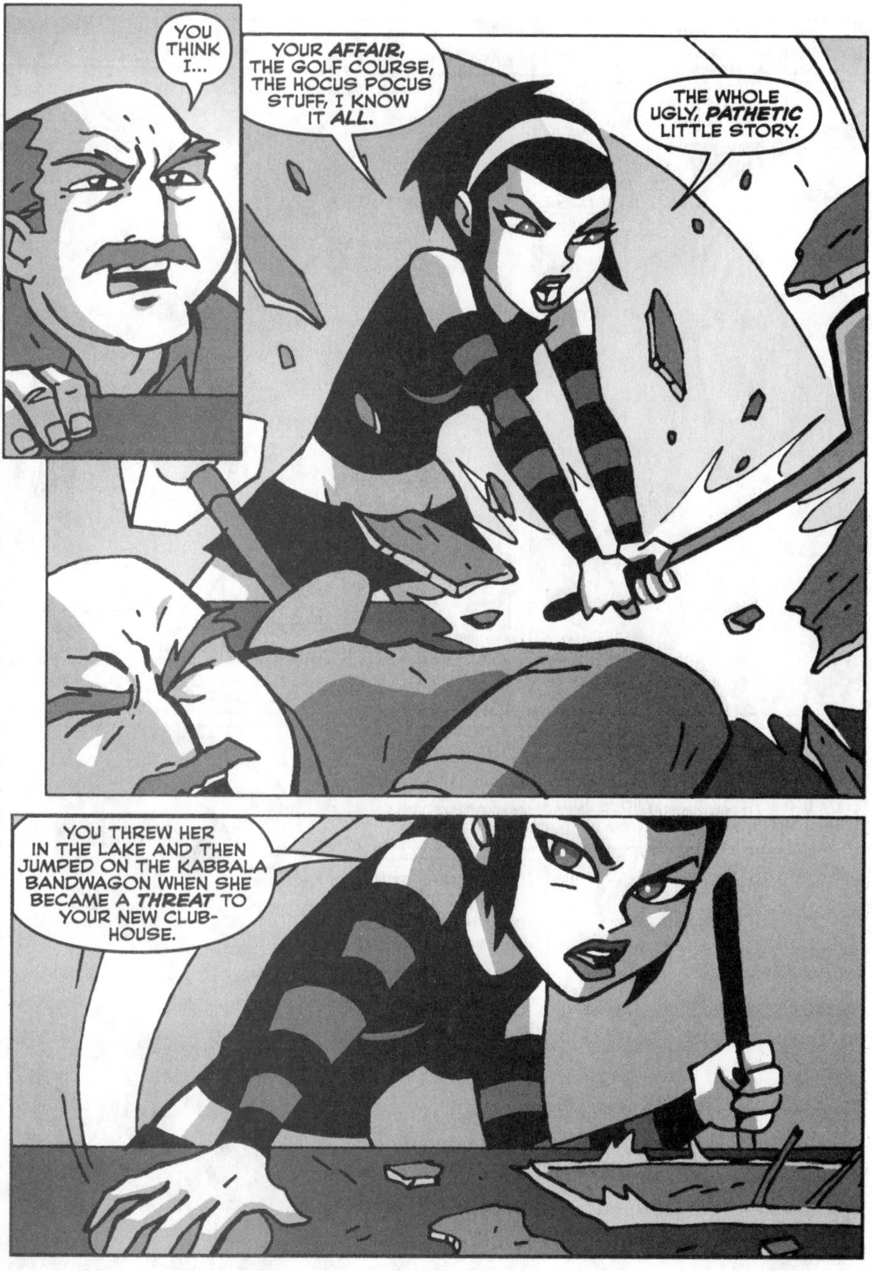
YOU THINK I...
YOUR ***AFFAIR,*** THE GOLF COURSE, THE HOCUS POCUS STUFF, I KNOW IT ***ALL.***
THE WHOLE UGLY, ***PATHETIC*** LITTLE STORY.
YOU THREW HER IN THE LAKE AND THEN JUMPED ON THE KABBALA BANDWAGON WHEN SHE BECAME A ***THREAT*** TO YOUR NEW CLUB-HOUSE.

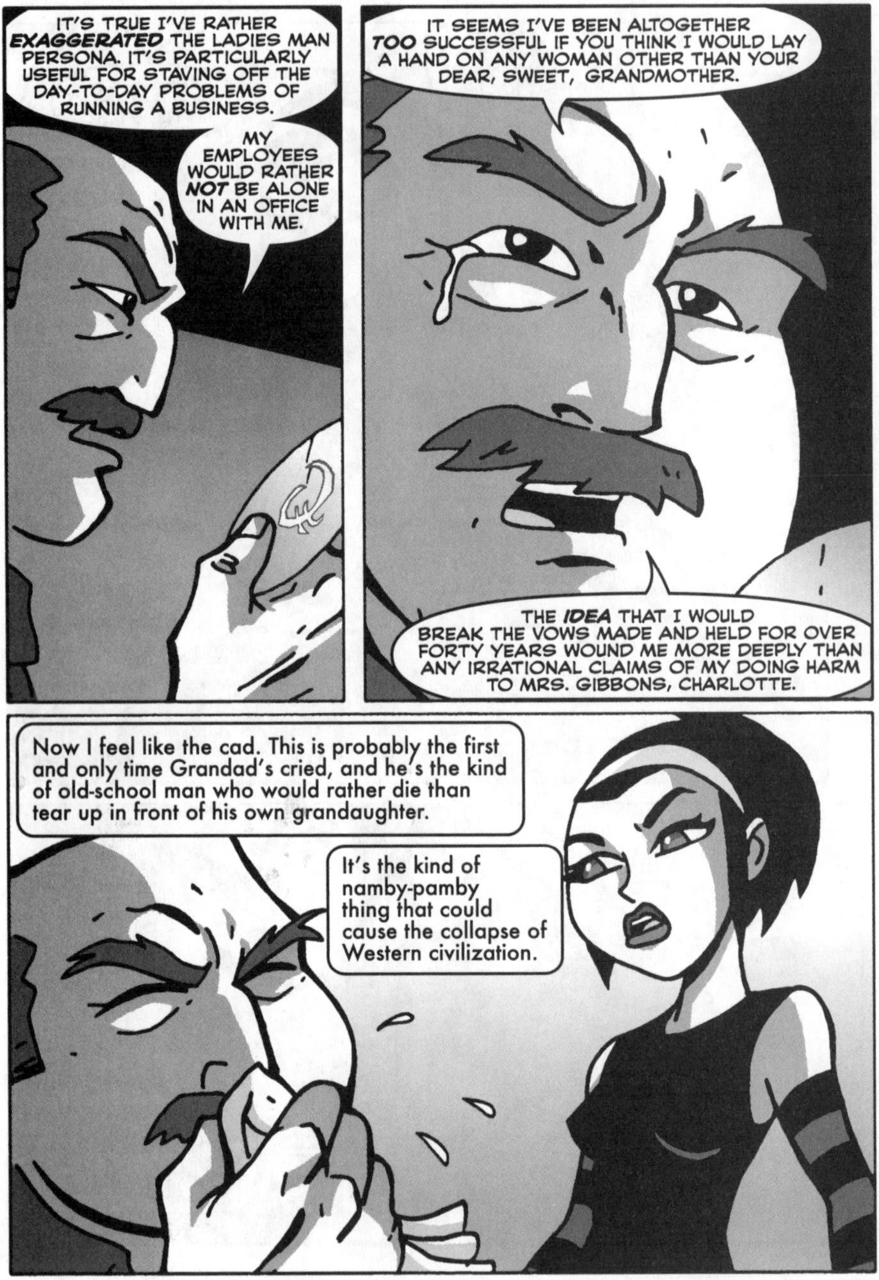
IT'S TRUE I'VE RATHER **EXAGGERATED** THE LADIES MAN PERSONA. IT'S PARTICULARLY USEFUL FOR STAVING OFF THE DAY-TO-DAY PROBLEMS OF RUNNING A BUSINESS.
MY EMPLOYEES WOULD RATHER **NOT** BE ALONE IN AN OFFICE WITH ME.
IT SEEMS I'VE BEEN ALTOGETHER **TOO** SUCCESSFUL IF YOU THINK I WOULD LAY A HAND ON ANY WOMAN OTHER THAN YOUR DEAR, SWEET, GRANDMOTHER.
THE **IDEA** THAT I WOULD BREAK THE VOWS MADE AND HELD FOR OVER FORTY YEARS WOUND ME MORE DEEPLY THAN ANY IRRATIONAL CLAIMS OF MY DOING HARM TO MRS. GIBBONS, CHARLOTTE.
Now I feel like the cad. This is probably the first and only time Grandad's cried, and he's the kind of old-school man who would rather die than tear up in front of his own grandaughter.
It's the kind of namby-pamby thing that could cause the collapse of Western civilization.

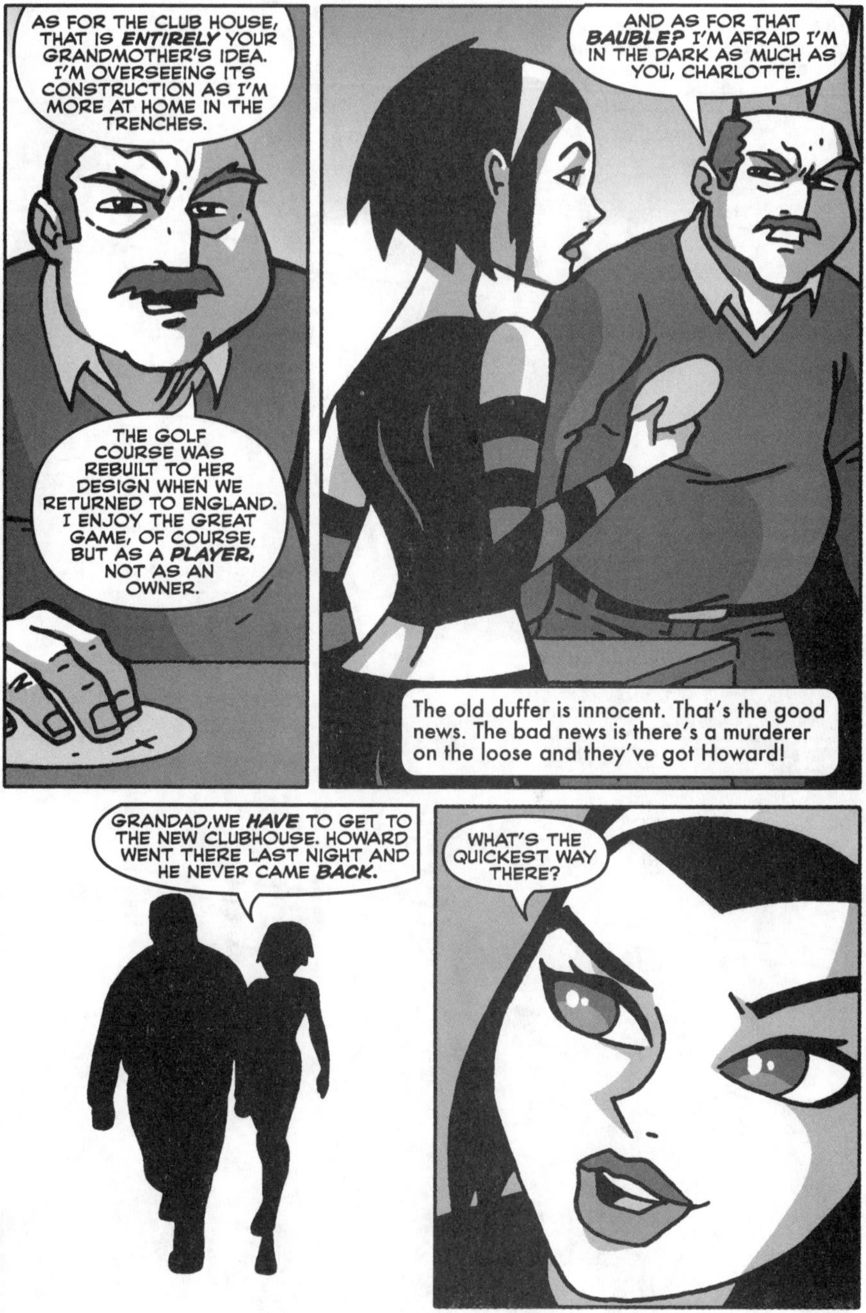
AS FOR THE CLUB HOUSE, THAT IS *ENTIRELY* YOUR GRANDMOTHER'S IDEA. I'M OVERSEEING ITS CONSTRUCTION AS I'M MORE AT HOME IN THE TRENCHES.
THE GOLF COURSE WAS REBUILT TO HER DESIGN WHEN WE RETURNED TO ENGLAND. I ENJOY THE GREAT GAME, OF COURSE, BUT AS A *PLAYER,* NOT AS AN OWNER.
AND AS FOR THAT *BAUBLE?* I'M AFRAID I'M IN THE DARK AS MUCH AS YOU, CHARLOTTE.
The old duffer is innocent. That's the good news. The bad news is there's a murderer on the loose and they've got Howard!
GRANDAD,WE *HAVE* TO GET TO THE NEW CLUBHOUSE. HOWARD WENT THERE LAST NIGHT AND HE NEVER CAME *BACK.*
WHAT'S THE QUICKEST WAY THERE?

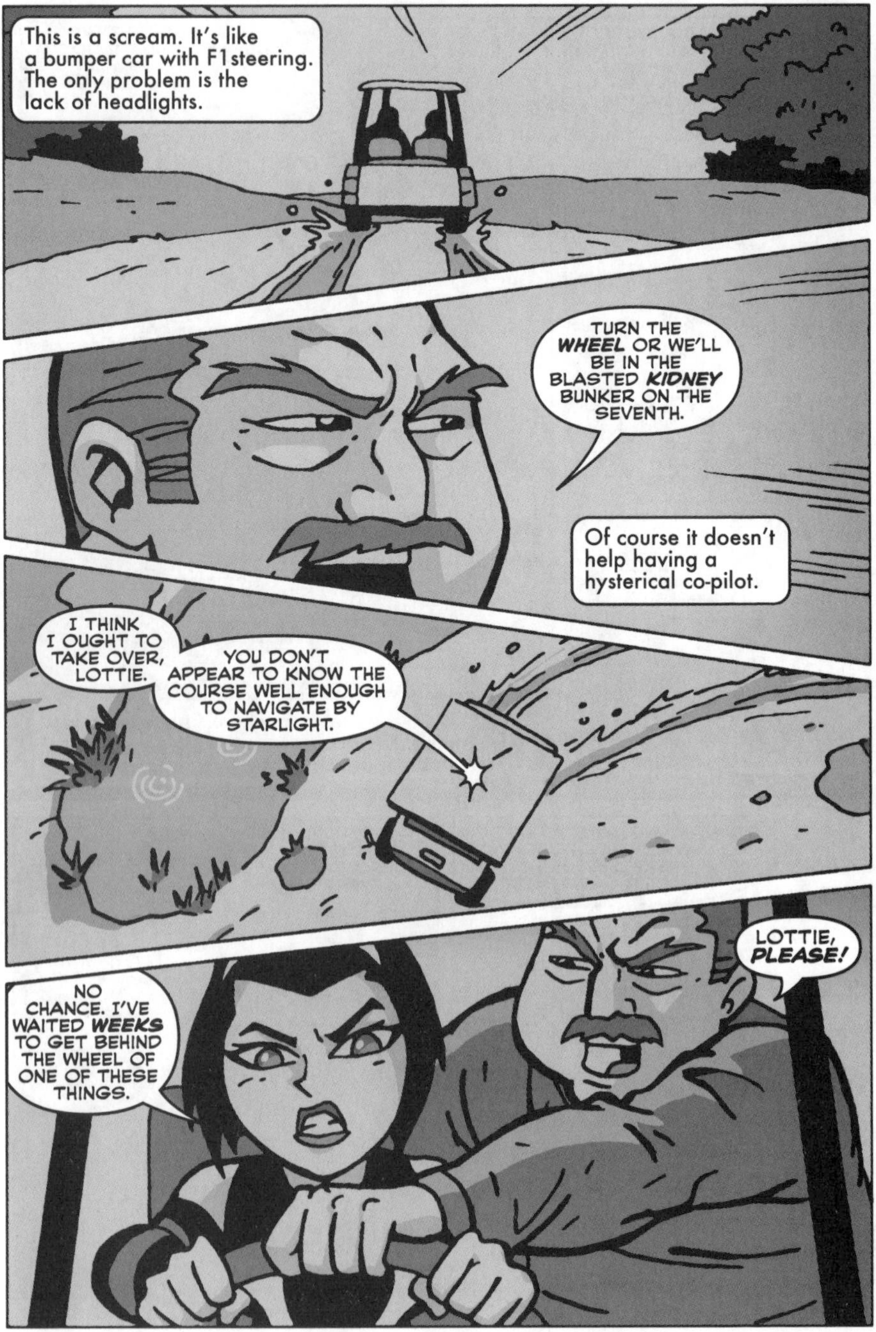
This is a scream. It's like a bumper car with F1steering. The only problem is the lack of headlights.
TURN THE WHEEL OR WE'LL BE IN THE BLASTED KIDNEY BUNKER ON THE SEVENTH.
Of course it doesn't help having a hysterical co-pilot.
I THINK I OUGHT TO TAKE OVER, LOTTIE.
YOU DON'T APPEAR TO KNOW THE COURSE WELL ENOUGH TO NAVIGATE BY STARLIGHT.
NO CHANCE. I'VE WAITED WEEKS TO GET BEHIND THE WHEEL OF ONE OF THESE THINGS.
LOTTIE, PLEASE!

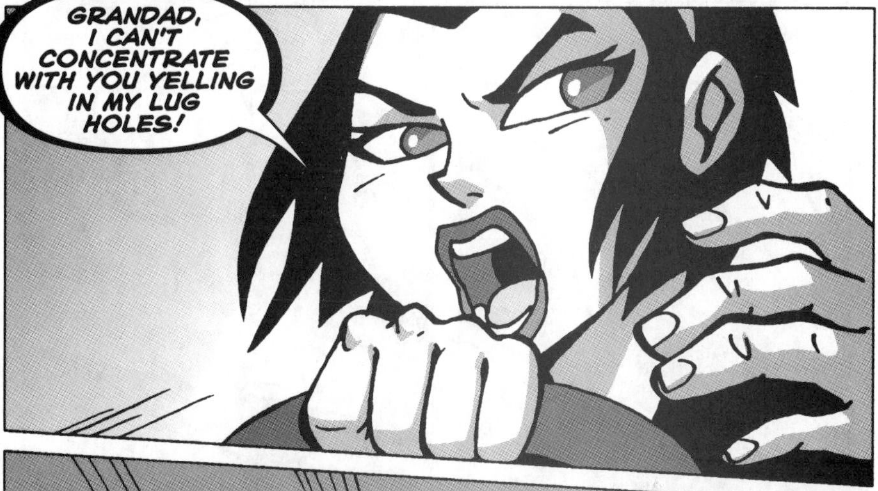
GRANDAD, I CAN'T CONCENTRATE WITH YOU YELLING IN MY LUG HOLES!

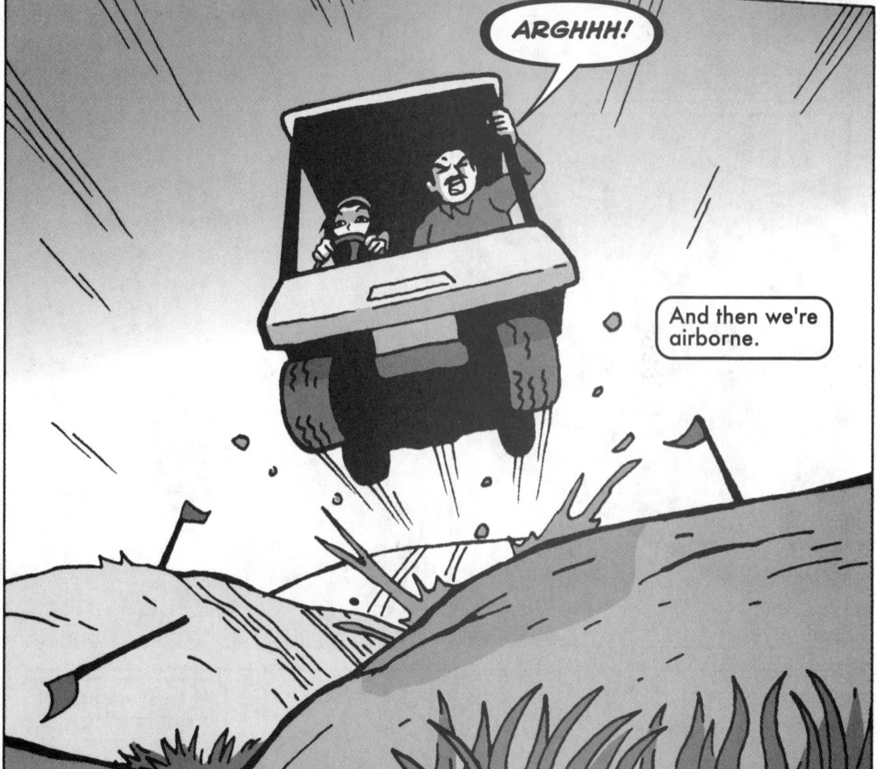
ARGHHH!
And then we're airborne.

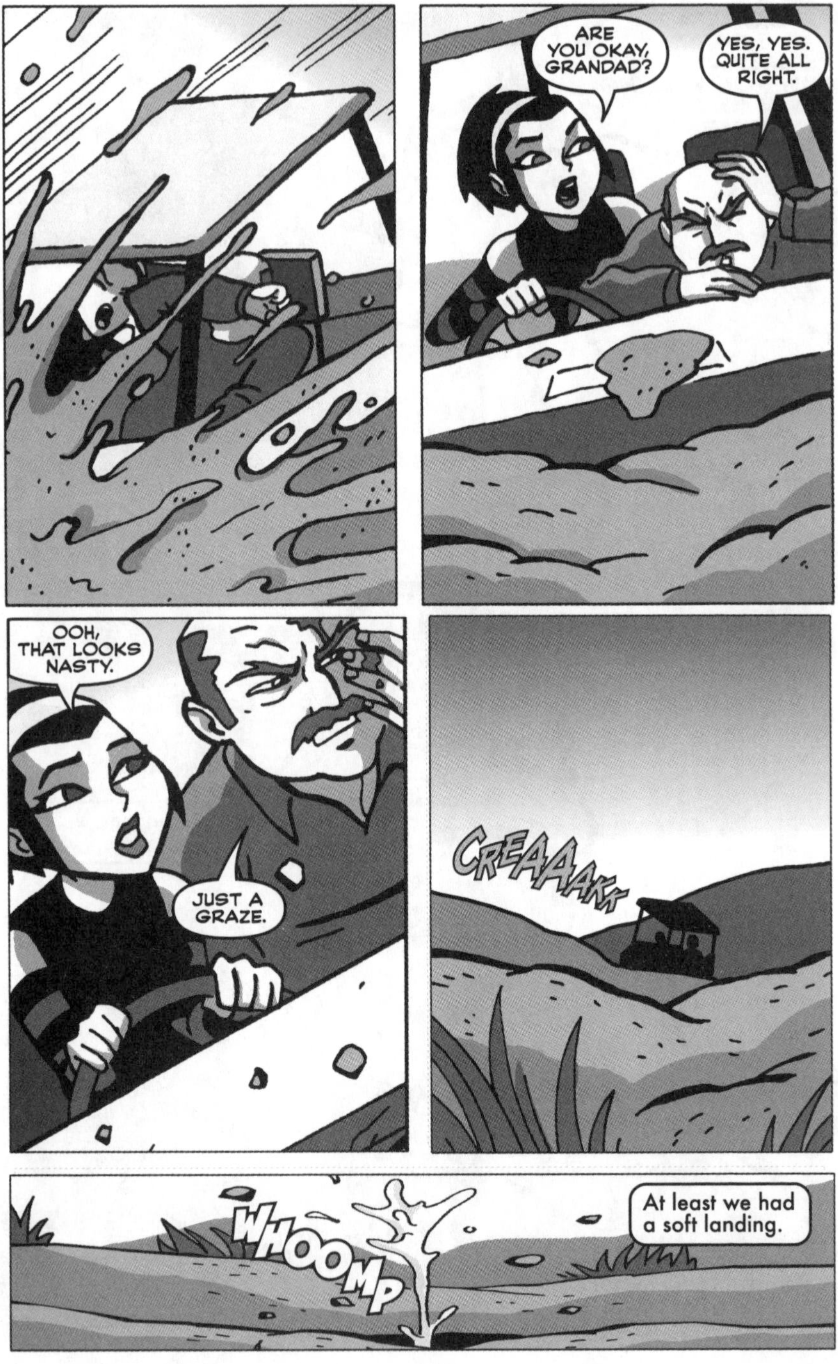
ARE YOU OKAY, GRANDAD?
YES, YES. QUITE ALL RIGHT.
OOH, THAT LOOKS NASTY.
JUST A GRAZE.
CREAAAKK
WHOOMP
At least we had a soft landing.

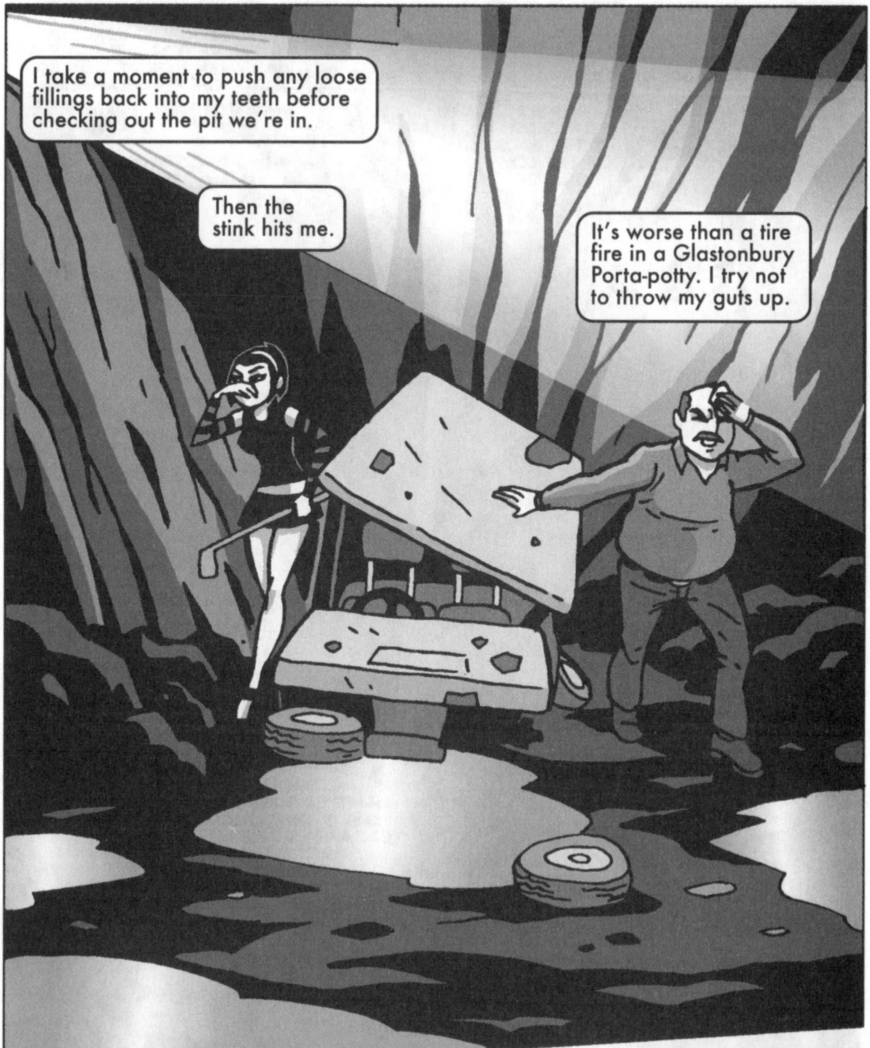
I take a moment to push any loose fillings back into my teeth before checking out the pit we're in.
Then the stink hits me.
It's worse than a tire fire in a Glastonbury Porta-potty. I try not to throw my guts up.

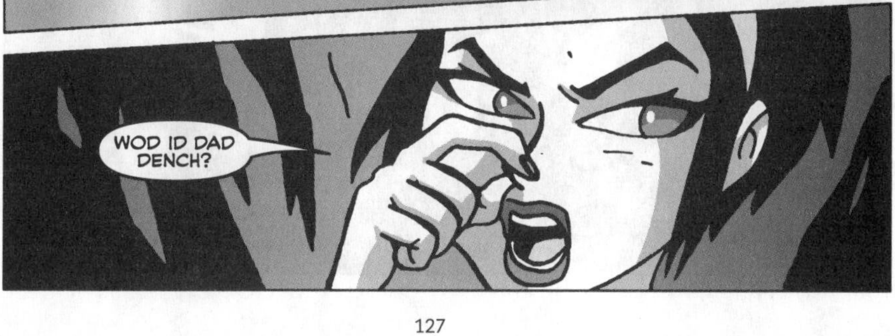
WOD ID DAD DENCH?

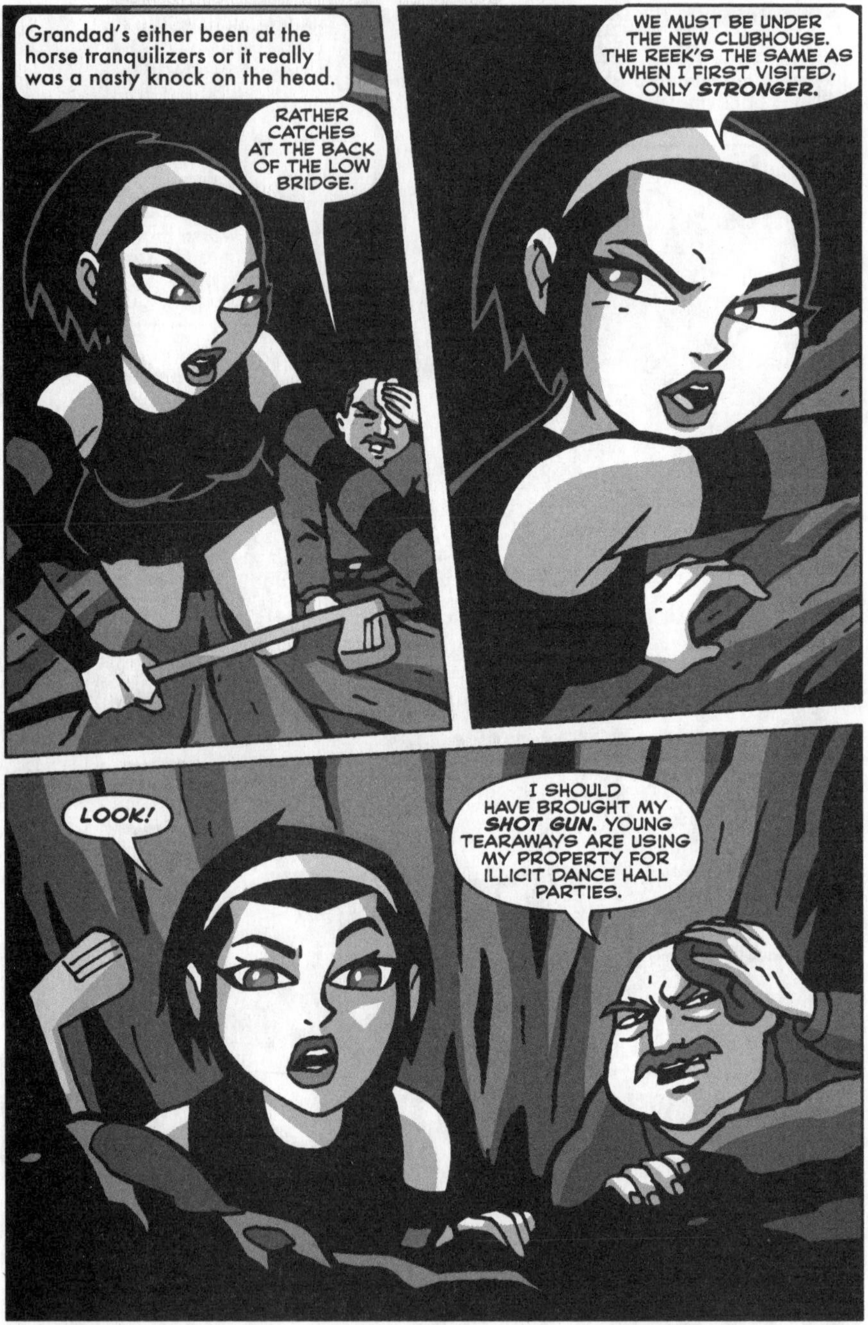
Grandad's either been at the horse tranquilizers or it really was a nasty knock on the head.
RATHER CATCHES AT THE BACK OF THE LOW BRIDGE.
WE MUST BE UNDER THE NEW CLUBHOUSE. THE REEK'S THE SAME AS WHEN I FIRST VISITED, ONLY *STRONGER.*
LOOK!
I SHOULD HAVE BROUGHT MY *SHOT GUN.* YOUNG TEARAWAYS ARE USING MY PROPERTY FOR ILLICIT DANCE HALL PARTIES.

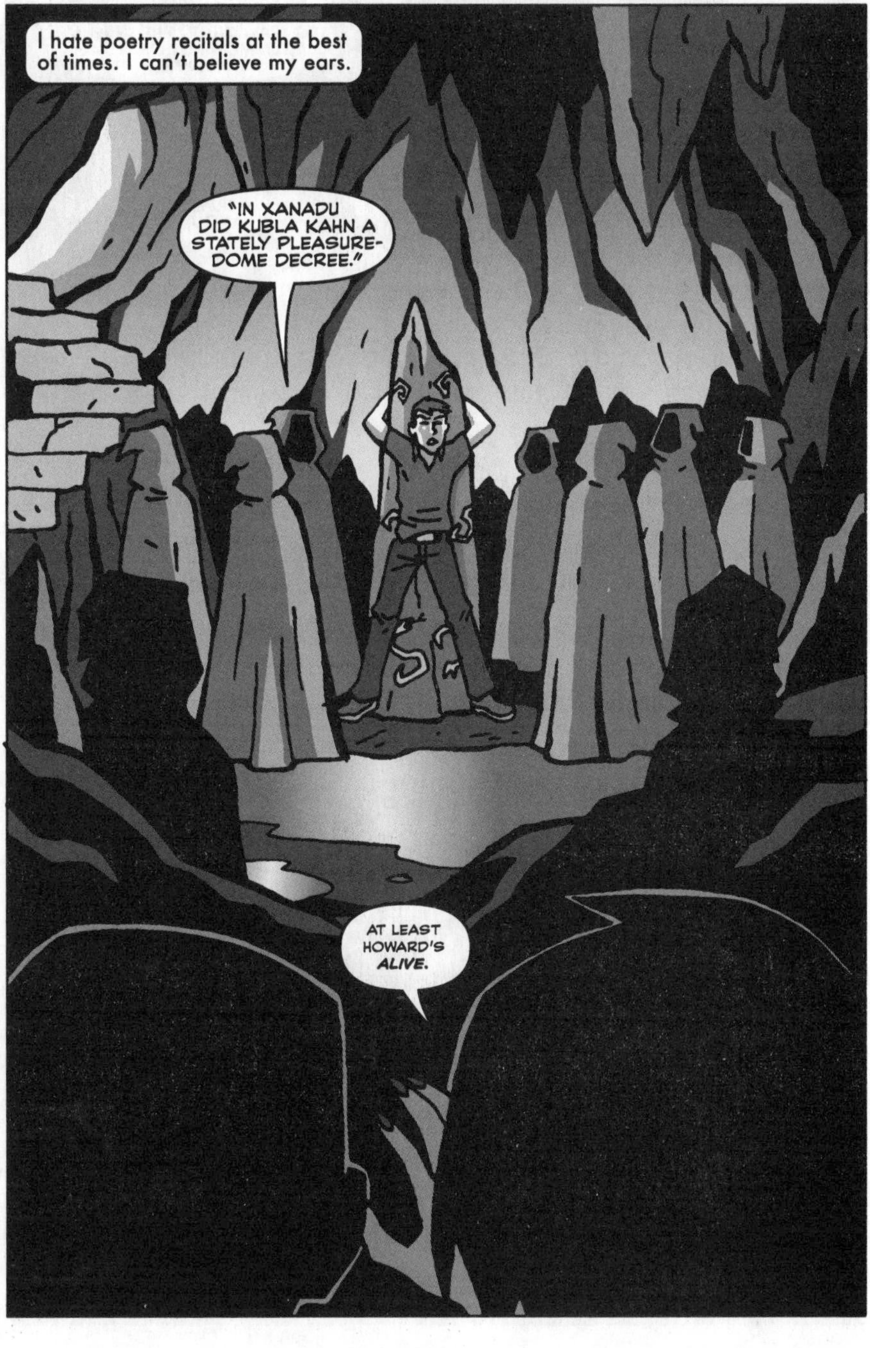
I hate poetry recitals at the best of times. I can't believe my ears.
"IN XANADU DID KUBLA KAHN A STATELY PLEASURE-DOME DECREE."
AT LEAST HOWARD'S *ALIVE*.

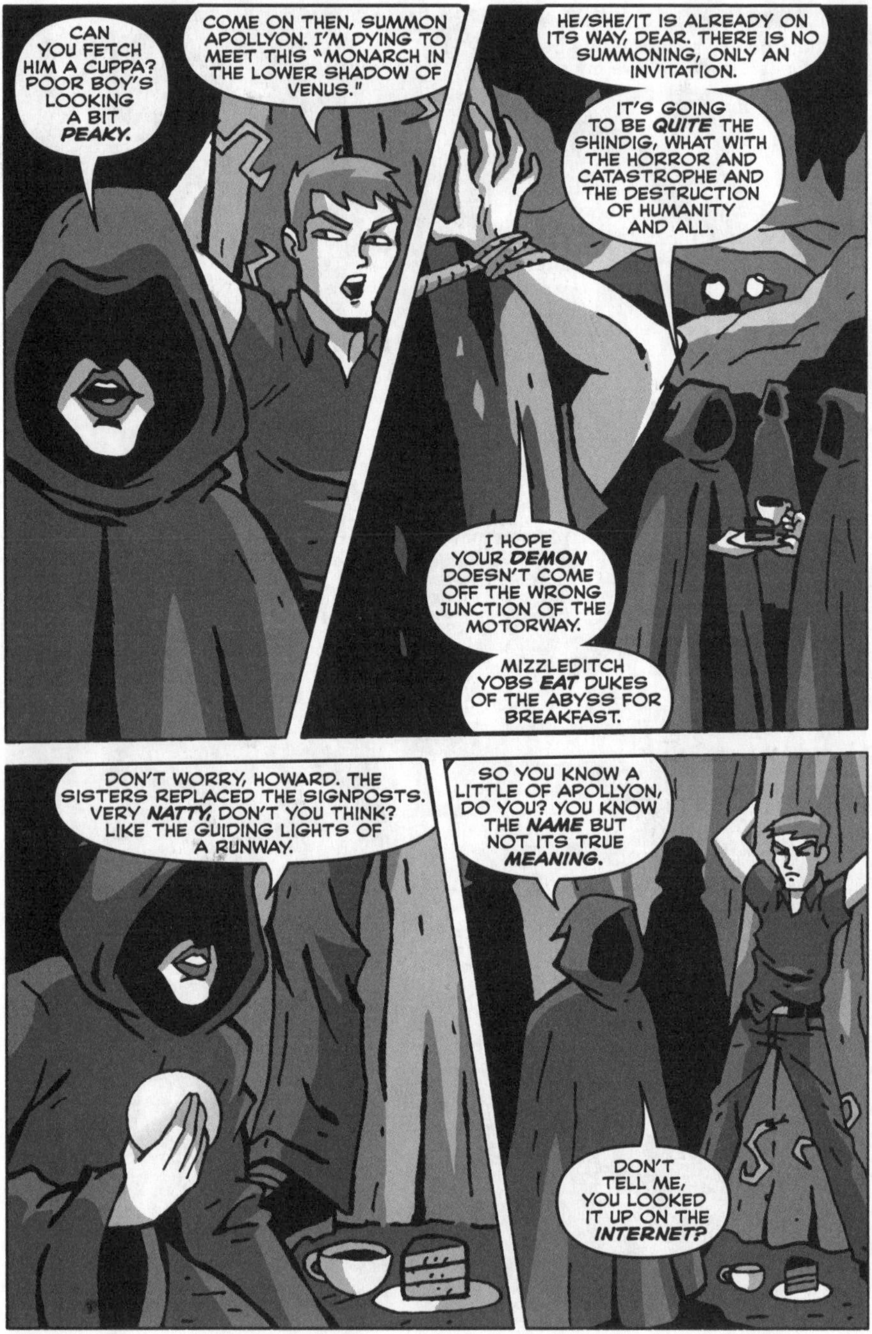
CAN YOU FETCH HIM A CUPPA? POOR BOY'S LOOKING A BIT **PEAKY.**
COME ON THEN, SUMMON APOLLYON. I'M DYING TO MEET THIS "MONARCH IN THE LOWER SHADOW OF VENUS."
HE/SHE/IT IS ALREADY ON ITS WAY, DEAR. THERE IS NO SUMMONING, ONLY AN INVITATION.
IT'S GOING TO BE **QUITE** THE SHINDIG, WHAT WITH THE HORROR AND CATASTROPHE AND THE DESTRUCTION OF HUMANITY AND ALL.
I HOPE YOUR **DEMON** DOESN'T COME OFF THE WRONG JUNCTION OF THE MOTORWAY.
MIZZLEDITCH YOBS **EAT** DUKES OF THE ABYSS FOR BREAKFAST.
DON'T WORRY, HOWARD. THE SISTERS REPLACED THE SIGNPOSTS. VERY **NATTY,** DON'T YOU THINK? LIKE THE GUIDING LIGHTS OF A RUNWAY.
SO YOU KNOW A LITTLE OF APOLLYON, DO YOU? YOU KNOW THE **NAME** BUT NOT ITS TRUE **MEANING.**
DON'T TELL ME, YOU LOOKED IT UP ON THE **INTERNET?**

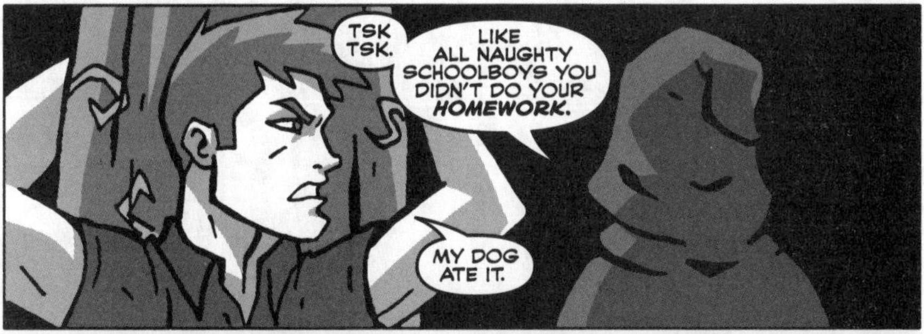
TSK TSK.
LIKE ALL NAUGHTY SCHOOLBOYS YOU DIDN'T DO YOUR **HOMEWORK.**
MY DOG ATE IT.

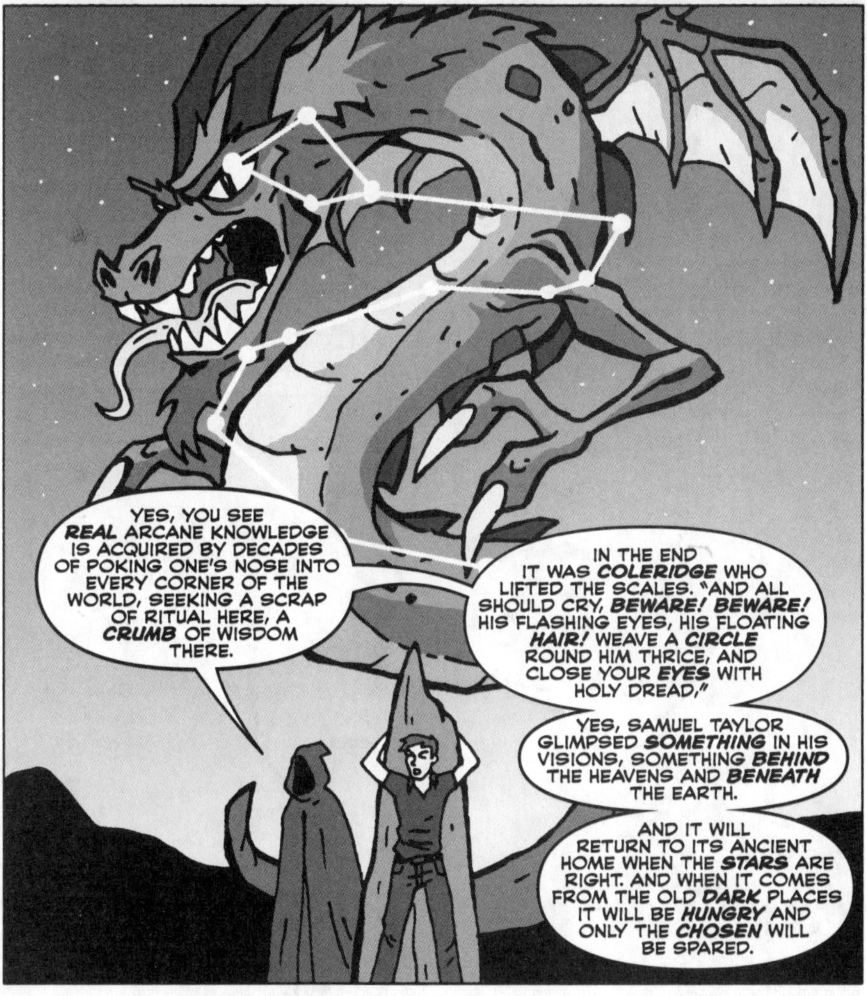
YES, YOU SEE **REAL** ARCANE KNOWLEDGE IS ACQUIRED BY DECADES OF POKING ONE'S NOSE INTO EVERY CORNER OF THE WORLD, SEEKING A SCRAP OF RITUAL HERE, A **CRUMB** OF WISDOM THERE.
IN THE END IT WAS **COLERIDGE** WHO LIFTED THE SCALES. "AND ALL SHOULD CRY, **BEWARE! BEWARE!** HIS FLASHING EYES, HIS FLOATING **HAIR!** WEAVE A **CIRCLE** ROUND HIM THRICE, AND CLOSE YOUR **EYES** WITH HOLY DREAD,"
YES, SAMUEL TAYLOR GLIMPSED **SOMETHING** IN HIS VISIONS, SOMETHING **BEHIND** THE HEAVENS AND **BENEATH** THE EARTH.
AND IT WILL RETURN TO ITS ANCIENT HOME WHEN THE **STARS** ARE RIGHT. AND WHEN IT COMES FROM THE OLD **DARK** PLACES IT WILL BE **HUNGRY** AND ONLY THE **CHOSEN** WILL BE SPARED.

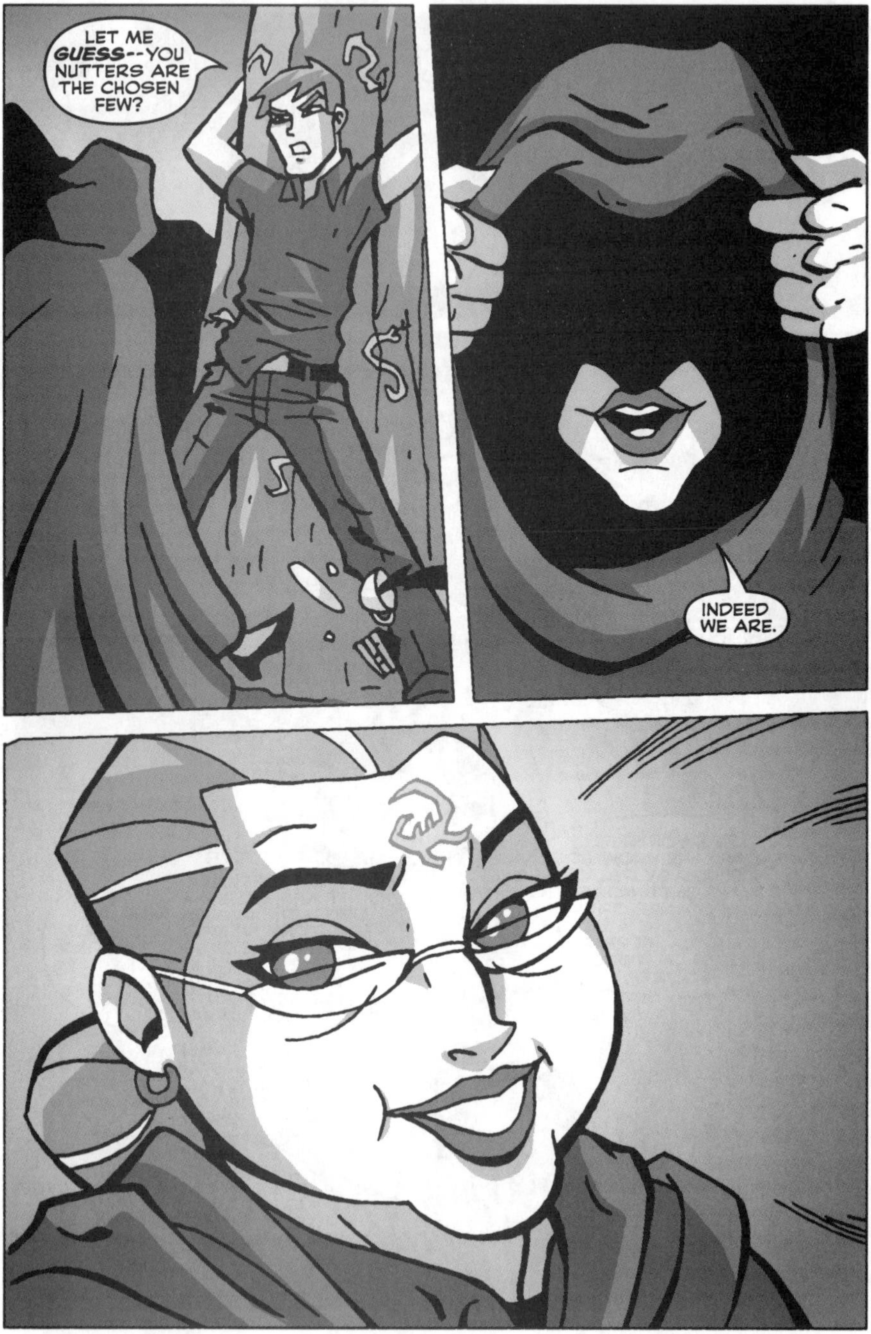
LET ME GUESS--YOU NUTTERS ARE THE CHOSEN FEW?
INDEED WE ARE.

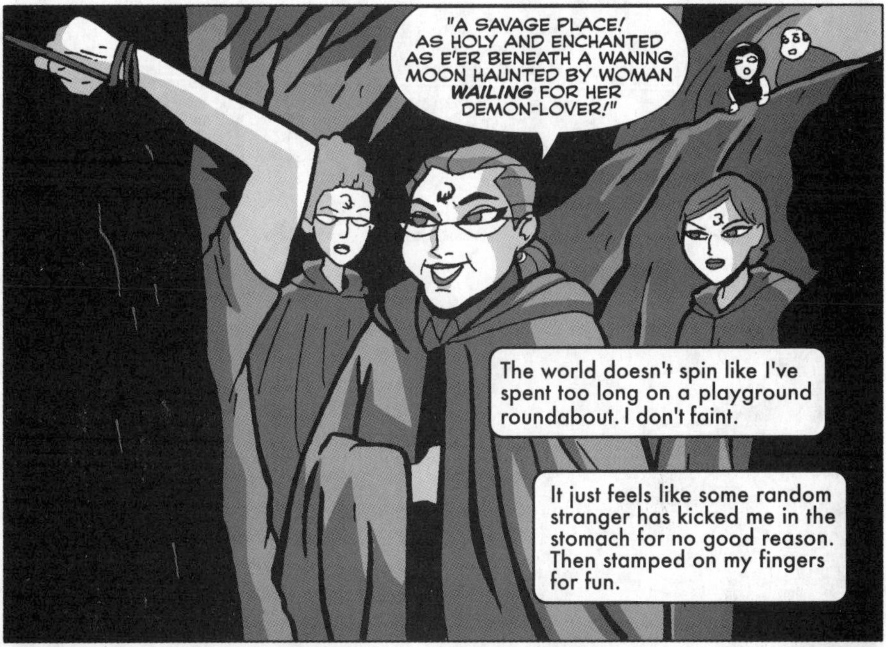
"A SAVAGE PLACE! AS HOLY AND ENCHANTED AS E'ER BENEATH A WANING MOON HAUNTED BY WOMAN *WAILING* FOR HER DEMON-LOVER!"
The world doesn't spin like I've spent too long on a playground roundabout. I don't faint.
It just feels like some random stranger has kicked me in the stomach for no good reason. Then stamped on my fingers for fun.

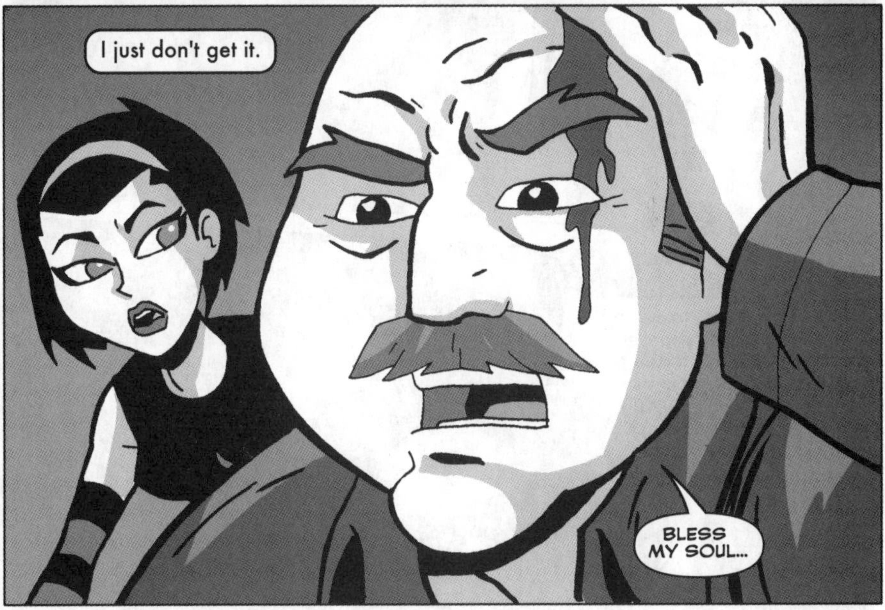
I just don't get it.
BLESS MY SOUL...

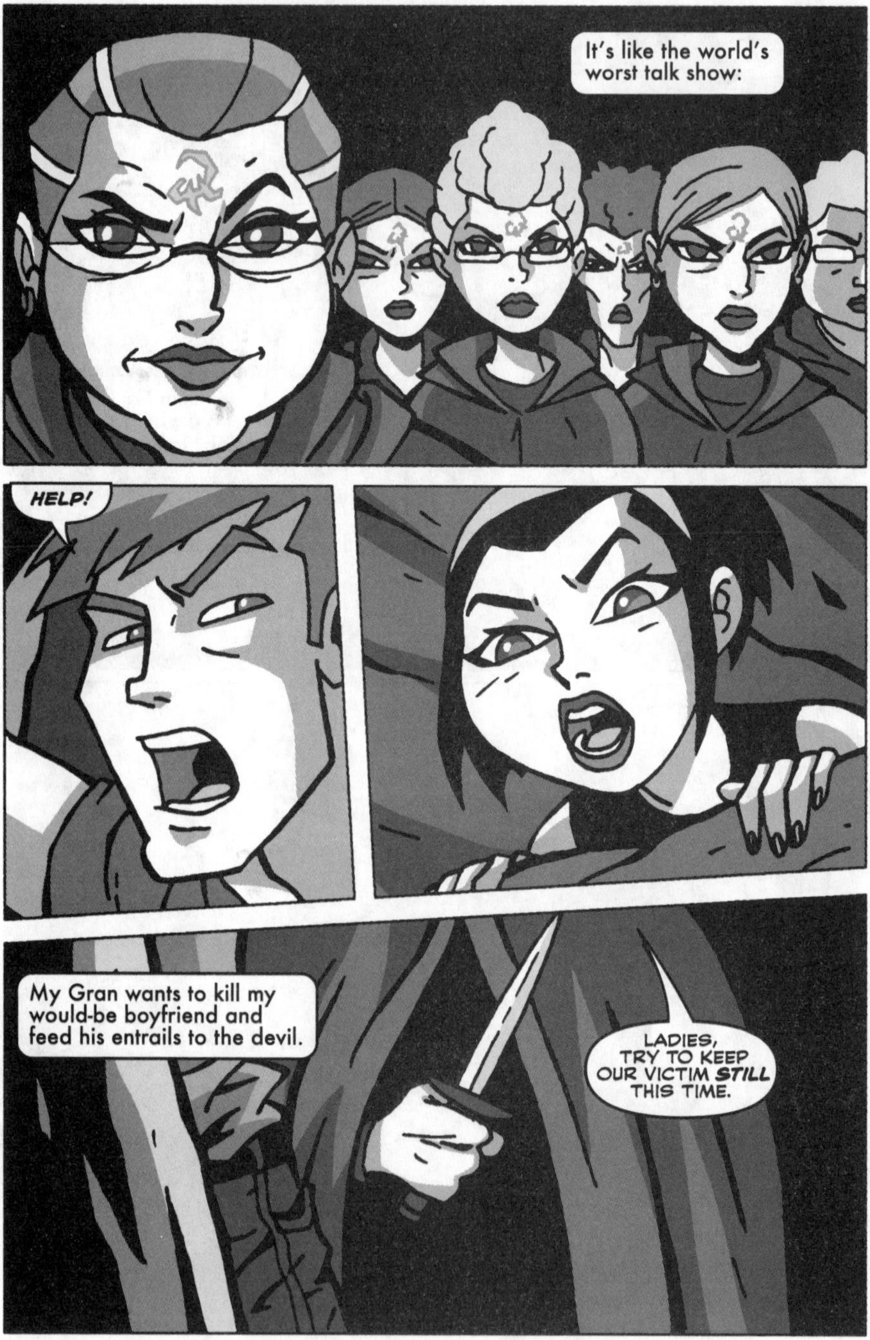
It's like the world's worst talk show:
HELP!
My Gran wants to kill my would-be boyfriend and feed his entrails to the devil.
LADIES, TRY TO KEEP OUR VICTIM STILL THIS TIME.

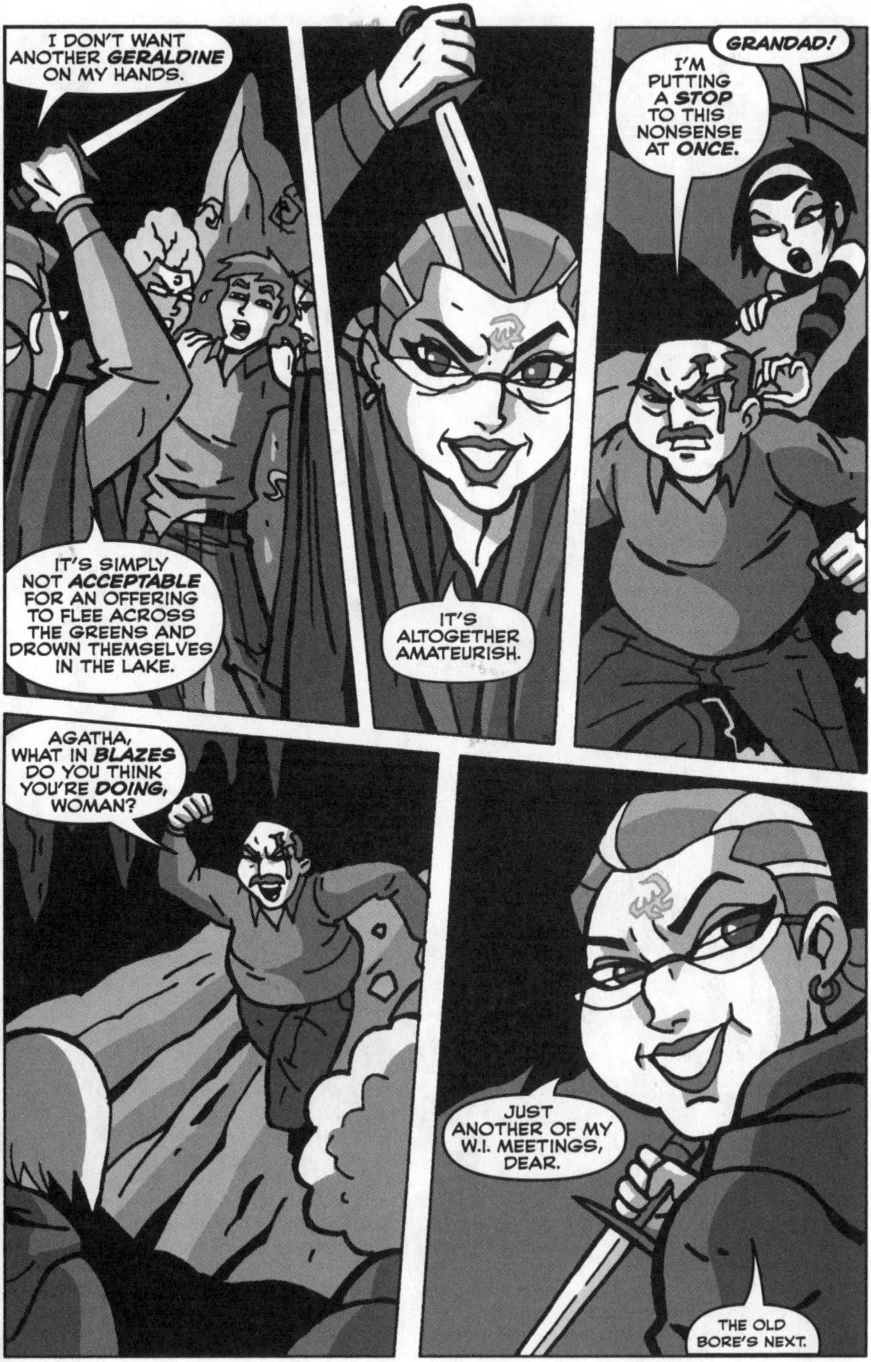

I DON'T WANT ANOTHER GERALDINE ON MY HANDS.
IT'S SIMPLY NOT ACCEPTABLE FOR AN OFFERING TO FLEE ACROSS THE GREENS AND DROWN THEMSELVES IN THE LAKE.
IT'S ALTOGETHER AMATEURISH.
GRANDAD!
I'M PUTTING A STOP TO THIS NONSENSE AT ONCE.
AGATHA, WHAT IN BLAZES DO YOU THINK YOU'RE DOING, WOMAN?
JUST ANOTHER OF MY W.I. MEETINGS, DEAR.
THE OLD BORE'S NEXT.

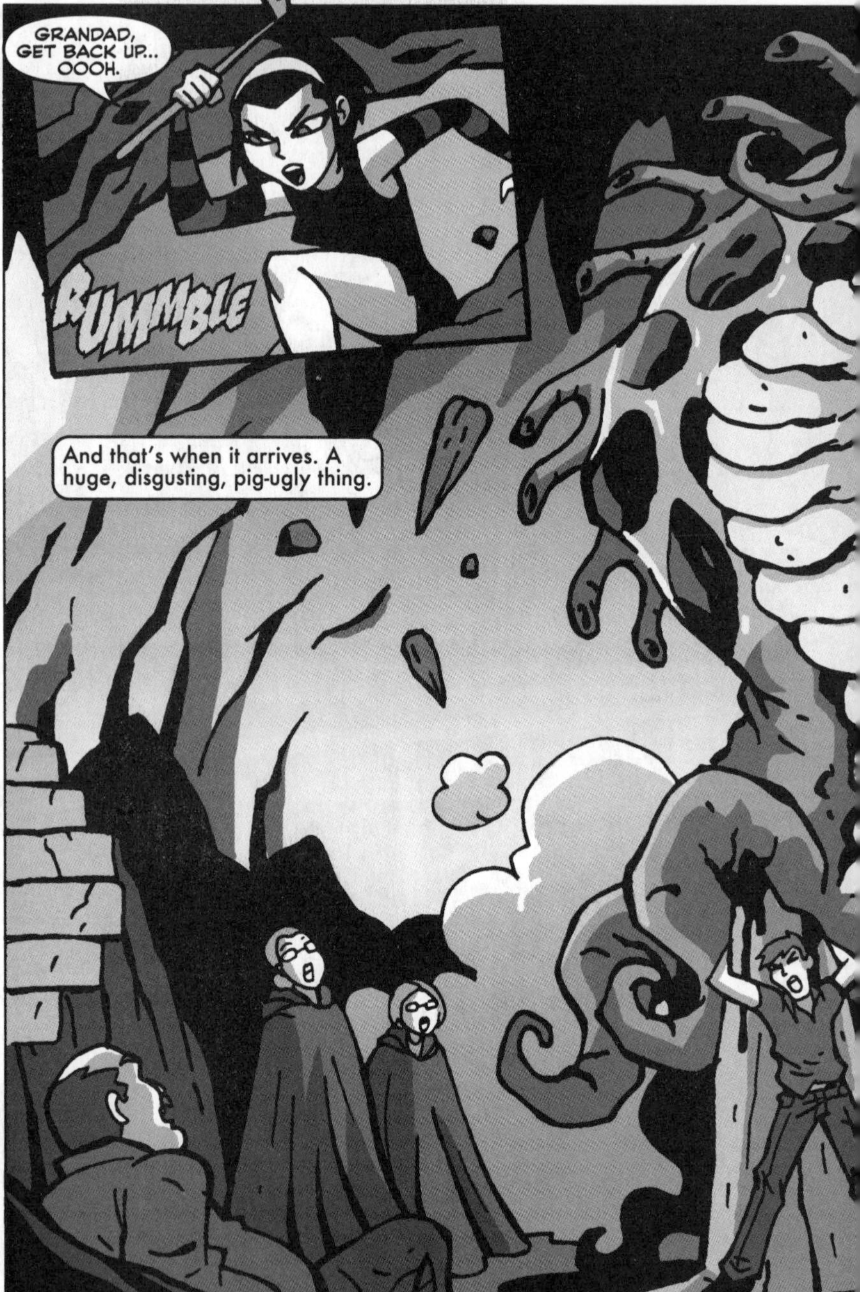
GRANDAD, GET BACK UP... OOOH.
RUMMBLE
And that's when it arrives. A huge, disgusting, pig-ugly thing.

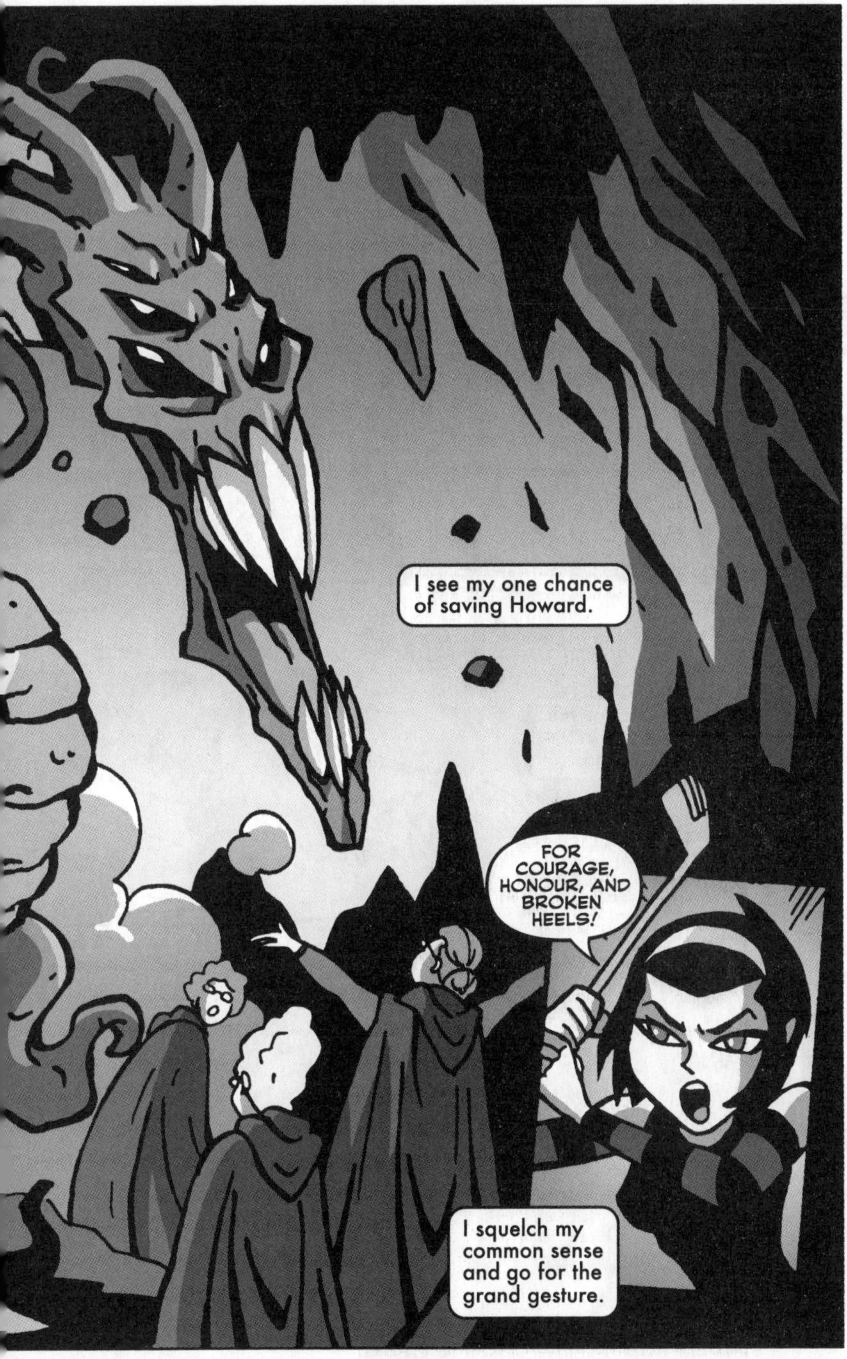
I see my one chance of saving Howard.
FOR COURAGE, HONOUR, AND BROKEN HEELS!
I squelch my common sense and go for the grand gesture.

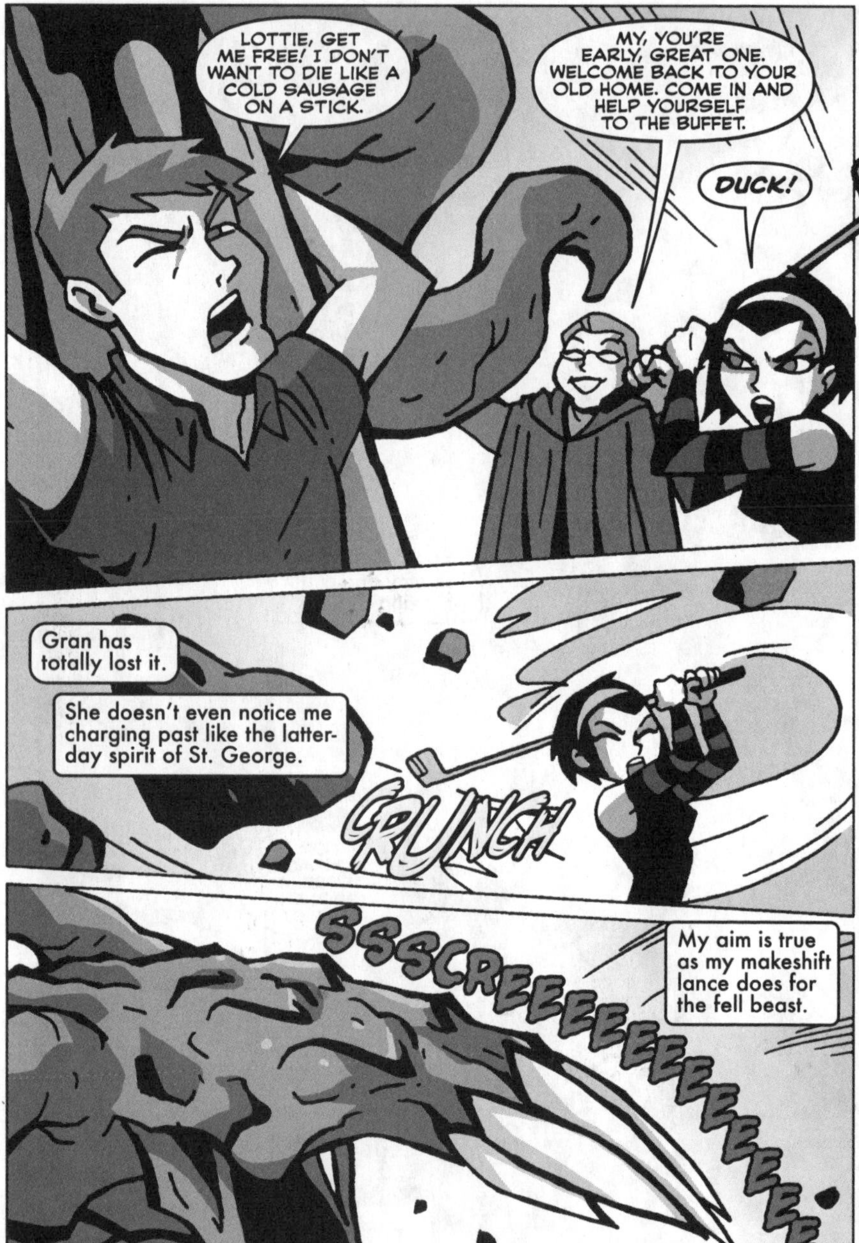
LOTTIE, GET ME FREE! I DON'T WANT TO DIE LIKE A COLD SAUSAGE ON A STICK.
MY, YOU'RE EARLY, GREAT ONE. WELCOME BACK TO YOUR OLD HOME. COME IN AND HELP YOURSELF TO THE BUFFET.
DUCK!
Gran has totally lost it.
She doesn't even notice me charging past like the latter-day spirit of St. George.
CRUNCH
SSSCREEEEEEEEEEEEEEEEE
My aim is true as my makeshift lance does for the fell beast.

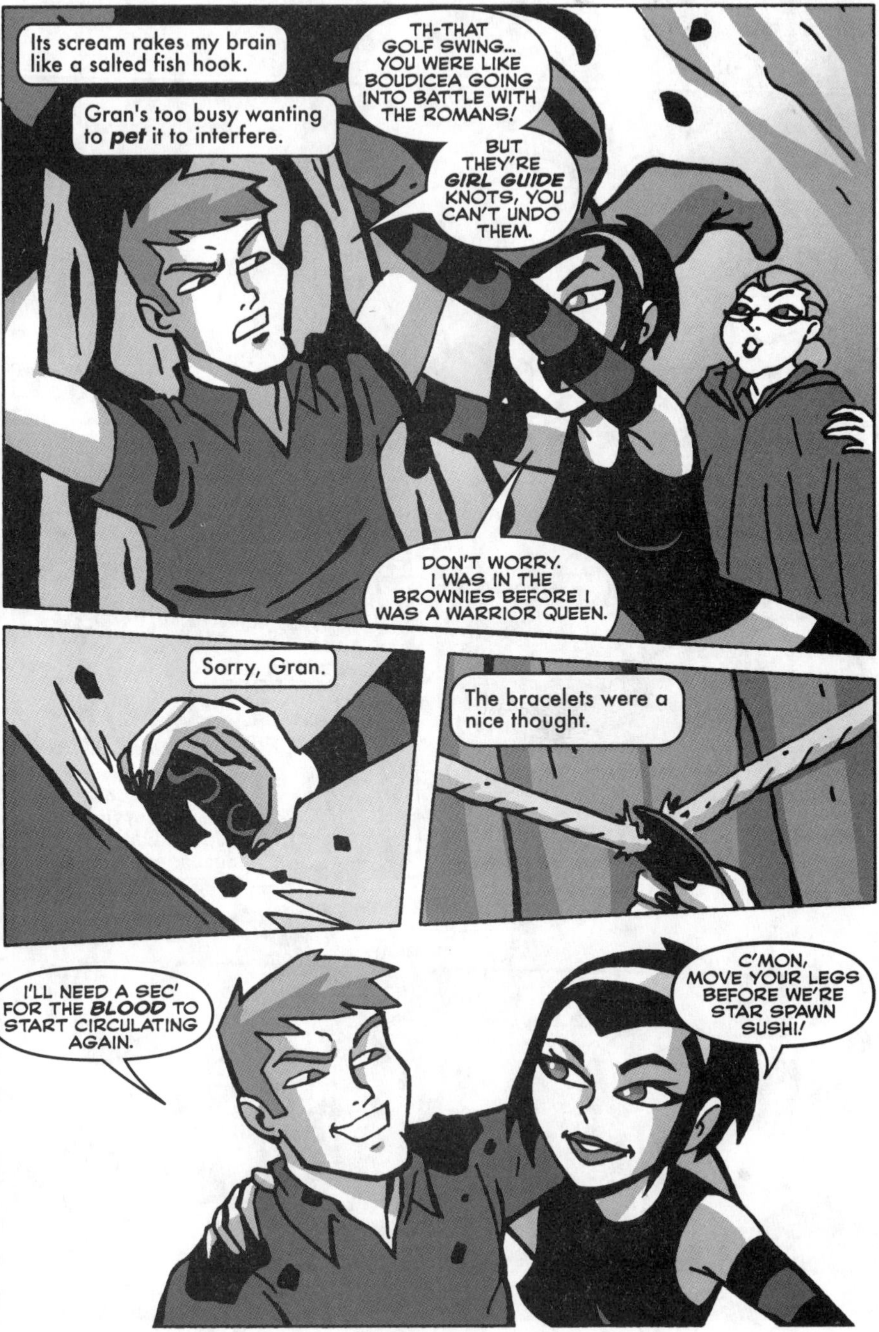
Its scream rakes my brain like a salted fish hook.
Gran's too busy wanting to ***pet*** it to interfere.
TH-THAT GOLF SWING... YOU WERE LIKE BOUDICEA GOING INTO BATTLE WITH THE ROMANS!
BUT THEY'RE ***GIRL GUIDE*** KNOTS, YOU CAN'T UNDO THEM.
DON'T WORRY. I WAS IN THE BROWNIES BEFORE I WAS A WARRIOR QUEEN.
Sorry, Gran.
The bracelets were a nice thought.
I'LL NEED A SEC' FOR THE ***BLOOD*** TO START CIRCULATING AGAIN.
C'MON, MOVE YOUR LEGS BEFORE WE'RE STAR SPAWN SUSHI!

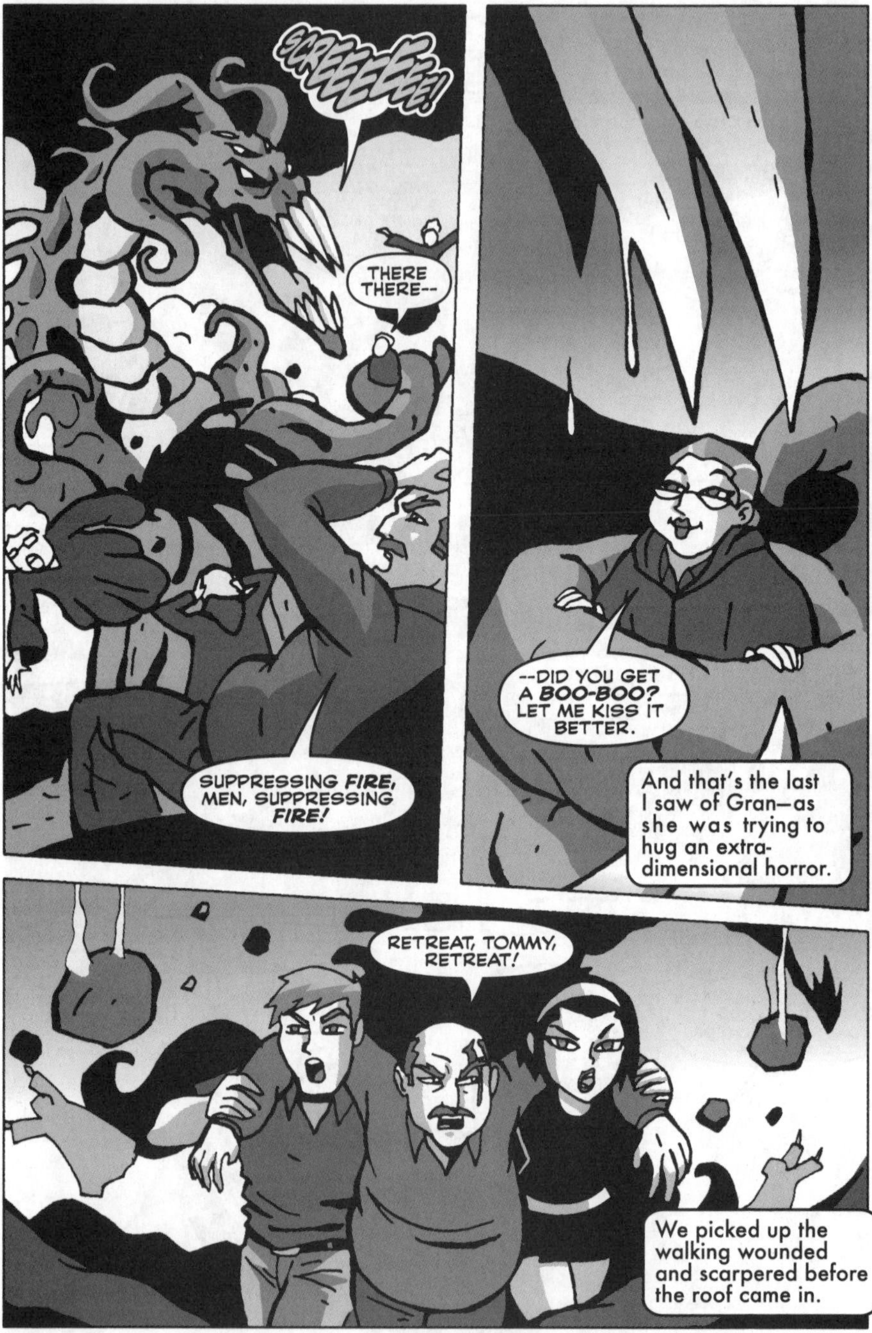
SCREEEEEEEE!
THERE THERE--
SUPPRESSING FIRE, MEN, SUPPRESSING FIRE!
--DID YOU GET A BOO-BOO? LET ME KISS IT BETTER.
And that's the last I saw of Gran—as she was trying to hug an extra-dimensional horror.
RETREAT, TOMMY, RETREAT!
We picked up the walking wounded and scarpered before the roof came in.

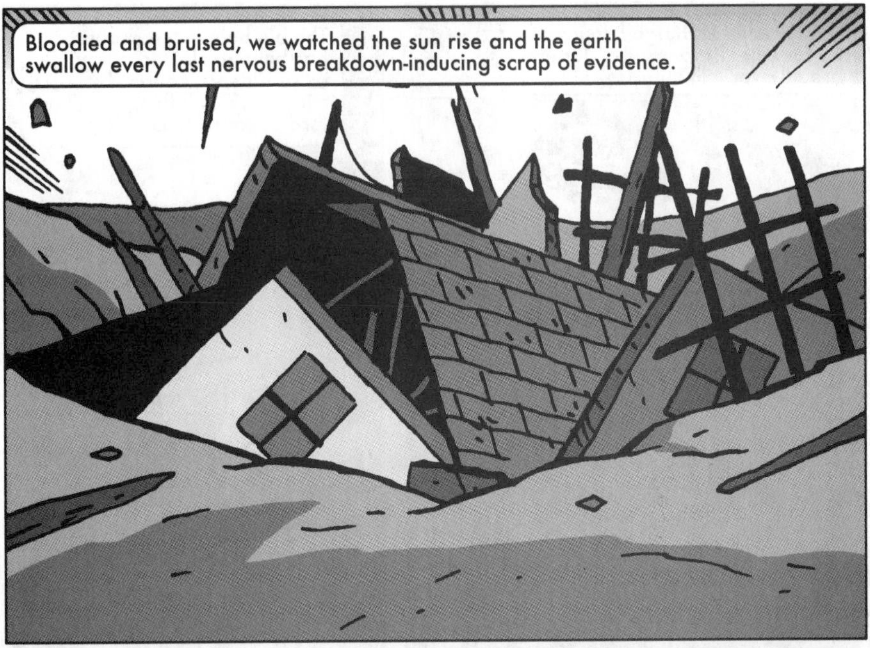
Bloodied and bruised, we watched the sun rise and the earth swallow every last nervous breakdown-inducing scrap of evidence.

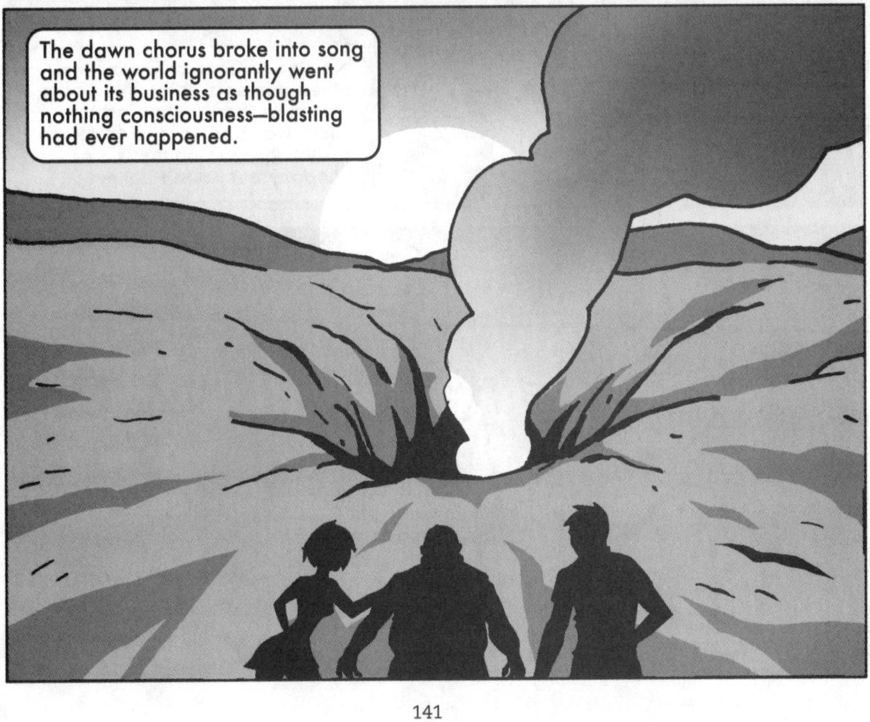
The dawn chorus broke into song and the world ignorantly went about its business as though nothing consciousness—blasting had ever happened.

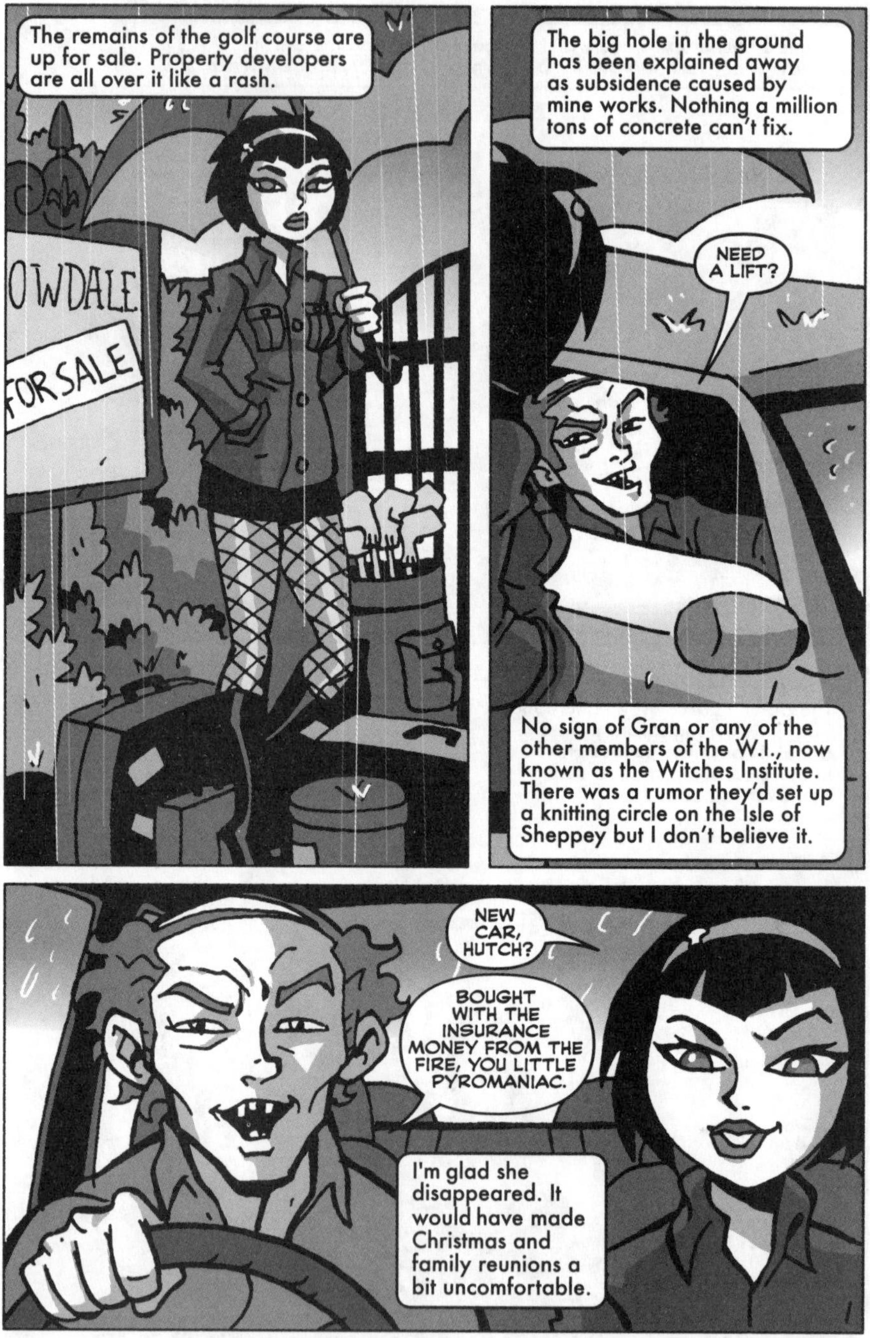
The remains of the golf course are up for sale. Property developers are all over it like a rash.
OWDALE
FOR SALE
The big hole in the ground has been explained away as subsidence caused by mine works. Nothing a million tons of concrete can't fix.
NEED A LIFT?
No sign of Gran or any of the other members of the W.I., now known as the Witches Institute. There was a rumor they'd set up a knitting circle on the Isle of Sheppey but I don't believe it.
NEW CAR, HUTCH?
BOUGHT WITH THE INSURANCE MONEY FROM THE FIRE, YOU LITTLE PYROMANIAC.
I'm glad she disappeared. It would have made Christmas and family reunions a bit uncomfortable.

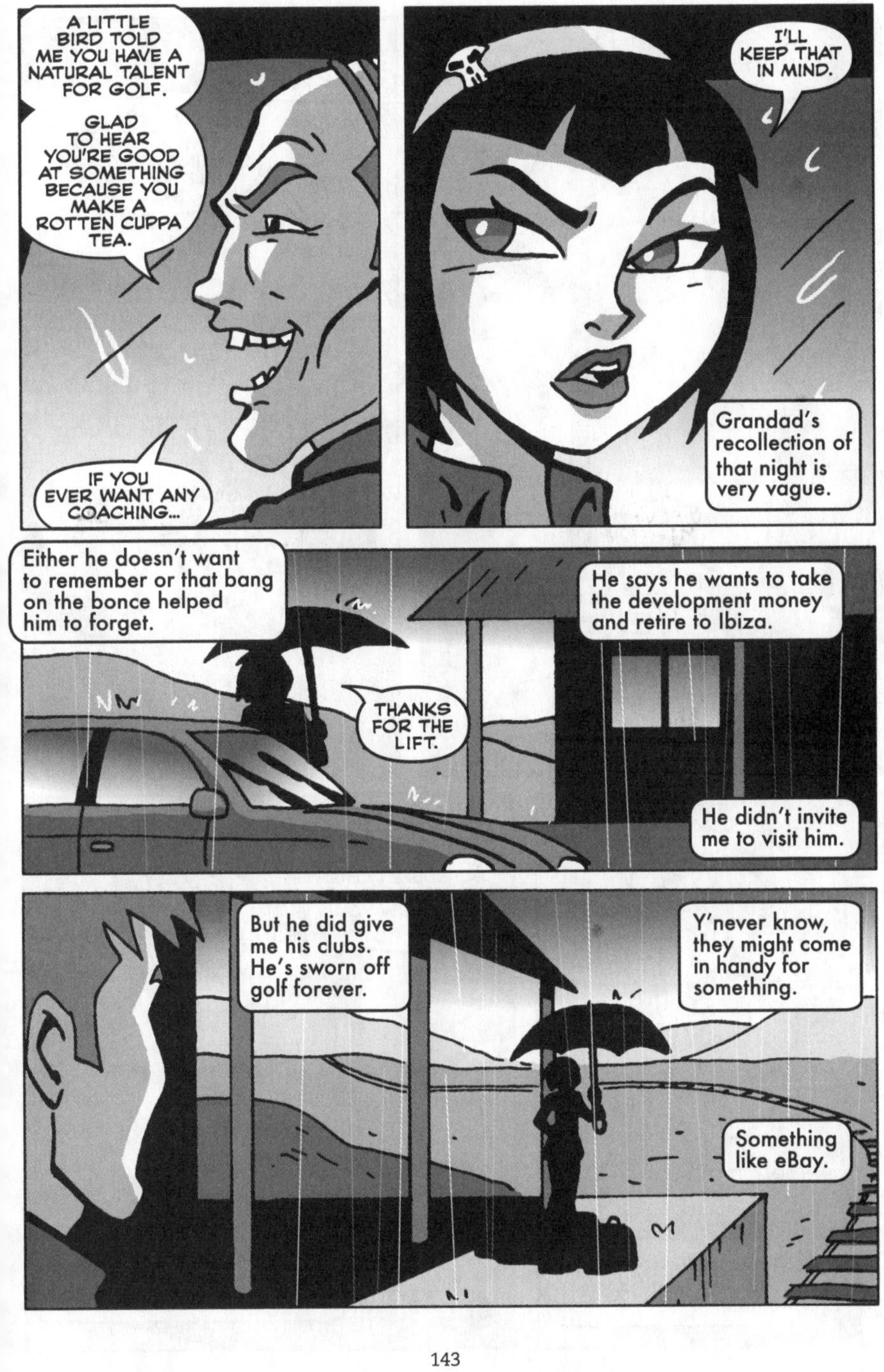
A LITTLE BIRD TOLD ME YOU HAVE A NATURAL TALENT FOR GOLF.
GLAD TO HEAR YOU'RE GOOD AT SOMETHING BECAUSE YOU MAKE A ROTTEN CUPPA TEA.
IF YOU EVER WANT ANY COACHING...
I'LL KEEP THAT IN MIND.
Grandad's recollection of that night is very vague.
Either he doesn't want to remember or that bang on the bonce helped him to forget.
THANKS FOR THE LIFT.
He says he wants to take the development money and retire to Ibiza.
He didn't invite me to visit him.
But he did give me his clubs. He's sworn off golf forever.
Y'never know, they might come in handy for something.
Something like eBay.

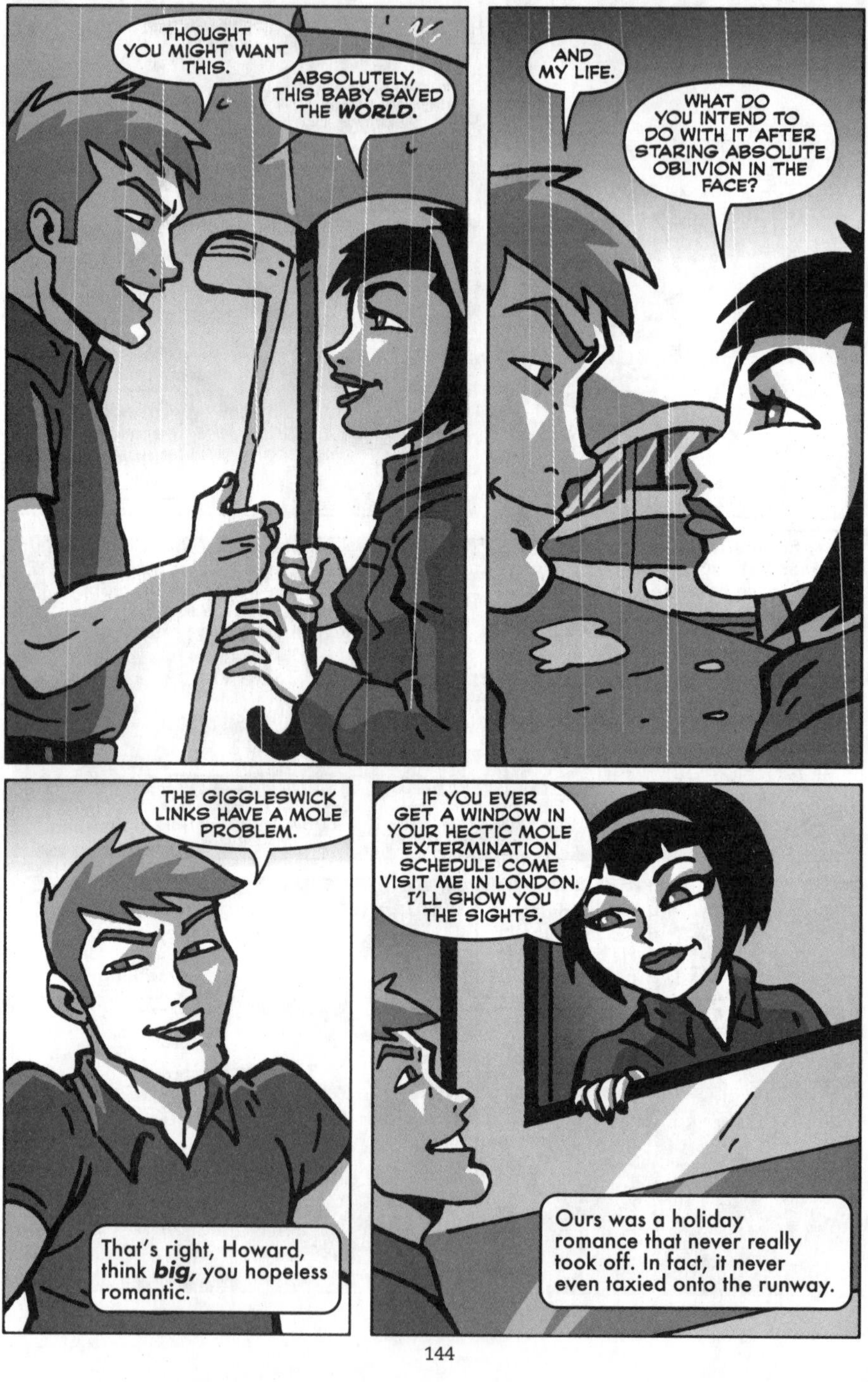
THOUGHT YOU MIGHT WANT THIS.
ABSOLUTELY, THIS BABY SAVED THE **WORLD.**
AND MY LIFE.
WHAT DO YOU INTEND TO DO WITH IT AFTER STARING ABSOLUTE OBLIVION IN THE FACE?
THE GIGGLESWICK LINKS HAVE A MOLE PROBLEM.
That's right, Howard, think ***big,*** you hopeless romantic.
IF YOU EVER GET A WINDOW IN YOUR HECTIC MOLE EXTERMINATION SCHEDULE COME VISIT ME IN LONDON. I'LL SHOW YOU THE SIGHTS.
Ours was a holiday romance that never really took off. In fact, it never even taxied onto the runway.

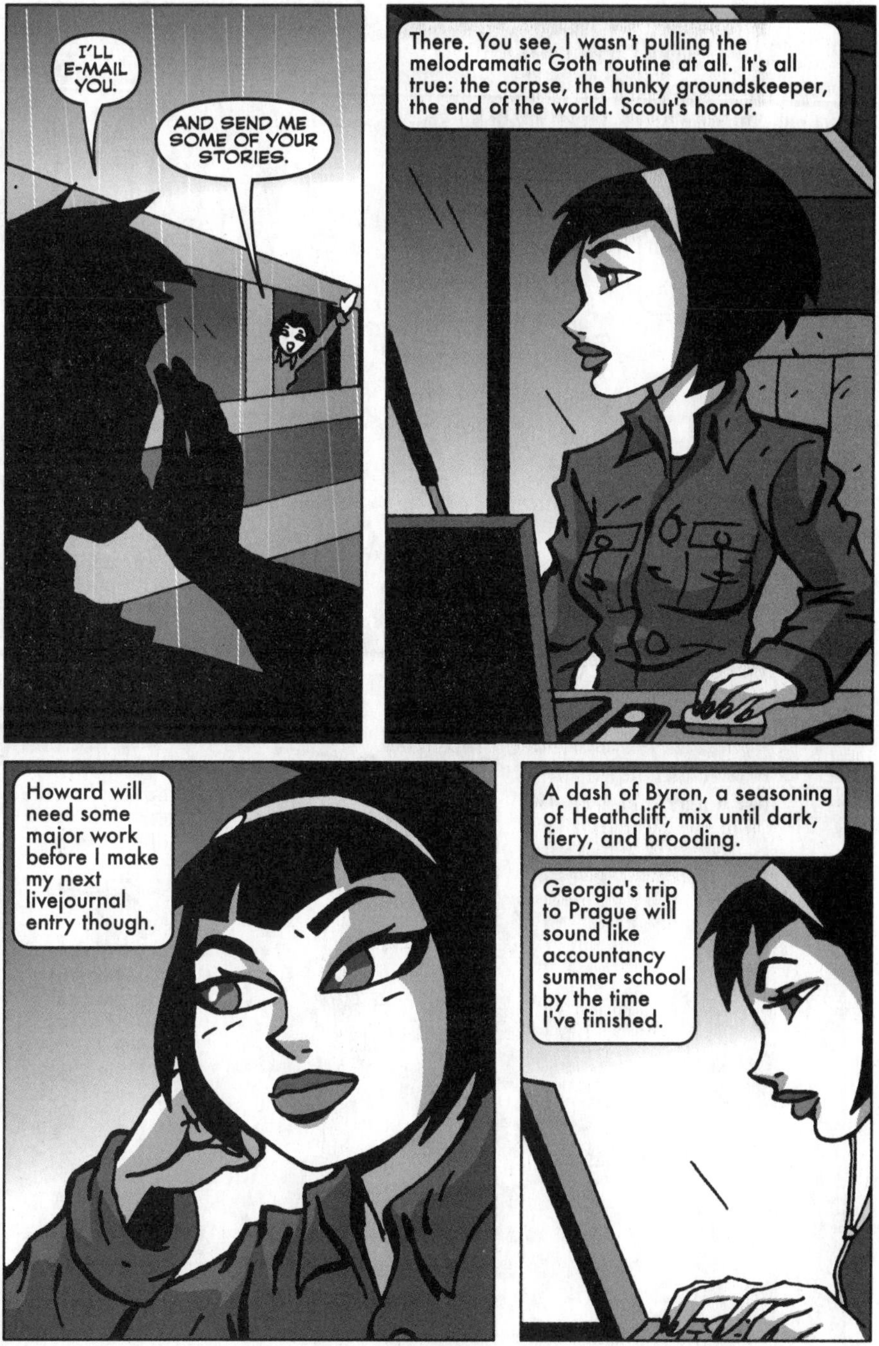
I'LL E-MAIL YOU.
AND SEND ME SOME OF YOUR STORIES.
There. You see, I wasn't pulling the melodramatic Goth routine at all. It's all true: the corpse, the hunky groundskeeper, the end of the world. Scout's honor.
Howard will need some major work before I make my next livejournal entry though.
A dash of Byron, a seasoning of Heathcliff, mix until dark, fiery, and brooding.
Georgia's trip to Prague will sound like accountancy summer school by the time I've finished.

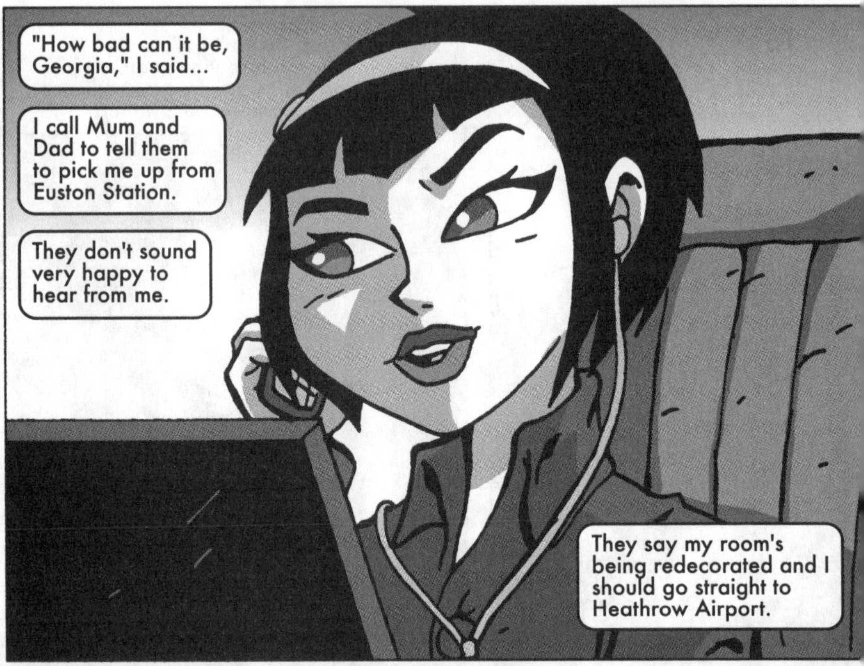
"How bad can it be, Georgia," I said...
I call Mum and Dad to tell them to pick me up from Euston Station.
They don't sound very happy to hear from me.
They say my room's being redecorated and I should go straight to Heathrow Airport.

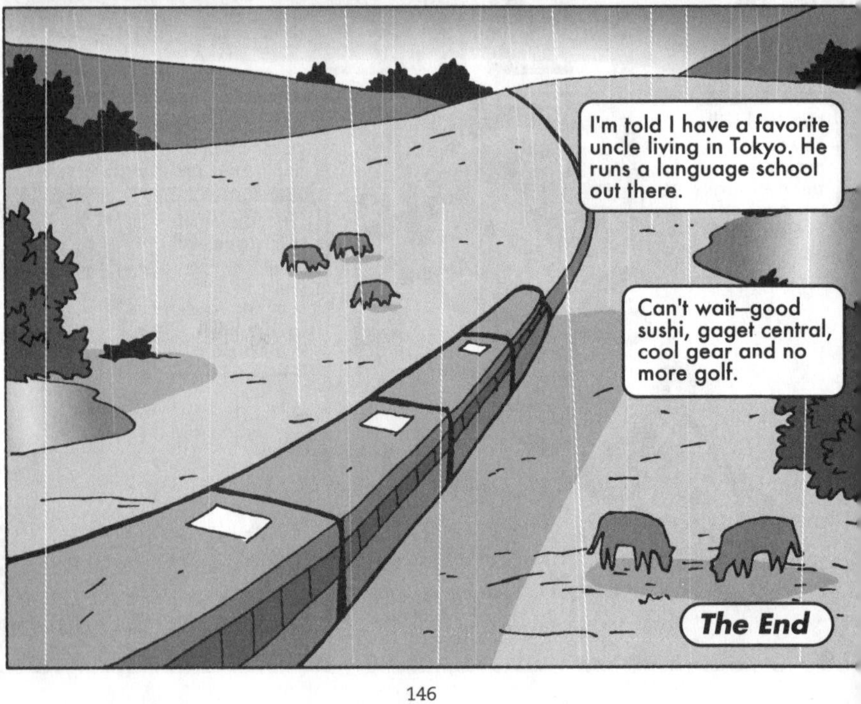
I'm told I have a favorite uncle living in Tokyo. He runs a language school out there.
Can't wait–good sushi, gaget central, cool gear and no more golf.
The End

lottie's lexicon

lottie's lexicon

Battled - struggled, wrestled with

David Beckham - world-famous footballer (soccer player), married to Posh Spice

Bedlam - insane asylum

Biddies - old biddies, old ladies

Big to-do - argument

Bit of a domestic - argument between the partners in a romantic relationship, a domestic row

Bogged off - gone away

Bonce - head

Bonkers - mad/crazy

Britishism - any custom, manner, characteristic, or quality peculiar to or associated with the British people

Butlins - old-fashioned holiday camp

Cheek - sassy, impudent

Cider - hard cider, with alcoholic content

Coleridge - Samuel Taylor Coleridge 1772-1834, romantic poet and pal of William Wordsworth. Lived in the Lake District

Compost - silage, animal fertilizer

Cuppa - cup of a hot beverage, usually tea or coffee

Dandelion & Burdock - peculiar to Britain, made from fermented dandelion and burdock roots

Darts - sport enjoyed by fat men in gaudy shirts

Laura Davies - successful woman golfer from Coventry, England

Down South - catchall term used in the north of England to categorize anyone hailing from south of Birmingham. Birmingham's in the middle.

Ear bashing - shouted at

Emmeline Pankhurst - 1858-1928, British suffragette. It was Emily Davison who stepped in front of the King's horse in 1913.

F1 - Formula One car racing

Franz Kafka - Czech funny-man who wrote hilarious tales about people turning into cockroaches and being persecuted by a surreal, bureaucratic state

Frock - dress

Full to the gunwales - full to overflowing

Funny-trousered - wearing unusual garments on the legs

Gee and Tees - gin and tonic cocktail, favorite of Bertie Wooster

Get stuffed - go away, get lost, remove yourself from my sight immediately

Giggleswick Links - fiendishly difficult eighteen-hole golf course, historically plagued by moles

Glastonbury - the granddaddy of all music festivals. Home to the smell of fried tofuburgers, wet hippies, and overflowing porta-potties

Gnome - Painted pottery garden gnomes were introduced to the U.K. in 1847 and are banned from the Chelsea Flower Show

Got its ferret teeth in me - Once a ferret has bitten you, it's difficult to dislodge it.

Hit you for six - In the game of cricket, hitting the ball over the boundary scores six runs. Hit hard.

Laddered - a run in tights or pantyhose

Lake District - U.K. national park in Cumbria in the North of England. Famous for mountains, rain, and...lakes

Lawnmower hospital - where ill grass-cutting tools go to get well

Long Meg - a Bronze Age stone circle

Lug holes - ears

The Mail - *The Daily Mail*, popular right-wing daily newspaper in the U.K.

Miss Havishams - the archetypal bitter spinster who was left at the altar in Charles Dickens's novel *Great Expectations*, published in 1861

Namby-pamby - soft/effeminate

Natty - clever/ingenious/smart

Nicked - stolen. Also means to be arrested by the police.

Nutters - mentally unstable individuals

Offy - off license, shop that sells alcohol and snacks

Oh my giddy aunt - Flippin' Eck! An exclamation of surprise without resorting to foul language

Old duffer - elderly individual

Panda Shandy - cheap soda, a mix of lemonade and a small amount of beer

Peaky - peaked/ill looking/under the weather

Pensioner - drawing their pension, an older person

Play the lie - hit the ball from the exact spot it came to rest

Playground roundabout - merry-go-round, used to spin children around until they are either thrown off or feel sick

Plods - P.C. Plod, the police

Pork scratchings - a snack made of deep-fried pig skin. Hutch prefers his with hair still attached.

Pound - pound sterling, the currency of the U.K., issued by the Bank of England. Also known as a "quid"

Rabbiting - talking incessantly

Rags - newspapers

Rosette - a rose-shaped ribbon given to competition winners

Ruskin - John Ruskin, 1819-1900, art critic and author famous for his bust-up with painter James McNeill Whistler

Scarpered - run away/fled

Septuagenarians - seventy-year-olds, old folk, retirees

Shop mobility trolley - small motorized vehicles used by those unable to walk for long distances/golf carts

Skivvying - doing menial domestic chores

Snogging - kissing

Stroppy - upset/cross/angry

Swotting - researching/homework/studying a subject

Taking the mickey - extracting the urine, making fun of

The Bill - U.K. cop show featuring bobbies on the beat

Tombolla - money raiser for charity. Dip your hand into a bucket full of tickets. Pull out a numbered ticket. Match the ticket to the same number stuck on to the prize. Weep when you discover your prize is a jar of homemade cauliflower chutney.

Top herself - commit suicide

Torchlight - by flashlight

Victoria sponge - cake with whipped cream and jam filling. A favorite of Queen Victoria.

Walkers cheese and onion crisps - chips

Waterproofs *(see Wellies)* - items of clothing that keep out water

Wellies - Wellington boots, galoshes, waterproof footware

What're you on about? - What are you talking about?

Women's Institute - members club for ladies, famous for selling jam and cakes at village fêtes and raising money for charity

Bernie Wooster - the archetypal well-meaning but chronically befuddled character created by P.G. Wodehouse

Wrong end of the stick - a misunderstanding

Wyrm - worm/dragon loosely based on the legend of the Lambton Worm

Yoofs - young people

Yorkshire puds - Yorkshire puddings. Made from similar ingredients as pancakes but cooked in the oven in small, circular, aluminum trays

Young offenders - juvenile prison

ANDI WATSON

Born & Bred: Leeds, England.
Art School: Liverpool.
Penniless post-grad: London.
Penniless cartoonist: Brighton,
California, Abingdon.
Cartoonist: Wolverhampton,
Stoke-on-Trent.
Graphic Novels: *Samurai Jam,
Skeleton Key, Geisha, Breakfast
After Noon, Slow News Day,
Love Fights, Paris, Little Star.*
Likes: books, cakes, tea, rain,
Brussels sprouts, Kate Bush.
Avoids: daytime telly,
exercise, celery.

www.andiwatson.biz

JOSH HOWARD

Josh is the artist and writer
of *Dead @ 17 (Viper Comics)*,
named by *Wizard Magazine* as
the #1 independent book to
watch in 2005. His other work
includes *Black Harvest (Devil's Due)*
and *The Lost Books of Eve
(Viper Comics)*. Josh lives in
Arlington, Texas with his wife
and two children.

S P E C I A L   B A C K S T A G E   P A S S :

If you liked the story you've just read, fear not: Other MINX books will be

available in the months to come. MINX is a line of graphic novels that's

designed especially for you — someone who's a bit bored with straight

fiction and ready for stories that are visually exciting beyond words —

literally. In fact, we thought you might like to get in on a secret, behind-

the-scenes look at a few of the new MINX titles that will aid in your escape

to cool places during the long, hot summer. So hurry up and turn the page

already! And be sure to check out other exclusive material at

minxbooks.net

By the highly acclaimed author of *Boy Proof* and *The Queen of Cool*

THE PLAIN JANES

CECIL CASTELLUCCI
and **JIM RUGG**

Four girls named Jane are anything but ordinary once

they form a secret art gang and take on Suburbia by painting

the town P.L.A.I.N. — People Loving Art In Neighborhoods.

AVAILABLE NOW! ■ Read on.

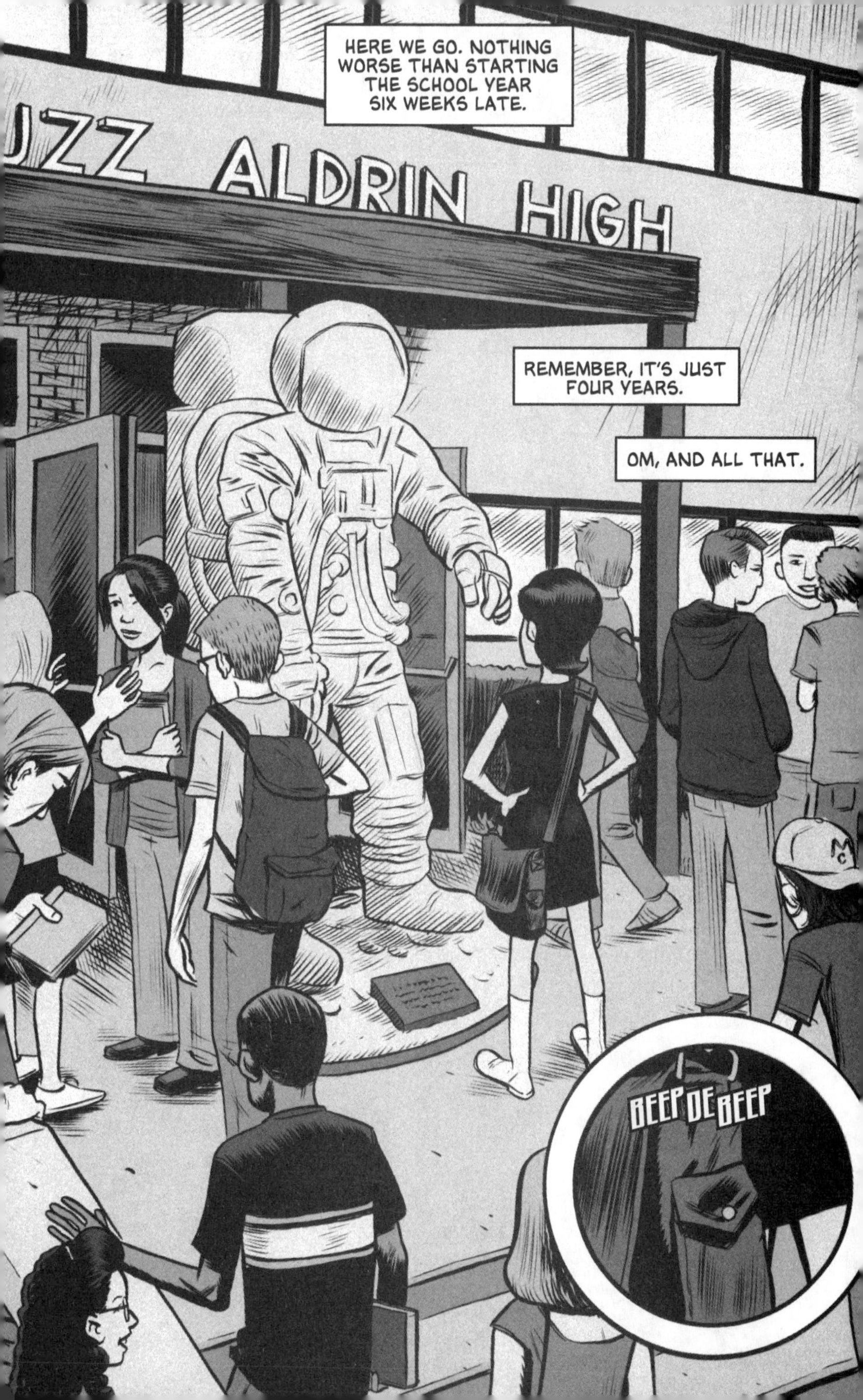
HERE WE GO. NOTHING WORSE THAN STARTING THE SCHOOL YEAR SIX WEEKS LATE.
UZZ ALDRIN HIGH
REMEMBER, IT'S JUST FOUR YEARS.
OM, AND ALL THAT.
BEEP DE BEEP

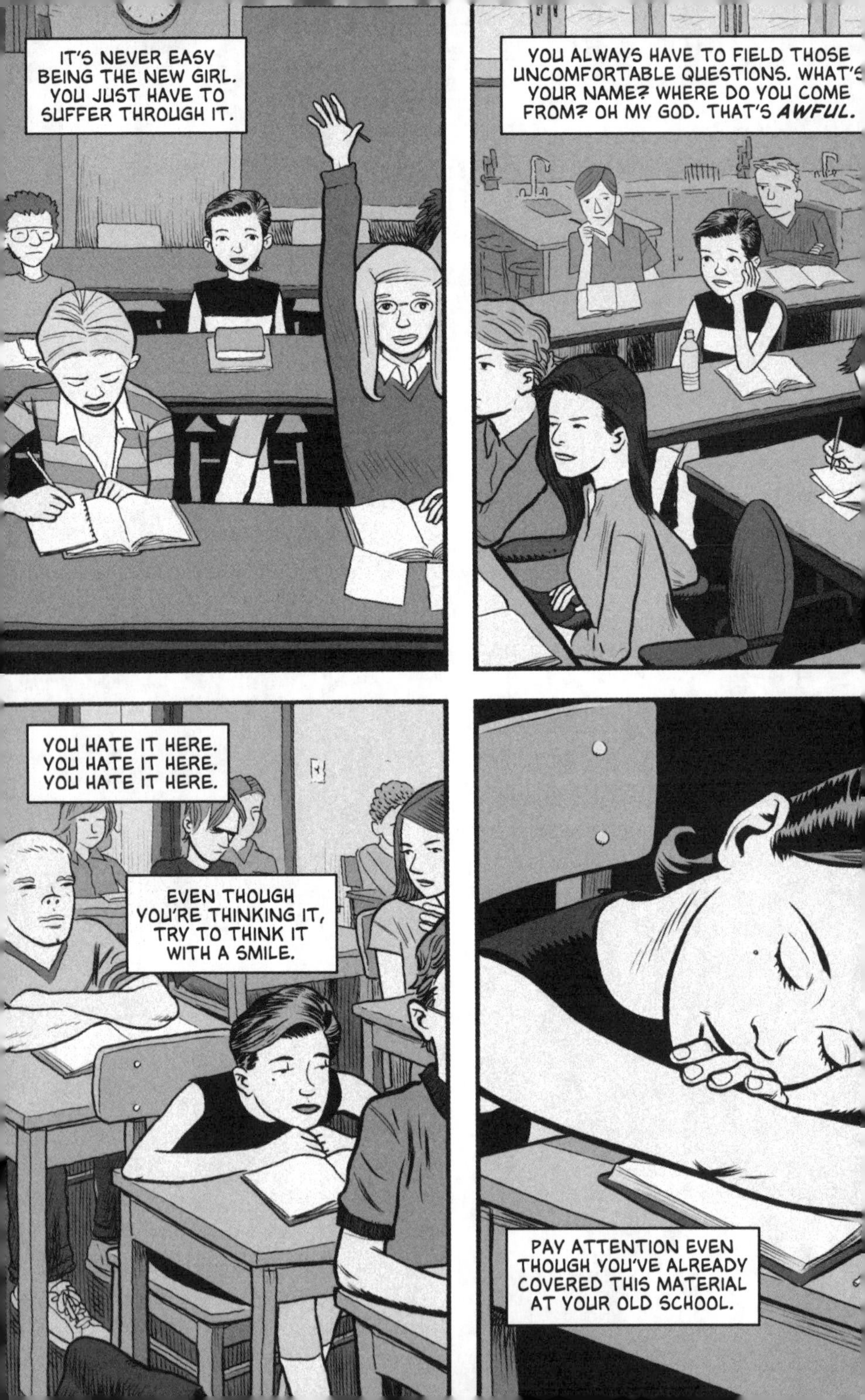
IT'S NEVER EASY BEING THE NEW GIRL. YOU JUST HAVE TO SUFFER THROUGH IT.
YOU ALWAYS HAVE TO FIELD THOSE UNCOMFORTABLE QUESTIONS. WHAT'S YOUR NAME? WHERE DO YOU COME FROM? OH MY GOD. THAT'S *AWFUL.*
YOU HATE IT HERE. YOU HATE IT HERE. YOU HATE IT HERE.
EVEN THOUGH YOU'RE THINKING IT, TRY TO THINK IT WITH A SMILE.
PAY ATTENTION EVEN THOUGH YOU'VE ALREADY COVERED THIS MATERIAL AT YOUR OLD SCHOOL.

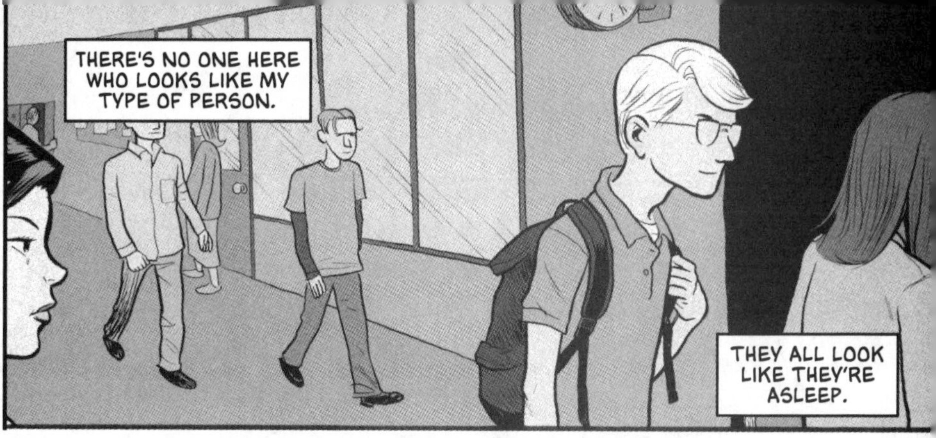
THERE'S NO ONE HERE WHO LOOKS LIKE MY TYPE OF PERSON.
THEY ALL LOOK LIKE THEY'RE ASLEEP.

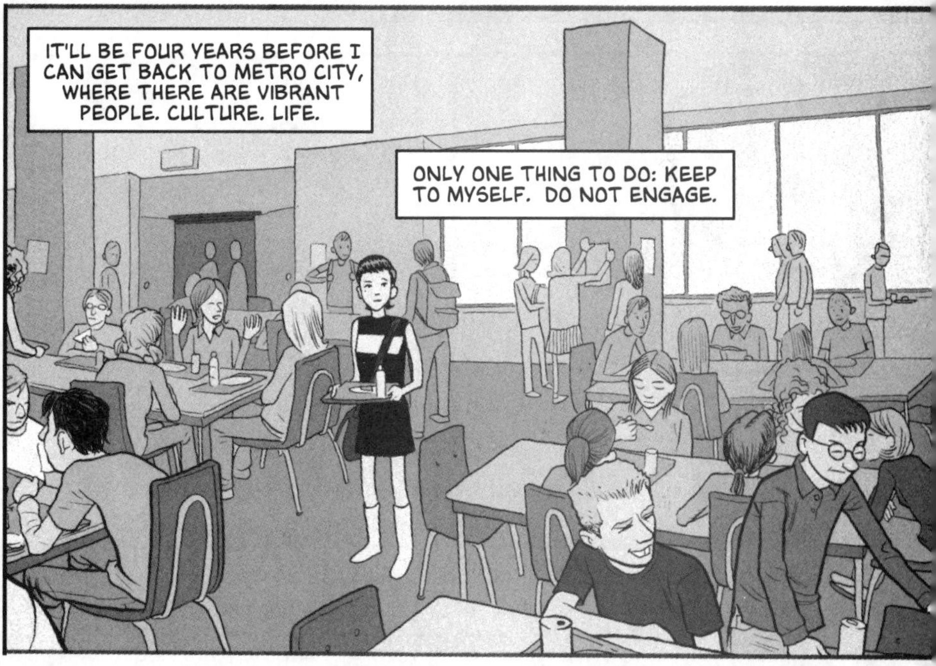
IT'LL BE FOUR YEARS BEFORE I CAN GET BACK TO METRO CITY, WHERE THERE ARE VIBRANT PEOPLE. CULTURE. LIFE.
ONLY ONE THING TO DO: KEEP TO MYSELF. DO NOT ENGAGE.

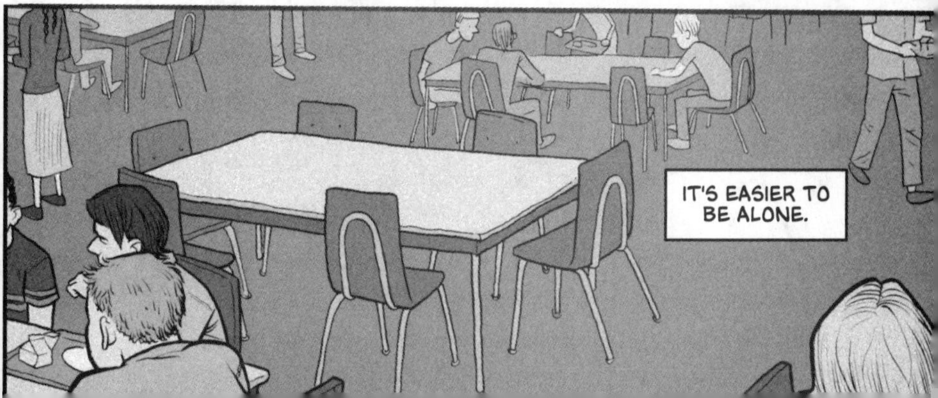
IT'S EASIER TO BE ALONE.

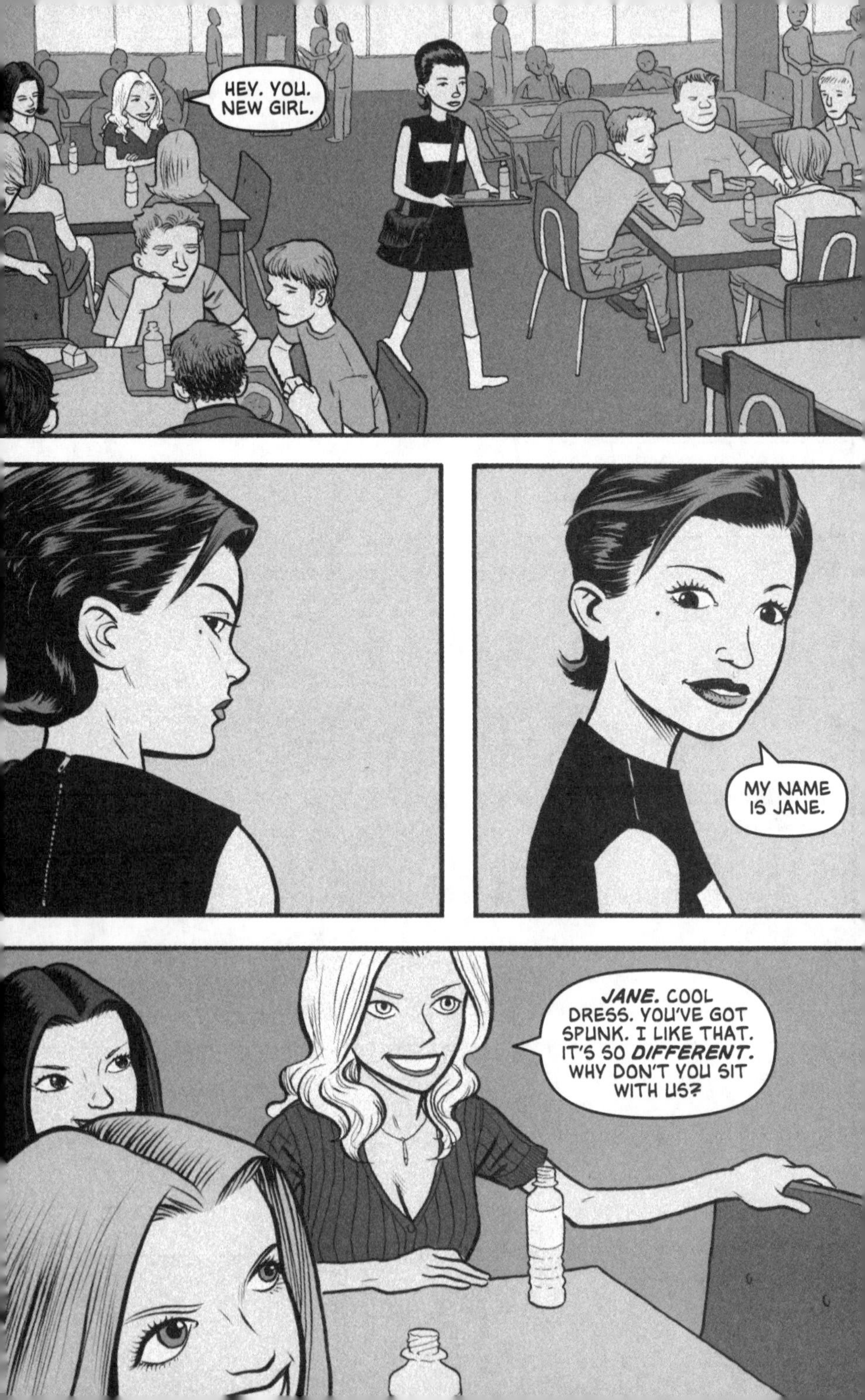
HEY. YOU. NEW GIRL.
MY NAME IS JANE.
JANE. COOL DRESS. YOU'VE GOT SPUNK. I LIKE THAT. IT'S SO *DIFFERENT*. WHY DON'T YOU SIT WITH US?

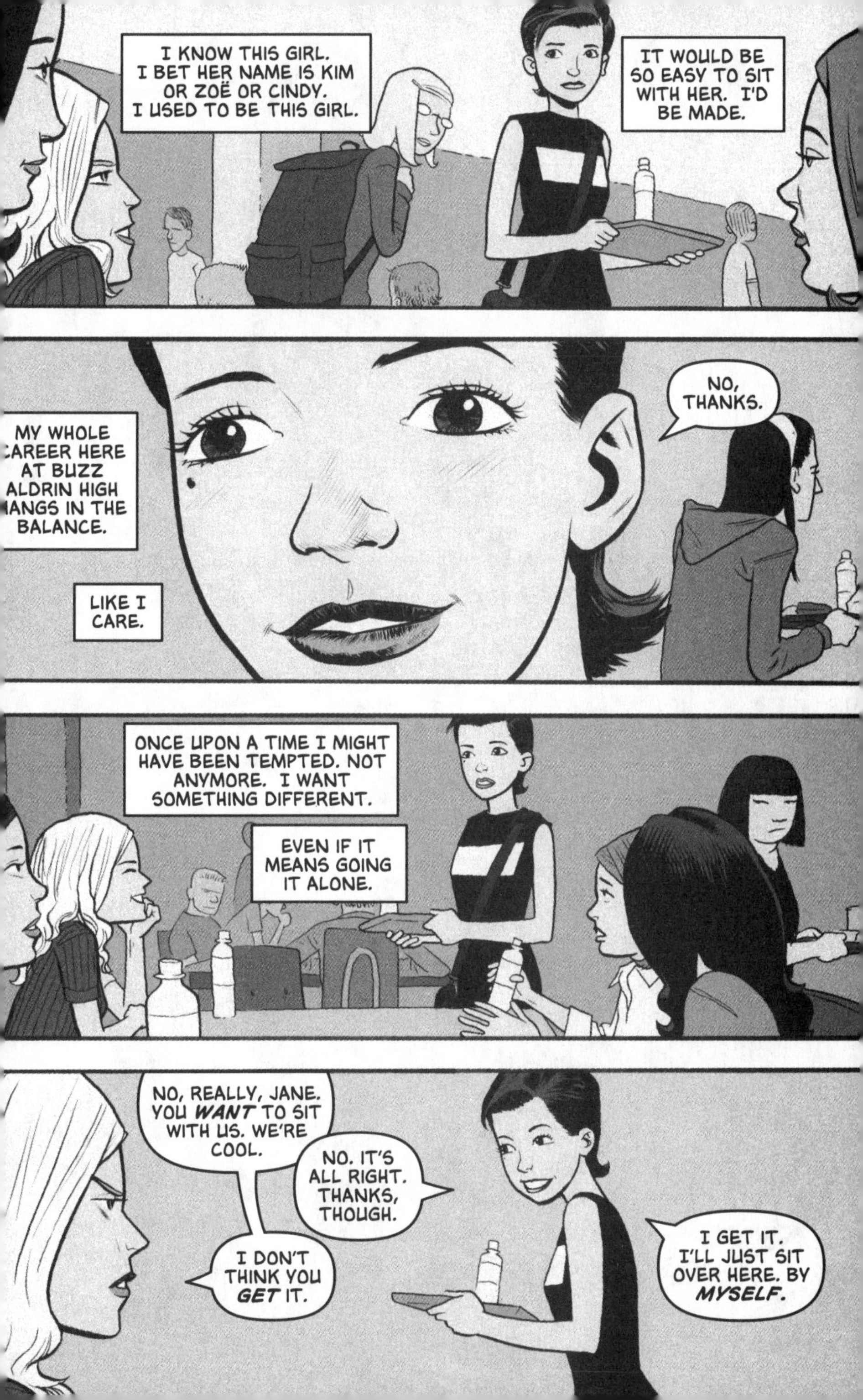

I KNOW THIS GIRL. I BET HER NAME IS KIM OR ZOË OR CINDY. I USED TO BE THIS GIRL.
IT WOULD BE SO EASY TO SIT WITH HER. I'D BE MADE.
MY WHOLE CAREER HERE AT BUZZ ALDRIN HIGH HANGS IN THE BALANCE.
LIKE I CARE.
NO, THANKS.
ONCE UPON A TIME I MIGHT HAVE BEEN TEMPTED. NOT ANYMORE. I WANT SOMETHING DIFFERENT.
EVEN IF IT MEANS GOING IT ALONE.
NO, REALLY, JANE. YOU *WANT* TO SIT WITH US. WE'RE COOL.
NO. IT'S ALL RIGHT. THANKS, THOUGH.
I DON'T THINK YOU *GET* IT.
I GET IT. I'LL JUST SIT OVER HERE. BY *MYSELF*.

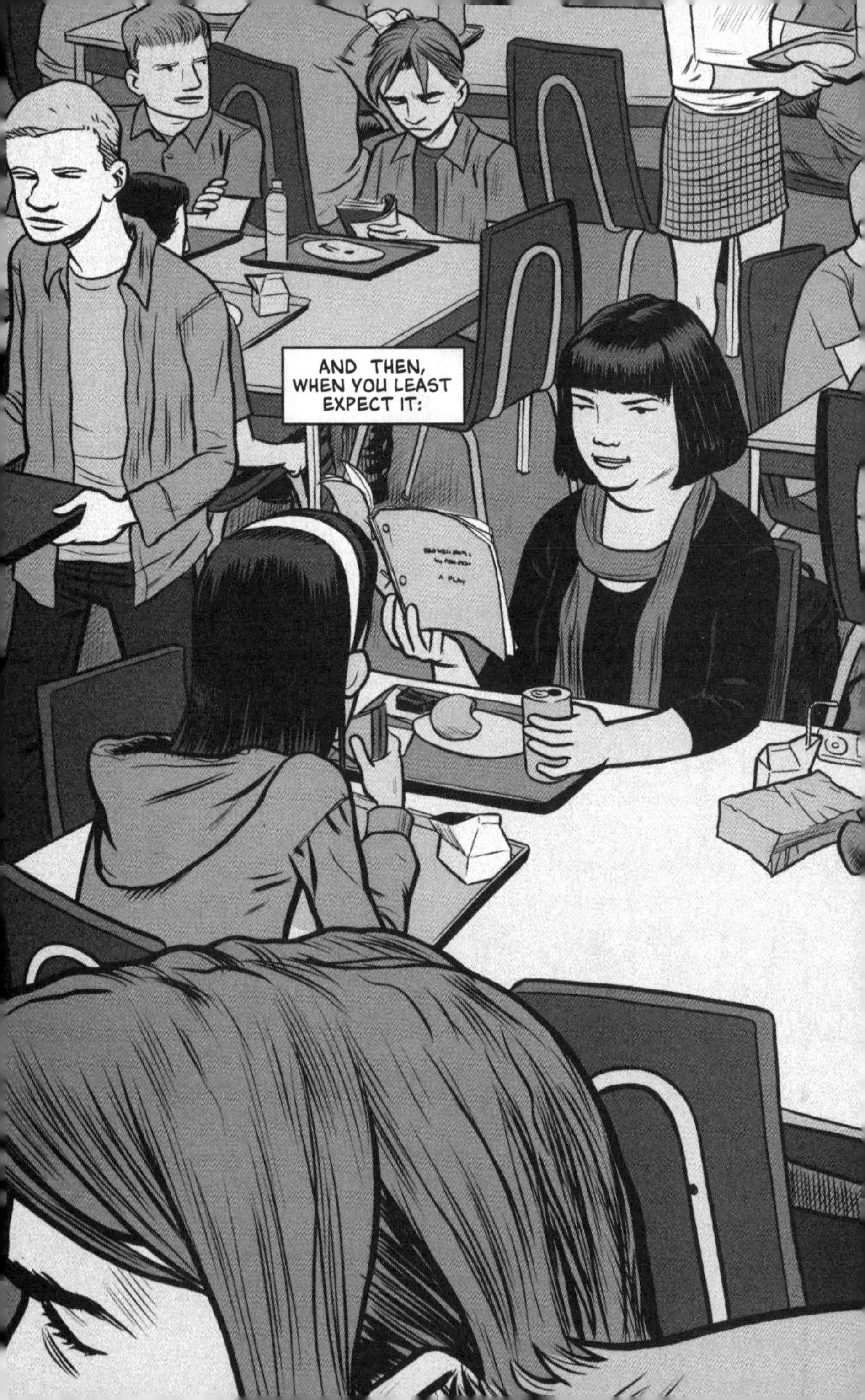
AND THEN, WHEN YOU LEAST EXPECT IT:

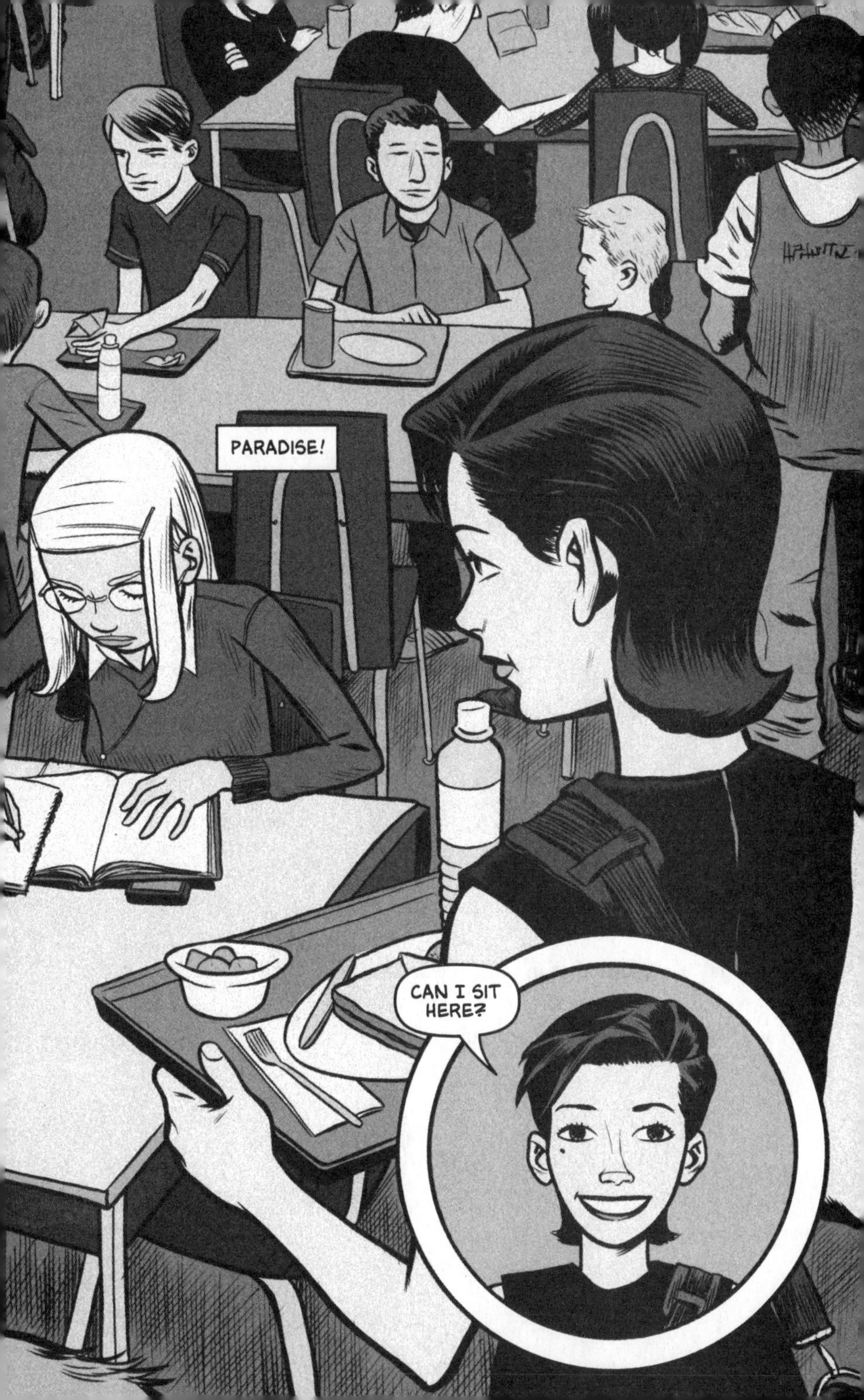
PARADISE!
CAN I SIT HERE?

A Korean-American California girl who's into

martial arts learns that in romance and recycled gifts,

what goes around comes around.

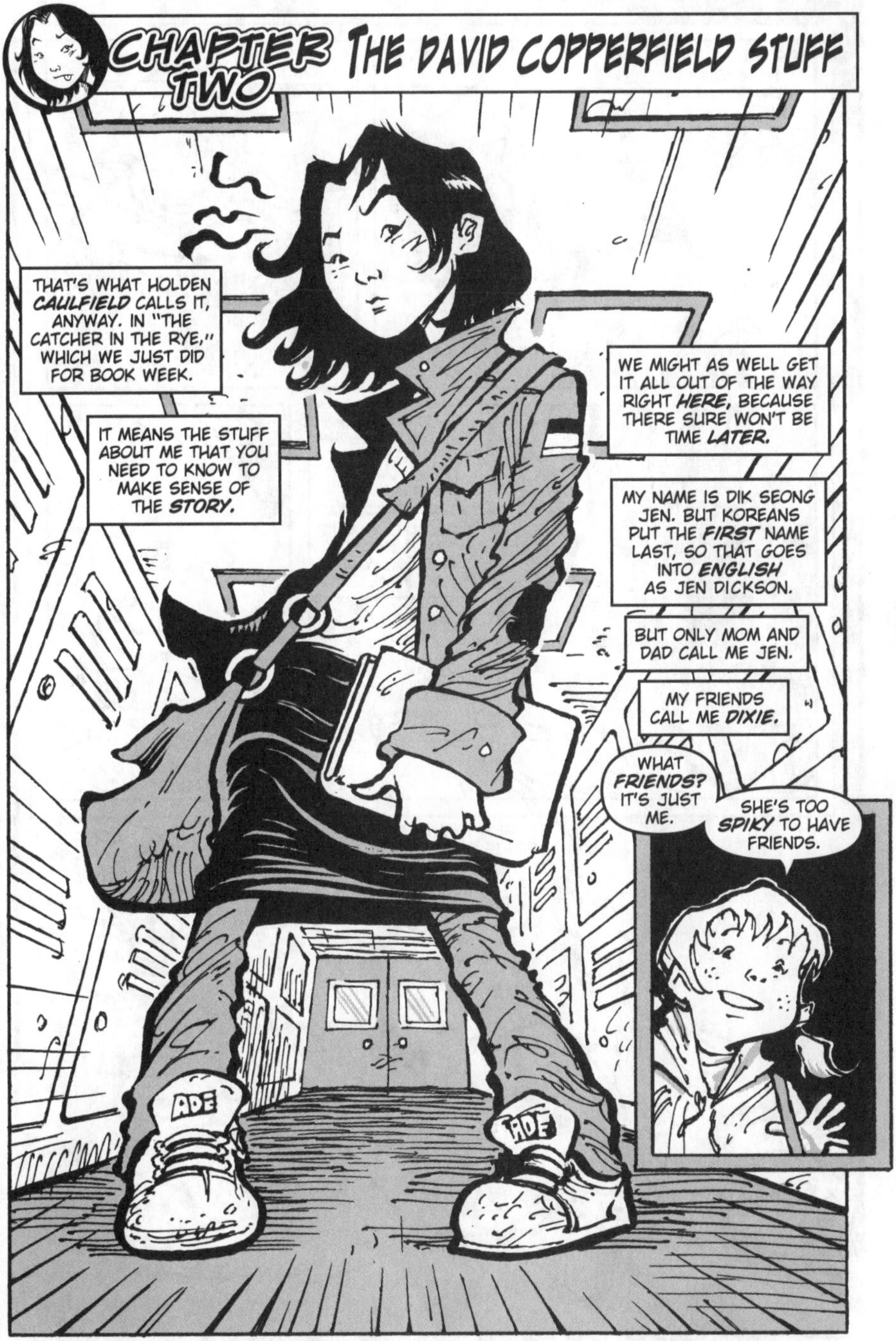
CHAPTER TWO THE DAVID COPPERFIELD STUFF
THAT'S WHAT HOLDEN CAULFIELD CALLS IT, ANYWAY. IN "THE CATCHER IN THE RYE," WHICH WE JUST DID FOR BOOK WEEK.
IT MEANS THE STUFF ABOUT ME THAT YOU NEED TO KNOW TO MAKE SENSE OF THE STORY.
WE MIGHT AS WELL GET IT ALL OUT OF THE WAY RIGHT HERE, BECAUSE THERE SURE WON'T BE TIME LATER.
MY NAME IS DIK SEONG JEN. BUT KOREANS PUT THE FIRST NAME LAST, SO THAT GOES INTO ENGLISH AS JEN DICKSON.
BUT ONLY MOM AND DAD CALL ME JEN.
MY FRIENDS CALL ME DIXIE.
WHAT FRIENDS? IT'S JUST ME.
SHE'S TOO SPIKY TO HAVE FRIENDS.

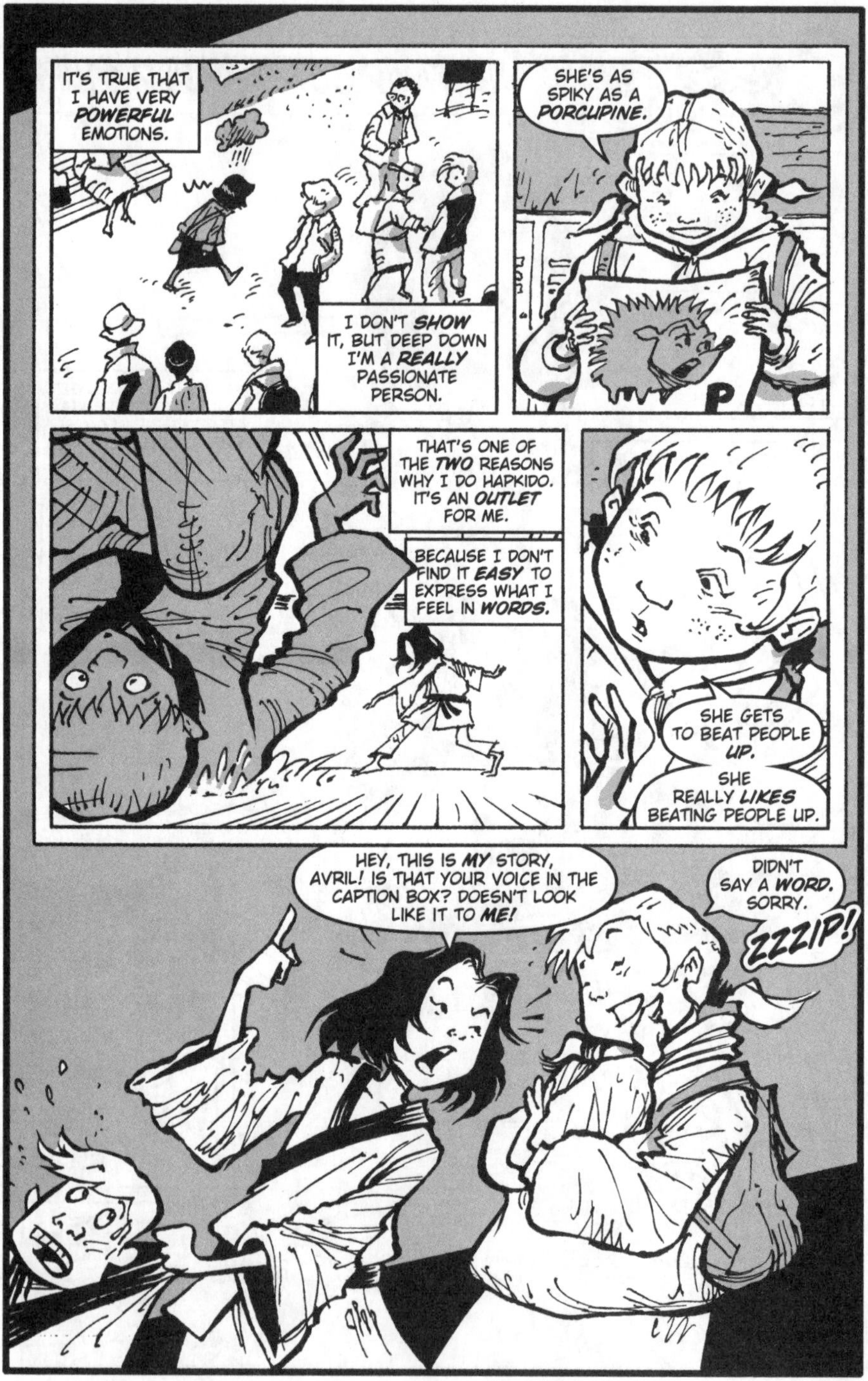
IT'S TRUE THAT I HAVE VERY POWERFUL EMOTIONS.
I DON'T SHOW IT, BUT DEEP DOWN I'M A REALLY PASSIONATE PERSON.
SHE'S AS SPIKY AS A PORCUPINE.
P
THAT'S ONE OF THE TWO REASONS WHY I DO HAPKIDO. IT'S AN OUTLET FOR ME.
BECAUSE I DON'T FIND IT EASY TO EXPRESS WHAT I FEEL IN WORDS.
SHE GETS TO BEAT PEOPLE UP.
SHE REALLY LIKES BEATING PEOPLE UP.
HEY, THIS IS MY STORY, AVRIL! IS THAT YOUR VOICE IN THE CAPTION BOX? DOESN'T LOOK LIKE IT TO ME!
DIDN'T SAY A WORD. SORRY.
ZZZIP!

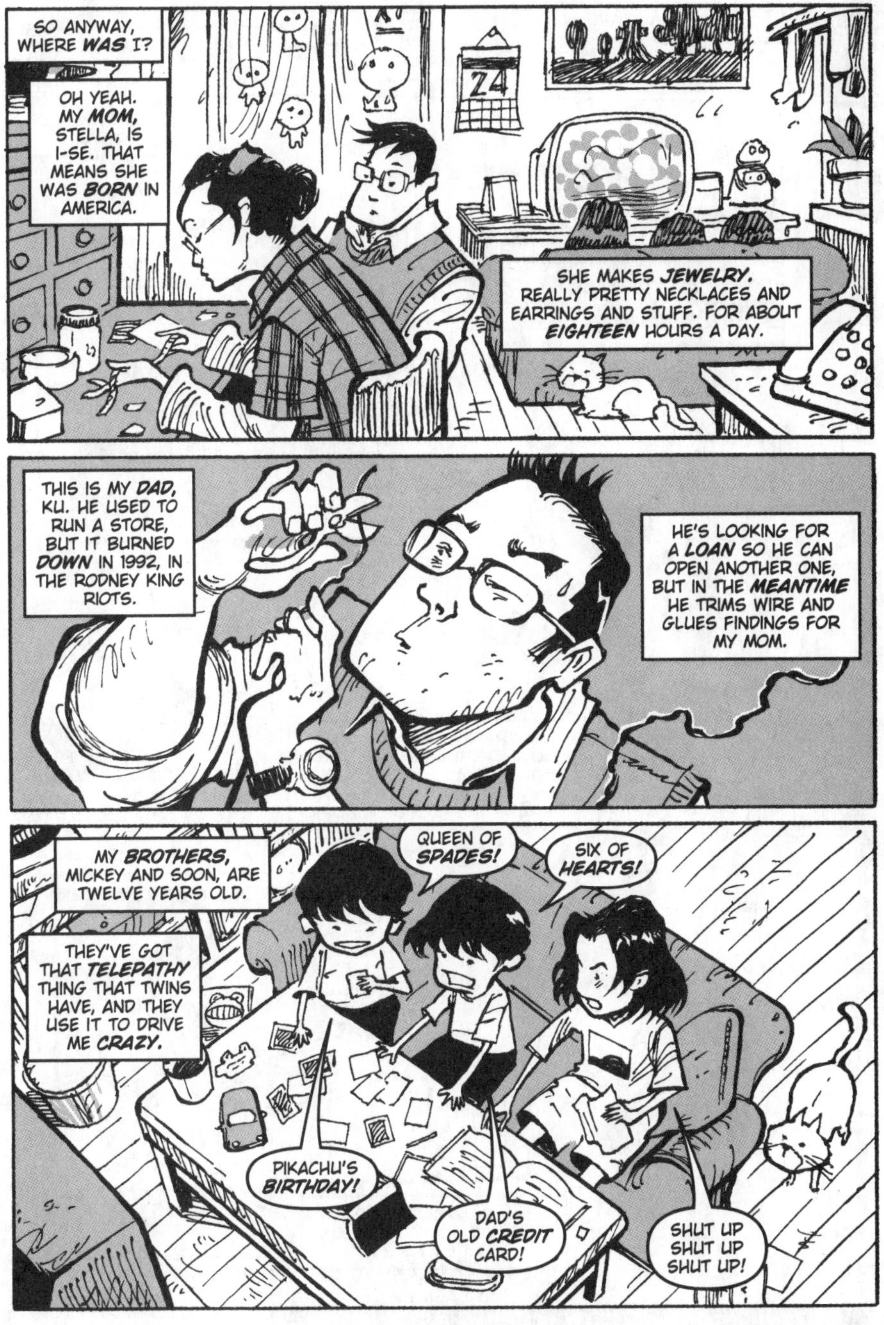
SO ANYWAY, WHERE WAS I?
OH YEAH. MY MOM, STELLA, IS I-SE. THAT MEANS SHE WAS BORN IN AMERICA.
SHE MAKES JEWELRY. REALLY PRETTY NECKLACES AND EARRINGS AND STUFF. FOR ABOUT EIGHTEEN HOURS A DAY.
THIS IS MY DAD, KU. HE USED TO RUN A STORE, BUT IT BURNED DOWN IN 1992, IN THE RODNEY KING RIOTS.
HE'S LOOKING FOR A LOAN SO HE CAN OPEN ANOTHER ONE, BUT IN THE MEANTIME HE TRIMS WIRE AND GLUES FINDINGS FOR MY MOM.
MY BROTHERS, MICKEY AND SOON, ARE TWELVE YEARS OLD.
QUEEN OF SPADES!
SIX OF HEARTS!
THEY'VE GOT THAT TELEPATHY THING THAT TWINS HAVE, AND THEY USE IT TO DRIVE ME CRAZY.
PIKACHU'S BIRTHDAY!
DAD'S OLD CREDIT CARD!
SHUT UP SHUT UP SHUT UP!

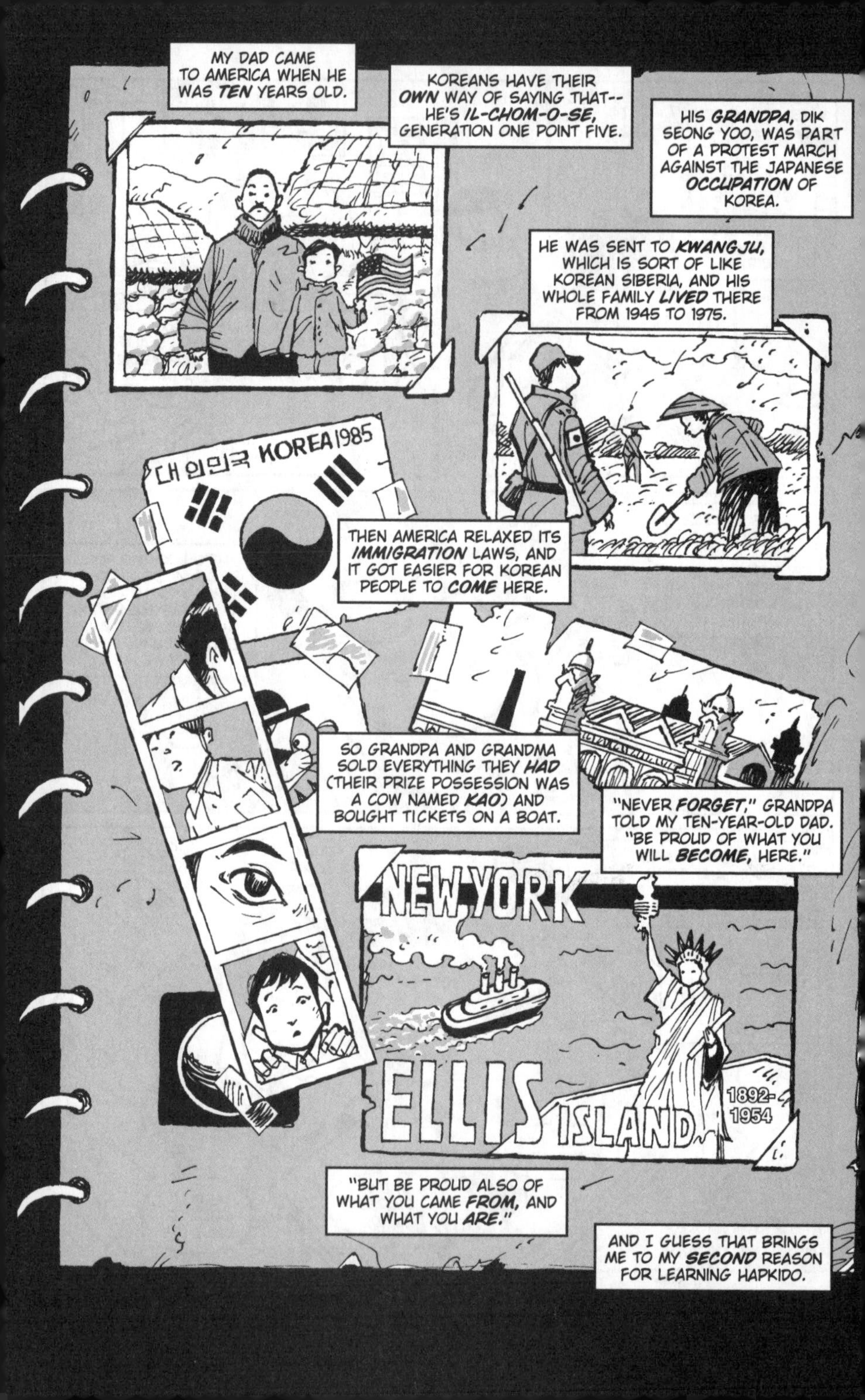
MY DAD CAME TO AMERICA WHEN HE WAS TEN YEARS OLD.
KOREANS HAVE THEIR OWN WAY OF SAYING THAT--HE'S IL-CHOM-O-SE, GENERATION ONE POINT FIVE.
HIS GRANDPA, DIK SEONG YOO, WAS PART OF A PROTEST MARCH AGAINST THE JAPANESE OCCUPATION OF KOREA.
HE WAS SENT TO KWANGJU, WHICH IS SORT OF LIKE KOREAN SIBERIA, AND HIS WHOLE FAMILY LIVED THERE FROM 1945 TO 1975.
대한민국 KOREA 1985
THEN AMERICA RELAXED ITS IMMIGRATION LAWS, AND IT GOT EASIER FOR KOREAN PEOPLE TO COME HERE.
SO GRANDPA AND GRANDMA SOLD EVERYTHING THEY HAD (THEIR PRIZE POSSESSION WAS A COW NAMED KAO) AND BOUGHT TICKETS ON A BOAT.
"NEVER FORGET," GRANDPA TOLD MY TEN-YEAR-OLD DAD. "BE PROUD OF WHAT YOU WILL BECOME, HERE."
NEW YORK
ELLIS ISLAND
1892-1954
"BUT BE PROUD ALSO OF WHAT YOU CAME FROM, AND WHAT YOU ARE."
AND I GUESS THAT BRINGS ME TO MY SECOND REASON FOR LEARNING HAPKIDO.

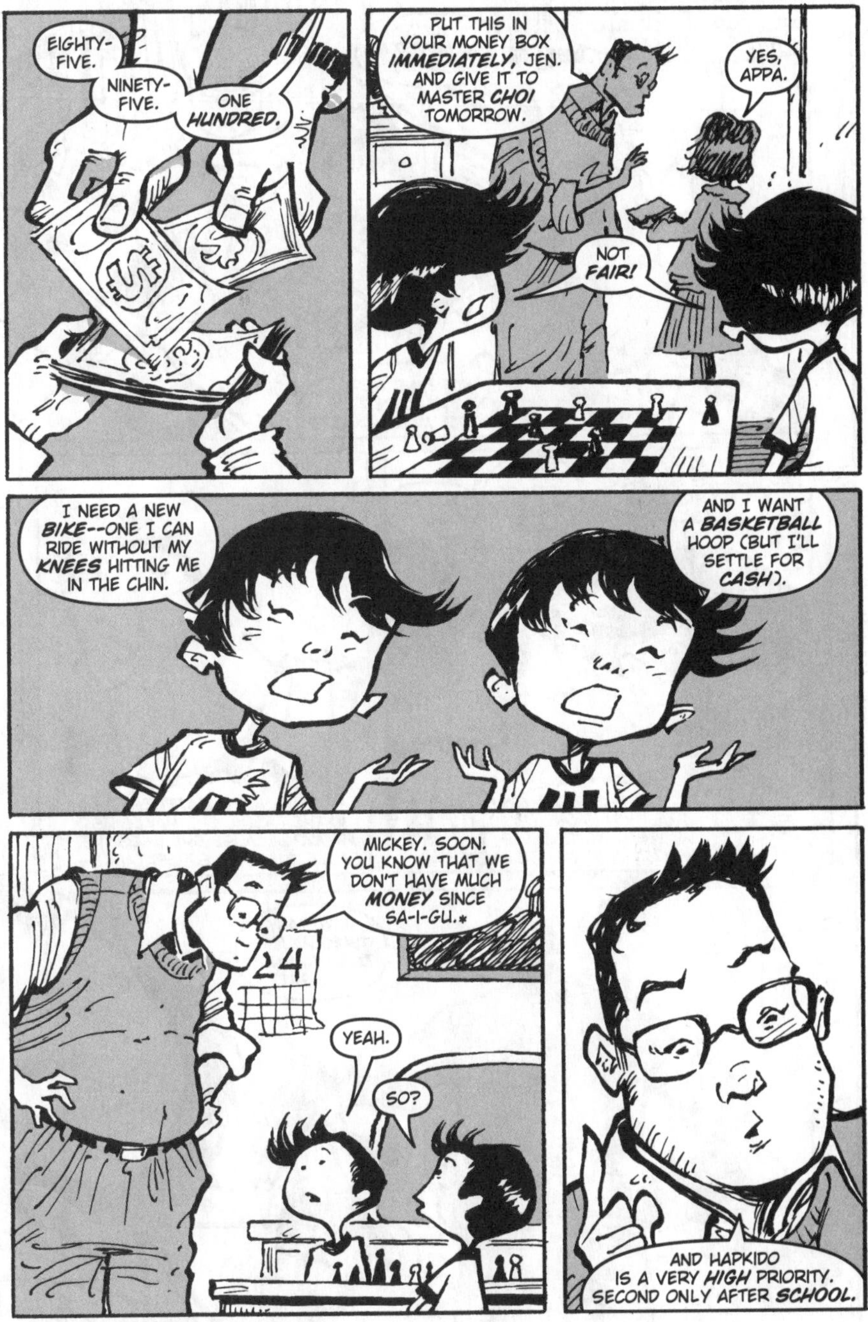
EIGHTY-FIVE.
NINETY-FIVE.
ONE HUNDRED.
PUT THIS IN YOUR MONEY BOX IMMEDIATELY, JEN. AND GIVE IT TO MASTER CHOI TOMORROW.
YES, APPA.
NOT FAIR!
I NEED A NEW BIKE--ONE I CAN RIDE WITHOUT MY KNEES HITTING ME IN THE CHIN.
AND I WANT A BASKETBALL HOOP (BUT I'LL SETTLE FOR CASH).
MICKEY. SOON. YOU KNOW THAT WE DON'T HAVE MUCH MONEY SINCE SA-I-GU.*
24
YEAH.
SO?
AND HAPKIDO IS A VERY HIGH PRIORITY. SECOND ONLY AFTER SCHOOL.

*WHAT KOREANS CALL THE RODNEY KING RIOTS--LITERALLY "APRIL 29TH."

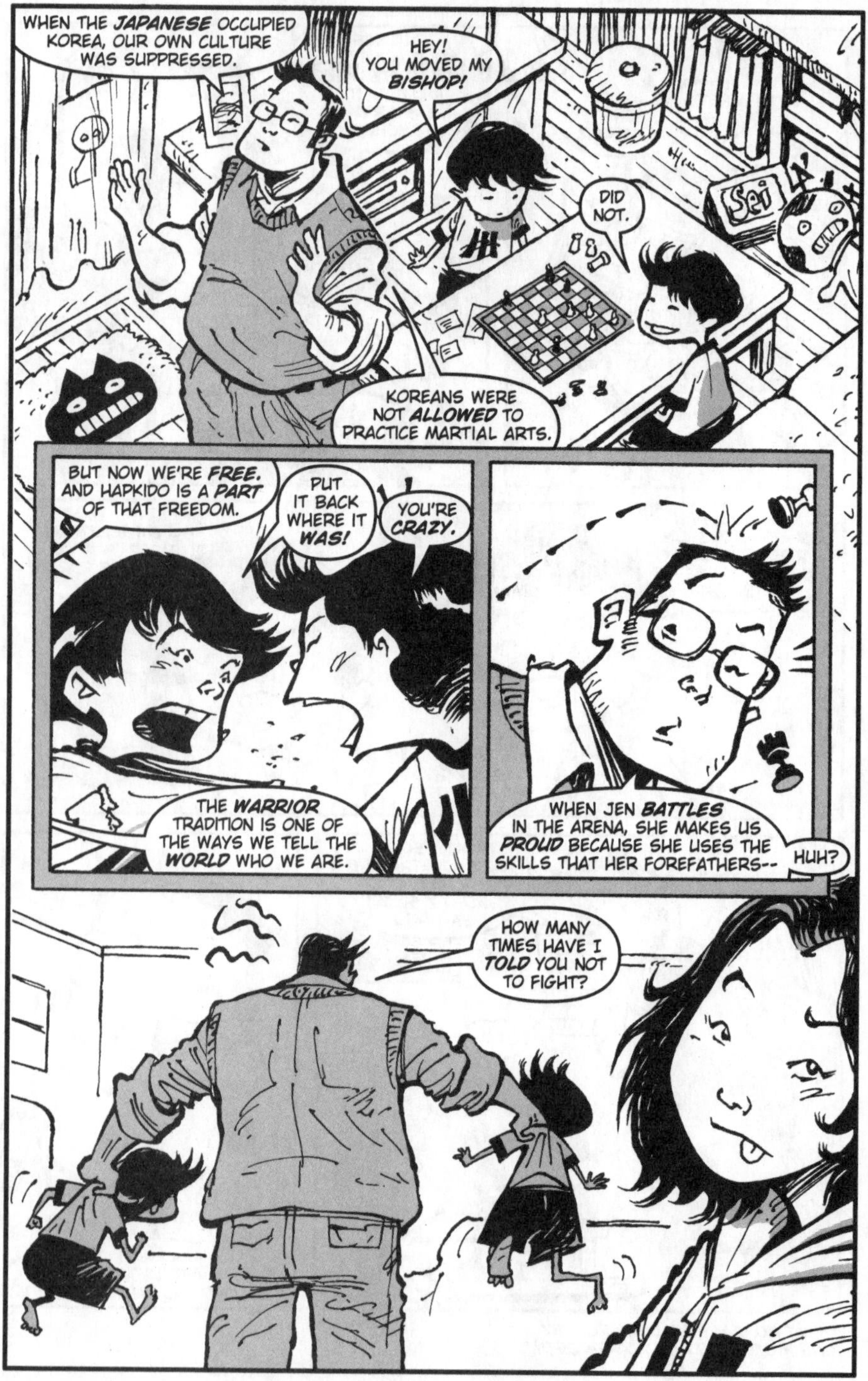
WHEN THE JAPANESE OCCUPIED KOREA, OUR OWN CULTURE WAS SUPPRESSED.
HEY! YOU MOVED MY BISHOP!
DID NOT.
Sei
KOREANS WERE NOT ALLOWED TO PRACTICE MARTIAL ARTS.
BUT NOW WE'RE FREE. AND HAPKIDO IS A PART OF THAT FREEDOM.
PUT IT BACK WHERE IT WAS!
YOU'RE CRAZY.
THE WARRIOR TRADITION IS ONE OF THE WAYS WE TELL THE WORLD WHO WE ARE.
WHEN JEN BATTLES IN THE ARENA, SHE MAKES US PROUD BECAUSE SHE USES THE SKILLS THAT HER FOREFATHERS--
HUH?
HOW MANY TIMES HAVE I TOLD YOU NOT TO FIGHT?

Derek Kirk Kim & Jesse Hamm

Good As Lily

What would you do if versions of yourself at ages 6, 29 and 70

suddenly became part of your already complicated

high school life?

COMING IN AUGUST 2007 ▪ Read on,

but please note: the following pages are not sequential.

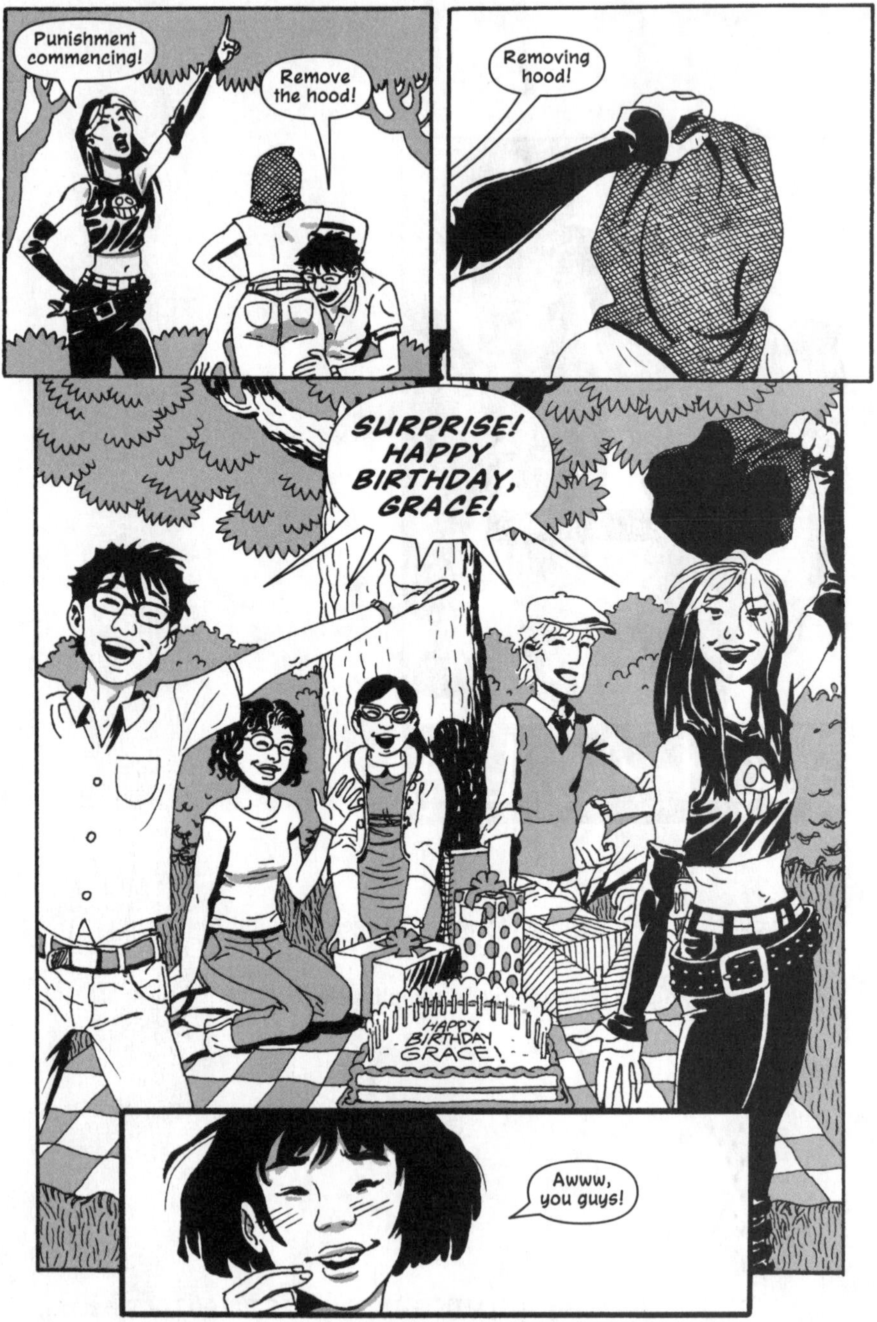
Punishment commencing!
Remove the hood!
Removing hood!
SURPRISE! HAPPY BIRTHDAY, GRACE!
HAPPY BIRTHDAY GRACE!
Awww, you guys!

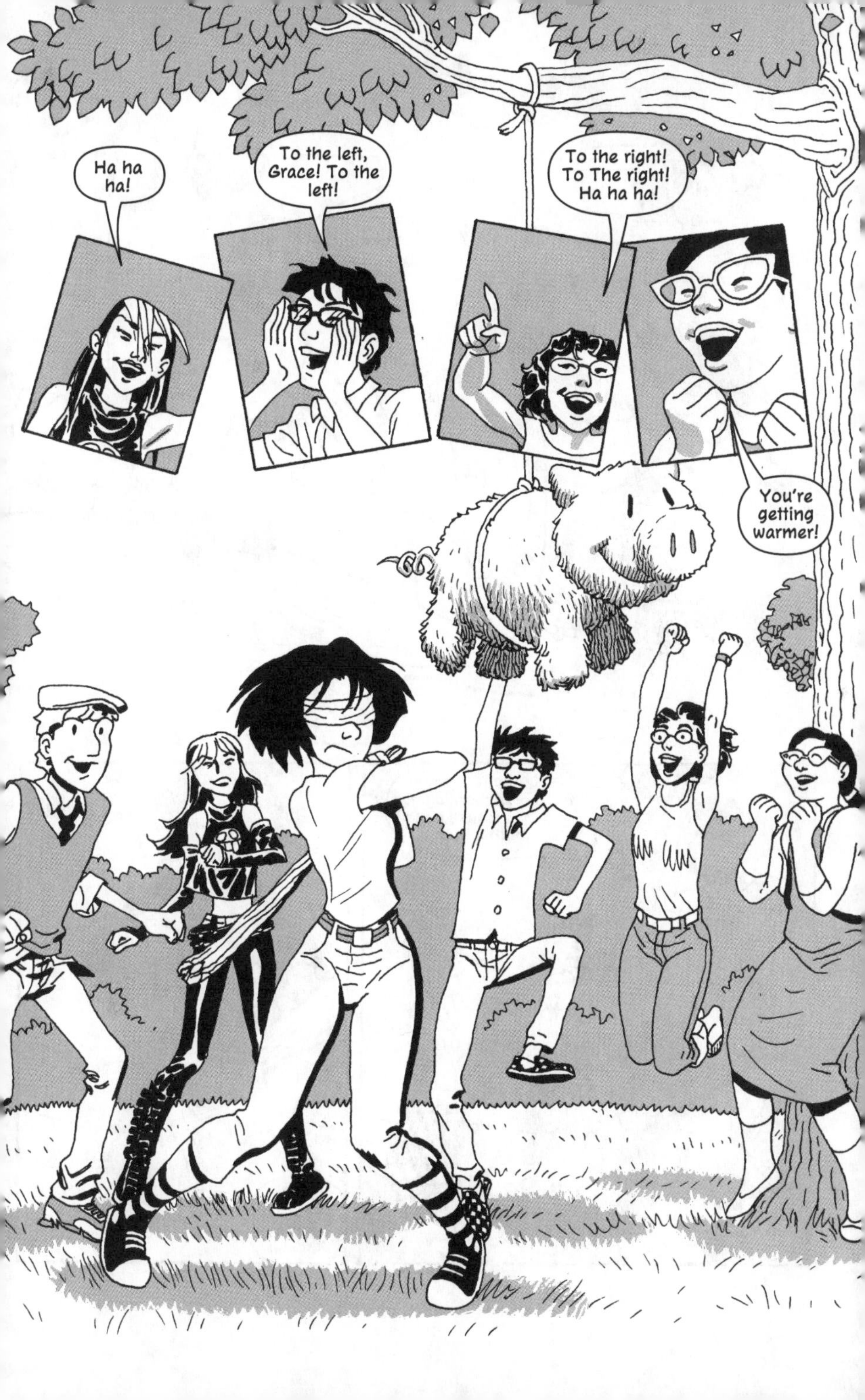

Ha ha ha!
To the left, Grace! To the left!
To the right! To The right! Ha ha ha!
You're getting warmer!

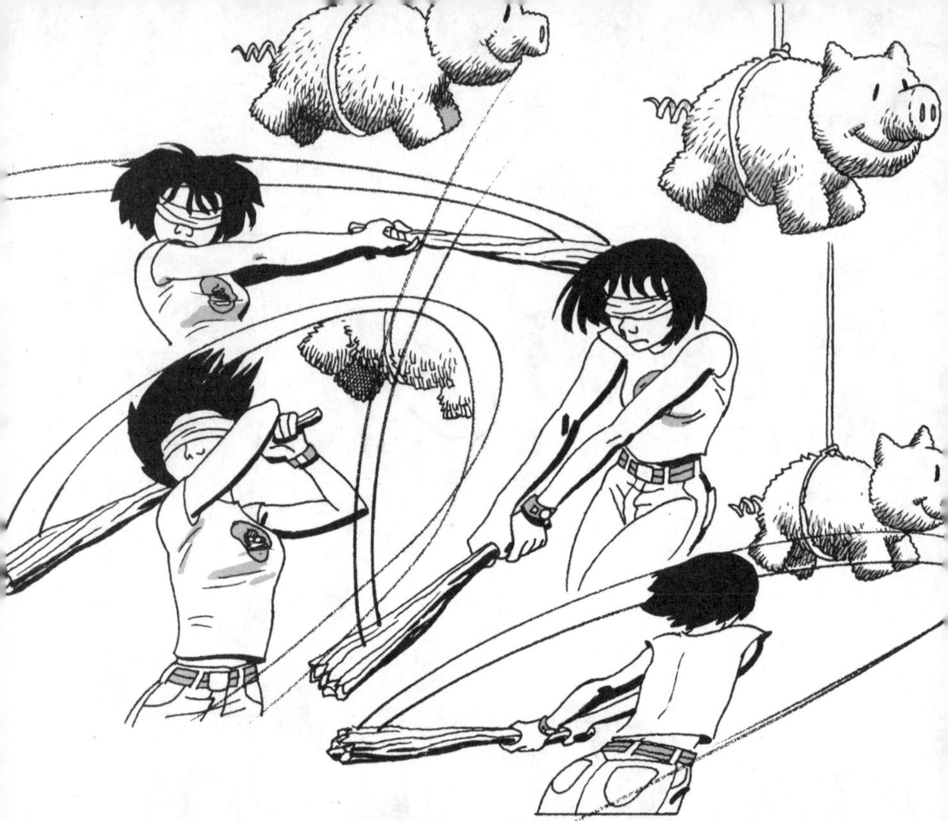

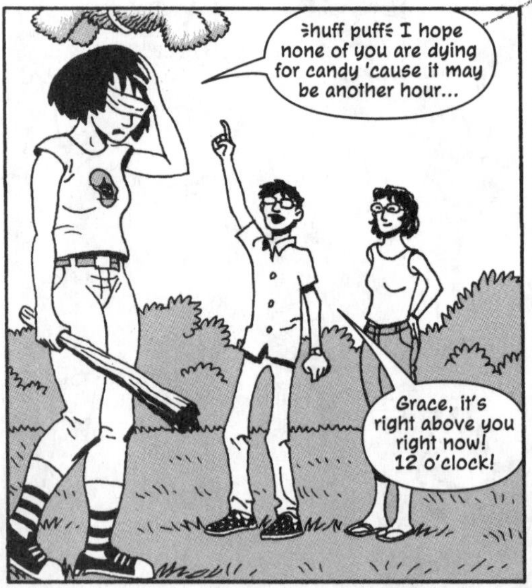
huff puff I hope none of you are dying for candy 'cause it may be another hour...
Grace, it's right above you right now! 12 o'clock!

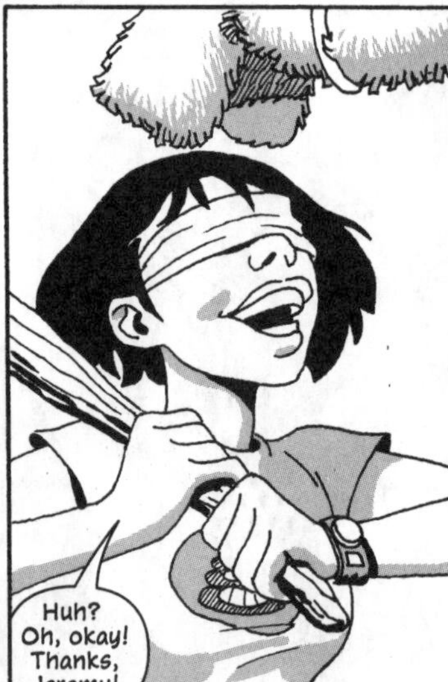
Huh? Oh, okay! Thanks, Jeremy!

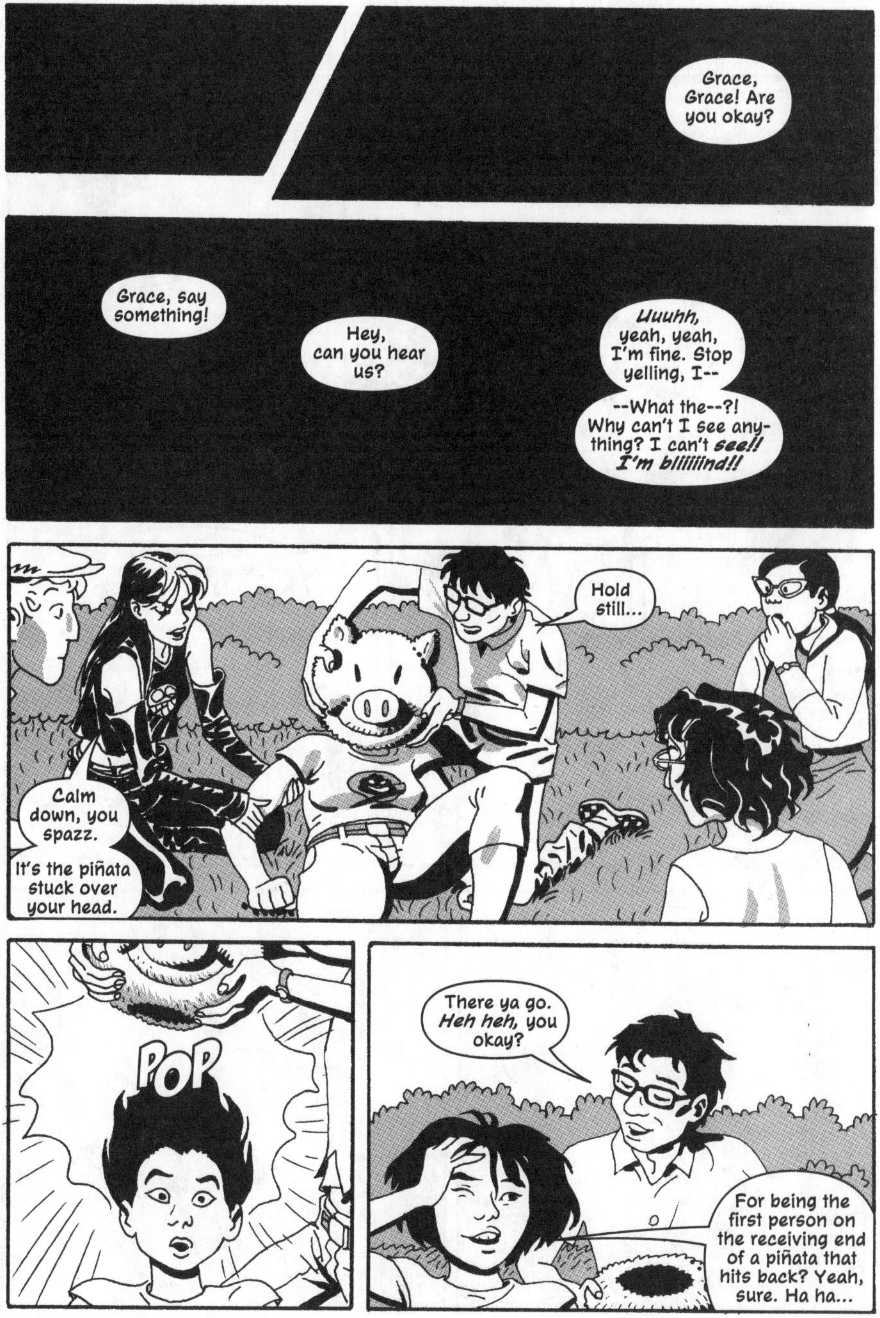
Grace, Grace! Are you okay?
Grace, say something!
Hey, can you hear us?
Uuuhh, yeah, yeah, I'm fine. Stop yelling, I--
--What the--?! Why can't I see any-thing? I can't ***see!!*** ***I'm bliiiiind!!***
Hold still...
Calm down, you spazz.
It's the piñata stuck over your head.
POP
There ya go. *Heh heh,* you okay?
For being the first person on the receiving end of a piñata that hits back? Yeah, sure. Ha ha...

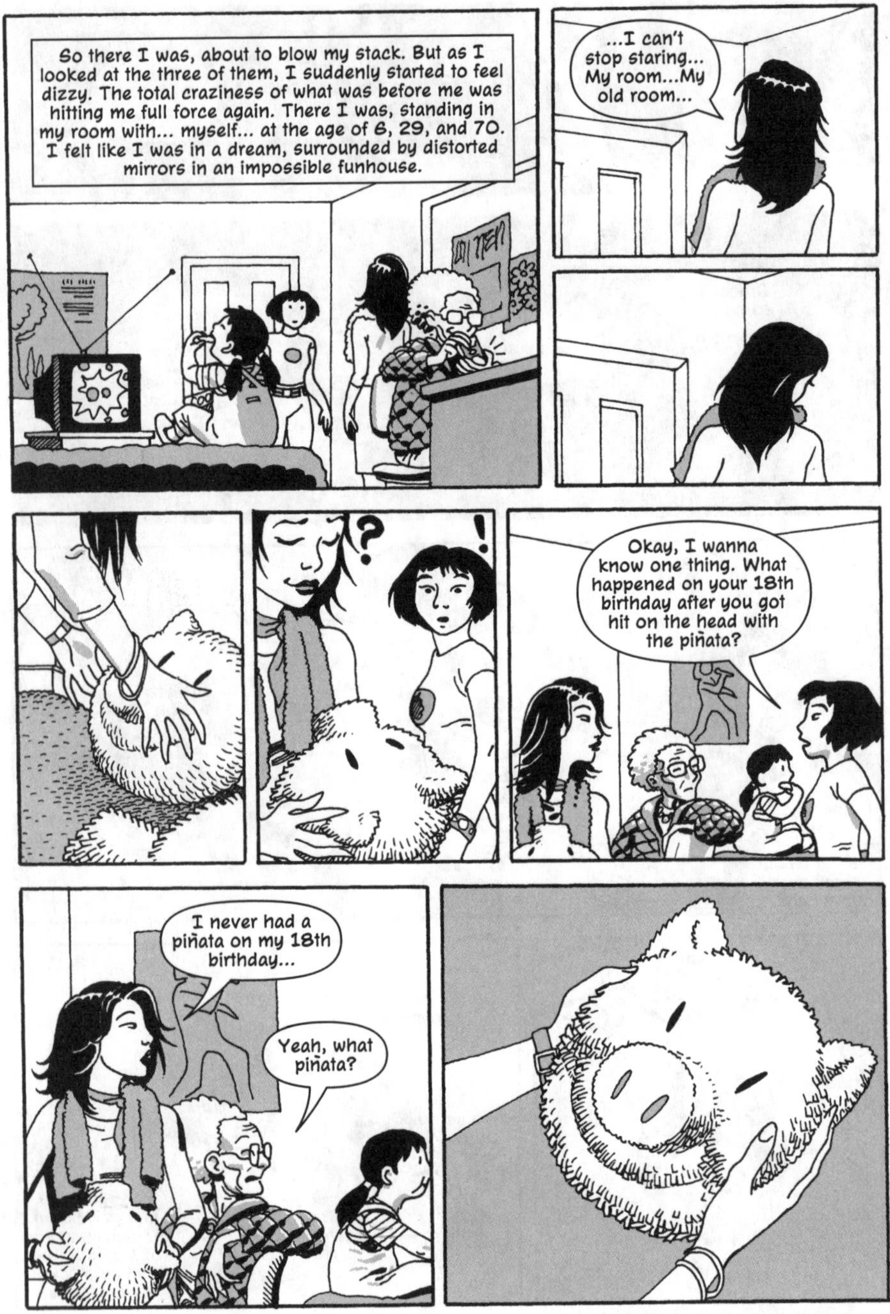
So there I was, about to blow my stack. But as I looked at the three of them, I suddenly started to feel dizzy. The total craziness of what was before me was hitting me full force again. There I was, standing in my room with... myself... at the age of 6, 29, and 70. I felt like I was in a dream, surrounded by distorted mirrors in an impossible funhouse.
...I can't stop staring... My room...My old room...
?
!
Okay, I wanna know one thing. What happened on your 18th birthday after you got hit on the head with the piñata?
I never had a piñata on my 18th birthday...
Yeah, what piñata?

Don't miss any of these upcoming  books:

CONFESSIONS OF A BLABBERMOUTH
By Mike and Louise Carey and Aaron Alexovich
September 2007

When Tasha's mom brings home a creepy boyfriend and his deadpan daughter, a dysfunctional family is headed for a complete mental meltdown.

WATER BABY
By Ross Campbell
October 2007

Surfer girl Brody just got her leg bitten off by a shark. What's worse? Her shark of an ex-boyfriend is back, and when it comes to Brody's couch, he's not budging.

KIMMIE66
By Aaron Alexovich
November 2007

This high-velocity, virtual reality ghost story follows a tech-savvy teenager on a dangerous quest to save her best friend, the world's first all-digital girl.

minxbooks.net

Go to
minxbooks.net
for exclusive interviews
and bonus artwork!

The Face of Modern Fiction